P9-DFR-939

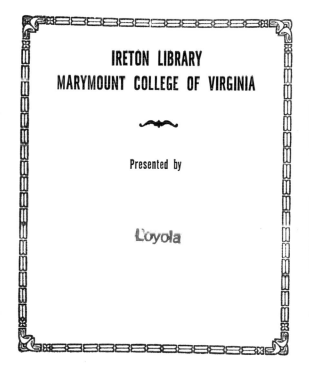

IRETON LIBRARY
MARYMOUNT COLLEGE OF VIRGINIA

Presented by

Loyola

Gender, Fantasy, and Realism in American Literature

GENDER, FANTASY,
and
REALISM
in American Literature

ALFRED HABEGGER

COLUMBIA UNIVERSITY PRESS

New York *1982*

74949

The publisher gratefully acknowledges the financial
assistance of the University of Kansas
in the publication of this book.

Library of Congress Cataloging in Publication Data

Habegger, Alfred.
Gender, fantasy, and realism in American literature
Includes bibliographical references and
index.
1. American fiction—19th century—History
and criticism.   2. Realism in literature.
3. Sex role in literature.   4. Fantasy in
literature.   5. Howells, William Dean, 1837–
1920—Criticism and interpretation.   6. James,
Henry, 1843–1916—Criticism and interpretation.
7. Women and literature—United States.
I. Title.
PS374.R37H3   813'.4'0912   82-1239
ISBN 0-231-05396-7   AACR2

Columbia University Press
New York *and* Guildford, Surrey

Copyright © 1982   Columbia University Press
All rights reserved
Printed in the United States of America

*Clothbound editions of Columbia University Press books are Smyth-sewn and
printed on permanent and durable acid-free paper.*

Contents

Preface

The old idea, most memorably worked out by Richard Chase in *The American Novel and Its Tradition,* that novelists in the United States have mainly written the symbolic romance has found less favor with critics over the last decade than it did with those who rose to prominence after World War II. My own volume joins those works of criticism and literary history that, opposing Chase, regard the realistic novel as a principal type of American fiction. Further, *Gender, Fantasy, and the Novel* attempts to make a case for seeing realism as the central and preeminent literary type in democratic society. But I am afraid that the shape of my argument as it has worked itself out will be so unlike anything the reader might expect that I would like to offer a brief summary.

The rarely questioned assumption that great art must be universal does not always seem applicable to great social novels. The most obvious difficulty preventing the modern reader from grasping and appreciating realistic fiction from the nineteenth century, especially that of W. D. Howells, is that this fiction not only dealt with a society unlike our own but generally assumed that the reader would know it well or even belong to it. Merely to get to the place where one can see that the fiction is in fact realistic requires independent knowledge of the society in question. Worse, the fact that many works of realism were written as conscious corrections of a large body of popular literature in the background leaves us with the unwelcome burden of reading that literature. It is simply impossible, as both Chase and Lionel Trilling have inadvertently shown in their imperceptive essays on Howells, fully to make sense of a realistic novel by sending the usual probes into the text alone. The critic has to find out certain things about the world that received the text—has to discover the books that were in the air at the time, the sort of people who read and liked these books, the social divisions within the reading public and the configuration of genres that appealed to these groups, the stereotypes of men and women that happened to be getting a lot of attention, and most important of all, the exact state of the ongoing concern about the nature of womanhood.

Because in the 1850s, 60s, and 70s, novels were read mainly by women, it is pointless to try to think about the novels of those years without also thinking about gender and its many ramifications within literature and society. Another reason why gender is primary is that the form of the novel itself was bound up with sex and courtship. Almost every popular novel from the 1850s exhibits an idealized hero and heroine (the latter far more important than the former), a noticeable element of "romance," and a final scene allowing the union of a man and a woman. Turning from this body of fiction to the actual social matrix, one is at once struck by the mounds of magazine articles and books dealing with domestic and marital concerns and changing norms of behavior for young women. Doesn't it seem plausible on the face of it—and I believe that my and others' studies bear out the hypothesis—that novels dealt with the same issues under another guise? That the novel as a literary type allowed readers to work out these problems in a way special to this genre? In fact, the novel became a daydream-book representing female hopes and fears by means of narrative that looked "domestic" in the eyes of contemporary readers but was really symbolic in a way not understood until the rebirth of feminism a decade ago.

The key to the symbolic nature of women's fiction is the concept of stereotyped character, or character-type. This concept has played an important role in feminist criticism, particularly in the early 1970s, when many women readers found the shallowness of fictional women characters very offensive. It was urged that, because readers tend to model themselves on people in books, this "sexual stereotyping" had a pernicious effect on women's lives. Although this polemic was off the mark in some ways, especially in failing to see that stereotypes, female or male, enter into every single fictional character in some way or other, at bottom the polemic made sense. Not only do many novels written by men rely on a few cartoon cut-outs of women, but more important, the feminist polemic gave renewed currency to an old and powerful truth about the act of reading fiction: lead characters are potential models for the reader. More precisely, character-types in fiction often appear to be versions of available gender roles in the reader's and writer's culture. Thus, the precise contours of any given story involving familiar character-types embodies a sustained and playful reflection, in narrative form, of the conflicts inherent in society itself. Stories about familiar types often amount to a symbolic assessment of mainstream gender roles. To the extent that Victorian readers, especially adolescent girls, were obsessed with fashioning an appropriate self-image, to read a novel was to try on a certain role—to think out with the help of a book-length narrative the potential life-consequences of being a given kind of woman. Novel-reading thus became one among many important life-processes for readers. (This perspective makes clear how finicky it is to try to understand novels by confining one's attention to certain formal features.)

It was in the 1850s that Howells and James struggled with the torment of their own adolescence and first began to define themselves as men and as writers. The fifties was the one decade in American history in which women wrote practically *all* the popular books. The full significance of the dominance of the "scribbling women" Nathaniel Hawthorne complained about is only now being explored. Those scribblers appear to have worked a revolution in American literature, and it was one of the aftershocks of this upheaval that Howells and James around 1875 began to pay so much more detailed attention to exact social nuance than Hawthorne, Melville, Poe, or Emerson had ever thought possible or necessary. The popular women-authored books of the 1850s all purveyed a certain complicated fantasy, but the fact that they embodied this fantasy in homely detail had incalculable consequences. To embody a daydream in dense social notation is to bring that daydream out into the world, to test it and to make it, with all its aspirations and distortions, a political force. Women's fiction posed a challenge to men, a challenge taken up in a definitive way in realistic fiction of the 1870s and 1880s. James and Howells, who have always been seen as somehow feminine, did not derive from Hawthorne, George Eliot, Balzac, Flaubert, or Turgenev. They were born to, and then established themselves against, the maternal tradition of Anglo-American women's fiction.

Because realism always struggles to push back the borders of fantasyland, many readers can't help but feel that it seeks to represent things as they actually are. Criticism has never cared to find a way to operationalize this widespread intuition, preferring to dismiss it as naive and to expatiate on the nonrepresentational conventions and structures of novels. Unless I am mistaken, my basic equation—character-types are a symbolic form of ideal gender roles—backs up this naive intuition and indicates a way to apply it in particular books. A book, then, is not realistic if it endorses the popular scenarios featuring standard character-types. The book *is* realistic if it gives individual features to the standard character-types and creates a plausible causal sequence departing from the scenarios they are often found in. A realistic novel thus appeals to our sense of how things go. Of course, if we have not acquired some sense of this, we are in no position to judge. Also, if we do not have a feeling for the daydreams the novelist is questioning, we will not notice what is at issue in the book.

One of the reasons why part 2 of this study investigates male and female humor in nineteenth-century America is that daydreaming and laughter are closely linked: laughter, like realism, punctures choice lies. The raw material of male comedy, whether in the humorists of the Old Southwest or in Mark Twain, was essentially male fantasy. Although most humorists were men, there were also a number of funny women, both in and out of books. Yet each gender's humor tended to exclude the other's. The bright, censorious humor that was felt to be appropriate for well-bred ladies was light-years removed from the self-burlesquing pattern of masculine humor. The male and female forms of humor, especially the tendency of certain character-types to become comedians or comic butts, illuminate the exact nature of the intimate bond between character-type and gender role. My entire discussion is framed by the instructive case of Penelope Lapham in Howells' novel *The Rise of Silas Lapham*. Penelope is instructive not only because she was the first female humorist to be featured as a romantic lead in a novel, but also because all characters in the novel including herself assume that Tom Corey prefers her beautiful, vapid sister, Irene, to her. Penelope and the subplot containing her put into narrative form a rich accumulation of social and literary custom involving male and female humor. And it is precisely because the subplot reflects society so richly and so beautifully that it has generally gone unappreciated in our time.

This, the difficulty of understanding Howells in the twentieth century, has no solution except detailed historical investigation.

The fact that Howells and James came of age at the end of "the feminine fifties" and during a brutal civil war edged them, in combination with other causes, into a social category that hardly exists today—sissy. The last two parts of this study deal with Howells' and James's struggle to win manhood and their effort to represent in narrative what it meant to grow up male in their time and place. Howells survived the terrors of male initiation much better than did James and went on to write a number of masterly fictions about the problem of being a man in a rough capitalistic society. His memoir of life in Hamilton, Ohio, offers a more circumstantial presentation, and a far more penetrating analysis, of the institution of the boyhood gang than anything written by Mark Twain. And Howells' account in *A Foregone Conclusion* of a Venetian priest with a gift for mechanics and a dream of freedom constitutes a brilliant study of the helpless, isolated, impractical man who is able to survive only in an artificial and hierarchical world. Howells has long been recognized for his many fine novels from the 1880s and early 90s that study the destructive effects of capitalism. But his self-mastery also enabled him to study with equal relentlessness the futility of altruistic reform and the evasiveness of genteel men. His fiction, so far from being genteel, tests the fantasies of liberal reformers of his time.

Howells was our great nineteenth-century novelist because his work alone, somewhat like that of the more brilliant Balzac, creates a large configuration of character-types in their true relations with one another. By the same token the reason James, with his great gifts, did not produce an oeuvre of first-rate realistic fiction between 1875 and 1890 was that he could not confront the full social reality of the United States. Looked at with a cold and skeptical eye, James's American novels appear to endorse some grave misconceptions about American life. The most influential of these is the notion that a country consisting of many races, immigrant groups, social castes, and codes of manners was in some way blank, uniform, devoid of interest. James's decision in 1876 to take up residence in London while continuing to write about Americans was a pioneering version of the modernist rejection of the ordinary or the bourgeois. By the same token James's disillusionment with realism after the mid-1880s—his growing tendency to regard social life from the perspective of an inner exile—anticipates trends even more evident in "The Love Song of J. Alfred Prufrock," *A Portrait of the Artist as a Young Man,* and *Ulysses.* This separatist mentality, I argue, precludes a dignified representation of basic human passions or an objective representation of society. Conspicuous in James, as in some later male modernists, is a fearful hostility toward the vulgar common *man.* Howells, who shared this hostility in his youth, fled America for Venice during the Civil War. But Howells came back. James did not and could not come back because he had never been able, in spite of repeated efforts in boyhood and youth, to join the male comitatus that was such an important boyhood institution.

My final chapter explores the moment in recent literary history, the 1940s, when James was pronounced the first great American master. The two influential groups who caused James to be canonized were the New Critics and the Partisan Reviewers. Because the influence and social conservatism of the former group seem obvious, I concentrate on the latter, particularly Philip Rahv and Lionel Trilling, who were not always candid in revealing the bases of their literary allegiances. These two critics considered *The Bostonians* a great masterpiece of social realism about an uprooted and invasive society, and they made the novel available in cheap modern editions. The reasons why they loved the book so much and put it back on the map was that it endorsed their own unacknowledged conservative commitments. Turning decisively away from politics of the Left, increasingly devoted to the sacredness of the private self and suspicious of "mass" society and all reform movements, Rahv and Trilling found in James's unsuccessful attempt to write an American novel a distinguished version of their own basic fantasy—the fantasy that no decent man can find a place in American political life. At the heart of the James revival lies the same highbrow depoliticization that was evident in the only political group James felt any kinship with, the non-party liberal reformers who gathered around *The Nation* in the Gilded Age and achieved little except to bequeath to later generations of highbrows the certainty that good men were doomed to fail if they entered politics.

Tied closely to mass-fantasies about the perfect mating, the novel has not often been able to tell the truth about the way life goes for most people. Mrs. Emma D. E. N. Southworth and Augusta J. Evans often attributed a wonderful efficacy to their powerful heroines;

Henry James, conversely, told of superfine minds who understood all at the cost of being alone and doing nothing. Either excess accompanies a particular delicious fantasy, and each fantasy has its devoted following. Narrative fiction that offers a consoling vision of the world and thus constitutes a special form of shelter from the wind will always find favor. But what about fiction that gives us the wind itself and the spectacle of humans struggling to remain upright in it? It is the premise of my study that only such fiction can exact one's respect as well as one's love.

In writing this book I have incurred many debts, which I cannot possibly pay by this meager form of acknowledgment. The typists who have helped me are Julie Higgins and Sarah L. King of Bloomington, Indiana, and Pam Loewenstein of Lawrence, Kansas. I have been given a wealth of usable information, advice, and correction by Roy E. Gridley, Stuart Levine, Michael Butler, Thomas O'Donnell, Donald Warders, Janet Sharistanian, Jack R. Cohn, Simon Habegger, Nellie Habegger, John Tibbetts, and, in particular, Ann Douglas. I am grateful for the kind assistance and many valuable leads given me by David J. Nordloh and Christoph K. Lohmann at the Howells Edition Center at Indiana University. Libraries that have facilitated my work by offering me the use not only of their collections but also of special facilities are the Huntington Library, the New York Public Library, the University of Washington Libraries in Seattle, and Watson Library at the University of Kansas. Finally, it is to the National Endowment for the Humanities that I owe the greatest obligation. Without the study fellowship I received from this agency in 1978, I would not have been able to write this book.

Gender, Fantasy, and Realism in American Literature

Part I

MARRIAGE

CHAPTER ONE

A Genre and Its Absorbed Audience

By the middle of the last century it was widely understood that the novel had become something that appealed to women more than to men. Many men purposefully relegated fiction to the ladies, apparently regarding all novels as inherently feminine—that is, juvenile, precious, or visionary. Even more cultivated men, such as David Masson, a professor of English at University College, London, lamented "the conversion of the Novel, in the hands of the majority of modern novelists, and especially of lady-novelists, into a mere love and marriage story."[1] According to an American critic and arbiter of manners, Oliver Bell Bunce, "the great vice of womankind" was to confine their "reading exclusively to novels."[2] Nathaniel Hawthorne, W. D. Howells, and Henry James often betrayed an uneasy sense that they were writing largely for a female reading public. Some women, in fact, openly proclaimed the novel the exclusive territory of their sex: "The privilege of deep research is man's right; with it we have no wish to interfere," but fiction is "woman's appropriate sphere, as much as the flower-garden, the drawing-room, and the nursery."[3] One of the basic facts in American literary history is that during the decade in which Howells and James came of age, the 1850s, the bestselling American works of fiction were written by, and probably consumed by, women.[4] Normally, one assumes that it is the dominant class that speaks to itself in print. Whether or not this assumption is in most cases correct, the fact that it would be erroneous one hundred and twenty-five years ago shows how important it is to try to sense what novel-reading once meant for women readers.

The only real difference between the novel and the short story or novella—that of length—is an index to what is special about reading a novel: it takes much more time. More time means two things for the reader: the novel's fictive world becomes more complete and engrossing than that of shorter narratives, and the impossibility of finishing the novel in one sitting gives this fictive world a status curiously different from that of a story or play. Because one returns to this world again and again, as one returns to a favored pastime, to read a novel is to become unusually absorbed in what one reads. There is plenty of evidence that in the mid-nineteenth century young women tended to get caught up in novels in an extreme kind of way, so extreme that their pastors, teachers, parents, and husbands took alarm.

Susan Warner, a novelist herself and the author of one of the most popular and pattern-setting novels of the 1850s, *The Wide, Wide World,* offers a perfect instance of the intensely absorbed reader. In adolescence, according to Susan's sister, the future novelist had "her head in a rosy dream of fiction half the time." At the age of fifteen Susan was perplexed when young Julia Ward Howe pointed out that "novels only shewed one the romance of life, not the reality." Throughout her life, "the latest page of her beloved book held her fast in dreamland." Even at the age of forty, long after her own bestsellers had held thousands of other readers, Susan was caught up in *Katherine Ashton* and *The Initials* (the latter novel simultaneously caught young Henry James at the age of eleven and young W. D. Howells at the age of sixteen). Most striking of all was the intensity of Susan Warner's reading experience: she "was passionately fond of stories: identifying herself with the characters in a way that must have been often more pain than pleasure, and taking much to heart the least seeming blemish in some favourite personage."[5]

The record suggests that Susan Warner's intense absorption in the fictive life of "some favourite personage" was not at all unusual. In the view of Noah Porter, a philosopher who became president of Yale, novelists like Warner acquired an insidious power over readers:

No class of writers exercises so complete control over their readers as novelists do. . . . The fascination which they exercise becomes of itself a spell. . . . A favorite novelist becomes, for the time being, often more to his enamored and enchanted reader than preacher, teacher, or friend, and indeed than the whole world besides. . . . The entranced and admiring reader runs to his favorite when he can snatch an hour from labor, society, or sleep. He broods over his scenes and characters when alone.

As Porter saw it, readers who brooded over novels tended to be inactive and without jobs: "the reading of novels is the chief occupation of a certain class of persons who are exempt from the ordinary claims of business or study."[6] This class would consist largely of young women who were not poor.

One of the most important aspects of the novel-reading experience, for both Warner and Porter, is that it washed over the reader's other experiences as well. The reader may have laid the narrative aside, but the narrative continued to live within her. Evidently, Edgar Allan Poe was not speaking for novel-readers in "The Philosophy of Composition" when he argued that a long narrative inevitably loses its hold on the reader when it is temporarily put down. *Paradise Lost* may have loosened its grip on Poe, but *The Wide, Wide World* did not release its readers. There is, in fact, an unanswerable piece of evidence for the absorption of nineteenth century readers in their novels, and that is the custom of installment publication. Fiction must have gripped its victims very hard to hold them month after month.

Why were novels able to absorb their readers? The most general answer to this question is that novels provide a more intense version of the experience made possible by all good stories—an escape from oneself. Reading, like daydreaming, has a profoundly regressive aspect. The vacant or rapt expression on the face of a child acting out a private drama or following a good story hints at what is happening to a grown-up interested in a novel. Why is it sometimes so hard to make contact with a person deep in a book? Because the person doesn't want to come back. The great appeal of stories is that they make possible a temporary and satisfying escape from the conditions of human existence. When we are caught up in a novel, we leave behind the pressures of life and the ego's fulltime vigilance. That is why, from Samuel Richardson on, novels have solicited readers to identify with a central and generally sympathetic person— that is, to substitute another person's troubles and triumphs for their own. That is also why, in so many popular novels, the central character approaches perfection; the reader needs a wonderfully idealized substitute self in order to lose interest for the time being in his or her own life. If the substitute self is badly flawed, the game won't work and the reader drops out of it.

At the heart of popular American fiction in the 1850s was the figure of the heroine. The fact that many novels were named after the heroine is a sign of her centrality. Publishers, perfectly well aware of her importance, often rechristened serials by replacing the original title with the heroine's name. Thus, Rebecca Harding Davis' *A Story of To-Day* became *Margret Howth*; Oliver Wendell Holmes's *The Professor's Story* became *Elsie Venner*. The double meaning of the word *heroine*—protagonist and champion—indicates her basic function for the reader: the heroine was the reader's champion in a struggle that was full of risk and in some way exemplary. In the 1850s the heroine enabled the reader to forget her own trying world for the moment and identify with the superior person who, as Nina Baym has shown, faced and triumphed over certain archetypal dilemmas.[7] Thus, compared to the reading of other literary genres, the reading of novels was not so much an aesthetic experience as an ego experience. It was partly because novels gave an enormous if indirect satisfaction to the ego that many critics, such as Oliver Bell Bunce, condemned novel-reading so harshly: "It's nothing more than looking in a mirror. The novel-reader crawls into the skins of all the heroes he admires; he fills them out, strides in them, and when he glorifies the original, is secretly glorifying himself."[8] If one disregards Bunce's moralistic acerbity, his view offers a valuable glimpse of what it once meant to read a novel.

Judging on the basis of the bestselling women's novels of the 1850s, it appears the heroine was not only the reader's alter ego but that she provided the reader with a full range of pleasures, ranging from the clean satisfaction of a lofty self-image to the final joy of surrendering to a clean man. Ethically, every single heroine had a moral character without spot or wrinkle. She was not necessarily pretty, through she was almost always bright, but the quality she had to have was a will and a capacity to do the right thing under all circumstances, no matter how difficult. If the heroine had been merely a saint, however, the novel would not have become a popular genre. It was because the saintly heroine always got her man that the novel worked. Ultimately, the reason why novels encouraged the reader to identify herself with an altogether superior heroine was to make possible the intensely pleasurable pay-off at the end, a climax not considered successful unless it produced a physical effect—happy tears.[9] Underneath everything else, women's fiction was a material aid for the enjoyment of certain complex fantasy with a strong erotic component.

CHAPTER TWO

Fantasy in the Novel

By *fantasy* I am not referring to the class of fiction shelved in Woolworth's next to the Harlequin Romances, but to the daydreams enjoyed by all people (and especially Harlequin Romance readers). Let us begin our analysis of fantasy and its place in the novel by taking another look, through Ann Douglas' eyes, at the passionately absorbed nineteenth-century reader:

> Numerous observers remarked on the fact that countless young Victorian women spent much of their middle-class girlhoods prostrate on chaise lounges with their heads buried in "worthless" novels. Their grandmothers, the critics insinuated, had spent their time studying the Bible and performing useful household chores. "Reading" in its new form was many things: among them it was an occupation for the unemployed, narcissistic self-education for those excluded from the harsh school of practical competition. Literary men of the cloth and middle-class women writers of the Victorian period knew from firsthand evidence that literature was functioning more and more as a form of leisure, a complicated mass dream-life in the busiest, most wide-awake society in the world.[1]

What was the nature of this "complicated mass dream-life," and why did the novel turn out to be the genre that stimulated it?

In a recent paper, "Dialectics of Fantasy," Marcia Westkott draws on Freud's "The Relation of the Poet to Day-Dreaming" to argue that:

> Fantasy not only opposes real conditions, but also reflects them. The opposition that fantasy expresses is not abstract, but is rooted in the real conditions themselves, in concrete social relations. As a negation, fantasy suggests an alternative to these concrete conditions.

By arguing that fantasy is closely allied with children's play and adult literature, Westkott builds a case for regarding fantasy as not necessarily regressive. It has, she insists, a creative potential and can lead to problem-solving activity:

> Fantasy, like play and all other imaginative activity, requires the active engagement of our energies and the full involvement of our mental lives. To bring to creative consciousness a memory of past gratification and a criticism of present domination is to engage in self-knowledge.[2]

I am going to claim more than Westkott that our fantasies are deposited in us by our culture. Yet her basic analysis is useful because of her insistence that the very idea of fantasy implies a background of unsatisfactory reality. Fantasy is not some febrile phantasmagoria but an energetic dramatization of a better future by people living in a concrete world.

With this basic understanding of fantasy, let us try to grasp the link between fantasy and the nineteenth-century popular American novel. One writer expresses a common view of the relation between the two:

> The typical conventions of the novel can be separated from those characteristic of both private fantasies and fantastic narratives. This separation can be seen most clearly in the representation of the conflict between social institutions and the imagined self. In general, novels tend to represent this conflict more directly and with less displacement than do fantasies . . . In fantasies we know what we want and learn how to get it. In novels we learn what is possible and get what we can.[3]

This distinction obviously applies to realistic fiction and many of the novels that have been admitted to the canon, but it does not apply to a large number of novels, including many bestsellers and most nineteenth-century women's novels, books which, as Nina Baym has shown, almost invariably show how the heroine triumphs over her hardships. Like so many theories of the novel, this one commits the error of trying to generalize about a genre on the basis of a few great and therefore exceptional instances.

The most ambitious attempt to understand the element of fantasy *within* fiction (and not as opposed to it) is Norman Holland's pioneering study *The Dynamics of Literary Response*. Unfortunately, the umbilical cord connecting this book with Freud was not severed. Holland understood that fantasies "occupy a special prior and primitive place in our mental life,"[4] but he limited his "dictionary of fantasy" to the developmental categories of psychoanalysis—oral, anal, and so forth. Holland made a further mistake: he omitted the latent and genital stages of development because they derived from preceding phases. Thus, he not only committed the logical fallacy of equating a phenomenon with its earlier or original form, but in omitting the last phase he ipso facto dismissed the fantasies that are so important for adolescents and adults and the fiction they read. Most serious of all, Holland's severely schematic approach necessarily ignored the fact that our fantasies are shaped by culture, class, economics, and history. There is little sense of history or culture in his book.

The best study of fantasy in literature and culture is John G. Cawelti's *Adventure, Mystery, and Romance: Formula Stories as Art and Popular Culture*.[5] This book deals with standardized story patterns in various popular American literary forms, particularly the mystery and the western. Cawelti analyzes these forms by "replacing the inevitably vague and ambiguous notion of myth" with the concept of "conventional story pattern or formula." The reason why certain formulas gain currency is that "they bring into an effective conventional order a large variety of existing cultural and artistic interests and concerns." Cawelti's careful study "rejects the concept of a single fundamental social or psychological dynamic," such as the Freudian concept of fantasy elaborated by Holland. Yet Cawelti also insists that formula and fantasy are closely related—"formulas become collective cultural products because they successfully articulate a pattern of fantasy that is at least acceptable to if not preferred by . . . cultural groups." The question he does not answer is why certain patterns of fantasy become popular.

Fantasy is clearly the key. But the key will not turn unless we can explain how something so private as our fantasies links up with something so communal as formulas. We need, in other words, a schematic social theory that places us in society and takes account of our personal daydreams, the "mass dream-life," and the novel. Let us try to work out such a theory by first looking at a vignette in Adeline D. T. Whitney's novel, *The Gayworthys* (1865), where we are shown a conventional middle-class family group sitting together and reading: "After the child had gone to bed, Mr. Gair being quite absorbed in his *Journal of Commerce*, Mrs. Gair took up the *Lady's Book*, and when she was reading, nobody ever talked. Gershom [an adolescent nephew] was rapt and happy in Ross's *Voyages*."[6] It is obvious that the three characters are intensely interested in very different things, and that each pursues his or her interest by means of the solitary, non-physical activity of reading. And what is very much to the point, we see that entirely different genres have evolved in order to satisfy the varying demands of husband, wife, and growing boy. The husband is in business, the wife has social ambitions (which she indulges by reading after she has got rid of her daughter for the night), and the boy, who will grow up to be a sailor, reads adventure. Age, gender, social role, and literary genre— these are the essential components for a simple theory designed to explain in general the appeal of certain narrative genres to their reading and listening clientele, and in particular the appeal of the novel to nineteenth-century women readers.

In this theory, gender is primary and fundamental. As we humans grow up, we begin very early to think of ourselves as male or female; and this early gender-identity soon becomes unalterable.[7] In nineteenth-century America, as in all known societies, adult social roles were determined in part by sex. A basic part of socialization, then as now, had to do with the child's progress toward certain idealized gender-based adult roles. Whatever conflicts these roles may have caused (and there were serious conflicts then too) the ideal gender roles inspired an intense allegiance and became the focus of a great effort, for it was only when individuals filled the contours of the role satisfactorily that they could be seen, and could see themselves, as successful men or women. People felt an intense desire to achieve a certain ideal gender identity, for its achievement would be a public triumph and self-vindication. This gender identity was at one and the same time very private and very public—private because it formed the individual's goal or idealized self or wished-for image; public, because it was after all a kind of copy of cultural norms. Fantasy, then, was nothing less than a private drama in which one put oneself into the ideal gender role. And the popular novel was a prop for standard fantasies.

It is because so many people are so constantly occupied with the dream of becoming a certain kind of man or woman that the story told by so many popular novels involves the final stages of a young person's growing up. It is probably unnecessary to label one kind of novel the *bildungsroman,* since most nineteenth-century novels fall into this category. Similarly, it is beside the point to belittle the final embrace or wedding or wrapping-up of the characters' lives: these were at one time genre qualities in the novel, and the reason they became genre qualities is that they completed the daydream at the heart of the novel—the daydream of becoming the right kind of man or, more pertinently, the right kind of woman. Girls, preoccupied with the basic human desire to grow up to be a certain kind of grown-up, shaped themselves on the basis of a particular cartoon-like self-image; adolescent girls, on the point of acquiring their adult identity, tried on various personalities and destinies by reading novels. And finally, as women, when they discovered that their dreams had not worked out, they relived their unsuccessful self-casting by reading yet more novels about the terrors of growing up. The female *bildungsroman* novel suddenly became a fantastically bestselling formula because the essential human business of working toward an ideal gender role had become such a critical problem for women.

Women's fiction was not the only genre with a core of fantasy in the nineteenth century. American humor, the first original American genre, dramatized the tall-talking backwoodsman who represented such a significant figure in male folklore. This humor worked, as I try to show in part 2, by provoking laughter at a grotesque form of the independence many men dreamed of even while knowing it was unrealistic. Male humor served to distance the laugher from an ideal gender role that had become impractical; women's fiction, which tended to outlaw laughter as something coarse and irreligious, worked on the basis of a passionate identification. By means of a model heroine who embodied the ideal feminine role, the novel secured the reader's total involvement and then provided her with a triumphant reenactment of her most cherished daydreams. The peculiar force of the novel lay in the fact that it gave daydreams a local habitation and a name and thus blurred the line between reality and desire. The dense realism of Susan Warner's fiction—the homely verisimilitude praised or deplored by contemporary readers—to some extent served the function of disguising the dreaminess of the story. This confusion explains the tremendous popularity of certain novels in the 1850s, the recurrent denunciation of novel-reading, and W. D. Howells' perception that there was a real danger in reading novels that weren't true to life.

One of the best literary studies I am aware of that regards particular genres as aids to particular fantasies has to do with the appeal of pornography. Robert J. Stoller defines pornography as "a complex daydream in which activities, usually but not necessarily overtly sexual, are projected into written, pictorial, or aural material to induce genital excitement in an observer." His way of defining the essential task of the writer of pornography has important implications for the study of popular novels:

> Especially helpful [in using pornography to study perversion] is the fact that since pornography, for its creator, is produced for money-making, he will be motivated in the highest to develop *a daydream that is not idiosyncratic.* If his pornography is to pay, he must intuitively extract out of what he knows about his audience those features all share in common ... He therefore has to create a work precise enough to excite and general enough to excite many.[8]

Stoller then examines a story intended for a rather limited clientele— male transvestites. In this story, a college boy joins his friends in a panty raid. His friends escape, but he is caught and held prisoner by the girls and then compelled to wear their clothing—nylons, heels, etc. The climax of the story occurs when the hero reflects that he is being made to impersonate a woman against his will.

As Stoller shrewdly points out, the ordinary reader might easily fail to notice the point at which the narrative culminates. That very difficulty should alert us to the possibility that less specialized forms of popular literature might also aim at a highly particular and recurring effect for their proper readers. I suggest that most popular women's novels of the last century tended, like transvestite pornography, to address a single erotic fantasy. Even though this female fantasy was more complex and appealing than the extremely specialized story of the college boy caught in a panty raid, readers who do not form part of the original clientele for women's fiction no longer recognize and respond to the fantasy. That is to say, readers who do not share certain mid-nineteenth-century assumptions—only in marriage can a woman sleep with a man, only by marrying a dominating man can a woman find satisfaction, and, paradoxically and most important of all, only a man can ruin a woman—will miss the crucial signposts in a genre that regularly forced the heroine to endure privations, anguish, and painful misunderstandings before entering the bliss of a happy marriage. Such readers will not feel like crying happily over the happy ending.

There is no better way to reveal the modern reader's difficulty in spotting the fantasy embedded in the nineteenth-century women's genre than to examine the actual responses of a contemporary reader. A recent article on Olive Schreiner tells how the nineteenth-century girl who grew up to be an early twentieth-century feminist read a certain novelist, a Miss Wetherell, largely for the pleasing fantasy of being carried off by a man:

> These fantasies, on occasion, possess definite erotic elements. In a charming letter to Ellis, Schreiner describes a story by a Miss Weatherall [sic], written for young girls, in which the central character, Daisy, breaks her foot. As the doctor carries Daisy in his arms she feels for one instant his moustache brush against her lip. Schreiner exlaims, "One longs that one had broken one's leg and been carried by the doctor, and felt the moustache brush one's lip!"[9]

And who was Miss Wetherell (to spell the author's pseudonym correctly)? None other than Susan Warner in disguise, lover of novels and author of *The Wide, Wide World*. The book that so impressed Olive Schreiner was *Melbourne House*, first published in 1864. The heroine, Daisy Randolph, breaks her ankle while hiking on a mountain with Captain Drummond. He carries her off the mountain. Although he does not brush her with his moustache, he later kisses her fervently on the forehead. The American edition has a striking illustration showing the girl, very white, lying in bed and looking up at the black-suited captain, who has a large moustache. Two hundred pages later, as Daisy is still unable to walk and must be carried by a doctor she has grown very fond of, she finally gets the moustache:

> "Dr. Sandford!" she exclaimed. "I shall tire you. Please put me on the floor and let me stand."
> "No—you cannot," said the doctor decidedly. "Be a good child, Daisy. Lay your head down and go to sleep again."
> And greatly to Daisy's astonishment the doctor's moustache brushed her lip. Now Daisy had always thought to herself that she would never

allow anybody that wore a moustache to kiss her; here it was done, without leave asked . . .¹⁰

I would not have guessed that there was such powerful fantasy material here, if Schreiner hadn't tipped me off. Of course, this particular fantasy may have been idiosyncratic. Nonetheless, it indicates the sort of response novels solicited.

Susan Warner herself felt that there was something a bit fishy about novels, even though she loved to read them and together with her sister (Anna, author of the familiar children's song, "Jesus Loves Me") wrote so many of them. In Susan's first novel, *The Wide, Wide World,* the second of three last requests the hero (a grown man) asks of the heroine (not quite grown up) is to "read no novels." What is the third question he will ask the girl once she has grown up (provided she has kept herself pure by not reading fiction)? That is coyly left to Ellen and the reader to figure out. "Ellen puzzled herself a little to think what could be the third thing John wanted of her; but whatever it were, she was very sure she would do it!"¹¹

It is always a mistake to underestimate the resources available to human animality. The terrible proscriptions of nineteenth-century life produced the duplicity evident in the conclusion of this incredibly bestselling book, which purveyed the erotic satisfaction customary in novels at the same time that it outlawed the entire genre. To see the precise outlines of the fantasy the novel-genre stimulated, we must now turn to the subject most serious discussions of fiction make a point of avoiding, love-interest and the happy ending.

CHAPTER THREE

Love-Interest

A full-page engraving in *Graham's Magazine* in 1854 titled "The Declaration" represents a young man and woman in a darkened interior, with the woman dressed in white and spotlighted in such a way as to suggest that she is the real subject of the scene and this is her apotheosis.[1] *Graham's Magazine,* at one time combined with *Burton's Gentleman's Magazine,* was not for women only. Forty years later, the prairie realist Joseph Kirkland wrote about weddings as if everybody had a fixation on them: "A wedding and a bridal trip. What an opportunity for the romancer! How easy to enchain all readers, of any age, sex, color, or previous condition of servitude! No need to be graphic, witty, picturesque in order to be interesting, the mere theme does it all."[2] A little less than a century later, John Updike would speak of love-interest as if it still had the power to hold our attention, and, more to the point, were closely bound up with the novel considered as a genre:

> The French say, "Without adultery, there is no novel," and while this may be more true of *their* novels than yours [England's], it is indeed difficult to imagine a novel, even one by Lord Snow, without its as the phrase goes "romantic interest."
>
> I would suggest that this is a *genre* trait of the Novel . . . The amassment of sums of money, fascinating in reality, acquires interest in a novel only if the acquisition of wealth advances the hero or heroine toward that eventual copulation that seems to be every reader's insatiable and exclusive desire.[3]

Granting this desire (though without implying that every fiction fiend is racked with lust), let us ask this question: what sort of novel would be most enjoyed by feminine readers living in a culture where it is assumed that to copulate with a man means pairing off with him for the duration of life?

The only serious flaw in Nina Baym's fine study of women's fiction in the United States in the 1850s is her overlooking the crucial importance of love-interest. Baym points out that the heroine of this fiction "stays aloof from the husband hunting of her peers, preferring, in an oft-repeated phrase, 'honest independence' to a mercenary marriage." She argues that "since the point of the fiction is the development of feminine self-sufficiency, the traditional rescuing function of the lover is denied to him." One of Baym's recurring themes is that families in popular fiction were generally unhappy or broken, and that the heroines tend to enter "a network of surrogate kin." Furthermore, the marriage with which

> most of these novels conclude . . . represents the institutionalizing of such [surrogate] families, for the heroine's new home includes not only her husband but all her other intimates as well. And her final 'domesticity' is defined as her relations with all these adults, rather than as childbearing and childrearing.[4]

This way of looking at the fiction clearly makes it possible for modern progressive readers to enjoy it and also explains many of its peculiar features. But Baym overlooks some of the primitive fantasy-content. Every single popular novel had an insistent, if sometimes damped, love-interest. The heroine may not chase men, but her mind inevitably begins to dwell on one particular man to the exclusion of all others, even though she may not speak of him. Calumny or misfortune causes him to remain misinformed about her true feelings, and for most of the novel, hero and heroine are separated by tragic accidents. In the end, inevitably, after the author has systematically harrowed the reader's desires and expectations, the reader gets her happy marriage. This marriage is emphatically not a marriage that includes "all her other intimates" and "all these adults." It is marriage with a man—a strong man who has a firm social identity and standing and is almost always richer, taller, and older than the heroine. The heroine may have stayed aloof from husband hunting, but neither the author nor the reader had left the business of match-making.

St. Elmo, the 1867 bestseller by Augusta J. Evans, is the perfect case in point, for no novel (except *Beulah*, also by Evans) had a heroine more interested in "honest independence" than is Edna Earl.

She flatly turns down the Satanic hero's proposal—"I can not lift up your darkened soul; and you would only drag mine down"—and goes to New York to become a governess and famous novelist. But silence and distance can not keep her from worshipping at her private shrine. The intensity of her love for St. Elmo is disclosed by a brief conversation with his mother, which briefly misleads Edna into thinking he has married the rival, Estelle:

> "My poor Edna! my dear little girl! why did not you tell me you were ill? . . . I should have been here a month earlier, but was detained by Estelle's marriage."
> Edna looked vacantly at her benefactress, and her lips whitened as she asked:
> "Did you say Estelle—was married?"
> "Yes, my dear. She is now in New-York with her husband. They are going to Paris —"
> "She married your—" The head fell forward on Mrs. Murray's bosom, and as in a dream she heard the answer:
> "Estelle married that young Frenchman, Victor De Sanssure, whom she met in Europe. Edna, what is the matter? My child!"
> She found that she could not rouse her, and in great alarm called for assistance.[5]

Illness is not the only cause of Edna's vacant gaze, whitened lips, forward falling head, and swoon. The author did not have to spell out the heroine's intense fixation on one particular man. The reader *knew*.

One of the features of women's fiction that would seem much more irrational to the modern feminist than to the nineteenth-century reader is that the heroine's remarkable accomplishments in taking care of herself almost always lead to marriage rather than to a career. To see why marriage was understood as the proper goal, one must grasp the basic representation of female life in popular novels. Not only do these books rarely offer a portrait of a marriage; they rarely tell about courtship. What they really tell about is some terrible frustration of the normal progress of courtship. The essential story, then, is how the heroine, by a great effort of will and duty, resolutely pursues the path of righteousness and thereby wins the man in the end. This is the story of girlhood probation under specially trying circumstances, the prize at the end being, of course, the perfect man who will take care of the girl for the rest of her life. After her unremitting endeavors, the heroine can at last relax. This partly explains her final passivity, as in Susan Warner's *Queechy*. Here the proposal takes place during the heroine's bitter night journey on a snowbound train. The hero's ingenious method of proposing is to insist that he will accept Fleda's Bible only if she gives herself with it. Saying nothing, Fleda accepts by merely giving him the Bible. He acknowledges their engagement by clasping her hands and the Bible and sitting there in silence and darkness with her. Now Fleda is safe: as the temperature drops inside the stalled car, the hero throws over her shoulders his expensive black fox cloak, an "emblem . . . of care and protection,—something that Fleda had not known for many a long day,—the making up of the old want. Fleda had it in her heart to cry like a baby."[6]

As the black fox cloak suggests, the heroine gets much more than security when she finally gets her man. The touch of fur, like the touch of mustache that Olive Schreiner never forgot, evokes the sensual delight that marriage promises. The most important thing to remember about the social context of popular fiction in the nineteenth century is that sex outside marriage was taboo for women. One strange consequence of this was that weddings and even proposals became shorthand for sex: no reader could have been unaware that following the wedding ceremony would come something . . . that could not be spoken of. The reason why the scene on which everything depended in the novel had to do with love and its dread ceremonies is that the heart of the novel was an anticipated act of copulation. In an age when a man's declaration, "I love you," was tantamount to a proposal, these three words formed, quite simply, the most interesting speech-act there was. Indeed, I suggest that a structural analysis of this speech-act (which always implies certain emotional intensities, complications, and social dynamics), would show that it constitutes the generative core of the novel.[7] In back of all the complications and impediments that in novel after novel delay the marriage of true minds lies both a strong and pervading desire and a strong and pervading sense of the danger of desire. It is the combination of desire and danger that accounts for the story told by so many popular women's novels—the girl's working so hard and denying herself so much and being so careful, all in order to legitimize the huge pleasure at the exit (she thinks) of the maze.

It was understood, of course, that male supremacy meant that the wife would to some extent be the servant of her husband. As Catherine Beecher wrote, woman "is *a subordinate* in the family state, just as her father, husband, brother, and sons are subordinates in the civil state."[8] Apparently unaware that the United States was, at least in theory, a republic where citizens governed themselves by electing legislators and governors, Beecher, like many women writers and readers, loved to celebrate the high and joyful calling of subordination. This is the calling that the heroine of Augusta J. Evans' *Beulah* (1859) finally acknowledges:

> The vows yet upon her lips bound her irrevocably to his side, and imposed on her, as a solemn duty, the necessity of bearing all trials for herself; of smoothing away home cares from his path; and, when her own heart was troubled, of putting by the sorrow and bitterness, and ever welcoming his coming with a word of kindness, or a smile of joy. A wife![9]

Evans was still single when she wrote this.

One of the basic social facts behind the novel's breathless interest in becoming "A wife!" was the Victorian ideology that considered love the basic female emotion. Even George Henry Lewes, who was less prejudiced against the scribbling females than most men of letters, insisted on this point: "Love is the staple of fiction, for it 'forms the story of a woman's life.'"[10] Mary P. Ryan has made a more cogent analysis of the complicated ways in which love appealed to women:

> Romantic love had a certain logic as a method of female socialization. This emotional extravagance, first of all, might bridge the ever-widening gap between the sexes. The euphoric leaps to romantic love could transcend the gulf between worldly men and retiring girls. The fragile, over-specialized female, furthermore, was helpless without a man to support her and accept her emotional riches in return. Romantic love conveyed the urgency of her search for a spouse. Intense heterosexual attraction also helped to wrench a young woman away from the maternal home . . . Finally, a glorified and overpowering sentiment like romantic love could disguise the inequitable relationships a bride was about to accept . . . The hope of "being paramount in one heart" was a major consolation.[11]

All this helps explain the great appeal of love-interest in the novel. But Ryan's and my account would be incomplete without a brief glance at one last consideration: heterosexual love leading to marriage, parenthood, and domestic life is a central human experience. Our impatience with the way Victorians inflated this kind of love too often leads to a rejection of the thing itself. Is the kind of love that leads to domestic life only one among various sexual life-styles? The answer, in the context of civil liberties, must be yes; the law must be blind to homosexuality, etc. But in another sense the answer is no. Marriage, defined as any child-rearing heterosexual group, is clearly the more usual and more nearly universal choice. Families are central in all human cultures, and what is more, by far the most common form of marriage is monogamy.[12] Along with monogamous marriage goes a universal and natural curiosity about the intimacies of family life and the ritualized gestures of sexual approach that lead to sex and marriage. Rituals, myths, and various literary genres from all times and places testify to our great interest in the coming together of a man and a woman. This is a basic human drama and necessity, given the fact that children require so much longer a period of nurturing and socialization than do the young of any other species. And stories about this coming together have a perennial appeal. Love-interest has an inherent importance and dignity.

In nineteenth-century America, the intense concern with marriage led to the emergence of a curious mythic drama—the courtship of Priscilla and John Alden. This drama turned into a ritual in which a significant ancestral mating was reenacted for a local community. As Kirkland showed in *Zury* (a book concerned with the making of a strong family in the wilderness), this drama was widely performed by amateur actors in school exhibitions. Anne Sparrow, a schoolteacher from New England, is the first to introduce "The Puritan Marriage" to a frontier settlement in Illinois. The farm folk who make up the audience are captivated when John Alden (played by the novel's hero) urges Captain Standish's suit and is told by Priscilla (Anne Sparrow) to ask for himself. The third act of this mythic drama brings down the house merely by representing John and Priscilla's wedding.[13] This interesting ritual is a culmination everyone enters into.

CHAPTER FOUR

Home Sweet Home

The novel dramatized the most important fantasy of women living in a culture where wifehood was not only idealized but seen as their *raison d'être*.

Living the fantasy of "a wife!", however, was not quite so simple. The very fact that women loved to fantasize a perfect mating shows that they had not achieved the ideal in their own lives. There is plenty of evidence, furthermore, suggesting that many nineteenth-century homes were not nearly as sweet as the old motto claimed. There is also evidence that outside marriage men and women often dealt with one another in extremely stylized and fearful ways. The enormous appeal of the John Alden–Priscilla story can be attributed to some extent to the intangible but strongly felt barriers between the sexes: here was a courtship, apparently doomed from the start, where the woman spoke out and broke through the barrier. Isn't it possible that the novel was popular for the same reason? That it enabled the hard-pressed reader to keep the impossible faith?

It has often been suggested that one of the causes of marital unhappiness in the nineteenth century was the bride's ignorance of the facts of life, and a general Victorian repression of female sexuality. One scholar cites an 1890 review of the book *Effect on Woman of Imperfect Hygiene of the Sexual Function* that claimed three out of four wives "suffer from sexual ill-health due to ignorance before and after marriage."[1] No doubt, many brides were as ignorant of the nature of sexual intercourse as was Edith Wharton, whose terrible mother froze with hauteur when her nervous daughter asked for information.[2] Perhaps the tendency for husband and wife to sleep in separate bedrooms is relevant here: in Ed Howe's *Story of a Country Town*, Joe Erring and Mateel apparently have different rooms *before* their marriage goes completely to pieces. Most pertinent of all is Robert Herrick's 1908 novel, *Together,* which, like Updike's *Couples,* studies the course of several deteriorating marriages. Herrick's narrative of the Falkner's disastrous honeymoon takes a daring look at the wife's fearful rigidity during the act of intercourse and her total rejection of what her husband is doing to her.[3] It is hard not to realize that any marriage beginning like this hasn't got very far to go. Yet skepticism is in order: how much, after all, is known of the sexual intimacies of marriages a century ago and more? Isn't it rash to assume that normal human animality can be suppressed as completely as the old stereotypes of Victorian life demand? Most important of all, there is the evidence provided by some early Stanford question-naires that Carl N. Degler has recently analyzed. Degler concludes that for middle and upper-middle class college-educated wives who married in the last years of the nineteenth century, sex was satisfying.[4]

Another popular explanation for domestic discord in the last century is the rise of industrialization, which supposedly divided the sexes by turning men into careerists and women into domestics. The one big objection to this view is that it overlooks the differentiation of sex roles that preceded the industrial revolution and the frequency with which domestic discord has been associated with farm life. New England folklore had it that a certain husband and wife were buried under a single tombstone—"Their warfare is accomplished."[5] Only in death could this warring couple be united. The same is surely true of the couple in Robert Frost's poem, "Home Burial"—a brilliant analysis of an exemplary kind of quarrel. The hating couple in this work shows how certain non-idiosyncratic gender traits lead to an irremediable conflict in the home (the title has more than one meaning). The man is practical, hard-working, extremely reserved about his grief for his child, and full of a belligerent common sense: "A man must partly give up being a man / With women-folk." The wife, excessively sensitive and absorbed in a nineteenth-century feminine way with death, sees her husband as a dolt: "I can repeat the very words you were saying. / 'Three foggy mornings and one rainy day / Will rot the best birch fence a man can build.' / Think of it, talk like that at such a time!"[6] Of course, this poem from *North of Boston* reflects many developments that came in conjunction with industrialism: Frost is not simply portraying a primitive agrarian household. But the poem does show—and there is a great deal of evidence all over the place to support this—that farm households have not generally been egalitarian utopias where husband and wife do all the work equally and together.

But if industrialization did not create specialization by gender, it did exaggerate it, blowing up to an enormous extent a distinction that was already (and always?) there. Edward O. Wilson has suggested that one of the links between culture and human biology is that a given institution may develop a biological trait to the point of hypertrophy.[7] When the Englishwoman Harriet Martineau visited the United States in the 1830s, she was shocked by the American "persuasion that there are virtues which are peculiarly masculine, and others which are peculiarly feminine. It is amazing that a society which makes a most emphatic profession of its Christianity, should almost universally entertain such a fallacy."[8] This bifurcation did not proceed so far in England, possibly because of the presence of social, religious, and intellectual elites that were not greatly affected, at least at first, by industrialization. But the United States, without the ballast of a landed aristocracy or a massive cultural inheritance, gave way to the pressures of industrialism in a most illuminating way: men were redefined in terms of business interests, women in terms of the home; and this separation in their spheres of activity tended to lead to separate goals, values, and ethical systems. Men respected men who were shrewd, aggressive, and self-seeking, while women, practicing the imitation of Christ, looked on love and nurture as the essential feminine traits.

In *The American Scene* (1907) Henry James gave a striking formulation of the chasm between men and women. The "great social fact" about the United States that impressed James more than anything else was that "the business-man" can "never hope to be anything *but* a business-man." Failing to develop "the so numerous relations with the world" that a "civilized being" must develop, he has left an "unexampled opportunity" to his mate, the American woman, who has reconstituted American life "in her image." Thus, because of the man's "default," the American scene has become "subject and plastic to his mate." In James's view, American women were "of a markedly finer texture than the men," who, in "facial cast and expression," tended to have a certain "business man" look. (In many nineteenth-century photographs of men, the jaw is set in a way that makes the lower lip jut. In Howells' 1889 novel, *Annie Kilburn*, it is a little surprising that a man who has "the face of the caricature American," with "curved vertical lines" enclosing his mouth, lacks "the slight frown of challenge and self-assertion which marks this face in the type.")[9] James was also struck by "the appearance of a queer deep split or chasm between the two stages of personal polish, the two levels of the conversible state, at which the sexes have arrived." James saw this split, correctly I think, "as *the* feature of the social scene" (italics James's). He felt himself "in danger of seeing" nothing else in the American scene but this strange incompatibility of the sexes— "this apparent privation, for the man, of his right kind of woman, and this apparent privation, for the woman, of her right kind of man." For James, "this failure of the sexes to keep step socially" was "more suggestive of interesting 'drama' . . . than anything else in the country."[10] The American man and the American woman were incompatible.

The fact that men and women had opposing values naturally led to enormous conflict, especially in the home. And the fact that the home was supposed to be a peaceful retreat and marriage a perfect union only obscured the reality. Men were more and more absorbed in the egotistic struggle for wealth, place, and power. While the home turned into a shrine, the rest of the world became a fierce, competitive arena for the rough and tumble of primitive capitalism. The books that dealt with this world—*Moby-Dick, Two Years before the Mast, Miss Ravenel's Conversion from Secession to Loyalty, The Red Badge of Courage*— all involve the idea of battle in one guise or another, an oppressive male hierarchy of some sort, and a man's great effort to survive. And in certain male literary forms such as humor, there is evidence that men did not always place the perfect lady on a pedestal. In humor, at least, they often evinced a notable contempt for gentility, fashion, and cultural imports from Europe or the East. If woman's place was the home, man's place would have been the cross-roads grocery or the big city wardheeler's bar, the steamboat saloon or the railroad smoking car. Man's place was *the tavern*, the only spot where men could casually get together behind frosted glass windows or their equivalent, and drink, smoke, chew, spit, swear, and laugh. Small wonder that a great female crusade arose in order to suppress this place.

Temperance crusaders were not willing or able to face the possibility that men patronized saloons partly because they weren't altogether at ease in their home sweet home. In *The Inebriate's Hut* Mrs. S. A. Southworth (not to be confused with Mrs. Emma D. E. N. Southworth) told of a home broken up by alcoholism and then blamed it on the tavern-keeper, the husband's weak moral resolve, and the devil in the bottle.[11] She didn't consider the likelihood that the husband felt more comfortable in the saloon than in his wife's neat parlor, or that he preferred to relax with his cronies. Temperance was the perfect woman's movement for the average respectable woman who didn't want to be considered a radical. In *Adventures of Huckleberry Finn,* the King exploits this situation: "I'd ben a-runnin' a little temperance revival thar 'bout a week, and was the pet of the women folks, big and little." It would be many years before the brilliant Charlotte Perkins Gilman would go to the heart of the problem in her perceptive study *The Home,* where she asked and answered the essential question: "What is the average workingman's attitude toward this supposed haven of rest? The statistics of the temperance society are enough to show us the facts." Those who seek to close the saloon, she wrote, "do not dream that it is the home which drives him [the erring husband] there."[12]

One of the few complaints by a man about the rarity of home comfort is a pair of articles written by Oliver Bell Bunce in *Appleton's Journal* in 1870. The articles claim to reproduce an argument between a married man and a blunt, rational bachelor who believes there is very little "domestic bliss" in most marriages. The bachelor builds his case by pointing out that "men and women, as a consequence of their distinct daily occupations, have very different aspirations and expectations in regard to matrimony." For women, marriage is supposed to be a "career, and hence within it centre all their ambitions, all their hopes, all the largeness of their future. But, with man, marriage is something very different. Men are out in the world, busy in the great battle of life." Hence, when a man comes home, he wants to relax and take it easy. His wife, however, wants to go out for her relaxation: "And so we see how a natural and radical antagonism may exist between man and wife as to the pleasures and the needs of home." What the bachelor objected to most of all was the tendency of so many wives to make the home far too neat and orderly "in blind servility to one of their gods, Propriety." Because of women's insistence on having a neat parlor—"damask furniture that must not be sat on, and all forms of finery that must not be warmed by good, honest fires, lest the dust alight on them"—women are not, "as they suppose, the source of domestic bliss, [but] they are radically and constitutionally its obstacles and enemies."[13]

I suspect that Bunce's fictive bachelor gave voice to a widespread masculine point of view that did not often see print. William Henry Milburn, a popular minister and lecturer, expressed a more conventionally acceptable view in his talk "An Hour's Talk about Woman." Milburn believed that "we have little or no true domestic life in this country." He fixed the blame on habits of conspicuous consumption (though of course without using Veblen's later phrase) in successful metropolitan families. The typical "New York merchant in flourishing business," Milburn wrote, would have a home full of showy objects that contributed nothing to domestic comfort—knickknacks, unread gilt-edged volumes, "magnificent" works of art. The consequence of this was that neither the husband nor the wife nor children could regard the home as a place of enjoyment. Milburn concluded: "Among the thriving mercantile and commercial classes of this country, the statement may be ventured without fear of exaggeration, that there is little or no domestic life."[14] Granting for the moment that Milburn was correct about New York, what about the rest of the country? Alexander Hamilton Sands, a Virginian "barrister" who reviewed Milburn, defended the South: "The picture our author draws of New York domestic life we accept as a truthful portraiture, but it is not a model of Virginian homes."[15] But Sands published this essay in 1859, at a time of tremendous sectional hostility and Southern defensiveness. Another book of the same year, written by a Southern woman, supported Milburn. Augusta J. Evans' frivolous character, Antoinette Graham, who "received the attentions and flattery of gentlemen as unreservedly, nay, delightedly, as though she had no neglected husband and child at home," is said to be typical of the married men and women in the Southern city where the story is laid: "this sort of conjugal indifference was in vogue."[16]

It is hard to know how much credence to place in the many laments in the 1850s and 60s that the family had fallen apart. Milburn, Evans, and other writers were undoubtedly determined to make the point that women should rededicate themselves to the home, and this purpose may have distorted the writers' perceptions. Yet the basic reason why they felt so strongly that women should be domestic may have been that home-life was indeed a shambles. Milburn knew perfectly well that most husbands were busy at work away from home and would not be inclined to help with the family even when surrounded by it: "the children," Milburn sarcastically said, "must not speak a word, for 'papa is busy.'"[7] It would therefore be up to the wives, if anyone, to save the home and reform manners and morals for the future. Wonderful as those Virginia homes may have been, even Sands felt a desperate need for an angel in the house: "There is need for a mighty transformation here; and none but woman can work it. Satire and ridicule, man's weapons, will not avail."[8] It is this sort of desperate concern that lies behind much of the talk about women's sphere. The family was sacred, not so much because it was a haven in a heartless world, but because people were afraid that the family itself was falling apart. In 1859 a magazine writer declared: "The Family, in its old sense, is disappearing from our land, and not only our free institutions are threatened, but the very existence of our society is endangered." In 1864 another writer put a painful rhetorical question to his readers: "Do any of you who may be our readers know half a dozen happy families in your circle of friends?"[9] To understand the ethical zeal and unrelenting correctness of so many fictional heroines in the nineteenth century, we must try to discern in the background the well-concealed outlines of a massive social upheaval.

It became obvious to many women at the time that an intense rededication to the family would not save it as long as husbands were so absorbed in their work and outside interests that they were for all intents and purposes strangers in the home. Mrs. Adeline D. T. Whitney would always be opposed to women's rights, yet in 1860 she could write:

> But just take a man,—
>   Shut him up for a day;
> Get his hat and his cane,—
>   Put them snugly away;
> Give him stockings to mend,
>   And three sumptuous meals;—
> And then ask him, at night,
>   If you dare, how he feels!

> Do you think he will quietly
>   Stick to the stocking,
> While you read the news,
>   And "don't care about talking"?[20]

The notion that men are incapable of performing or enduring women's work is a common theme in folklore. Whitney's poem, a commentary on a Mother Goose rhyme, illustrates one connection between proverbial wisdom on the nature of men and women and the new social conditions of mid-century.

Some of the bitterest complaints about male abdication from the home came not from the women's suffrage radicals but from two very popular domestic advice columnists, Gail Hamilton and Fanny Fern (pen names for Mary Abigail Dodge and Sara Payson Willis). One of Fanny Fern's main contentions was that men should spend more time with their children, especially in "their government and *home* education."[21] In her biography of Gail Hamilton, Fanny Fern quoted with approval one of her bitterest complaints: "*You* go out to your shop, or sit down to your newspaper, and forget all about it [housekeeping]. She sits down to her sewing, or stands over her cooking-stove, and meditates upon it with indescribable pain." Gail Hamilton also wrote:

> When papa comes in, the children are often hurried out of sight and sound, for they will 'disturb papa.' . . . I am amazed at the folly of women! Kept from disturbing papa! Rather hound them on! . . . Let him come into close contact with his children, and see what they are, and what they do, and he will have far more just ideas of the whole subject than if he stands far off. . . . His children will elicit as much love and interest, together with a great deal more knowledge, and a great deal less silly, mannish sentimentalism.

Fanny Fern rightly called this last sentence "one of the choicest and most sensible verses in Miss Gail's new gospel."[22] It is interesting to note that Gail Hamilton had a very intense correspondence with Henry James, Sr., in 1864–65. She wrote, "Mr. James, you are head and shoulders above your kind, a Saul among the brethren, in this matter of women."[23] Even more interesting, she was the first person to pronounce a benediction on Henry James, Jr., solely from reading him:

> Young Henry James, I think, is one of the most promising writers we
> have. His stories are studies. He has a way and a thought of his own.
> How much there is in this last story of his just begun. All his stories have
> body. His women, if they are wicked or foolish, have their own way of
> being so. They are not the old block women handed down by tradition.[24]

In some of her essays, Fanny Fern clearly saw herself as a kind of
universal advocate for suffering wives:

> Married men should everywhere, and in all classes, remember, that it is
> very discouraging for any wife and housekeeper, when, for the same
> efficient labor which she expends under her own roof, she could earn
> for herself at least a competence, to be obliged to go as a *beggar* to her
> husband for the money which is justly her *due*.[25]

In another essay she begged editors not to discontinue the "Poet's
Corner," a feature that gave solace to the tired wife:

> As she reads, a tear gathers in her eye; she dashes it quickly away with
> an "ah—me," and laying her head back upon the chair, and closing eyes
> that were once much bluer than now, she is soon far, far away from the
> quiet home where her treadmill round of everyday duties has been for
> many years so faithfully performed, and, perhaps, alas! so thanklessly
> accepted.

Abruptly, the vignette turns into a story when the wife's reverie is
interrupted by "a heavy and familiar footstep"—her husband. He
picks up the newspaper clipping, and she says,

> "It was only a bit of poetry, John." Now, there are more Johns than one
> in the world, but he don't think of *that*, as turning to some political
> article he says, "Oh, you are quite welcome to all that sort of stuff;" nor
> does he know how much that other John had to do with her crying over
> those verses, which somebody certainly must have written, who, like
> herself, had married the wrong John.[26]

The sudden colloquial bitterness here is extremely illuminating,
disclosing a vast social landscape of suppressed marital unhappiness

and unacknowledged regret. The critic understands nothing if he dismisses the wife's tearfulness by means of the epithet *sentimental*.

The potency of the mythology about marriage, along with the inadmissability of divorce in respectable society, led to a widespread falsification—a point a number of realistic writers would make from 1880 on. One of the stories James tells in the last third of *The Portrait of a Lady* is how Isabel finally stops trying to convince her closest friends that she and Gilbert Osmond are happy. She admits part of the truth to Henrietta, her old girlfriend. But she discloses her real misery only to the dying Ralph. Her strong impulse to hide the truth about her wretched marriage shows how the lofty mystique of the home served to obfuscate the facts of the matter. It was this sort of wretchedness that actually induced fiction-writers to glorify marriage. In a later novel, Jack London's *Martin Eden*, the hero's sister turns into a drudge for her husband, the tyrannical and small-minded sole owner and proprietor of Higginbotham's Cash Store. Martin's short stories disappoint this unhappy wife precisely because they are true to life:

> "That story was perfectly grand," she announced, straightening up from the wash-tub with a tired sigh and wiping the sweat from her forehead with a red, steamy hand; "but it makes me sad. I want to cry. There is too many sad things in the world anyway. It makes me happy to think about happy things. Now if he'd married her. . . ."[27]

This character is caught in more than one trap. Her misery accounts for her need to fantasize, but the sacredness of romance makes any realistic appraisal out of bounds. Caught in a double bind, she represents the common female reader of the nineteenth century in her need for a regular dose of escapism. She is a genuine addict and she has to take her fiction fix in periodical installments. In *The Minister's Charge* (1887), Howells sketched a group of wives living in a residential hotel. Uprooted and sickly, with few children, no social life, no occupations, no function of any sort, these women would be the envy of Martin Eden's overworked sister; yet they wander vacantly through the corridors with novels "clasped to their breasts with their fingers in them at the place where they were reading; they did not speak of them, and apparently took them as people take opium."[28] A great deal of nineteenth-century women's fiction was a brew laced with opium, alcohol, a pinch of wormwood, and buckets of molasses. It was the moral equivalent of soothing syrup (the male drug being alcohol).

The problem was, there was a dreadful double bind in marriage itself. The less interest men took in their homes, the more domestic the wives had to become. And the more dutifully the wives tried to make their homes the heaven on earth they were supposed to be, the more alienated became the husbands. According to Mary P. Ryan, "the social-psychological function" of the good woman was "internal control of the economic lust and antisocial tendencies of the middle-class male."[29] That was certainly the theory. But in practice, it appears, men and women were not complementary but antagonistic. Instead of creating a single coherent culture, they tended to create two separate nations, male and female. Love-interest tried to cover up this chasm.

But the chasm always revealed itself in novels, particularly in Mrs. Emma D. E. N. Southworth's fiction, where there is a powerful and sometimes ludicrous death-dealing aspect to the conflict between the sexes. In one of her early novels, *The Curse of Clifton,* an old drunkard attempts to reform and swear off liquor. But a doctor tells him he will not get well unless he takes brandy, a single glass. The drunkard asks his saintly granddaughter, the heroine of the novel, for advice. She tells him to pray. That night he prays. The next morning, the doctor arrives and refuses to modify the prescription: "unless you consent to save yourself by taking alcohol, you must die." But the heroine wins. "Then I will die*!" replies the reformed sinner, and he does. The asterisk calls the reader's attention to a laconic testimonial at the bottom of the page—"A Fact."[30]

One of the oddest accounts of the impasse between the sexes is the short story "Mlle. Olympe Zabriski," by Thomas Bailey Aldrich. A New York blue-blood, Ralph Van Twiller, falls in love with a trapeze artist. Ralph knows he should have nothing to do with a woman so much below him, but he is bored with proper young ladies. Echoing an observation that was widely made from *The Scarlet Letter* on, Ralph complains that modern American women have "no physique. They are lilies, pallid, pretty,—and perishable. You marry an American woman, and what do you marry? A headache." Mlle. Zabriski is so different—"a lithe, radiant shape out of the Grecian mythology, now poised up there above the gas-lights, and now gleaming through the air like a slender gilt arrow." So Ralph Van Twiller finally breaks down and sends this lovely shape an expensive bracelet as a token of his esteem. He receives the following grateful note in reply:

> Mr Van Twiller Dear Sir—i am verry greatfull to you for that Bracelett. it come just in the nic of time for me. The Mademoiselle Zabriski dodg is about plaid out. My beard is getting to much for me. i shall have to grow a mustash and take to some other line of busyness, i dont no what now, but will let you no. You wont feel bad if i sell that Bracelett. i have seen Abrahams Moss and he says he will do the square thing. Pleas accep my thanks for youre Beautifull and Unexpected present.
>
> > Youre respectfull servent,
> > Charles Montmorenci Walters[31]

The story is basically a familiar male joke at the expense of a man who has innocently done something that can be construed by his comrades as homosexual. Yet the story reflects a genuine male problem: if all good young ladies are going to grow up to be invalids, it might make sense for a young man to marry a healthy boy.

There is much, much more of the secret hostility between men and women in the novels of the 1850s, 60s and 70s.[32] We must now look more closely at the way certain novelists attempted to deal with what Charlotte Perkins Gilman called "the bitterness of feeling which has arisen between the sexes in this century."[33] Many writers, after all, made an effort to tell the truth in their work, particularly Elizabeth Stuart Phelps and John William De Forest. Yet these writers, like all the other novelists I've read before James and Howells, were unable to reconcile the truth they saw with the genre demands of love-interest. The fact that love-interest was essential in the novel, a part of its form and substance, meant that novels *ipso facto* preached that love was the most important passion. Howells understood that the novel's heroine "*taught by example*, if not precept, that Love . . . was the chief interest of a life, . . . that it was lasting . . . that it was worthy of every sacrifice."[34] Any reader caught up in a novel automatically consented, if only for the time being, that there could be no more happy resolution than satisfied love, no matter what else the work in question might have to say. But what could this mean, given the pervasive hostility between the sexes, the disintegration of the home, the elaboration of two separate nations, except that there was an emptiness at the heart of the novel and a confused evasion in the novel-reading experience? Is it at all surprising that the first two full-scale realistic novels—*The Portrait of a Lady* and *A Modern Instance*—focussed squarely on bad marriage? Or that the authors of these works were themselves the products of happy families?

CHAPTER FIVE

Domestic Bitterness as Presented in Popular Women's Novels

"These American novels," Mrs. Gaskell wrote in 1857, "unconsciously reveal all the little household secrets; . . . we hear their kindly family discourse, we enter into their home struggles."[1] Edith Wharton, looking back from 1920, might have wanted to excise the word *kindly*, though she agreed that "they all lived in a kind of hieroglyphic world, where the real thing was never said."[2] The secret never told but conveyed in hieroglyphics again and again and again was that domestic life was intolerable.

In *The Wide, Wide World* the heroine's father, Captain Montgomery, is an authoritarian absentee ruler. On Sundays he either goes out or—and here is one of Mrs. Gaskell's household secrets—stays "in bed, the whole day." He suddenly tells his wife to send their daughter away, and when he finds a way to dispose of her, his wife watches his movements in terror:

> *He* seemed very well pleased; sat down before the fire rubbing his hands, partly with cold and partly with satisfaction; and his first words were, "Well! we have got a fine opportunity for her at last."
> How little he was capable of understanding the pang this announcement gave his poor wife![3]

Here, the husband is the enemy of the home, which Warner generally pictures as a warm, dry, fire-lit refuge against a nasty cityscape and bad weather. And contrary to expectation, the husband is not even a provider; one of the events that throws the heroine out into the wide wide world is the discovery that the father has just lost an important lawsuit.

When the husband is at home, it's generally bad enough, but when he leaves, things get worse. One of the basic stories novels told was the poverty or anguish suffered by a wife when her husband deserted her. In Susan Warner's second novel, a man who begins as a respectable figure, Mr. Rossitur, ends up deserting a wife who is so helpless she would not survive if it weren't for the heroine's exertions.[4] Desertion, as Helen Papashvily has pointed out, is a highly charged event in Southworth's novels. In *The Curse of Clifton*, Zuleime, accidentally abandoned because she is thought to be dead, practically starves during the winter. In *Ishmael* Herman Brudenell walks out on his English wife when she suddenly shows up at Brudenell Hall. For years afterwards she walks every day to a certain turnstile waiting with her "woman's heart" for her man to return. According to Papashvily, one of the big fantasies in Southworth's novels is that the devoted wife will triumph over the deserting husband in the end. "Hagar! I have not one word to say for myself! Not one excuse to offer for my weakness! Not one syllable to breathe in palliation of my fault! Hagar, I am a bankrupt!"[5]

In E. W. Howe's bitter study of home-life on the frontier, *Story of a Country Town*, two men desert their wives—Damon Barker (Captain Deming) and Rev. John Westlock. And Howells' first realistic study of a disintegrating modern marriage would lead up to the husband's desertion. But these two realistic works would not have a happy ending.

There is a more subtle desertion in those novels that tell of a man's divergence from the ideal union he enjoyed with the heroine in childhood. In *Beulah*, the heroine and Eugene had an understanding before he went to a German university. But now Eugene is fallen away, as the author, Augusta J. Evans, discloses:

"Beulah, as a man, I see the world and its relations in a far different light from that in which I viewed it while a boy."
"It is utterly superfluous to tell me so!" replied Beulah, bitterly.
"I grapple with realities now, and am forced to admit the expediency of prudent policy. You refuse to see things in their actual existence, and prefer toying with romantic dreams. Beulah, I have awakened from these since we parted."
She put up her hand deprecatingly, and answered:
"Then let me dream on! let me dream on!"[6]

Man reneges, but woman keeps the faith.

In Whitney's novel, *The Gayworthys: A Story of Threads and Thrums*, there is a much more perceptive analysis of the divergence of a young couple. Sarah and Gershom begin as playmates. Then Gershom goes to sea and becomes a man. When he returns he has a sailor's scorn for Sarah's stylish boots, dress, and behavior. The elegance she hopes will please him is all "frippery and sham." Sarah is very disturbed. The author's understanding of the gap that has opened between these two is more profound than Evans'. While "Gershom has seen the world—a sailor's sight of it—over and over," Sarah "had lived on in her world: half a dozen streets; a couple of score of drawing rooms; four houses, perhaps, where she was intimate enough to go up stairs when there was no party." She had "achieved [,] it seems [,] nothing but her growth, her bloom, and her woman-garb. Nothing else, that Gershom could apprehend. She could but put on her pansy-robe and come to him, so, with her best."[7] Whitney handles the girl's inevitable disappointment with great understanding. In the end, unfortunately, she mates this poorly matched pair.

The Gayworthys traces the fortunes of four separate couples, always emphasizing the "thrums"—the unjoined ends of threads. Like all of Whitney's work, this novel was full of didactic advice partly because it addressed itself to what were believed to be actual problems—the impediments that prevented lovers' meetings and the possibilities of marrying the wrong person. One of her couples has to wait seventeen years before coming to an understanding. Another couple never does get together. It was this kind of failure that formed the subject of Whittier's famous poem, "Maud Muller":

> For of all sad words of tongue or pen,
> The saddest are these: "It might have been!"[8]

Bret Harte's parody—

> If, of all words of tongue and pen,
> The saddest are, "It might have been,"
> More sad are these we daily see:
> "It is, but hadn't ought to be."[9]

dealt with the more common tragedy of the mismated couple. One of the oddest literary pieces to emerge from the widespread concern with domestic discord was *Six of One by Half a Dozen of the Other: An Every Day Novel.* This work was written by six writers (three men and three women including Stowe, Whitney, and Edward Everett Hale) about three mismatched young couples who finally get straightened out so that they all marry the Right Person.[10]

One of the most intriguing studies of a bad marriage is Whitney's portrait of a childless old farm couple in *The Gayworthys,* Wealthy and Jaazaniah Hoogs. Wealthy has worked so hard all her life that she has scarcely had the leisure to discover "that there was something unresponsive in her sphere, that she had not found—I am half ashamed to use the word—her 'affinity;' that she was a mismatched, misplaced woman." But she still does her duty and tries to love her husband "faithfully"—a word that apparently means "forbearingly, for the most part." He is not her companion but simply "the man whose name and home she shared." Bright and questing, eager to read, philosophize, talk, Wealthy almost looks as if she were a superior being. She is compared to a bent apple tree struggling to rise from underneath a rock. Her husband is of course the rock— "slow-moving, literal Jaazaniah came out of the dairy, his arms strung with milk pails, and took his plodding way down the path toward the barnyard, wrinkling his brows in the level-glancing afternoon sunlight, with never an apparent outglancing of any light within kindled of all those heavenly shafts illumined."[11]

The portrait of the Hoogs's marriage justifies to some extent the claim of *The Gayworthys* to be a realistic novel. Yet in this couple we see one of the favorite myths of a great many women's novels: man is a coarse, literal-minded beast, and woman a glorious spirit who lives on sunshine and metaphor. It was precisely this myth that vitiated so many women's novels, for even as the author attempted to sketch an accurate portrait of contemporary life, her better angel whispered to her that realism was only a coarse male habit after all. And so she compromised her artistry by choosing the old path of ideality and hopefulness and a glorious model of what true marriage should be or what the true woman was. Only a coarse man like Theodore Dreiser could penetrate the confusion:

> The maiden and the matron as well has been schooled to believe that she is of a finer clay than man, that she was born to uplift him, and that her favors are priceless. This rose-tinted mist of romance, having nothing to do with personal morality, has brought about, nevertheless, a holier-than-thou attitude of women toward men, and even of women toward women.[12]

CHAPTER SIX

John William De Forest
vs. Elizabeth Stuart Phelps

John William De Forest, wrongly billed as the pioneering American realist (the honor goes first to Caroline Kirkland, then Susan Warner), is notable as the first American novelist to offer realistic representations of the Civil War, the officer class, the Southern gentry, and lower-class manners in the South. Elizabeth Stuart Phelps made history with her bestseller *The Gates Ajar* (1868) and later wrote the first important American novel about a failed marriage, *The Story of Avis* (1877). Together, De Forest and Phelps make a fascinating study in literary and sexual polarities. De Forest apparently had much more firsthand knowledge of men and manners than all earlier or contemporary American writers of fiction, including Herman Melville. He traveled widely in Europe and the Middle East, was at home in New England as well as the South (which he knew before, during, and after the Civil War), saw action in the war, and was appointed by the Freedman's Bureau to maintain law and order in Greenville, South Carolina. He apparently fought with his wife about her spending. His best novel, *Miss Ravenel's Conversion from Secession to Loyalty,* has as good a claim to being the Great American Novel (De Forest coined the phrase) as anything before Dos Passos' *USA.* Unhappily, *Miss Ravenel's Conversion,* like all of De Forest's books, did not sell and went quickly out of print. Elizabeth Stuart Phelps's books were far more popular than his. In the United States alone, *The Gates Ajar* may have sold one hundred thousand copies by 1884;[1] the copy of *The Story of Avis* I borrowed from the Seattle Public Library was checked out fifteen times in 1926 and 1927—fifty years after publication. An extremely "poetic" writer who was keenly alive to the

suffering of women, Phelps apparently had a large, devoted following. At the age of forty-four, after writing her most successful books,
she married a man seventeen years younger than herself. This
marriage appears to have been even less successful than De Forest's.

Phelps was often asked how she happened to write *The Gates Ajar*.
She would answer, "The angel said unto me 'Write!' and I wrote."
This is not the complete story. She wrote the book in her early
twenties when she was still living at home. At the time, as she recalled,
she "had no interest at all in any especial movement for the peculiar
needs of women as a class." Yet she was consumed with a feeling that
"creeds and commentaries and sermons were made by men. What
tenderest of men knows how to comfort his daughter when her heart
is broken?" This animus against male ministers was caused partly by
her rebellion against her Calvinist father, but in addition the house
was full of "noisy boys," mainly stepbrothers. She would always
remember going downstairs and discovering that the dining-room
had been converted into a play-church and the boys were delivering
sermons. She fled upstairs to her cold unheated room, put on her
dead mother's fur pelisse, and worked on *The Gates Ajar*, which, not
too surprisingly, would turn out to be a denunciation of male rule
and an affirmation of tender femininity.[2]

The tenderness accounts for some of the striking contrasts between
the way De Forest's best novel treated the Civil War—the war that
took more American lives than all our other wars put together and
the way *The Gates Ajar* treated it. Phelps's book took the form of a
journal kept by a girl who has lost her brother in the war. The story's
central figure is Aunt Winifred, from Kansas, a consolation-figure
who persuades the mourning girl that she will be reunited with her
brother after death and paints the most delicious pictures of heaven.
It is Aunt Winifred who holds the gates of heaven ajar for grieving
mortals. Dr. Bland, the official minister, offers no comfort at all in
his dry, rationalistic sermons. This man is dull, maladroit, and
oppressively self-satisfied, at least until his wife is burned to death.
Then he learns his lesson. The other men are worse, and one of
them, Deacon Quirk, is beyond redemption, for he has an "obstinate
old face with . . . stupid, good eyes and animal mouth."[3] His son
Aminadab is an "uncouth specimen of six feet five" straight out of
the laboratory of Hawthorne's "The Birthmark." When Aminadab
dresses up, he combs his hair "into two horizontal *dabs* over his ears"

and breaks the cardinal color rule by wearing a "green-gray coat" and "blue-checked shirt-sleeves" (p. 117). In contrast to these grotesque males, Aunt Winifred is a "white, finely cut woman . . .—every inch of her, body and soul, refined not only by birth and training, but by the long nearness of her heart to Christ" (p. 104). This classy, tasteful angel gathers an admiring group of Sunday School girls around her and develops a close, tearful, idealistic friendship with some of them. Together they talk and dream of heaven, while the stupid, bumbling men go about the base world's business.

The Gates Ajar was a bestseller partly because it offered the refined and idealistic fantasies that many women demanded from literature. At one point a girl, Little Clo, comes to Aunt Winifred for solace. Little Clo has for two years been in love with a man who hardly knows of her existence, a former summer boarder and thus a person above her and the farm boys in wealth, status, and sophistication. Little Clo knows that her love is hopeless, and she's afraid that even in heaven she won't be happy: "What is going to become of me up there?" (p. 138). Although Aunt Winifred knows that there is some affection between Little Clo and big Aminadab, she strengthens the girl's infatuated obsession by promising her she'll actually get her man in heaven—the ultimate happy ending. Thus, by encouraging Little Clo to ignore real people in anticipation of a heavenly rendezvous with the summer boarder, Aunt Winifred comforts the girl in the most pernicious and silly way. The whole book, in fact, responds to the ugly tragedy of war by seeking refuge in dreamland. Phelps begins with the agonies of bereavement but then turns away to dwell in rapture on the joys of the hereafter, when all good people will get their one big wish. *The Gates Ajar* suggests one of the reasons why so few novelists wrote about the most destructive war in American history: the gentle reader did *not* want to know the facts.[4]

In 1867, the year before Phelps published her rhapsody, John William De Forest brought out *Miss Ravenel's Conversion from Secession to Loyalty*. This novel provided the most detailed accounts of combat to be found in American fiction, up to Kirkland's *Captain of Company K* (1891) and Crane's *Red Badge of Courage*. The dominating figure in De Forest's novel is Colonel Carter, Virginia aristocrat and West Point officer, a hard-drinking, worldly, competent man who embodies many ideal masculine traits. His social poise, virility, and blunt military bearing prove irresistible to young Lily Ravenel, who easily falls for him.

There is another man interested in Lily, young Colburne, who comes from a New England college town named New Boston. This virginal Puritan cannot compete with the mature Southerner, who marries Lily. Only after Carter has died in battle and Colburne has lost "the old New Boston innocence" and acquired an "authoritative demeanor,"[5] does Lily fall in love with the younger man. She falls in love, but not because she changes in any important way—the title is very misleading. Rather, Colburne *earns* her; by facing death in armed combat, he has become a man and attracts women as easily as Carter did.

Colburne's development bears out one of the fundamental laws of American manhood. While a female is born to womanhood, manhood is never given. It must be fought for on the battlefield or in some other competitive arena. Thus, although the author shows and laments the horrors of war, he can't help missing them when all is said and done:

Those days are gone by, and there will be no more like them forever, at least, not in our forever. Not very long ago, not more than two hours before this ink dried upon the paper, the author of the present history was sitting on the edge of a basaltic cliff which overlooked a wide expanse of fertile earth, flourishing villages, the spires of a city, and, beyond, a shining sea flecked with the full-blown sails of peace and prosperity. From the face of another basaltic cliff two miles distant, he saw a white globule of smoke dart a little way upward, and a minute afterwards heard a dull, deep *pum!* of exploding gunpowder. Quarrymen there were blasting out rocks from which to build hives of industry and happy family homes. But the sound reminded him of the roar of artillery; of the thunder of those signal guns which used to presage battle; of the alarums which only a few months previous were a command to him to mount and ride into the combat. Then he thought, almost with a feeling of sadness, so strange is the human heart, that he had probably heard those clamors, uttered in mortal earnest, for the last time. Never again, perhaps, even should he live to the age of threescore and ten, would the shriek of grapeshot, and the crash of shell, and the multitudinous whiz of musketry be a part of his life. Nevermore would he hearken to that charging yell which once had stirred his blood more fiercely than the sound of trumpets: the Southern battle-yell, full of howls and yelpings as of brute beasts rushing hilariously to the fray: the long-sustained Northern yell, all human, but none the less relentless and stern; nevermore the one nor the other. . . . After thinking of these things for an hour together, almost sadly, as I have said, he walked back to his home; and read with interest a paper which prattled of town elections, and advertised corner-lots for sale; and decided to make a kid-gloved call in the evening, and to go to church on the morrow. (pp. 345–346)

A sentence from another nineteenth-century novel about the Civil War serves as an apt commentary on this passage: "To the average American [man] brutal battle is better than irksome idleness."[6]

While regarding war as a test and arena for manhood, De Forest renders Lily as a grown-up little girl, privileged and pampered. When playing whist, she "stole glances at her opponent's hand" and "screamed with delight when she won." Breaking "all the venerable rules," she is gladly tolerated: "was she not queen and goddess, Semiramis and Juno?" (pp. 355–356). When Lily speaks, she generally "prattles." She expects her father to know everything. She is shallow, pretty, and uninteresting, as De Forest blithely acknowledges near the end of the novel:

> Here she is, at twenty-thrèe, with but one child, and only at her second husband. Two-thirds of her years and heart history are probably before her. Women are most interesting at thirty: then only do they in general enter upon their full bloom, physical, moral and intellectual: then only do they attain their highest charm as members of society. (p. 519)

This is a fatal admission, confirming that De Forest doesn't care for his "charming" heroine nearly so much as he pretends. It wouldn't be at all surprising if he actually resented her. While his male lead has to risk his life in battle merely to become a man, the female lead gets to remain a girl even after marrying twice. In fact, she wins lasting devotion precisely by remaining immature, while Colburne has to face death before he can make any impression at all on her.

The Gates Ajar and *Miss Ravenel's Conversion from Secession to Loyalty* are the literary expressions of two opposed systems, woman's sphere and man's world. Rather than being complementary, the two systems seem hostile to each other. Placed side by side, the two novels do not really say that woman is dependent and man protective. Rather, the woman's book says that the meek will be taken care of, while the man's book says that Colburne must learn to take care of himself. The woman's book turns its authoritative males, Dr. Bland and Deacon Quirk, into clumsy, mismanaging grotesques, and the man's book turns the charming, dependent heroine into a lightweight chatterer with the political consciousness of a baby: Lily votes with the strong man in her life. The title of the woman's book is religious and metaphorical, while the title of the man's book jocularly secular-izes conversion. Elizabeth passionately dwells on the joys of heaven and thus dreams of a fantastically benign autocracy in which God pets us every one, but John, still exhilarated by war, offers scenes of combat that form a seductive alternative to peacetime life. Both writers yearn for another world, but not the same one. Worst of all, their books adumbrate a deep-seated hatred between the sexes. What makes the hatred so poisonous is its covert nature, for neither novelist will admit in the end that the hatred exists. Instead, *Miss Ravenel's Conversion* concludes with a scene of domestic bliss between Colburne and Lily; while the narrator of *The Gates Ajar* looks forward to a final reunion with her brother (and Aunt Winifred) and Little Clo keeps herself pure for the heavenly summer boarder.

Given the extent of De Forest's experience and great literary talents, it is unfortunate that he could not or would not realize that he was working against the grain of the novel. His one other novel which has received frequent praise, *Kate Beaumont,* written about five years after *Miss Ravenel's Conversion,* shows that De Forest was moving in the wrong direction. The hero and heroine of this book, Frank McAlister and Kate, are much more conventional and dull than Colburne and Lily. As James F. Light has pointed out, "the real interest" lies in the novel's "variety of characters."[7] A case in point is Mrs. Chester, the aging flirt (one of the author's favorite types). This middle-aged woman has "passed twenty-five years in no other habit of mind, than that of love-making" (p. 195) and now she makes an ass of herself by chasing the good-looking hero. Best of all, there is a rich variety of types of men, generally defined in terms of family hierarchies and tribal or political affinities. De Forest wrote about the tired old business of feuding and dueling as no one ever has: he was deeply interested in political chess games in old patriarchies, and he brilliantly narrates the delicate diplomatic steps involved in the defusing of an ancient enmity. Also, I cannot think of another writer who has captured a certain kind of touchy Southern masculinity as well as De Forest in the characters of Peyton Beaumont and his sons. Sadly, the realistic characters and actions are so good they leave us all the more dissatisfied with the noble traits De Forest absent-mindedly rubberstamps *Approved* in the figures of his hero and heroine. His exposure of Mrs. Chester's foolish love enables us to detect his excessive valuation of the heroine's romantic attachment. And his analysis of the Beaumonts' and McAlisters' sensitive male pride makes it all the more surprising that he is taken in by Frank's adolescent heroics, as when De Forest lets this young man rescue Kate from drowning with the promptness of an automaton.

There are hundreds of good things in *Kate Beaumont,* such as the heroine's maneuvering her alcoholic father by rubbing her "satin forehead against his bull neck" (p. 167). But elsewhere there is also a pervading falseness. De Forest clearly found the novel an uncongenial form and was considerably oppressed by what he knew or thought he knew his readers would demand. His best writing is often closely related to his journalistic accounts rather than fictive convention,[8] and seems to reflect a thoroughly secular, mockingly highbrow angle of vision. One always senses that if he had let himself go and ceased paying lip service to the idealized courting couple at the heart of his novels, he might have written a devastatingly fine book on the order of Howells' 1887 novel, *April Hopes,* which tells the story of a courtship that leads to marriage, the difference being that it is all wrong and that the couple is doomed to destroy one another. But De Forest chose a different path. He threw a sop to his readers by giving them a conventional pair of lovers, and then he poured his best efforts into a large cast of subsidiary characters, mainly men.

Many critics have wondered why De Forest failed to attract readers or produce a significant body of work. The reason often given is that he was a man's man trying to write for women: in a letter to Howells, De Forest himself blamed "a female or a very juvenile public" that would rather read "*Helen's Babies* and *That Husband of Mine.*"[9] James F. Light adds another important reason—the opportunism with which De Forest tried one gimmick after another to form his public. But the basic reason seems to me that De Forest evaded the questions at the heart of the novel. How do men and women come together? And what is it that so often separates them? He knew some of the answers to the second question, as we see in the one marriage he looked at closely in *Kate Beaumont*—the squalid marriage between the heroine's sister and the depraved gentleman, Randolph Armitage. After the heroine sees her sister's misery, she wonders: "Could it be that the degrading and miserable tragedy which she had looked upon was marriage? What might be her own future . . . ?" (p. 281). These were the questions De Forest refused to face head-on.

Elizabeth Stuart Phelps did face them, in her popular and controversial *The Story of Avis* (1877). In *The Gates Ajar* the discordances between contemporary men and women were only implicit. In *The Story of Avis* they are at the center. The title character is a gifted painter who would like to devote herself to her talent. After studying in Italy and France, she returns to the United States and begins painting, only to be pursued by a determined young professor, Philip Ostrander. Eventually, after making sure that he understands she intends to pursue her career, Avis marries him. Then she discovers that the usual household distractions—stopped drains, undependable domestic help, crying babies—will not permit her to concentrate on her work. Worse, her husband turns out to be a philanderer and a big baby himself, and she ends up nursing him full-time in a Florida convalescent colony. After his death, she finds she can no longer paint, even though she is still in her early thirties: "'It is of no use,' said Avis wearily, 'my pictures come back upon my hands. Nobody wants them—now. They tell me that my style is gone.'"[10] She ends up devoting herself to her one surviving child, Wait, whose name indicates the only apparent present course of action for woman.

Clearly, *The Story of Avis* was a women's novel in a new sense: it emerged from a strong sense of shared suffering and it regarded traditional masculine prerogatives as highly oppressive for women. It of course had no program for the future (though what good novel does?), but it had the merit of turning a powerful searchlight on the opposition between man and woman. The fact that the woman wanted to devote herself to a career makes the novel all the more appealing to modern feminists. Christine Stansell has written: "Today unjustly forgotten, *Avis* is . . . a probing exploration of the possibilities for survival for a woman who tries to preserve her human wholeness."[11] The controversy that arose on the book's publication was reflected in the anonymous comments W. D. Howells published in the *Atlantic Monthly*'s "Contributor's Club." Some of these comments were extremely negative, some not. One favorably disposed writer duly noted the book's "feverish intensity and occasionally vicious rhetoric," but approved of its "brave, clear intent." This unknown contributor was surprised by the hue and cry of critics who accused the book of bristling with "hatred of marriage *per se,* disdain of homely duties, and all the other ugly appurtenances of a presumedly 'woman's rights' creation."[12] The writer felt the book should be presented to engaged couples.

As far as I know, Howells never entered the controversy *Avis* stirred up. But as editor of the *Atlantic,* he saw and accepted every item in the "Contributors' Club." He may have endorsed Harriet W. Preston's review, which interpreted the novel as saying that "gifted women must not be fettered by domestic ties."[13] There is every reason to suspect that Howells was greatly engaged by the first serious attempt to depict a broken marriage in a novel. I think that *A Modern Instance* would have been a very different book without the precedent-breaking example of *The Story of Avis,* and I also think that Phelps's novel was one of the many threads James gathered together in *The Portrait of a Lady.*[14]

The Story of Avis is an important document for nineteenth-century literary and social history. It prepared the way for our classic realistic novels. The reasons why it was only a precursor and not itself a classic, not even a very good novel when all is said and done, are illuminating. The basic defect in *Avis,* I believe, is that it was too feminine. That is to say, it was written for women, in defense of women's interests and in support of women's myths and values, and was therefore a highly partisan book that set out to attack one side, the men, in aid of the other side, the women. It was not an exploration of the bitter antagonism between men and women; it was itself bitterly antagonistic.

One does not have to read very far in *Avis* to discover that the author has not abandoned the idea pervading *The Gates Ajar:* that men are crude animals and women, at their best, lovely spirits. The basic metaphor in the book is the bird (Avis) that dashes itself against the lighthouse. Phelps establishes this metaphor early in the novel in her gaudiest prose:

Some homeless bird took wing for the burning bosom of the reflector, and straight, straight—led as unerringly as instinct leads, as tenderly as love constrains, as brutally as Nature cheats, with a glad fluttering at the delicate throat, with a trustful quiver of the flashing wings, like the bending of a harebell, like the breath of an arrow—came swaying; was tossed, was torn, and fell. (pp. 24–25)

And what, or rather who, is the lighthouse against whose burning "bosom" the bird kills itself? Here is the author's answer to this question, in the passage describing the moment at which Avis consents to marry Philip Ostrander:

Slowly at first, with her head bent, as if she resisted some opposing pressure, then swiftly, as if she had been drawn by irresistible forces, then blindly, like the bird to the lighthouse, she passed the length of the silent room, and put both hands, the palms pressed together as if they had been manacled, into his. (p. 201)

Here, as in Whitney's portrait of Wealthy and Jeremiah Hoags, man's inevitable effect on woman is to stifle her.

It is partly because man is beast and woman angel (or at least bird) that Phelps sees her heroine as essentially faultless. Avis not only has an amazing genius, but she achieves her initial successes with astonishing rapidity. After her first painting is exhibited, her old master tells her that "New York has gone wild" (p. 372). In Paris, after she has finished her course of study, Couture enters the studio and declares, "Mademoiselle, I will give you two years to make a reputation" (p. 67). Vindicated, she shows a "magnificent, rare pallor" and thrusts out "her empty hand with a gesture" that Couture admires. We do not learn the nature of this gesture, though we are told it reminds her master of a painting of Roxana. Evidently, Avis is not only a wonderful painter but she is a beautiful and natural model as well. When we first meet her, she is disposed against a lustrous carmine drapery, as if she's the subject rather than the artist. Her "certain native daintiness" (p. 89) is noted, as are her various outfits (pp. 15, 90). Even when she falls asleep, worn out, she is picturesque: "She had thrown herself down with the especial grace which great exhaustion gives to a lithe figure. Avis was too much of an artist ever to choose an awkward pose" (p. 307).

But we must entertain at least a passing doubt about a heroine who poses even while sleeping. Do painters really live such wonderfully picturesque lives? Phelps's answer appears to be yes, judging by the scene in which Avis gets the inspiration for her one great work, the Sphinx. Alone in her room, she tosses off a shot of a French liqueur, a "cautious dose" (p. 144) to be sure, and soon begins hallucinating. She sees Egyptian vases, waterlilies, ferns uncoiling delicately, waves. These she rejects. Then faces and hands of the working poor materialize. But her heart protests; "I am yet too happy, too young, too sheltered, to understand. How dare I be the apostle of want and woe?" (p. 140). Next she sees a procession of women: "they sang to their babes; they stooped and stitched in black attics; they trembled beneath summer moons" (p. 150). Finally she sees a desert, a departing caravan, and "in the foreground the sphinx, the great sphinx, restored." It comes alive: "The mutilated face patiently took on the forms and the hues of life; the wide eyes met her own; the dumb lips parted; the solemn brow unbent. The riddle of ages whispered to her. The mystery of womanhood stood before her, and said, 'Speak for me'" (p. 150). Like so much of the novel, this episode has a definite power and an immitigable absurdity. One is both impressed and put off by the belletristic quality of the hallucinations[15] and the completely unchecked megalomania. It seems illegitimate to create a character capable of solving the riddle of the ages, but then to blame her failure to do so on someone else's interferences. This attributes too much power to her at first and not enough in the end, and it enables author and reader to drink deep of the pleasure of feeling persecuted.

And what sort of person does Avis marry? At first Philip is said to look "like a young Scandinavian god" (p. 89). But he rapidly metamorphoses into a selfish and dishonest cad. His essential quality is perhaps his willingness to appear weak in order to secure an advantage over others. Also, he has a very defective sense of responsibility: he refuses to understand why he is fired, he doesn't tell Avis before their marriage of the $3,000 he owes, and he makes his need of her seem wholly impersonal when he pushes for an early wedding date: "I do not wish to press any claim or want of mine unduly, . . . but there *is* my work" (p. 227). He is very insensitive: "Tired?" he asks his wife after unexpectedly inviting four guests for dinner. He is also a snob: he sees that his countrified mother is not allowed to attend his wedding.

After the marriage is established, even though Philip continually abrades his wife's fine nerves, she never complains. Her splendid endurance weighs on him so much that he finally begs her to speak out:

> "I wish you would!" he cried hotly. "I wish you had! I think I should feel better if you would out with it, and tell me what a contemptibly weak fellow you thought me. . . ."
> "O, hush!" said Avis in her rich maternal voice. (p. 409)

Here one sees another advantage in Avis' "maternal" endurance of her boyish husband: she not only gains the upper hand but convinces him that he is about as worthless as it is possible for a person to be. The more nobly she stoops to nurse and humor him, the more paltry he feels. He is finally reduced to saying, "It does seem to me that there must have been something in me worth loving, or you wouldn't have cared for me in the first place" (p. 421).

One of the amusing aspects of the bitter quarrel at the heart of the novel is the change in the two main characters' relative stature. After the first quarrel, when Philip tries like the scoundrel he is to make up with his wife, "her bent figure heightened grandly, and her unwon maiden eyes seemed to look again from a great height down upon him" (p. 282). When she catches diptheria and realizes that her death might saddle her children with an uncongenial stepmother, she decides to live: "magnificently, she set herself moment by moment to conquer death" (p. 331). When she surprises her husband dallying with another woman, Avis, planted "in the doorway, haggard from her mortal illness, stood colossal" (p. 337). She silently points the other woman out the door. Her husband watches her "as a dumb animal watches a human face" (p. 339), and she looks down on him as if he were "small and far, like a figure seen in the valley of an incoherent dream" (p. 342). Now Avis knows that she is like one who "had suddenly stepped into a world of pygmies, and had a liliputian code to learn" (p. 342).

Finally, in the light of the heroine's genius, beauty, forbearance, and all-around superiority, one must raise the question: in which sense, finally, is *Avis* a women's novel? Is it ultimately the realistic, and thus moral and political, book it pretends to be, or is it finally an old-fashioned fantasy-purveying novel in spite of the fact that it lacks a happy ending and addresses an endemic incompatibility between the sexes? The second alternative seems the more likely. Avis is only one more in a long line of idealized heroines, and the sympathy the novel solicits for her is uncritical and wholly out of control. The tendency apparent in women's novels from at least *The Wide, Wide World* on to articulate women's views, dreams, prejudices reaches a kind of climax in *Avis,* where the reader is invited to indulge her grievances by entering deeply into Avis' defeat. Sexual politics, in this book (not in all books, of course), is window dressing: the real thing is an intense desire that one's will may prevail in the wide, wide world and an equally intense bitterness that the world is stronger than the self. In *The Gates Ajar,* the author had indulged her dream of the perfect never-never land where all needs are taken care of by a benevolent provisioner. *Avis* is a wail of regret that it is so hard to reach this land.[16] Narcissistic self-pity has an insidious appeal to women (as it would to men) when they are mythologized as intoxicating girls or good angels and yet subjected to distinct social disadvantages as compared to men. In Phelps, this combination of de jure superiority and de facto handicap led to an off-centered analysis of feminine misery.

But the prime influence on Phelps's analysis was probably her mother.[17] Still single at the time she wrote *Avis,* Phelps was obsessed by the memory of this unhappy and driven woman, who died at the age of thirty-seven. The parallel between Mrs. Phelps and Avis is unmistakable and arresting. Mrs. Phelps had been the daughter of a professor at Andover Theological Seminary, the leading Calvinist school; Avis is the daughter of an antiquated sort of metaphysician who teaches at "Harmouth University." When the mother married a minister who then accepted a professorship at Andover, she returned, like Avis, though even less willingly, to the home town she thought she had escaped. Mrs. Phelps managed to become a popular writer in spite of her invalidism and domestic responsibilities. She also had "a passionate taste for painting and statuary," according to her husband's biography, "A Memorial of the Author." Even as a child, her "first serious enthusiasm" had been for painting; later, after she was married and settled in Andover, she chose to celebrate her wedding anniversary each year by leaving home, traveling to Boston to view the canvases exhibited in the Gallery at the Athenaeum. According to her awed widower, "the resistance of disease by force of will, had been a habit with her for years."[18] Along with her powerful will and invincible sense of duty, Mrs. Phelps had a

Calvinist's anxiety about her own salvation, and for much of her life she struggled with religious doubt. Dying, she actually worried whether she would go to heaven. The one passage where *Avis* explicitly refers to its biographical sources concerns Avis' temporary "syncope" of faith. The novelist wrote: "To dwell upon this phase of her experience would seem to copy the rude fault of those biographers that break faith with the personal confidence of the dead who can no longer protest" (p. 366). This recriminatory passage alludes to Austin Phelps's open discussion of his wife's religious uncertainties in his "Memorial." The daughter evidently regarded his candor as an act of treason, one more instance of rude masculine insensitivity.

Like the story of Avis, the story of Mrs. Phelps was one of lifelong frustration and intense self-discipline. According to her husband, Mrs. Phelps's "literary pursuits . . . were religiously subordinated to her duties 'at home.' This was not a mere sentiment in her mind — it was her daily study; it cost her thought and labor, and was achieved only by an indomitable resolution."[19] Yet the violence with which she forced her life into a domestic channel seems to have made her an oppressively unnatural mother. She practiced a methodical sort of buoyancy because of an "habitual fear that her family might suffer for the want of a cheerful, sunny home." Significantly, when her husband quoted one of her notes in order to show what she was like "at home," the piece turns out to be about her hope of literary success.[20] It seems clear from her husband's "Memorial" that she regarded her children as a real burden. This suspicion finds corroboration in the most celebrated story she ever wrote, "The Angel Over the Right Shoulder," which discloses the mother-author's terrible inner battle by condemning the very ambition that produced the story.

The fictive mother who is the protagonist of "The Angel Over the Right Shoulder" tries to spend two hours a day in study, but her children, husband, and servants frustrate her by their insistent demands. Discouraged, she falls asleep and has a dream in which she sees a woman crossing a broad plain toward a splendid horizon. Children surround this unknown woman and impede her progress. Every time she does something, however trivial, to assist the children in the journey, the angel over the right shoulder gives her a good mark; but every time she tries to reach the golden land alone, the angel over the left shoulder records the act of selfishness. The dreamer eagerly reaches out to inform the traveler of the recording angels, but on touching the traveler's shoulder the dreamer recognizes herself. She then wakes up in tears; we learn that it is New Year's Day; and the mother rededicates herself to her children. Nothing more is said of the two hours' study a day. Apparently, the mother has given up her own time.

This story, I believe, opens a window on the hidden life of the girl who would grow up to write *The Story of Avis*. Just before the mother falls asleep and has the dream that supposedly resolves the conflict between ambition and family, she wonders in agony whether there is "some better way of living." She wishes that "she could shield that child from the disappointments and mistakes and self-reproach" that torment her, and she hopes "that the little one might take up life where she could give it to her—all mended by her own experience." Although the mother has another child, a boy, the girl appears to be the only one qualified to inherit the mother's "mended" life. Thus it happens that in the crisis of her regret the unhappy mother "*leaned over her child*" and "*her tears fell fast upon its young brow.*"[21]

Wonderfully, Mrs. Phelps's own little girl would one day narrate the same event in *Avis*, presenting it from the daughter's point of view. It is little Avis who innocently precipitates the event by asking her mother why she didn't stay in theater if she wanted to be an actress. This question causes Avis to be first rebuffed, then passionately hugged—"put down from her mother's knee . . . , then impulsively recalled, snatched, kissed, and cried over with a gush of incoherent words and scalding tears." For the rest of her life Avis would recall this moment "with incisive distinctness." The memory would stand out all the more clearly as the daughter "never saw her mother cry before or after that" (p. 44).

In Ursula Le Guin's excellent fantasy narrative, *The Tombs of Atuan*, a little girl named Tenar is taken away from her family at the age of five, given a traditional name, and gradually initiated into a deathly vestal cult until she almost forgets who she was.[22] *The Tombs of Atuan* tells in a nonrealistic way exactly what happened to Mrs. Phelps's helpless little girl, who never came out of the shadow after her mother leaned over her, never resumed her own name after being rebaptized in her mother's tears. The scene narrated by mother and daughter alike tells how the one compelled the other to shoulder a heavy emotional burden. Unfortunately, the daughter never had a chance to assess her mother from the vantage point of an adult and equal, for the mother died when the daughter was only eight years old. Her death, Elizabeth Spring believed, "was no common loss."[23] This one can well believe in the light of the fantastic thing that was done to the bereaved child. Her own original name, Mary Gray, *was taken away*, and she was given another name—her mother's. Thus, when Elizabeth Stuart Phelps died, little Mary Gray died too, and Elizabeth Stuart Phelps was born again, along with her bitter grievance. The difficulty one has in knowing by what name to call the daughter at this juncture no doubt reflects her own uncertain sense of identity. Although it is not known who determined the change in name, I suspect that the mother at least willed it, tampering with her daughter's identity in order to pass on her own "mended" life. What is known is that "in the same breath in which she requested that her daughter might be carefully instructed in the fine arts, she requested, also, that her two little boys might be trained for the work of foreign missionaries."[24] (One of these future missionaries was not yet one year old, but even so he would one day annoy his sensitive sister with his mock sermons.) Thus, the daughter was absorbed into the cultic worship of a mother whose aesthetic tastes and aspirations had been thwarted by her Calvinist heritage, unsatisfying marriage, and early death. Twenty-five years after she was interred Elizabeth Stuart Phelps II would fictionalize—and falsify—her mother's bondage in *The Story of Avis*. Yet this book would adumbrate a form of servitude much more insidious than the one it dealt with on the surface. For where was Mary Gray? Did she ever suspect that the story of *her* life had been buried beyond recovery?

Both the strengths and the weaknesses of *Avis* stemmed from the author's strange identification with a mother imagined as less successful, more sinned against, and much more pure than she in fact was. The bereaved daughter's cultic worship of her mother was an important theme in American life a century ago. Thus, in Harriet Beecher Stowe's *Pearl of Orr's Island* (1861) there are two daughters who cling to the memory of their dead mothers—Mara, named for her mother, and Dolores, who wears a peculiar bracelet made from her mother's hair. Significantly, these names signify *bitter* and *sorrow*. It is tempting to blame Phelps's devotion to the cult of the dead mother for the many flaws in her best novel—its religiosity, poetic intensity, stiff female partisanship, consistent hatred of men,[25] in fact its entire tendency to palm off the history of a particular family as social analysis. But this explanation would overlook the many other aspects of the book and the writer's life and times. Certainly, this much can be said of *Avis*—that its author was too wrapped up in her subject. She may have opened the way for James and Howells to write their first realistic analyses of bad marriage, *The Portrait of a Lady* and *A Modern Instance,* but she could not approach their level of achievement.

Phelps's biographer, Elizabeth T. Spring, sensed the connections between these two novels and the more popular *Avis.* Spring much preferred the latter, seeing its heroine as a representative up-to-date woman: "Avis is a woman such as one has seen—strong, gentle, true, with a genius for painting." The author too was great: "only a pure and exalted soul could have conceived" of the novel. By comparison with Avis, Marcia Gaylord and Isabel Archer were not at all noble:

> We have Marcia in 'A Modern Instance,' weak, passionate, unreasonable Marcia, swept under by the first swell in the domestic flood. Mr. James has drawn Isabel Archer best of all the women he has tried, and he has made her almost lovable, or would if he knew about women's souls. Despair and flight are her resort when disenchantment is complete, and pain grows heavy. He makes us sympathize with her; but she seems vague, shadowy, and weak beside the nobler figure of Avis. It is impossible to imagine poor Marcia being anything else than petty; unfit to reform Bartley and unworthy of the better man's [Ben Halleck's] devotion; and with all that is genuine and earnest in Isabel Archer, it is difficult to think of her in Avis' place, bending with conscientious good sense to conquer the homely details of housekeeping, or substitute with so silent a gentleness the maternal for the wifely feeling towards the weaker nature which failed her.[26]

This preference for the wife who has a "maternal" relation to her husband, and for noble role models over mixed and realistically seen characters, was, I believe, the attitude that did more damage to women's fiction than any other single attitude. This veneration of the superior woman explains what is so surprising about nineteenth-century American fiction—the fact that no great woman novelist emerged from the enormous number of women writing in America. Our first great realists *had to be men,* and the reason why they had to be, as Howells and James show us in their best work, is precisely that

the noble and maternal ideal was all wrong. It was this ideal that had
sabotaged Elizabeth Stuart Phelps from at least as early as the age of
eight, when the little girl was brought to dedicate her life to the
memory of a perfect mother she could never really know. And it was
because James and Howells didn't always take feminine self-right-
eousness at face value that they were so often accused in the early
1880s of something the modern reader never sees in them—cynicism.

CHAPTER SEVEN

Henry James and W. D. Howells as Sissies

But if it was going to be up to men to create the realistic novel in the United States, neither De Forest (a Hemingway without histrionics) nor any other highly masculine writer would be the man for the job. Albion Tourgee, a Reconstruction lawyer and novelist, also failed to bring about any significant change in American fiction, though he tried. Given the prevailing literary and social conditions in the post-Civil War period, our first good realistic novelists *had* to be fugitives from the rough masculine world—a world that was a lot rougher in a day when boys routinely owned firearms, scores of people were killed in accidents every Fourth of July, fighting if not dueling was still common, politics was intimately associated with saloon cliques, and business was apparently more of a free-for-all than today. Only a couple of rather effeminate men—in sympathy with the best feminine values but still in a position to criticize women's sphere from the outside—were able to understand and fictionalize the crazy quilt of American life. Essentially, Howells and James seized a popular women's literary genre, entered deeply into the feminine aspirations it articulated, yet brought to bear on them the critical sense of reality that was at that time basically masculine. Only a couple of sissies, so to speak, could perform such a balancing act.

Sissy! Baby! Crybaby! These taunting insults, so inadmissable in civilized life, are the key to many aspects of masculine American culture. They are the key because they name the fear that is one of the chief operative causes of the classic forms of masculinity. The only critic I am aware of who has attempted to deal with the fact that James and Howells were sissies was the eccentric and intelligent Alexander Harvey in 1917:

"Sissy," is not defined in the average dictionary. It is a somewhat slangy term, handed down from one generation of schoolboys to the next. A boy who was called a sissy was supposed to excel in feminine traits rather than in masculine traits. A sissy, as his playmates often admit, will be the clever boy of his class, gifted. Howells is at the head of the sissy school of American literature.[1]

To understand the significance of *sissy,* we must pass beyond Harvey's insight and look for the social causes of "feminine traits" and "masculine traits." The feminine traits that are stigmatized by the word *sissy* are the traits developed by boys excluded from the most active and turbulent masculine clique within a given cohort. It is because femininity is often the shadow of masculinity that a sissy is an effeminate boy, one who is too timid, careful, considerate, polite, or unwilling to join the rough play of other boys. He is thus seen by them as a weak male unable to earn the accolade theoretically open to any male—manhood—and for that reason he is scorned. Chances are, he is more closely bound to his mother than are other boys and more sympathetic to her way of seeing things. Thus, he is dismissed as a mama's boy and the insults applied to him—such as *pantywaist*—derive from characteristically feminine articles of clothing.

Howells and James became sissies partly because they were born into loving families rather different from the norm. Leon Edel has given proper emphasis to the large and close connections between James's uncles and aunts. The Howells clan seems to have been equally close. There were frequent visits up the Ohio river to Howells' maternal relatives, and the relationships within the family itself were apparently affectionate. James's father was independently wealthy and thus, unlike almost all American men, without a job or career; he lived on the fringe of man's world. Howells' father had to work, but he was unusually literate and supported his family in Hamilton, Ohio, by writing and printing a newspaper. His work as printer removed him from the male world almost as much as did James Sr.'s inherited wealth. The country printer's fellow citizens, Howells would later write,

see him following his strange calling among them, but to neither wealth nor worship, and they cannot understand why he does not take up something else, something respectable and remunerative; they feel that there must be something weak, something wrong in a man who is willing to wear his life out in a vocation which keeps him poor and dependent on the favor they grudge him.[2]

Henry James, Sr. and William Cooper Howells both felt a kind of scorn for businessmen, and both had very liberal political opinions, the Howells parent being an early opponent of slavery in a section of Ohio where there was strong Southern feeling. Significantly, both fathers were Swedenborgians who disapproved of "egotism" and associated it with capitalistic enterprise. Both men had a theoretical commitment to socialism, James adopting an eccentric form of Fourier's utopianism. Howells Sr. actually spent a year in a family milling commune with his brothers at a time when Will was thirteen years old. In his son's fictionalization of this quixotic venture, *New Leaf Mills*, the mother has the practical mind, while the father, a dreamer, philosopher, and ideologue, is always full of hope and speaks in a mild and lofty tone reminiscent of Bronson Alcott. His wife keeps him going: "She had always had to fortify him for his encounters with the world, and she understood how in this retreat from it he had felt a safety and peace that he had never felt in its presence."[3] It is striking that the fathers of our first important realists both deviated in the same significant way from masculine norms. Appropriately, one of the basic issues in their sons' fiction would be the legitimacy of selfish desire.

Henry James, Sr., spent a lot of time at home. His second son would recall the relief the father would often evince upon returning to the family circle. This home had in effect two mothers, for Aunt Kate, Mrs. James's sister, lived with the family. The older boy, William, was evidently a very masculine kind of child, adventurous, intrepid, energetic. Henry James defined himself partly against his older brother and partly by means of his warm attachment to his mother, aunt, and younger sister.[4] He was the good son, known in the family as the "angel." Even when he was nearing his thirtieth birthday, he still sent his mother accounts of expenses from Europe. He seems to have been rather miserable and aloof from other boys in his childhood, and he formed virtually no friendships outside the family until moving to Newport at the age of fifteen. At that crucial age he entered a kind of coterie with Thomas Sergeant Perry and John La Farge, who was much admired by James as a "European" dandy. James became an "observer" who "dawdled and gaped"[5] through a world he was prevented from joining. He became an observer because he could become nothing else in a world where boys and men were supposed to be bellicose and mean, to get in there, hustle and fight. The ghost or alter ego who threatens Spencer

Brydon in "The Jolly Corner" is nothing less than the archetypal American man, a millionaire, a fighter. This man kept James out of law, money, the entire male sphere, and chased him to England, where a man who was not in business could breathe more easily.

Howells was more of an ordinary kid than James, but he would also fail certain proverbial American tests of manhood. In childhood he ran wild along with the other boys in Hamilton, Ohio, becoming a full member in good standing of the separate "savage" culture Howells called "a boy's town." But when the family moved elsewhere, Howells fell away from the boyhood comitatus. When he happened to visit Hamilton some time later, boy's town seemed flat and stale. Howells had dropped out of the male sphere. He became dreamy, studious, and absorbed in literature. He seemed strangely amorphous, his handwriting undergoing a complete change from day to day. In his adolescence, "it was decided" by the local male loungers "at an evening session in one of the dry-goods and grocery stores" that he "would be nowhere in a horse-trade."[6] The first time he left home and mother, at the age of sixteen, he was so homesick he had to return. Like James, Howells also had an older brother, in his case older by several years, and this person was the "man" among the children. Among his siblings, Howells was most closely attached to his sister Victoria.[7] In Columbus, what he liked to do most of all was "call at some house where there were young girls waiting and willing to be called upon, and to join them in asking and saying whether we had read this or that late novel or current serial."[8] A youthful letter to Oliver Wendell Holmes reveals Howells' sympathetic feeling for a girl he worked alongside in a print-shop.[9] His awareness that unbridled male sexuality often represented a real threat to women led him to print in the *Atlantic Monthly* Harriet Beecher Stowe's article "The True Story of Lady Byron's Life." When the article caused a scandal, Howells defended his editorial decision in a letter to his father: "The world needed to know just how base, filthy and mean Byron was, in order that all glamour should be forever removed from his literature."[10] Those men who, like Sinclair Lewis, have ridiculed Howells for his feminine identification—"Mr. Howells was one of the gentlest, sweetest, and most honest of men, but he had the code of a pious old maid whose great delight was to have tea at the vicarage"[11]—seem to assume that female interests are inherently trivial. Howells knew better from late boyhood on.

Unlike De Forest and Tourgee, Howells and James took little

interest in the issues of union and slavery at the time of the Civil War. *Miss Ravenel's Conversion* sheds an interesting light on their detachment, especially James's, in a passage telling of Carter's failure to secure many volunteers among

> the young gentlemen of New Boston, the sons of the college professors, and . . . the city clergymen. The set was limited in number and not martial nor enthusiastic in character. It had held aristocratically aloof from the militia, from the fire companies, from personal interference in local politics, from every social enterprise which could bring it into contact with the laboring masses. It needed two years of tremendous war to break through the shy reserve of this secluded and almost monastic little circle.[12]

Of course, James did try on one occasion to help the volunteer fire company in Newport, an effort that gave him a weird sense of participation in the war itself. But neither this episode nor the war broke through James's shy and monastic reserve. He spent the duration with his parents in Newport and his brother William in Cambridge. Howells spent the war years in the most improbable place of all, Venice. The first sentence of one of several books he set in Venice indicates his uneasy, evasive feelings in 1861: "Every loyal American who went abroad during the first years of our great war felt bound to make himself some excuse for turning his back on his country in the hour of her trouble."[13] Even though Howells wrote two campaign biographies, of Lincoln and Hayes, and entered the lists against capitalism in the later eighties, he remained temperamentally apolitical: in his old age, he confessed: "I was never at a meeting, a rally, or a convention; I have never yet heard a political speech to the end."[14] In 1884, when he voted for Blaine and against Cleveland, whose illegitimate child had become a campaign issue, it was partly because of Cleveland's macho qualities: "Besides I don't like his [Cleveland's] hangman-face. It looks dull and brutal."[15]

The aspect of James's and Howells' fiction that made them famous, tagging them with their public image in the late seventies and early eighties, was their meticulous study of American girls. James's one hit was "Daisy Miller." His first consciously "big" book was *The Portrait of a Lady*, the American edition of which had a tasteful arrangement of flowers in gold and brown embossed on the cover.[16] Henry Adams' blunt wife, Clover, who was closely attached to a strong father, didn't care for the novel and sneered at its author by calling him Henrietta. Howells also became known as a writer who wrote about women. In 1883 Ambrose Bierce called him and James "two eminent triflers and cameo-cutters-in-chief to Her Littleness the Bostonese small virgin."[17] Howells' 1870 novels hinged on delicate social embarrassments—a girl's accidentally taking a strange man's arm in *A Chance Acquaintance*; another girl's isolation among a boatful of men in *The Lady of the Aroostook*, an Austrian officer's unauthorized courtship of Lily Mayhew in *A Fearful Responsibility*. Like "Daisy Miller," these works all dealt with a young woman's unintentional violation of the code. In this early fiction, as one reviewer noted, "there is the more than masculine, almost feminine, touch to be found."[18] After reading one of Howells' plays, Charles Dudley Warner wrote: "You must have been a woman yourself in some previous state, to so know how it is yourself. You are a dangerous person. Heaven grant you no such insight into us men folk."[19] A hostile male critic wrote, "Mr. Howells is never exciting; the most nervous old lady can read him without fear."[20]

The man who wrote this didn't see that many ladies, old or young, disliked Howells. In the early eighties, he moved beyond decorum into a sustained critical analysis of American femininity. According to Hamlin Garland. "All through the early eighties, reading Boston was divided into two parts,—those who liked Howells and those who fought him, and the most fiercely debated question at the clubs was whether his heroines were true to life or whether they were caricatures."[21] In 1886, after reading *The Minister's Charge*, De Forest wrote Howells:

> I admire most of all, your honesty & courage. How dare you speak out your beliefs as you do? You spare neither manhood nor womanhood, & especially not the latter, though it furnishes four fifths of *our* novel-reading public. It is a wonder that the females of America, at least the common born & bred of them, do not stone you in the street.[22]

Mark Twain also found it hard to believe that Howells was actually getting away with his demystifying treatment of sacred American womanhood. The reason Howells was able to get away with it was his preliminary sympathy.

De Forest did not feel the same kind of sympathy, for he was truly oppressed by female culture. In writing about the virile Colonel

Carter, he admitted he could not reproduce the actual speech the character would have used: "I suspect that I have not yet enabled the reader to realize how remarkable were the Colonel's gifts in the way of profanity."[23] Of course, you can't keep a good man down: De Forest still had the temerity to show a glimpse of Carter dallying after a battle with two "bold-browed, slatternly girls" (p. 347) at the same time. Howells didn't feel De Forest's urge to circumvent the censor. When he dealt with adultery or prostitution he tended to adopt an unctuous tone that is hard to take nowadays: his essay on the Boston police court refers to a prostitute as "the lost soul" and a madam as "the yet more fallen spirit."[24] For his part, James wrote more than one work of fiction in which a sensitive virginal hero— Winterbourne, the narrator of *The Sacred Fount*, Lambert Strether— is obsessed with the question of a woman's purity. In fact, the characteristic male type in American realistic fiction would be the fussy, anxious man whose delicate sense of morality stands in vivid contrast to the greedy egotism of some other person, often a virile man like Paul Muniment, who easily gets on in the world. The novel James considered his "best all round," *The Ambassadors*, had a belle-tristic hero who is obsessed with the question of defining the exact nature of the connection between a pair of lovers and ascertaining his own duty in the case. This hero was modeled on Howells, and even more on James himself.

As the prevalence of the anxious, ethical male in Howells' and James's fiction reminds us, these two writers may have been sissies, but they were not female. They wore trousers, earned money, supported others (James gave his inheritance to his sister). They *had* to try to find a public male role. The powerful literary ambition that drove both writers from adolescence on is evidence, I believe, that the idea of becoming a great man of letters was attractive partly because it offered them an escape from both the threat of feminization and the pressures of normal masculinity. Passing through adolescence in the "feminine fifties," as Fred Lewis Pattee named the decade, Howells and James knew all the time that they would have to live a man's life. The solution was to enter literature, which promised to be at one and the same time a pleasant feminine pursuit and a public career.

James's death-bed dictation would disclose his Napoleonic fantasies, the megalomania fermenting inside the creator of Roderick Hudson,

Christopher Newman (*the* American), and Adam Verver (founder of American City). Also, both writers undoubtedly responded to the great male dream of power and conquest, a dream which became far more compelling in an age of rapid industrial expansion and incredible opportunities. Howells, thinking of himself, well understood the compulsion, the desperation, young men felt to "get ahead.":

> Throughout his later boyhood and into his earlier manhood the youth is always striving away from his home and the things of it. With whatever pain he suffers through the longing for them, he must deny them; he must cleave to the world and the things of it; that is his fate, that is the condition of all achievement and advancement for him. He will be many times ridiculous and sometimes contemptible, he will be mean and selfish upon occasion; but he can scarcely otherwise be a man; the great matter for him is to keep some place in his soul where he shall be ashamed. . . . No man, unless he puts on the mask of fiction, can show his real face or the will behind it.[25]

This remarkable passage says that a boy *must* abandon and violate his home in order to make his way in the world, but that if he is good he will always be ashamed of himself. Meanness, shame, guilt, an inner lack of integrity or simplicity—all of these belong, unavoidably, to the masculine condition. Here one sees the terrible split in Howells, who as a youth experienced both homesickness and ambition and as a man was torn between his parents' altruistic values and the necessary egotism of man's world. The young man couldn't respect himself unless he joined in the "blind struggle"[26] for a place in the world, but the old man found that he couldn't respect himself for having succeeded.

The split in Howells was the condition that made it possible for him to become a realist. He was painfully double, both male and female, and his sexual doubleness gave him an objective perspective on the undeclared war between the sexes, the vast impasse between two opposed systems. At the same time his duplicity was a source of real uncertainty and wavering, and it often made him hypocritical, two-faced, or compromising. It is fitting that he chose the odd word *complicity* as the base of his ethics in the late 1880s.

James, though also trapped between man's world and women's sphere, was different. He never succeeded, as did Howells, in winning manhood as it was understood in the United States. Of course he supported himself, by writing fiction, but he was fired by the New York *Tribune* in his only salaried job; he never had an editorial position or worked for an organization of any kind; he never married or entered into any kind of stable domestic living arrangements with anybody outside his family, aside from servants; he left his native country; and late in life he admitted to a friend that "the port from which I set out was, I think, that of the essential loneliness of my life."[27]

In spite of all differences, Howells and James were alike in their deep opposition to their culture's central gender roles. Their uncompromisingly competitive, hard-driving men—Caspar Goodwood, Basil Ransom, Bartley Hubbard, Royal Langbrith—are never seen sympathetically. Their idealistic women—Isabel Archer, Olive Chancellor, Florida Vervain, Grace Breen—are apt to be misguided and occasionally destructive. And both writers would be obsessed most of all with the sensitive outsider, male or female, who cannot find a satisfying niche in the social order—Fleda Vetch, Maisie Farange, Lambert Strether, Helen Harkness, Annie Kilburn, Theodore Colville, Lemuel Barker. Howells and James were odd men out, and their realism arose in part from a passionate desire to grasp the system that had excluded them. That is why they became our first critical realists.

One of the consequences of the development of two separate spheres for men and women in the United States in the first half of the nineteenth century was that literature, generally a male preserve in earlier American and European history, came to be defined as feminine. By 1886 the men in the Albany Hotel in *The Minister's Charge* would regard Lemuel Barker's love of reading as "a womanish weakness, indicating a want of fibre."[28] The novel had become feminine. Critics and historians have often lamented this fact and pointed to the example of Melville, supposedly driven out of the market by female sentimentalists. But Melville tends to become the object of a cult. Great as he was, there was a self-destructive aspect to his writing which cannot be overlooked. Melville grew more and more distrustful of the power of fiction at the same moment a large body of cultivated women readers was being formed.[29] Also, one of the basic procedures in *Moby-Dick* (as in *Walden*)—the search for the symbolic meaning of natural objects—is notoriously unscientific and pre-Darwinian and not by accident responsible for many of the worst passages in both books. Moreover, the Doubloon chapter in Melville's one great book casts a grave doubt on the whole enterprise of trying to find the correct meaning of natural objects. *The Confidence Man* is also a fine book, but it reveals the ambiguous impasse to which Melville's symbolism led.

In fact, the symbolism that was such an important part of the American Renaissance represented a dead end. It was one of the consequences of the decay of Puritanism, and it necessarily disallowed the concept of causality or a scientific approach to nature. The *live* tradition at the end of the American Renaissance was represented by women writers. There is no denying the artistic mediocrity of most of the novels in this tradition. But neither is there any denying their tremendous vitality. What is most important in the present context is that only a recognition of the basic significance of women's fiction enables us to see the origin of American realism, which did not descend from Hawthorne, Emerson, George Eliot, Turgenev, or Flaubert. American realism descended from popular women's fiction by way of two sissies.[30]

After Howells and James exhausted their American material in the 1880s and early 90s, having explored the noble and self-sacrificial woman and the powerful American man to the best of their ability, they were succeeded by a group of writers (superficially called naturalists) who pushed the exploration of American masculinity much farther. Dreiser, Norris, Garland, London, Stephen Crane, Richard Harding Davis, and David Graham Phillips were interested most of all in depicting men under conditions of intense struggle, whether in war, in the capitalist economic system, on the frontier, or anywhere else away from the constraints of female civilization. With these writers, the enormous rift that had opened up in the heart of American life in the early 1800s—the split that made the novel far more feminine than it had ever been before and in effect banished our rough American masculinity from polite fiction—began to close. Women's fiction led to James's and Howells' realism (and in another direction, to the triumphs of local color), and realism led to "naturalism." The split in gender roles had banished the American man from the parlor; two or three generations later, he would be allowed back in. Howells and James, two distinctly unmasculine figures, were the crucial middle men—and the best writers—in this large historical movement.

CHAPTER EIGHT

The Portrait of a Lady

In writing no other novel did Henry James have the sense of undertaking something momentous that he felt when he began *The Portrait of a Lady*. In letters home he spoke of the novel as his first big bid for fame and excellence.[1] Appropriately, the book he wrote, as William Veeder has argued, was the culmination of his fiction in the 1870s and of a large tradition of popular fiction. Veeder sees Isabel as a mixture of familiar character-types, especially the Perfect Victorian Lady and the independent American Girl. Osmond belongs to a large and complex popular tradition of villainy: energetic and lethargic, capable of both violence and ennui, he is simultaneously the Victorian Paterfamilias and the nineteenth-century Dandy. James' great insight, Veeder argues, was to combine these two entirely different types and then to demonstrate the man's vicious tyranny and explore the failure of his marriage with Isabel: "Without mounting a soapbox or waving a placard, Henry James makes us experience what honest Victorians knew—that the ideal of Victorian marriage, the dream of reciprocal mastery [that is, she ruling his heart, he ruling her mind] was culpably remote from the social reality."[2] To a great extent, Veeder has tried to show what I must show at this stage of my argument—that the *Portrait* represented a thorough appropriation of a large and popular novelistic tradition and that James's great achievement was to combine the styles and character-types available to him in order to reveal the suffocating lies in marriage.

Veeder's book is one of the best there is on James, even though, as Nina Baym has shown, his understanding of popular fiction seems inadequate.[3] The specific point where I must take issue with him here involves Gilbert Osmond's role in the novel. This character is simply too special to represent the Victorian father, and Pansy is too mutilated in a peculiar way to be the Victorian daughter. Veeder grasps an important thread in noticing that Osmond is both father and dandy. Yet it is hard, finally, to see how this formula explains his functioning in any generalized analysis of Victorian marriage. Osmond is so much an individual, so peculiar and special, that he would seem to undermine the representative aspect of the book—the aspect highlighted by the title. How could James call attention to Isabel's fate as *Lady* if her husband and antagonist were unique?

I will argue that Osmond, like Isabel, does in fact have a general or exemplary value, but that this value cannot come into clear focus without recognizing his nationality. Osmond may look perfectly cosmopolitan at first—"he was one of those persons who, in the matter of race, may, as the phrase is, pass for anything"[4]—but he comes from American parentage, his mother having been, not cultivated or aristocratic, but a typically giddy lady of the 1840s who was known as the American Corinne. Osmond's apparent uniqueness notwithstanding, he is a definitely American type in James's gallery of masculine types—Ralph Touchett the Disinterested and Appreciative Friend, Caspar Goodwood the Square-Jawed Suitor, Lord Warburton the Gentle Lord, Ned Rosier the Aesthetic Pantywaist. Osmond is the Cruelly Perverted Expatriate. He and the other men represent the categories available to Isabel—categories and combinations of wealth, virility, inherited status, taste, and goodnatured affection. On the basis of this gallery of potential husbands, and with the addition of Madame Merle the False Confidante and Henrietta Stackpole the True but Gawky Girlfriend, James told the old story of courtship and marriage. The difference was, James took the heroine's situation seriously. He exploited love-interest to the hilt, not to satisfy his readers' fantasies but to explore and understand the heroine's tragic doom. And the most important agent in her doom was to be a displaced American with a secret and very American fantasy of absolute rule over others—a dream of kingship.

The *Portrait* was a study of what it cost to become and remain a lady. James's first important story about the American Girl, "Daisy Miller: A Study," had told of a brash, independent, and inexperienced person who ran afoul of the system on the threshold of adulthood, and died. Beginning the *Portrait* a year or so after "Daisy Miller" and completing it two or three years later, James answered the question, what would happen to the spunky American girl if, instead of dying, she had to find a place for herself in woman's sphere? In answering this question, James made his central character a more cultivated and conscientious person than Daisy was. Isabel does not flirt, tease, or brag. She is a much greater departure from the norm than is Daisy, and James establishes her by means of her surprising and challenging gestures and assertions. In her efforts to explore, to cultivate her mind, she forms a pointed contrast with Lilian, a dutiful and dull married sister. Isabel has a strong admiration for Henrietta, the New Woman as journalist, and is determined not to fix her hopes on a particular man. She refuses to daydream about romance. Like other progressive girls, she had a—

> collection of opinions on the question of marriage. . . . She held that a woman ought to be able to make up her life in singleness, and that it was perfectly possible to be happy without the society of a more or less coarse-minded person of another sex. (p. 44)

Isabel is not fashionable or pretty: nineteen persons out of twenty consider the third sister, Edith, "infinitely the prettier of the two" (p. 27). Of course, the cultivated twentieth person, the author, and the reader (here, as always, easily led) all prefer Isabel, who is worth making an "ado" over precisely because of those exceptional, break-away qualities that are present in all heroines of women's fiction.[5]

Tracing this model heroine's passage from girlhood to adulthood, James is concerned to show what adulthood is going to mean. He begins to show us in chapter 37, where, after following busy little Ned Rosier, we see Isabel for the first time since her marriage to the man who has struck us (thanks to the author's manipulations) as rather a sinister person:

> She had lost something of that quick eagerness to which her husband had privately taken exception—she had more the air of being able to wait. Now, at all events, framed in the gilded doorway, she struck our young man as the picture of a gracious lady. (p. 321)

This is the one passage in the novel that refers to the title. The tableau—a patient woman framed by a doorway inside her home—defines in a new way the character who first appeared by stepping outside a door. Marriage has made her, at least for the moment, a motionless feature of the interior of her husband's impressive house. A true portrait, she is even surrounded by a "gilded" frame. She is visibly less energetic and vital and seems more proper, subdued, even generalized. She is, momentarily, "the picture of a gracious lady."

And then she steps out of the picture, and goes about the business of her life once again. What the last third of the novel shows us is the uncertain, tyrannized, and muffled state in which she must now move and live. She doesn't know how much she can tell Henrietta, or how much she is obliged to assist her husband in engineering a match between Pansy and Warburton. She cannot be the self-abnegating wife her husband wants her to be, but neither does she think it right to defy or challenge him. Worst of all, this sinister marriage has become a barrier between her and the person she cares for most of all, Ralph Touchett. Yet the spell Osmond casts is so effective, so noxious, that she would not have been able to disobey her husband's lawful order and see Ralph before his death, if she had not learned from Osmond's sister the truth about Pansy's parentage and her own manipulation by Osmond and Madame Merle. At the end, when Isabel returns to her dreadful home, it is because there is no other choice. A variety of considerations (well summarized by Veeder)[6] compel her to return to Rome. Isabel had begun by challenging the definition and limits of conventional womanhood (as embodied in her sisters). But the world she set out to explore shrinks at the end to "a very straight path" (p. 519), with the evil figure of her husband at the far end. Isabel will not, presumably, cave in to him, but neither will she run away from or openly defy him. For the American girl to become a lady means the suffocation of her heart's desire, a final acceptance of an absurd set of constraints, an endless checkmate with a husband who hates her and whom she hates in return.

The terms under which Isabel must live with Osmond are set before us with infinitely greater honesty than the terms Phelps fantasized in *The Story of Avis*. Philip Ostrander was basically a crude boyish scapegrace. It was all too easy for the fine heroine to lavish her unselfish and noble maternal nature on him. But Gilbert Osmond is real and strong, and there is no way his wife could salvage the marriage by doing what Elizabeth T. Spring wanted her to do— "substitute with so silent a gentleness the maternal for the wifely feeling towards the weaker nature which failed her."[7] James understood what Spring and Phelps and many, many other women novelists in America could not understand—that this substitution was emphatically *not* the remedy, that it was actually the cause of Isabel's downfall.

Although Isabel is a victim of others, she is also a victim of certain delusions and inflated ideals James points out to us in the beginning of the book. In particular, although Isabel flatters herself that she is not as other women are, and holds as one of her "collection of opinions" (an ironic phrase) that there is no indignity in remaining single and thus becoming that object of ridicule, an old maid, Isabel does indeed share the tendency so common and so admired in contemporary women's fiction of mistaking maternal protectiveness for love. She herself comes to realize this in her midnight vigil:

> A certain combination of features had touched her, and in them she had seen the most striking of portraits. That he was poor and lonely, and yet that somehow he was noble—that was what interested her and seemed to give her her opportunity. There was an indefinable beauty about him—in his situation, in his mind, in his face. She had felt at the same time that he was helpless and ineffectual, but the feeling had taken the form of a tenderness which was the very flower of respect. He was like a sceptical voyager, strolling on the beach while he waited for the tide, looking seaward yet not putting to sea. It was in all this that she found her occasion. She would launch his boat for him; she would be his providence; it would be a good thing to love him. And she loved him—a good deal for what she found in him, but a good deal also for what she brought him. As she looked back at the passion of those weeks she perceived in it a kind of maternal strain—the happiness of a woman who felt that she was a contributor, that she came with full hands. (p. 373)

As this passage suggests, Isabel was very much a woman of her time and place. Conventional definitions of Victorian womanhood—nurturer, mother, even savior and domestic "providence"—run all through this passage, which explains better than any other one passage in the entire novel why Isabel fell for Osmond. The truth, as she suspects with a burning cheek, is that she married "on a factitious theory" (p. 374). Yet she didn't fully realize she had substituted the maternal for the "wifely," that what she felt for Osmond had little in common with sexual love. As James wrote, "The depths of this young lady's nature were a very out-of-the-way place, between which and the surface communication was interrupted by a dozen capricious forces" (p. 28). For a variety of reasons, love was too big a risk for Isabel to take. So she took the mother's way, the Victorian way, and lost.

Isabel is thus a victim of large cultural ideals and currents. But even though she is a product of her times, instead of the free spirit she pathetically imagines, James as moralist makes us understand that she is still responsible for what she does at any given moment in the present. In spite of Ralph's and Mrs. Touchett's warnings, she still chose Osmond; and in spite of his evil nature, it remains impossible for her to avoid urgent occasions for choice, and the responsibility for her choices. It is helpful to recall James's 1865 review of *Emily Chester,* one of the few novels James is known to have asked to review. He came down very hard on the heroine, who, like Isabel, does not care at all for her husband. James attacked the book for justifying the wife's emotional infidelity on the basis of "temper ament" and the "constitutional harmony of two congenial natures." James insisted that when one accounts for behavior, not in terms of choice, but in terms of "unaccountable attractions and repulsions, loathings and yearnings,"[8] one inevitably scuttles all question of moral responsibility. This was one of James's most important reviews. Fifteen years later, he would embody Emily Chester's approach in the gay lightweight, Countess Gemini, who acts largely on impulse and daring. Isabel represents the more responsible position. She is both free agent *and* product of society, a "delicate, desultory, flame-like spirit" *and* an "eager and personal young girl."[9] Similarly, even though James weights her with so many faults that "she would be an easy victim of scientific criticism," he expects her "to awaken on the reader's part an impulse more tender and more purely expectant" (p. 43). In other words, we judge Isabel in a tough-minded way, but we *still* identify with her in a very tender and primitive way. The conclusion of the novel observes the same delicate balance, placing Isabel in a terrible bind and generating great melodramatic excitement, but also turning, finally, on her own act of choice. Not what is done to her but what she herself decides to do forms the novel's proper conclusion. James regards her as both object and agent, not wholly the perfect and powerful heroine of women's fiction nor wholly the helpless victim of the naturalism that was to follow James in the 1890s. This balanced view of the self as both free and conditioned was one of the basic fictional conventions of realism.

The oddest aspect of the *Portrait* is that although it tells a conventional story of courtship and marriage, yet, conspicuously, there is not a single example of reciprocal love, except near the end.[10] James in fact emphasizes the point that Isabel's deepest feeling toward the opposite sex was a kind of wariness—as if something had happened to destroy the basis for trust. Caspar Goodwood repels Isabel because of his flatness, his pushing, insistent will, his hardness and forcefulness, and his desire to have her. As a successful cotton mill owner and inventor, he is as much a modern representative American man in the novel as Christopher Newman is in *The American*. In fact, Isabel wants to keep Goodwood at a distance precisely because of his all-too-American masculinity. Warburton the English nobleman seems more amenable—more easygoing, tolerant, pleasant. But as a hereditary aristocrat in the most powerful country in the world, he is backed by a complex and overwhelming society, which even his "radical" views cannot affect. He could never leave his society behind in any way, Isabel feels, and if she married him she would inevitably have to live with him on his terms. Neither Goodwood nor Warburton could allow Isabel to follow her own free will. So she turns them down and in doing so refuses to accept the conditions of contemporary feminine life. But neither will she accept the only alternative, the one chosen by Henrietta Stackpole—the masculinization of a male career. Her basic quandary—what shall I do with myself?—remains unsolved until she meets Gilbert Osmond.

Isabel dwells on this quandary much less than the narrative that is devoted to her. Yet when she meets Osmond, she is immediately swept away. There are many reasons for this, but one of the basic ones is that he promises to solve her dilemma. Although he lays his true character on the line when he admits that the only men he envies are the Sultan of Turkey, the Czar, and the Pope—all somewhat sinister figures in contemporary Protestant America—she fails to listen. She also misses a signal when he tells her that "woman's natural mission" is to be "appreciated" (p. 231). The reason Isabel overlooks these and other signals is that she desires to marry and at the same time go free and retain the total (and impossible) autonomy she innocently dreams of. Osmond looks safe to her, because he lacks the fundamental tokens of masculinity—a career, a visible occupation, a place in the world of men. Unlike Goodwood, a maker and shaker who places his imprint on the world, Osmond seems to have a graceful placidity, living with an imperfect world instead of changing it. Rather than trooping with the other males, he lives alone on his hilltop. Isabel is captivated by the image of the distinguished, rather lonely man looking down on the crowded city of Florence. The tableau of Osmond and Pansy, father and daughter, living in retirement from the world, has a potent and mysterious appeal for Isabel, and not simply because she finds freedom a burden and would like the strong paternal protection she has never known. The main reason she finds Osmond a possible mate is that he doesn't seem to belong to a power-based world. For Osmond is (or pretends to be) a spectator:

> "I never in my life tried to earn a penny, and I ought to be less subject to suspicion than most people. . . . My dear girl, I can't tell you how life seems to stretch there before us—what a long summer afternoon awaits us. It's the latter half of an Italian day—with a golden haze, and the shadows just lengthening, and that divine delicacy in the light, the air, the landscape. . . ." (pp. 307–308)

Isabel is reassured by Osmond's detached pose, his apparent view of life as a beautiful, late afternoon landscape and not as a field of battle. In fact, the long summer afternoon, as in the book's opening paragraph describing an English tea, stands at the center of the book in every way, being the best time of the best season, both scene and symbol of an unhurried, contemplative, ceremonial way of life. Surely, one of the finest aspects of *The Portrait* is the way its leisurely movement slowly evokes for us a sense of this kind of life. As we read the first thirty-five chapters we too want to give way to the spell and begin dreaming of a world without aggression, where we might be left alone to cultivate beauty and friendship, as in *Friends: A Duet*, the book Phelps wrote soon after *The Story of Avis*.

After marrying Osmond, Isabel finds out that he is indeed an American man, a perverted one whose thwarted dream of supreme rule has turned into an evil need to trample on the helpless. One of the most important passages in the novel is the long section analyzing Osmond that was deleted for the New York edition. Originally occurring in chapter 29, this passage may have been deleted because it destroys some of the suspense, or at least uncertainty, by frankly revealing Osmond's master passion—ambition. Osmond wants power and place, and he wants them more than anything else. The secret truth about him is that he, too, dreams of being number one—"the first gentleman in Europe" (p. 376). The only men he envies stand at the top of rigid, repressive, Byzantine hierarchies. In essence, Osmond's dream is the male American dream of supremacy, though the realm in which he wants to be supreme is more rigid and artificial than the economic marketplace in which the ordinary American hustler fought to get ahead. Aside from this, Osmond and the robber baron are brothers, because Osmond's refinement does not offer an alternative to greed, but merely a vindication of it. His wonderful taste is intended, "not to enlighten, or convert, or redeem" the world, but "to extract from it some recognition of one's own superiority" (p. 376). That is exactly why Newport became what it did in the 1870s.

Osmond is humiliated when his ambitious plans of marrying his daughter to Lord Warburton fall through. He is humiliated when Isabel sees through him: "How much you must wish to capture him!" (p. 415). And he is humiliated most of all when Warburton pays a final visit before departing for England: Osmond "had had a great hope, and now, as he saw it vanish into smoke, he was obliged to sit and smile and twirl his thumbs" (pp. 417–418). Here Osmond bluffs his way through the supreme male defeat, something corresponding to the feminine degradation of shame—he feels outwitted and publicly faced down by a far more successful man. The minute Warburton leave, Osmond accuses his wife of "trying to humiliate" (p. 421) him. This is only his paranoia. But paranoia is not unexpected in someone with Osmond's suppressed dream of supremacy.

The Portrait of a Lady is a deeply anti-masculine book. It may in its quiet way reverse many of the usual feminine ideals and formulas, but it attacks masculinity more than it attacks femininity. The fact that the one remarkably decent man should be Ralph Touchett only confirms the truth of this. (For brevity, I am overlooking Warburton, even though he offers confirmation: he too is "good" partly because of his weaknesses—his self-doubts, his absurdly ineffective radicalism.) Ralph is an invalid. His illness prevents him from playing an active role in life. Also, unlike Osmond, who feigns indifference, Ralph is a true bystander: "A certain fund of indolence that he possessed came to his aid and helped to reconcile him to doing nothing" (p. 32). Compelled to be inactive, he finds that "observation" has a "sweet-tasting property" (p. 33). This passive son of an aggressive Yankee banker has no career; he lovingly cares for his old father and also looks after Isabel's prospects; he is nurturing and self-sacrificial, giving up half his own inheritance. In all these ways Ralph appropriates an ideal feminine identity. All the other men— Goodwood, Warburton, Osmond, even Rosier and Bantling—are known by their last names. Ralph, like single heroines in nineteenth-century novels, is identified by his first name. (This distinction reflects the difference between male and female identity. The heroine was a directly known personality whom the gentle reader understood from the inside. The hero was known primarily as a member of a group—the family lineage in which he was born [hence the last name] or the occupation in which he found his level. If he happened to see action in a war, he would be lastingly identified with his military rank. Often, the use of his title or last name is an indirection that distances a potentially dangerous person.)

Ralph loves Isabel, but because he is dying and therefore cannot court her, his love does not threaten her autonomy. His disability makes him the only man whose love cannot oppress her. But because of this same disability, their love (for she also loves him) can never pass out of the state of potentiality.[11] Here, precisely, is the explanation of the frustrated matings one finds at the end of so many Jamesian novels. For James, a good man cannot mate with a good woman: male sexuality necessarily means a violation of the female. There is strong evidence of this in the contrast between Isabel's final embraces with Ralph and Goodwood. Ralph's declaration of love— "'And remember this,' he continued, 'that if you have been hated, you have also been loved'"—not only puts the declaration that was at the heart of the novel genre ("I love you") into the passive voice but in the *present perfect passive*. Is there any way to deliver this important speech with a smaller degree of assertiveness? Ralph's speech makes the minimal claim for himself. Isabel's reply—"Ah, my brother!" (p. 507)—confirms the impotence of their love. And this is the *only* reciprocal exchange of love between a man and a woman in the novel.

A total contrast to Ralph, Caspar Goodwood tells Isabel again and again in the imperative to be passive and dependent: "Trust me as if I had the care of you" (p. 518). His forceful insistence shows her that "she had never been loved before" (p. 517). Here, then, we find out what masculine love really is. The erotic content of Goodwood's love is greatly amplified in the New York Edition: "This was different; this was the hot wind of the desert. . . . It wrapped her about; it lifted her off her feet, while the very taste of it, as of something potent, acrid and strange, forced open her set teeth."[12] Goodwood greatly weakens Isabel's resolve and even, in a way, threatens her integrity. In fact, if we pay attention to the imagery, diction, the rising series, James does not seem to be describing a kiss but an act of rape and a pulsing orgasm:

> He glared at her a moment through the dusk, and the next instant she felt his arms about her and his lips on her own lips. His kiss was like white lightning, a flash that spread, and spread again, and stayed; and it was extraordinarily as if, while she took it, she felt each thing in his hard manhood that had least pleased her, each aggressive fact of his face, his figure, his presence, justified of its intense identity and made one with this act of possession.[13]

Of course, it is not rape but only a kiss. Yet James's description of the way Isabel experiences the kiss conveys the real meaning in this novel of male heterosexual love. This love seems to be by nature an aggressive act of possession that seeks to deprive the woman of her independence and stamp her with the man's own identity.

Isabel responds to Goodwood's love, up to a point, and then she feels a panicky claustrophobia.[14] She remembers how much she has always feared and hated Goodwood, and she realizes that life with him could not possibly bring her the independence he insists it would. She would only be exchanging one master for another. So she escapes. But in breaking away from him, Isabel is rejecting male sexuality, *and thus her own*, once and for all. She returns to Osmond because there is nothing else to do—"there was a very straight path" (p. 519). Now she has finally abandoned the dream of self-fulfillment that animated her in the first half of the novel and made her a worthwhile character for the "ado" James made about her. In going back to Rome, she takes up a way of life defined by social convention, full of duty to the childlike Pansy, and devoid of personal satisfaction. And so Isabel completes her development: after beginning as a hopeful, unconventional American girl, she grows up to be a lady, tightly corseted in a prison-like home.

Am I overlooking the moral triumph of Isabel's final choice and the significance of her entire growth in selflessness, maturity, responsibility? Many critics place a great deal of stress on this growth. I cannot accept it at face value, however, and for the same reasons that W. D. Howells would not accept the morality of self-sacrifice at face value. There is no question that Isabel becomes more considerate, patient, and supportive, and much less shrill and assertive. The question is, whether this kind of development is moral growth. To some extent James definitely implies that Isabel's triumph over her own callow will is a signal achievement. But of course James *has to* imply this, given his deep repugnance for masculine egotism—the pushing, dominating force that compels Isabel, living in a world a man like Goodwood considers "very large" (p. 518), to tread a very straight and narrow path. The novel represents a thorough repudiation of egotism.

The one serious flaw permeating the *Portrait* is its view of masculine sexuality, which is seen as the epitome of selfishness. James's insistence on Goodwood's unremitting *pushing* makes this person a very rigid caricature. It surprises me that Judith Fryer's recent book, *The Faces of Eve*, should assert that Isabel and James's other female characters are not "real women,"[15] but should then remain silent about Goodwood. Of course, if one really expects to find a "real" person between the covers of a book, or is simply applying an ideology, then there is little more to say. But even without understanding that stereotypes enter into all literary characters, even Edna Pontellier, it should be easy to see that Goodwood is nothing but a straw man. Students often call attention to the fact that he does nothing but tear back and forth across the Atlantic Ocean in single-minded pursuit of Isabel. Horace Elisha Scudder called him "the jack-in-the-box of the story."[16] And if the man is an inventor, as James claimed, why aren't we told what he has invented and why? How can James ask us to take something so special on faith? Howells' inventor, the out-of-place Venetian priest in *A Foregone Conclusion*, is one of the finest realistic characters in American literature. Merely to mention him, or call to mind an actual nineteenth-century industrialist, is to see Goodwood for the stick—or *prick*—he is.

James's complete failure with this character matters a great deal, given Goodwood's representative macho qualities and his place in Isabel's life. This is not the time to discuss James's altogether fearful and hysterical sense of American masculinity (see part 4). But it is time to say that the *Portrait* is a faulty novel to the extent that its defective view of masculinity underlies its analysis of the prison of womanhood.[17] There is, furthermore, something very ominous in James's distrust of masculine egotism as such. If the male self is fundamentally oppressive, illegitimate, or somehow all wrong, then unless the strong man constantly holds himself back, he is going to oppress others, especially women and weaker men, in everything he does. There is no good act, in this view, except a self-checking, self-frustrating act. The ultimate consequence of trying to live this way would be a contemplative and self-denying or renunciatory way of life. This was in fact the path taken by Buddha, who followed it precisely because of his feeling (the same feeling James had) that desire was evil by nature.

James was the most devout Buddhist in American literature. Increasingly, after the *Portrait,* and especially in the late 1880s and the decade from 1895 to 1905, his fiction avoided representing physical action between people and focused on spectatorial heroes and heroines, inner decisions and epiphanies, and acts of renunciation. Over the course of James's life, there was a genuine and profound turning away from the world Caspar Goodwood represented, and one odd result of this was that when James came to revise the *Portrait* in 1908, he developed in an extraordinary way the forceful and erotic qualities of Goodwood's kiss. Looking at this kiss in the cold light of common day, one sees at once that James's description of it is absurdly melodramatic, maybe even hysterical. "White lightning" is not only redundant but foolish. There is clearly something wrong in the revised scene. If we ask why James inflated the kiss in 1908—the period in which he was dredging up the prepotent alter ego who rages in the jolly corner—the question answers itself. James inflated the kiss precisely because of the pushing, American masculinity that had originally caused him to leave America for England and slowly, over the course of his life, to move in his own original manner down the negative way discovered so long ago by the most influential person ever to struggle with the problem of evil, aggression, and the unending suffering endured by so many humans. But there is no reason to take leave of common sense: an exaggerated fear of aggression will naturally look for an issue in an exaggerated form of withdrawal. If one must finally remain suspicious of the authenticity of Goodwood's aggression, one must also question the wisdom of what that aggression justifies—Isabel's acceptance of a self-denying way of life.

Most pertinent here is the implication for realism. A novel whose finest characters, Ralph and Isabel, withdraw from the world of desire and attachment is inevitably going to qualify its realism in a very searching way. The *Portrait* is realistic in that it tests and finds wanting so many male and female fantasies and ideal types. It is realistic in portraying the pernicious effect of aggressive, supremacy-seeking men and the feminine substitution of the "maternal" for the "wifely." But it is unrealistic in its picture of The Man and its endorsement of a central feminine myth, the fine, self-effacing lady. The novel's unbalanced femininity limits its value as critical realism and prevents James from really scizing one of his most important masculine characters, who remains a very crude symbol.

CHAPTER NINE

Their Wedding Journey

Howells' early work, animated by a lighthearted readiness to leave the past behind and explore the modern world, bore as its safe conduct or badge of respectability a conspicuous narrative daintiness. *Venetian Life* (1866), his first book, registered more facts, more carefully observed behavior, than all of James's travel books on Europe put together; yet this work was held together, unlike the ordinary guidebook, by Howells' delicate humor and play of sentiment and fine tuning—qualities which became his early trademark.[1] His Venetian book, like his first American book, *Suburban Sketches* (1870), was a gay patchwork gathered up by an obviously cultivated observer who found the modern world a fascinatingly mixed place. Whether he was looking at Venice or modern Cambridge, Howells evinced very little nostalgia. In *Suburban Sketches*, he was glad to move from one home to another:

> There is no house to which one would return, having left it . . . ; for those associations whose perishing leaves us free, and preserves to us what little youth we have, were otherwise perpetuated to our burden and bondage. Let some one else, who has also escaped from his past, have your old house.[2]

This only superficially resembles Thoreau, for Howells was speaking after all of a newly developed section of Cambridge. He was the first important American writer to pay attention to the look of a barren suburb or the feel of being part of a large urban crowd ("By Horse-Car to Boston," "Jubilee Days").[3] His detached exploration of these topics was accompanied by a conscious severance from traditional pieties—the old home, the old neighborhood, romantic love. Unlike

James, who worked out his variety of realism by recombining aspects of the tradition of the novel, Howells began by picking through the ashes and diamonds of the current scene.

But there was an odd discrepancy in Howells' early sketches. Even when he paid such close attention to the common world around him, he let the reader know in every sentence how fine and elegant he was. Although he used Americanisms from the start—"notions" and "loafing" in *Venetian Life*—they would inevitably be bracketed in some way.[4] This fastidious double consciousness is apparent in the familiar question raised in his first book-length work of fiction, *Their Wedding Journey*: "Ah! poor Real Life, which I love, can I make others share the delight I find in thy foolish and insipid face?"[5] The question is precious, and one wonders why someone who relishes this insipid face should take the trouble to display such a cultivated one. Howells undoubtedly had something of a camp sensibility in the 1860s and early 70s. He was able to appreciate mankind "in his habitual moods of vacancy and tiresomeness" (p. 55) because he himself was so bright and active and wide-awake inside. His early realism was a dandy's realism, a slightly perverse cultivation of the common man, not reality but a half dreamy reality trip. This odd angle of vision enabled Howells to touch on many ordinary experiences in a delightfully novel manner, for instance, the fun of staying in a luxury hotel: "One has there the romance of being a stranger and a mystery to every one else, and lives in the alluring possibility of not being found out a most ordinary person" (p. 63). Absolutely right, but there is still a discrepancy between the narrator's insistence that he is a most ordinary person and his obvious refinement. And there is the underlying desire to escape himself.

The course of Howells' development from the publication of *Their Wedding Journey* in 1872 to *A Modern Instance* ten years later would involve a remarkable modification in the refinement of his prose, in his carefully maintained distance from ordinary people, and in his rather brittle internal equilibrium. Considering the kind of man Howells was, he took incredible risks in writing his realistic masterpieces of the 1880s and early 90s.[6]

The insights Howells would somehow reach through his nervous delicacy are particularly apparent in his treatment of Isabel and Basil March's marital relationship in *Their Wedding Journey*.[7] Howells convinces me that this "modern" couple is well mated. Near the beginning of the Marches' trip, Isabel gets together with her friend Lucy Leonard and the two wives happily compare notes on their husbands: "They reassured one another by every question and answer, and in their weak content lapsed far behind the representative women of our age, when husbands are at best a necessary evil, and the relation of wives to them is known to be one of pitiable subjection" (p. 25).

Howells' irony may not be apparent. He does not think the wives are "weak" for being contentedly and happily married. On the contrary, he is ridiculing the current stereotypes about oppressed wives. What makes his point about the two wives' satisfaction all the more telling is that they are married to distinctly modern types of men: Basil is an insurance executive and Lucy's husband works on Wall Street and commutes like the "vast numbers of prosperous New-Yorkers who love both the excitement of the city and the repose of the country" (p. 26). I believe this is a more glowing picture of "upper middle-class" life than was conventional at the time.

As the honeymoon proceeds, Howells unfolds an analysis of marriage that is much more penetrating than anything promised by this early scene. The longest and most important chapter, located approximately in the middle of the book and representing the place farthest west in the Marches' trip, tells of their three-days' visit to Niagara. The central fact about this place, which is so full of "happy pairs" and which "perpetually renews itself in the glow of love as long as the summer lasts" (p. 105), is horror. The Marches tarry too long at Niagara and begin to appreciate its inhuman scale and its very real dangers. The waterfall "gradually changes from a thing of beauty to a thing of terror" (p. 96). To some extent, terror has been present from the beginning of the journey—the violent thunderstorm in Boston, the old invalid lying in the depot, the possibility of a train wreck on the way to New York, the Trinity Church cemetery, the man prostrated by heat in a drugstore, the collision with a towboat going up the Hudson, and the man fatally burned by steam who utters "a hollow, moaning, gurgling sound, regular as that of the machinery" (p. 49). Even this collision, fearful as it is, doesn't quite break through to the happily married couple.[8]

But Niagara reaches them. Isabel says:

> "When we first arrived I felt only the loveliness of the place. . . . but ever since, it's been growing stranger and dreadfuller. Somehow it's

begun to pervade me and possess me in a very uncomfortable way: I'm tossed upon rapids, and flung from cataract brinks, and dizzied in whirlpools; I'm no longer yours, Basil; I'm most unhappily married to Niagara. Fly with me, save me from my awful lord! (p. 103)

In delivering this charming speech, Isabel "lightly burlesqued the woes of a *prima donna*, with clasped hands and uplifted eyes." She is playing, but her act, as Basil sees, clearly reveals "a reality" (p. 103). Niagara has entered deeply into her imagination and aroused the fear of catastrophic death. She realizes once again that she is mortal, in this sense "married" to Niagara. Most interesting is the fact that her tie to Basil is seen as an act of running away, an artificial refuge from a natural and inescapable state. Her rightful lord is Death, while the bond between her and Basil is a fragile, willed connection, a civil contract that emerges out of fear and loneliness. But Howells the truth-teller also insists that marriage involves a certain denial of fact: "'But now,' she added triumphantly," after escaping Niagara, "'I'm rescued from all that. I shall never be old again, dearest; never, as long as you—love me!'" (p. 105). Here, Isabel has plainly gone too far in her not wholly playful effort to forget the fact that she may die prematurely and must grow old if she doesn't.

Howells is abundantly clear that in this particular marriage, a marriage so important in his fiction that it appears in nine novels and stories in all, Isabel finds more of a refuge than does Basil.[9] Her endearments often have a child's confiding impulsiveness, while Basil acts as the senior partner, protector, rescuer. His shielding her from a dangerous world allows her to be playful, irresponsible, inconsistent. On the trip down the rapids of the St. Lawrence, Isabel, like the other ladies, has no sense of danger and rather delights in the fun: "As to Isabel, she looked upon the wrecked steamer with indifference, as did all the women; but then they could not swim, and would not have to save themselves. 'The La Chine's to come yet,' they exulted, 'and that's the awfullest [rapids] of all!'" Basil, meanwhile, wonders how it would "fare with all these people packed here upon her bow, if the Banshee should swing round upon a ledge?" (p. 119). Like Howells himself, Basil has a sense of danger that is all the sharper because he knows his wife refuses to share it.

Inevitably, tension builds up between Basil and Isabel as they proceed on their journey. Basil loses patience momentarily at Niagara when Isabel refuses to leave an island by walking across a fragile bridge. Other strains appear. Suddenly, before they know what is happening, they have their First Quarrel. Isabel insists on hiring two horses to draw a carriage, while her practical husband refuses to indulge such an unnecessary extravagance. Isabel gets angry at his lack of consideration and generosity; he gets angry at her unreasonableness. They separate. Now "all was over; the dream was past; the charm was broken." Basil is furious, then abruptly repentant: "'On our wedding journey, too! Good heavens, what an incredible brute I am!'" (p. 130). He apologizes, in fact makes "all the concessions" (p. 132). Isabel holds no grudges (unlike Avis, who is far too good to forgive anything), but she does say something rather odd after her husband apologizes: "I knew you'd come back" (p. 131). This unconciliatory remark reflects her ladylike assumption that she has the right to insist on certain arrangements even while demanding that her husband take care of her. The Marches are well married, but there is a nagging inequity in their contract that the male author insists on pointing out.[10]

Basil and Isabel patch up their quarrel. They do not mend their faults or revise their basic accommodation with one another (Howells was no fool), but they do get a clear view of each other's character. Isabel compares her husband to the humorous Colonel Ellison: "He's funnier than you, Basil, and he hasn't any of your little languid airs and affectations." Basil acquires a clearer sense of his wife's irrationality and ultimate sanity. In comparing her to Fanny Ellison, he says, "She is a good deal like you, but with the sense of humor left out. You've only enough to save you" (p. 175). Significantly, the Ellisons seem to be very close to Howells' sense of the American norm. Mrs. Ellison, in particular, is typically exacting, proper, bossy, and irrational. Compared to these norms, the Marches are, not the ideal (Howells never trades in this article), but a good, sensible, above-average compromise. The best thing about the Marches' marriage is the sincere pleasure they take in each other; the next best, their candid and reciprocal recognition of the nature of the contract binding them. When Isabel affectionately criticizes her husband's "languid airs" and "affectations," and Basil allows that her humor barely saves her, it is easy to believe that this couple is well matched.

Their Wedding Journey is obviously a less substantial book than *The Portrait of a Lady*. But Howells' book is better than is generally understood. If one compares it to *The Golden Bowl*, that ornate study of marriage lost and regained, it seems clear that Howells' early novel-travelogue has infinitely more knowledge of how people actually get on in a working marriage than does James's work. The modern writer who comes closest to Howells' sense of marriage would probably be John Updike, who also shares his predecessor's fastidiousness, devotion to New England, latent religiosity, and fantastic gift for sensing how all kinds of people work. "The Crow in the Woods" in *Pigeon Feathers* is a miniaturization of Howells' chapter, "A Day-Break Ramble" in *Venetian Life*. *Rabbit Run* is like, but not a match for, Howells' first great novel about a collapsing marriage, *A Modern Instance*. But unlike Howells, Updike has never got control of his preciosity. Howells' enormous achievement in *A Modern Instance* was to relinquish that carefully refined distance that he had always worn so conspicuously. He wrote plain and straight about people he and his *Atlantic* readers regarded as beneath them. Isabel's candid assessment of the fastidiousness so apparent in her husband—and her author—augured as well for the future domestic life of the one as for the coming novels of the other.

CHAPTER TEN

A Modern Instance

In Edith Wharton's *The Age of Innocence* (1920), which looks back to the early 1870s, there is a brief conversation that suggests just how brave Howells was in undertaking a novel about divorce in the middle of that decade:

> "I hear she means to get a divorce," said Janey boldly.
> "I hope she will!" Archer exclaimed.
> The word had fallen like a bombshell. . . .[1]

Howells got the idea for *A Modern Instance* from seeing a performance of *Medea*, according to an interview he gave in 1908. "'I said to myself, "This is an Indiana divorce case,"' said Mr. Howells, and the novel was born."[2] He apparently began writing it in 1876; but, just as James was to make a false start on his first big novel, *The Portrait of a Lady*, Howells had to lay his own book aside for several years. When he finally wrote it in 1881 and 1882, he abandoned his original title, *The New Medea*. It may be assumed that he departed from his original idea in many other ways as well. Yet there are at least two important respects in which *A Modern Instance* could still be titled *The New Medea*: Marcia, the tragic wife, has an archaic ferocity that breaks out in fits of jealousy; and the novel as a whole focuses on a life-destroying enmity between husband and wife. There is a systematic representativeness about the central couple in *A Modern Instance* that gives their unhappy marriage a far-reaching significance. Marcia is at first the beautiful village belle, later the dependent, domestic, passionate wife. Her husband Bartley is the successful young man on the make in the city. The novel Howells finally wrote does not focus on the issue of divorce so much as the process by which these two far from singular people tear each other to pieces in marriage. Howells also traces the effects of their failed marriage on others. As the title hints, the novel tells a typical contemporary story—what happens when the plastic hustler marries "one little woman."[3]

One of the great things in *A Modern Instance* is that even though it was the first American novel to take a close look at the degenerative potential in modern city life, it did not for one moment suggest that the trouble began in the city. Much more than the present city generation seems to be falling apart. The previous country generation was also a failure. Marcia is presented as the product of a home as suffocating as the one she and Bartley make. Her father follows what was for his generation the chief masculine profession—the law. He is a leading man in the small town of Equity; he spends his days reading in his office adjacent to his home; in character he is shrewd, skeptical, laconic, and fierce. Marcia's mother, isolated in her house by the deep Maine snows and her own settled lethargy, lives a "silenced" life (p. 34) and lacks any perceptible identity. A remote event in the father and mother's marriage has cast a pall over the life of the family: the atheist-father somehow brought the Christian-mother to mothball her faith: "She gave up for him, as she believed, her soul's salvation" (p. 89). Thus, she utterly fails to live up to the role of wife as conceived in contemporary ideology; for instead of converting or restraining her husband, she has become profane herself.[4] Whether her sacrifice was caused by his force or, as seems more likely, her own weakness, this sacrifice is the slowly spreading rotten spot in the Gaylord family. The mother withdraws emotionally: "she padded herself round at every point where she could have suffered through her sensibilities." Living "soft and snug in the shelter" of her husband's "iron will" (p. 89), she goes so far as to lose interest in her youngest child, Marcia, who grows up depending on her father and developing an extremely close attachment to him. It is partly because of this withered mother and vigorous father that Marcia becomes a one-man woman with a strong predisposition to jealousy. She has always enjoyed the exclusive possession of a strong man. If it isn't father, it must be Bartley.

Elizabeth T. Spring was no doubt correct in seeing Marcia as "weak" and "petty."[5] When Marcia first meets Atherton, "she found herself talking on, about boarding, and her own preference for keeping house" (p. 208). She echoed her husband's opinions, and "her conversation had the charm and *pathos* of that of the young wife who devotedly loves her husband, who lives in him and for him, tests everything by him, refers everything to him" (pp. 208–209; italics mine). She is, in Atherton's words, "honest and sensible and good; simple in her traditions, of course, and countrified yet, in her ideas, with a tendency to the intensely practical" (p. 213). She has good taste, is an excellent housekeeper, and furnishes the Clover Street house quite economically. She takes pleasure in looking after Bartley and comes to life in a new way when Flavia is born. Her worship of her husband is revealed in the scene where she bends and kisses the doorknob he has touched.[6]

But how could such a weak and simple person possibly be a tragic heroine, let alone a new Medea? Howells' great stroke was to impute a powerful but suppressed will to the apparently unaspiring girl. Thus, what makes Marcia's marrying a jerk like Bartley so sad is that it means the forfeiture of a queenly potential which she does not know she has in her and which can emerge only in passionate acts of destruction. One of the many signs of this potential is the "superb sort of style" (p. 212) Atherton sees in her looks. Marcia's black hair, strong eyebrows, and unusual aquiline nose are the marks of her regal, antique beauty. When she wears a certain maternity robe, the narrator says she looks like "a Roman patrician in an avatar of Boston domesticity" (p. 215). Marcia's father's title, Squire, and her own maiden name, Gaylord, hint at a noble ancestry. She is very proud, and of course resents Clara Kingsbury's well-meant patronizing. She has a notable archaic capacity for resentment and ferocity. There is also a sensual streak in Marcia, as William M. Gibson and Kenneth S. Lynn have seen,[7] and this repressed sensuality is like the fertile beauty of the Maine river valley which Howells establishes in the novel's opening paragraph, only to obliterate it in the next with the snow that covers the plain for half the year. But the deepest thing in Marcia is not sensuality but her antique, pre-Christian will.

In 1876, the year Howells made his first attempt to write the story of the new Medea, Henry Adams delivered a lecture at the Lowell Institute on the topic, "Primitive Rights of Women."[8] In this lecture Adams argued against some of the received ideas among "writers on Primitive Institutions" (p. 1)—the ideas that primitive women were slaves, that marriage was a form of property in women, and that the wedding ring was a relict aspect of an ancient proprietary institution.

In arguing against these views, Adams cited the marriage institutions of Native Americans, the ancient Egyptians, the Greeks as seen in the assumptions apparent in Homer's treatment of Penelope and Odysseus, and the Germanic tribes as their customs were preserved in the Icelandic *Njalsaga*. In every case, Adams showed that women, however dependent or inferior in status, retained definite rights and privileges even after entering marriage. The ring was not the token of a sale but a civil contract, being the husband's "earnest money" (p. 35). What clearly interested Adams most of all was the murderous independence of Hallgerda in the Icelandic poem: "Surely a woman of this stamp was no slave, no descendant of slaves, no possible connection of slaves. All the fierce and untamable instincts of infinite generations of free, wild animals were embodied in her" (p. 31).

In its own mild way, Adams's essay was written in praise of this animal ferocity that underlay the legal fictions he handled so deftly. Most striking is Adams's clear perception of the misogynous tendencies of the Catholic Church in the Middle Ages:

> The Church established a new ideal of feminine character. Thenceforward not the proud, self-confident, vindictive woman of German tradition received the admiration and commanded the service of law and society. . . . In reprobation of these the Church raised up, with the willing cooperation of the men, the modern type of Griselda,—the meek and patient, the silent and tender sufferer, the pale reflection of the Mater Dolorosa. . . . For her and such as her was the kingdom of heaven reserved, while a fate of a very different kind was in store for the defiant heroine of the heroic age. (p. 38)

I do not know whether Howells heard or read this lecture before writing his novel about "a Roman patrician in an avatar of Boston domesticity," a very impatient Griselda. To some extent the idea of woman's fettered independence was common property in the 1870s. Certainly it appears in *The Story of Avis* and in the novel James began at least as early as 1878 about the Diana-like Isabel Archer. But there seems to be a special kinship between Adams's lecture and Howells' study of the new Medea. While James saw no alternative but for his heroine to resume her life of responsible bondage, and Phelps of course saw to it that her heroine became the complete incarnation of the self-sacrificing Mater Dolorosa, Howells had the audacity to make his heroine a modern post-Christian pagan whose strong native will bursts the bonds of her Boston domesticity and shatters her marriage. Of course one of the distinctive qualities in her paganism is that it is completely unconscious; also, she is to a great extent the product of a decayed Christian culture. Yet it is made clear that she has received no religious indoctrination. So ignorant is she about religion that she thinks she can find stability simply by joining a church—any church, as Ben Halleck finds out:

> "I suppose you would want to believe in the creed of the church, whichever it was."
> "I don't know that I should be particular," said Marcia. (p. 248)

Marcia's bland ignorance shocks the Calvinistic Mrs. Halleck:

> I couldn't have believed . . . that there was any person in a Christian land, except among the very lowest, that seemed to understand so little about the Christian religion, or any scheme of salvation. Really, she talked to me like a pagan. She sat there much better dressed and better educated than I was; but I felt like a missionary talking to a South Sea Islander." (p. 254)

The reason Marcia becomes interested in religion is that she is anxious to get a handle on her irrepressible ferocity: "I can't control myself at the very times when I need to do it the most, with—with—When I'm in danger of vexing—When Bartley and I—" (p. 253). Her abrupt incoherence reveals an inadmissible struggle against a bondage she can't realize.

One of the finest aspects in Howells' rendition of the relationship between Marcia and Bartley is this picture of her futile resistance against a subjection she is helpless to grasp. After watching her with her husband, Atherton thinks she looks "as if she were naturally above him, and had somehow fascinated herself with him, and were worshipping him in some sort of illusion" (p. 213). Atherton is correct, for one of the more striking bonds between this unhappy pair is the admiration Marcia feels for Bartley's phony side. When he ridicules some of her parents' books but then appears to discriminate by reading a poem "with studied elocutionary effects," she is impressed with a "sense of his intellectual command" (p. 10). Bartley easily overwhelms her with his cheap worldliness:

> "Chicago," he said, laying the book on the table, and taking his knee between his hands, while he dazzled her by speaking from the abstraction

of one who has carried on a train of thought quite different from that on which he seemed to be intent, "Chicago is the place for me. I don't think I can stand Equity much longer. You know that chum of mine I told you about: He's written to me to come out there and go into the law with him at once." (p. 10)

Here Howells not only seizes the theatrical, self-promoting masculinity of the Gilded Age that James would have considered beneath him to try to get on the page, but he shows how the theatricality is a conspicuous form of male prowess and serves to fascinate an admiring girl. Bartley's speechifying works as male display and has the effect of capturing Marcia. When she asks him if he was ever afraid she didn't care for him, he shouts "No!":

> She had risen and stood before him in the fervor of her entreaty, and he seized her arms, pinioning them to her side, and holding her helpless, while he laughed and laughed again. "I knew you were dead in love with me from the first moment."
> "Bartley! Bartley Hubbard!" she exclaimed. "Let me go! Let me go, this instant! I never heard of such a shameless thing!" But she really made no effort to escape. (p. 48)

Originally Howells had written that Bartley "now flung his arms round her, pinioning her own" (p. 540). Thus, Marcia would have been placed in durance by a hearty embrace. But the final version drops the embrace and substitutes a kind of handcuffing. This revision makes her acquiescence all the more arresting, especially if we notice that this tableau of the woman in willing captivity to the man constitutes the end of the chapter that tells how they got engaged. Physically, Marcia is in a position comparable to Avis', who, at the moment she consents to marry Ostrander, places her hands in his, "the palms pressed together as if they had been manacled."[9]

In the character of Bartley Hubbard, Howells came closer than James or any other American writer before Dreiser to creating a truly representative American man. Like these other writers, Howells suspected there was something latently brutal in male sexuality. He wrote Hamlin Garland that *The Forester's Daughter* was "a fine, courageous book" and praised the author for having "the courage to recognize the man's brute instinct for the woman. It is an important book."[10] Howells' portrait of Basil March and other men shows that he understood there was such a thing as a good man. But his portrait of Bartley shows how well he understood the bad. Bartley is competent, cynical, and invariably self-serving. He has no sense of deference for others, and no dignity himself. He sees himself as the self-made man, hoping to get ahead in the world by means of that "smartness" (p. 20) that is so admired in Equity.[11] And get ahead he does, making himself an indispensable part, for a time, of a big Boston newspaper. He fits the rags-to-riches pattern all the more closely in having been an orphan.

And yet, as Howells shows, Bartley is not nearly so "self-reliant and independent" as he believes.[12] His foster parents may have taught him "to think of himself as a poor boy, who was winning his own way through the world" (p. 27), but they also brought him up quite comfortably so that he has become the sort of man who automatically exploits or leans on others. He advances his own career in journalism by writing up Kinney's life. Appropriately, this man whose life Bartley steals has the genuine old self-reliant integrity that Bartley mimics so superficially. Even in emotional transactions, Bartley shifts his burdens to others: when a flirtatious Canadian woman snubs him, he recovers from his humiliation by making Kinney feel bad. His impulse to share suffering with others actually leads him to declare his love to Marcia. Feeling out of sorts, he goes to her to be babied—"for a little petting" (p. 46) from her, as she perceives. But when he doesn't get it, he shifts the discomfort to her, trying to make her feel all the more guilty by adding that he loves her:

> "Marcia, do you blame me for feeling hurt at your coldness, when I came here to tell you—to tell you I—I love you?" With his nerves all unstrung, and his hunger for sympathy, he really believed that he had come to tell her this. "Yes," he added bitterly, "I *will* tell you, though it seems to be the last word I shall speak to you. I'll go, now." (p. 39)

Emotionally and economically, Bartley is a grotesque parody of self-reliance. With enormous skill and penetration, Howells shows that the successful man may not be strong and protective, like Christopher Newman or Caspar Goodwood, but just the reverse—a parasite who feeds on others, his wife included. If one turns from Goodwood to Bartley, one turns from a myth swallowed whole to an authentic man behind the myth.[13]

Another difference between Bartley and Goodwood is that the latter is strangely single-minded in his pursuit of the woman he wants. In this respect Goodwood resembles his fellow Americans, Christopher Newman and Basil Ransom, who set about winning their women with a self-possessed deliberation that is almost as unrealistic as Roger Lawrence's plan in *Watch and Ward* of bringing a young girl up to be his wife. In *The Story of Avis* Phelps conceived of Ostrander in the same way, as a single-minded pursuer. Howells understood male courtship a lot better than Phelps or James. Bartley's playful dallying with Marcia has an impressive authenticity. Bartley doesn't really need Marcia. He courts her because she is the prettiest girl there and he has nothing better to do. He is like the man in the song, "Old Joe Clark":

> I never did see a pretty little gal
> But what I loved her some.

His sexuality is promiscuous and cool and anything but monogamous. He is as ready to flirt with Hannah Morrison or Mrs. Macallister, or even Clara Kingsbury, as with Marcia, who is jealous partly because she is hot where he is cold. When Bartley quotes the familiar tag from Byron—

> "Man's love is of man's life a thing apart—
> 'Tis woman's whole existence" (p. 10)—

he is summing up one of the essential differences between himself and his wife-to-be, who has an overt and concentrated passion.

Bartley's cool sexuality is part of his casual and uncommitted personality. This casualness, a very important aspect of Howells' portrait of the man, is what enables him to become a cog in a modern metropolitan newspaper. Bartley fits in with the new journalism that Witherby represents precisely because Bartley has that slick adaptability that makes him immune to "future shock." One of the basic reasons James could not create a convincing portrait of the American man was that he did not know how to establish him in his native habitat—his work. And questions of gender aside, Bartley is superior to all of James's journalists—Henrietta Stackpole, Matthew Pardon, Flack in *The Reverberator,* and Maud Blandy and Howard Bight in

"The Papers." (Merton Densher in *The Wings of the Dove* is a well individualized character, though he is never shown working.) In general, James's portraits of journalists are too hostile and symbolic, bent on showing how the press invades privacy or sensationalizes events or debases the public mind. Further, James's portraits reveal no sense of craft or guild. Howells shows exactly how Bartley begins as a free lance reporter in Boston, and how he then makes professional acquaintances, gains entry into a professional club, gets on with Ricker and Witherby, makes his mark, and eventually drops out of sight. None of the details are missing in his rapid rise and fall. We also see how the rise of cheap journalism intersects with the fortunes of an ambitious opportunist. Bartley is clearly made for city journalism; and it is made for, and even partly by, him. As we discover in *The Quality of Mercy* (1892), the mark Bartley makes turns out to be a mark on history: ten years later the Boston *Events* would remain what he

> had made it, and what the readers he had called about it liked it to be: a journal without principles and without convictions, but with interests only; a map of busy life, indeed, but glaringly colored, with crude endeavors at picturesqueness, and with no more truth to life than those railroad maps where the important centres converge upon the broad, black level of the line advertised, and leave rival roads wriggling faintly about in uninhabited solitudes.[14]

The differences between Bartley and the journalists created by James illustrate a far-reaching distinction between the two writers' imaginative treatment of men. Howells' men are located in history, while James's men have only a superficial connection with their times. Warburton is "radical" and Goodwood is in manufacturing; but beyond a few details we get no sense of their public or business life. With Christopher Newman, James's most ambitious portrait of the new industrial lord, we get more information, but it is hard to fit together. The novel opens in 1868. At the end of the Civil War Newman had been penniless. In the three intervening years he has not only made an enormous fortune, but operating mainly in San Francisco, St. Louis, elsewhere in the West, and occasionally in New York, he has been active in copper, railroads, oil, wash-tubs, leather, and the New York stock market. These facts cannot explain themselves, let alone Newman. The narrative of his struggle to get ahead, presented as a summary of Newman's own account,[15] seems about as convincing as Huckleberry Finn's attempt to describe life in Sheffield, England. Now, Howells' various businessmen and professional women—Lapham, Gerrish in *Annie Kilburn*, Dryfoos, Fulkerson, Dr. Breen—are each locked into time and place, and this historicity helps confer on each of them a rich, particular identity. Each person is quite different from the others, with his or her own manners, speech, and personal style. James, who could never quite get into the stream of history, did not discover what Howells always took for granted: that in a rapidly evolving industrial society, people who work take a large part of their identity from their particular historical moment.[16]

A Modern Instance was so perceptive, so right, about the pervasive large-scale and personal disintegration of modern life that its author seems to have lost his nerve in the last third of the book. Instead of continuing to look squarely at Marcia and Bartley, Howells gave his attention to a peripheral matter, the ethical issue that agonizes Ben Halleck—does he have the right to court Marcia? This issue seems academic, given Marcia's fixed attachment to Bartley. Also, it is hard to enter into Ben's infatuation. Worse, the answer to Ben's question seems so obvious that his tortured doubt and Atherton's lofty conservatism become rather hollow. The answer to Ben's question must be yes precisely because the novel demonstrates so circumstantially that marriage has become profane and can no longer be seen as sacred. The difficulty that Ben and Atherton, and Howells himself, have in reconciling the sacred tradition with the profane facts serves to derail the novel. The cause of all this anxiety is the taboo against divorce, which, like some other taboos, unfortunately brought out the fussy, irrational side of Howells.[17]

But that anxiety is not the only thing that explains why Howells allowed Ben Halleck to take over some of the concluding chapters of the novel. There is an additional explanation. Ben Halleck and Bartley Hubbard go together; Howells could not conceive of one without the other. The two men have the same initials.[18] They went to college together, love the same woman, and dislike one another. Bartley once loses his temper and knocks out a weaker man whose "womanish weakness" (p. 68) is revealed by his tears of rage; Ben was once knocked down by a bully at school, and he has been lame ever since. Bartley rapidly wins his way in the world; Ben, by not going to Harvard, has somehow lost step with his contemporaries, and he now lacks ambition, a job, cronies. Bartley does pretty much as he pleases and generally gets what he wants; Ben is conscience-stricken, ineffective, and unhappy. Bartley gets Marcia without trying or even wanting her very badly; Ben has apparently been mooning over her face ever since he happened to see her photograph in a shopwindow. Bartley relies on Ben to bail him out of difficulties— drinking, borrowing money, what to do with Marcia. Each time he leans on Ben, Bartley goes his way unperturbed, while Ben tries in fear and trembling to restore order. The reason Ben takes up so much room at the end of *A Modern Instance* is that he is Bartley's double and therefore has to clean up, or at least try to clean up, the mess left by his ungovernable Mr. Hyde. Only a double's irrational *complicity,* the key term in Howells' unsatisfactory ethical system of the late 1880s, could explain Ben's compulsive heart-searching.

But what is complicity if not guilt? Ben and Bartley represent the two opposed gender ideals that divided Howells. Ben is the decent man, closely associated with the female members of the family, especially his sister Olive. He cannot make a place for himself in the world of men, and in desperation chooses the pulpit. Bartley, admired by Kinney, Henry Bird, young Andy Morrison, and virtually all other men and boys in Equity, Boston, and Tecumseh, at least until they get to know him better, is the popular ideal. Ben was the better half of Howells, decent, prudish, and feminine. But Bartley was the man, and had the lion's share.[19]

These opposed masculine ideals were to reappear in a great number of paired men in Howells' fiction. *The Shadow of a Dream* is partly about the curious friendship between a virginal minister and a practical politician. *The Landlord at Lion's Head* would pair a prim New England landscape painter with a bluff, successful businessman. One of Howells' earliest novels, "Private Theatricals," introduced a similarly contrasting pair of friends. Howells' paired men are sometimes friends, sometimes enemies. Generally, one of them is a minister, a painter, or a rich drifter at loose ends, and the other is a lawyer, a businessman, a journalist. The most striking pair is in *A Counterfeit Presentment* (1877), which deals with two men who look exactly alike, one of them a scoundrel, the other a gentleman. This work, intended originally for the stage and written at the time Howells first laid *A Modern Instance* aside, shows his incredible skill in dealing with serious matters in a light, fantastic vein; he himself called *A Counterfeit Presentment* a "comedy-romance."[20] The scoundrel jilts the heroine after leading her to fall in love with him; she goes to pieces, her feminine pride so badly injured that she actually begins to wonder if her father has ever liked her; the gentlemanly look-alike then falls in love with her, restores her self-esteem, and makes everything work out happily.[21] *A Modern Instance*, dealing less prettily with the same triangle as *A Counterfeit Presentment*—vulnerable girl, scoundrel, decent man—showed, without any of the usual let's-pretend, that the good man could not undo the damage done by his darker side. As a matter of fact, it seems that, because masculinity had come to signify a certain kind of jaunty aggression, Howells was fundamentally uncertain whether it was right to be a man. Only a person whose gender loyalties were deeply divided could have undertaken such a penetrating study of a characteristic bad modern marriage, yet this division in the writer also caused the messy guilt that Ben Halleck parades through the last half of the novel.

The split in Howells caused another problem as well. The main characters in *A Modern Instance* fall into two opposed classes, the one consisting of the main actors—the Squire, Marcia, and Bartley—and the other limited to the moral bystanders—Ben and Olive Halleck and Atherton. There is a difference between these classes which I think would normally have been quite embarrassing to Howells. The people in the first class are so richly characterized and so well located in the American social landscape that their behavior has an inevitable and even driven quality. But the people in the second class exercise a detached moral concern that somehow goes along with their great wealth, leisure, cultivation, and avoidance of dialect or vernacular.[22] One can easily imagine Dreiser writing a novel about the first group without finding it necessary to introduce any leisure-class angst. Can one imagine the finicky author of *Their Wedding Journey* doing this? I don't think so. In the decade between his first novel and *A Modern Instance*, Howells' understanding of the coarse modern scene that had fascinated him from the start grew by leaps and bounds, but it was clearly going to be impossible for him to get rid of that fastidious mentality that had shaped his initial narrative voice. What he evidently did in his first serious attempt to write a realistic novel about marginally moral people was to embody his own fine consciousness in a group of moralizing Brahmins. This solution had an aristocratic implication that could not have satisfied Howells, who knew better, for it implied that questions of moral choice were relevant only for the aristocracy. In his next good novel, *The Rise of Silas Lapham*, Howells corrected this implication. *Silas Lapham* continued to deal with the opposition between demotics and Brahmins, but it insisted that no social class had a corner on decency.

Although the concluding chapters of *A Modern Instance* are saturated with an uncontrollable sense of guilt, it seems most important, finally, to emphasize the book's essential strength—the clarity and insight with which it traces the inevitable breakup of a typical marriage and the wife's ultimate defeat. One gains a proper sense of Howells' achievement if one recalls the self-indulgent lies in *The Story of Avis* or the stupidity of the suggestion by a cultivated reader like Elizabeth T. Spring that Marcia is "unfit to reform Bartley." Given the pervading falsity in the bond between Marcia and Bartley, reform can never be at issue. Even in the scenes where the couple make up after quarreling, everything is all wrong. After the party at Clara's, for instance, Marcia returns home in a fury and slams the door of her room. Bartley doggedly enters and embraces her until the arms which "she had kept rigidly at her side" (p. 228) relax and twine around his neck. She cries, he tries to jolly her up, and before long she is giggling so hard that Howells dryly says of her: "Marcia was not in the state in which woman best convinces her enemies of her fitness for empire" (p. 229). Not even in this couple's reconciliation is there much to admire. In their periods of closest intimacy, as after Flavia's birth, the best they can manage is to try to make up for the past to each other. As a gesture of restitution, Bartley offers to invite the old Squire for a visit and to name the baby after him. More sickeningly, Marcia is always looking for an excuse to celebrate her husband to his face—"How good you are, Bartley!" (p. 235)—an opinion with which Bartley is in heartfelt agreement.

One of the nineteenth-century myths Howells scotched in the novel is the redemptive function of the wife. At the very beginning, Bartley carelessly mouths this myth: "I believe you could make me do anything; but you have always influenced me for good; your influence upon me has been ennobling and elevating." Ironically, this affirmation of idealism is nothing more than a hustler's line of goods, as Marcia's fervent response makes clear: "She wished to refuse his praise; but her heart throbbed for bliss and pride in it; her voice dissolved on her lips. They sat in silence; and he took in his the hand that she let hang over the side of her chair" (p. 13). Much later, just before the quarrel that impels Bartley to run away from Marcia, she finds herself frozen into the old double bind: she cannot approve of her husband's shiftiness, but her obligation to uplift him leads her to blame herself and try even harder to "show perfect faith in him by perfect patience" (p. 342). She has "perceived that he was not her young dream of him; and since it appeared to her that she could not forego that dream and live, she could but accuse herself of having somehow had a perverse influence upon him" (p. 341).

But of course Marcia cannot completely subdue herself to this "Boston domesticity." The archaic wildness breaks out in the form of jealousy when she suspects Bartley of carrying on with Hannah Morrison, now a Boston streetwalker. The marriage breaks apart, Bartley takes off, and Marcia suddenly finds herself in the role made familiar by hundreds of nineteenth-century novels and didactic fables—the deserted wife. The difference is, Howells does not render her as the Sad But Faithful Wife but as a person who has been hit on the head with a maul:

> She seldom left the house, which at first she kept neat and pretty, and then let fall into slatternly neglect. She ceased to care for her dress or the child's; the time came when it seemed as if she could scarcely move in the mystery that beset her life, and she yielded to a deadly lethargy which paralyzed all her faculties but the instinct of concealment. (p. 273)

Even after recovering from the shock, Marcia is unable to learn anything from her desertion. Everything remains shrouded, she is always telling Flavia about Bartley and trying to canonize him, and she refuses to move to a more suitable house for fear her husband won't be able to find her when he returns. Again, Marcia sinks beneath the huge mass of culturally sanctioned lies.

Only one thing can rouse her from her stupor. When her father artfully suggests that Bartley intends to marry another woman, Marcia's deeply suppressed anger brings her back to life. The same ancient animal fury is evident in her father's face and her own: "His was dark and wrinkled with age, and hers was gray with the anger that drove the blood back to her heart; but one impulse animated those fierce profiles, and the hoarded hate in the old man's soul seemed to speak in Marcia's thick whisper, 'I will go'" (p. 412). The brief revival of Marcia's spirit is matched by the spring weather. But she cannot sustain her anger; even on the train trip west, she anticipates returning to "the hills at home, which must be still choked with snow" (p. 420). All her father wants, however, is one chance at Bartley Hubbard: the old man "looked down mechanically at his withered hands, lean and yellow like the talons of a bird, and lifted his accipitral profile with a predatory alertness" (p. 421).

In the courtroom at Tecumseh, Indiana, Marcia is at first a bystander at a process that derives from ancient ritual combats and is marked by stately ceremonies, protocol, and the lawyers' hired artillery.[23] But her avenging father is in his element. The procedures by which he requests and is granted the privilege of the bar have the anticipatory power of the introductory rituals at a prizefight, and when he makes his peroration it is evident that speech, here, is a form of battle:

> "Two days ago, a thousand miles and a thousand uncertainties intervened between us and this right, but *now* we are here to show that the defendant, basely defamed by the plea of abandonment, returned to her home within an hour after she had parted there with the plaintiff, and has remained there day and night ever since." He stopped. "Did I say she had never absented herself during all this time? I was wrong. I spoke hastily. I forgot." He dropped his voice. "She did absent herself at one time,—for three days,—while she could come home to close her mother's dying eyes, and help me to lay her in the grave!" He tried to close his lips firmly again, but the sinuous line was broken by a convulsive twitching. "Perhaps," he resumed with the utmost gentleness, "the plaintiff returned in this interval, and, finding her gone, was confirmed in his belief that she had abandoned him." (p. 443)

The Squire's oration, a perfect blend of art and nature and the culmination of his entire career, is, as Howells makes us understand, somewhat antiquated. But however dated, it is still a very moving piece of eloquence, partly because it is such an artful expression of a passion for self-vindication. But it is at precisely the moment when Marcia finally understands the significance of her father's ferocity— the fact that it is for real, that Bartley may be imprisoned on a felony—that she commits her one last act. The modern wife finally suppresses "the proud, self-confident, vindictive woman of German tradition" (Adams, p. 38); she stands up and declares in the presence of the Court that she doesn't want to "harm" (p. 445) Bartley and in so doing publicly repudiates and humiliates her father; and as the old man collapses with a stroke that will leave one side of him "palsy-stricken" (p. 449), Bartley, saved once again by his wife, escapes and heads for the timber. Thus, in the end, the modern wife satisfies the Victorian scenario and redeems her husband. But the fact that she only saves him from the penalties of the law rather than his own wickedness shows how deeply compromised the wife has become. Even her mercy is a form of corruption.

In the end Marcia and the virile father she has destroyed return to the snows of Maine, where the old routine resumes. Love, for Marcia, had originally seemed like a thrilling conspiracy against the deathly ways of this routine. Love promised a way out. Now Marcia takes up the kind of "unmolested life" her dead mother had lived. Marcia hardly sees even her father and daughter: "Two or three times a day she ran out to see that they were safe; but for the rest she kept herself closely housed, and saw no one whom she was not forced to see; only the meat-man and the fish-man could speak authoritatively concerning her" (p. 449). The "deadly lethargy which paralyzed all her faculties" after Bartley left now had her *and* her father in its grip. Marcia will live the rest of her life in the modern stupor that was known as dullness and melancholy in so many nineteenth-century novels—the stupor against which Howells' realism itself represented a concerted, though apparently doomed, act of defiance.

In Marcia's life, Howells set forth the terrible dialectic between the dream of bliss and the withered life, which he saw as products of each other from generation to generation. Unlike James, who generally did not let his couples get together   Roderick and Christina, Newman and Claire—Howells was able to tell how and why men and women were driven to form a couple and then to tell the story of their life together, for good or bad. James lived the life of art and never really got past the threshold of sexual attraction. One of his best stories, "The Beast in the Jungle," concerned a man who did not learn until it was too late that in failing to care for May Bartram he had failed to come to life. Each one of James's leading characters seems to be a distinguished refugee from some not very interesting place, while Howells' people are only too familiar and confused. James's work has the enameled perfection of an artist who mastered his genre and sailed to Byzantium, at the price of never living except in potentiality. Howells' work has the vitality of an artist who sacrifices style and form in order to tell the story his readers must hear. James would gradually abandon realism in the late 1880s. After his work in the theatre from 1890 to 1895, he became the Master whose wonderful late novels helped shape a generation of British modernists during the teens and twenties and a later generation of American critics, readers, and writers in the 1940s and 50s. Howells worked harder and harder and produced a series of novels in the 1880s and early 90s that were the best realistic novels his country had to show. Much of his later fiction then lapsed into a strange lethargy, and he has since then had very little influence on anyone.

CHAPTER ELEVEN

Realism

What *was* realism, exactly? Up to this point I've assumed that we share a rough sense of what it was. If the reader has followed my contentions without any uneasiness over what I understand by realism, then all is well; there is communality. But if there is only uneasiness, then it is high time I admit that I have adhered all along to René Wellek's description of realism as "the objective representation of contemporary social reality."[1] Wellek offers this formula as a period concept, strictly appropriate to nineteenth-century European and American literature. With the proviso that there is no reason for not generalizing the concept (in order to take in twentieth-century non-Western literatures, for instance), I find Wellek's formula satisfactory. But it must be understood that it is only a definition based on a well-informed survey of the subject, and not anything more. Too many studies of American realism tend to confuse definition, which serves to point out and distinguish a group of objects (in this case, realistic novels) and to classify them by their common denominator, with certain other activities an intellectual may reasonably undertake to perform with them.[2] In particular, there is no reason why Wellek's concept cannot lead to the sort of analysis that makes use of the most far-reaching thought on the subject of realism, that of Georg Lukács.

A definition of a period concept in literature is useful if it opens the way to a fuller sense of literary and historical processes, cleavages, identities. Wellek's definition is particularly valuable in enabling one to get past the confusion concerning Mark Twain. If we entertain the idea that this artist was something other than a realist, we find ourselves following an irresistible line of thought. The widespread, though by no means universal, opinion that the *Adventures of Huck-*

leberry Finn is a realistic book begins to look rather questionable. Not only does this work not deal with contemporary society, it presents a view of antebellum life along the Mississippi that is highly colored. The picture of Pokeville or Brickville may be factual and pointed, but it does not seem realistic. The Grangerford chapters are wonderful, but whatever they are they are not realistic, as one immediately sees in comparing them to De Forest's sensitive exploration of a family feud in *Kate Beaumont*. In none of Mark Twain's "novels" was he "objective" or "contemporary." No doubt a debunking factuality was one of the tricks in his trade, but I doubt whether his trade was realism. He was too close to popular and folk art to enter that line of work. Mark Twain was a preacher, public exhorter, moralist, satirist, prankster, entertainer, yarn-spinner, and public fool, not to mention newspaperman, traveler, pilot, prospector, investor, and writer-businessman. My wife's grandfather, born into a farm family, was named Mark Twain by an enthusiastic parent. Would that baby have been so named if his eponym had been a realist?

Another consequence of Wellek's definition is that the body of writing known as local color, which flourished after the Civil War, can be sharply distinguished from realism. These two forms were born together and remained in close touch, but the difference—local color's adherence to old times rather than the passing scene—cannot be too much emphasized. James, and to a much lesser extent, Howells looked down on local color fiction (though James came to admire Jewett).[3] To some extent they were justified in taking this attitude. Local color's devotion to odd places and speech-ways and curious veins and outcroppings from the past all reflected a deep rejection of the contemporary world. Howells and James knew how important it was for the novel to try to come to terms with modern urban, "middle-class," civilized life. The local colorists were animated by a nostalgia that is easy to sympathize with, even though it disqualifies their literature from the centrality realism aspired to. The local colorists were well aware of their peripheral status, for they invariably dealt with regions, cultures, and vernaculars that were picturesque survivals. Certainly *The Grandissimes* is that rare thing, a good historical novel, Mary E. Wilkins Freeman's stories are wonderfully accurate and moving, Harriet Beecher Stowe's *Oldtown Folks* or *Oldtown Fireside Stories* preserve rural life in fine artistic form, and Sarah Orne Jewett remains one of the best American writers. A story like "The White

Heron," where a country girl protects a bird from a city scientist, deals in an indirect but uncompromising way with the destructive tendencies of modern life. But can modern life, no matter how bad, be understood from a position somewhere off the map? Realism, at any rate, insists that it can't be.

The third and most difficult exclusion is within James's own corpus of fiction. James was a realist for a time—roughly 1876 (*Roderick Hudson*) to 1890 (*The Tragic Muse*). But he neither began nor ended as one, and the failure to see this has undermined many investigations of American literary realism. In James's early disdainful reviews of Trollope and Rebecca Harding Davis, or his first disparaging references to Flaubert, his original antipathy to realism seems clear.[4] He later changed his mind on the two male writers and realism, but he never abandoned a certain contempt for lowlife characters, and on the whole his realism remained conservative. It was always modified by a predisposition to picture the world as a high-minded and finely conscious person would picture it. Sometimes James would upset the high-minded view; sometimes he would endorse it. His ambivalence in this matter corresponds to the sort of ambivalence toward Europe that he dramatized in "A Passionate Pilgrim" and analyzed in his memoirs with such tender irony. His 1884 essay, "The Art of Fiction," is by no means a defense of realism (as it makes a case for Robert Louis Stevenson), but a defense of artistic freedom and an attack on all rules, orthodoxies, cliques, and schools, including the realists. The essays James wrote soon after, on Howells and Constance Fenimore Woolson, clearly anticipated his approaching repudiation of realism in the 1890s, when he wrote a number of rich interiorized fictions. These late books offer a fascinating vision of the world rather than an objective representation of it. I do not see how they can be considered realistic.

The exclusion of Mark Twain, the local colorists, and James's later novels limits the field but still leaves a large corpus of realistic fiction by James, Howells, H. H. Boyesen, E. W. Howe, Joseph Kirkland, John Hay, Henry Adams, Alice Wellington Rollins, and Constance Fenimore Woolson (one of the best of the novelists on the border between local color and realism). The most important and productive of these were clearly James and Howells.

With the field properly marked off, we can now move on to a brief analysis of some essential qualities of the American realistic novel.

And first, we must supplement Wellek's definition with a more explicit recognition of the dialectical nature of realism. Wellek concluded his chapter by suggesting that "the theory of realism is ultimately bad aesthetics because all art is 'making' and is a world in itself of illusion and symbolic forms."[5] This objection must be reckoned with, for it points out that no art can be defined simply by referring to its subject matter, even if that subject matter is objectively represented. The proper response is to recognize that realism was not an independent genre or independent symbolic form or anything of the sort. It belonged to the mid-nineteenth-century genre of the novel, but bore in part an adversary or corrective relation to a major type of novel, women's fiction. Women's fiction was characterized by an idealized heroine, a strong appeal to the reader's fantasies or daydreams, a great deal of "domestic" social and psychological detail, and a plot based on love interest that led up to a decisive speech—"I love you." As a social institution, this genre was closely tied in to contemporary female roles and definitions of marriage. Once realism is seen as an inevitable reaction *within* the novel genre, the problem brought up by Wellek vanishes. The detailed verisimilitude, close social notation, analysis of motives, and unhappy endings were all part of a strategy of argument, an adversary polemic. These techniques were the only way to tell the truth about, to test, to *get at,* the ideal gender types, daydreams, and lies that were poisoning society and the novel. Realism was an analysis of quiet desperation. Attempting to break out, and to help their readers break out, of a suffocated, half-conscious state, Howells and James had to be circumstantial. It was the only way to make their case. One of James's early views, which he would never abandon, was that "when once a work of fiction may be classed as a novel, its foremost claim to merit, and indeed the measure of its merit, is its *truth*."[6] The book that made James sound this battle cry was a woman's novel, *Azarian,* by Harriet Prescott Spofford. Several years later, James would see that the only way to tell the truth was by means of realism. And several years after that, when American women's fiction no longer dominated the field, realism, for James, also lost its appeal.

But why would James and Howells be so concerned to oppose popular women's fiction? Why would a high mimetic art go to the trouble to be so aware of, so responsive to, an often cheap fantasy art? John G. Cawelti's excellent study of formula stories, *Adventure,*

Mystery, and Romance, points to the answer. As Cawelti shows, most formula stories enable the reader to enjoy the pleasures of escape and entertainment by offering him or her a familiar set of stereotypes, a superior protagonist that takes us out of ourselves "by confirming an idealized self-image," and "an imaginary world that is just sufficiently far from our ordinary reality to make us less inclined to apply our ordinary standards of plausibility and probability to it."[7] It may be hard to imagine a supremely talented writer going to all the bother of resisting such literature. The writer might actually enjoy it. But if we imagine a formula literature that insisted its world was not at all imaginary, that exhibited an unusual richness of verisimilitude and contemporary detail, that stimulated a very emotional identification and then appealed to the most respected ethical and religious ideals, the case is altered. Escape literature characterized by an intensely felt confusion between fantasy and reality might easily arouse the best talents to resistance.

There is thus a noticeably rational element in realistic fiction. Full of sober and comprehensive assessments, Howells and James were very different from the euphoric women's novels that preceded them. These earlier books were full of extreme highs and lows, a passionate brooding over the problem of being female. The male realists tried to deal with this and other problems more dispassionately. But unlike Oliver Wendell Holmes, Sr., and his "medicated" novel about the neurotic Elsie Venner, Howells and James were anything but prying Hawthornesque scientists poking at patients they saw as wholly other. As I have already argued, these two men were themselves strangely feminine and were deeply implicated in their own heroines. The strength of their best realistic work lies in their equilibrium between the passionately felt identity characteristic of women's novels and the detached judgment that was an essential component of realism.

This detachment has misled many later critics, who have been ignorant of the popular fiction against which Howells and James established themselves. One of the serious flaws in many accounts of realism is an extreme emphasis on its rationalistic or scientific component—determinism, environment, heredity, Darwinian evolution, and the evolving technological society in the background.[8] One must not overlook such matters, but they did not so much inspire the realists as authorize them.[9] What inspired them was something much deeper, much more strongly felt. One gains a sense of the real animus in realistic fiction only by considering the society and popular art of the time. In particular, the gender roles that were implied both by the major social institutions and the lineaments of the novel's idealized hero and heroine formed the basic source of realism. How did it happen that some of the major realistic novels in various countries—*Anna Karenina, Madame Bovary, Middlemarch, The Portrait of a Lady,* and *A Modern Instance*—all told the story of a bad marriage? The source of realism lay right on the surface—love interest—and yet ran far deeper than intellectual history can reach.

Of course, one dares not overlook the intellectual currents in Howells and James. To some extent these realists worked to deflate the self-assertive romantic ego. The anti-egotism James got from his father enabled him to study the romantic agony of a Roderick Hudson or the suicidal transcendentalism of the Bostonians. James's strong aversion to the self-culture symbolized by Concord entered deeply into his fiction. Howells attacked romantic egotism in both its overt form and its ironic masks. His adolescent enthusiasm for Heine suggests that his mature realism represented a solution to a malaise not far removed from that in twentieth-century modernism. Yet I think we approach the heart of the matter if we take our cues from the novel as cultural artifact rather than the novel as intellectual history. Essentially, the realists refused to give their readers the sort of satisfaction the novel generally afforded.

Women's novels offered a heroine who the reader could playfully and temporarily become. Popular fiction of all kinds—the sensation novels, Beadle's dime novels, working-girl fiction of the 1880s and 90s, the historical romances of the latter decade—all spotlighted a single leading character, who was of greater intrinsic interest than anyone around her or him. Fiction worked by offering the reader an alternative ego. Thus, the pleasure the reader experienced at the end was an ego-pleasure—a happy embrace, a successful coup, a completed journey, a threat finally averted. This satisfaction, and the fantasies containing it, reflected to some extent the atomization of society, the individual's increasing alienation, and the well-publicized success of a few great achievers. The surge of industrial activity in nineteenth-century America puffed up the ego with dreams of stunning personal success, of inevitably triumphant personal nobility. Realism was a critical response to the simultaneously inflated and privatized ego that was made hungry by contemporary society and fed by the fantasies in popular fiction. That is one of the reasons realism was often "pessimistic"—it insisted that the self was limited and conditioned and not capable of the apotheosis promised by mass fantasy. James told stories in which the protagonist often had to do without his heart's desire. Howells did the same, but he also tried a more radical idea. He prevented the reader from identifying with any one character. James did this in one realistic novel, *The Bostonians.* Howells did it in a dozen.

This particular difference between the two writers is worth noting. While James studied Isabel in great detail so that she became "an easy victim of scientific criticism," he also hoped the reader would feel "an impulse more tender and more purely expectant." That is to say, James still allowed us, though just barely, the old pleasure of "becoming" Isabel and getting some of the traditional shivers of fear, anticipation, anxiety, and so forth. But Howells did not permit the reader to feel much tender expectancy in *A Modern Instance.*[10] Refusing to tell a story that lined up with a major fantasy, he began with a familiar courtship situation that gradually petered out into a naturalistic world devoid of satisfaction or unity and with an inherent centrifugal tendency. Hoping to sever the novel from its rooted daydreams, he wrote time-bound narratives populated by people infinitely richer than those of any other nineteenth-century American writer.[11] Yet the mainspring at times seemed broken. Unlike James, who told a familiar story over and over, Howells told the non-story of people trying to live by false ideals and fantasies and getting tripped up by them. The *point* of the novel was to let us escape into a fully imagined world, one held together by a single thread of narrative movement and thus assimilable by an ego reading in time. Howells insisted that the novel was not dessert but meat and potatoes, for he wanted to use it to represent a people partly ruined by the dream of transcendence.

The strong ethical concern in American realism has often been noted. Ben Halleck, Silas and Penelope Lapham, Isabel Archer, and Hyacinth Robinson all have to make a difficult decision with important consequences for themselves and others. The distinctive contribution of realism in representing ethical choice was to insist on its importance even while hedging it about with enormous material and obligatory compulsions. In realism the self was free, but just barely.

All the characters listed here can and must choose, but each of them has only two choices, and only one of these (except for Ben) seems in each case to be correct. Even more striking is the fact that in every case except Penelope's, the correct choice enforces a painful discipline on the self (in Hyacinth's case, death). Here we see a reflection of the massive Victorian content in Howells' and James's realism—but we also see a denial of the faith, dramatized in so many popular novels, that the straight and narrow path leads to warm embraces and valuable stock certificates. American realism was an extremely moral fiction. But its insistence that we live in society rather than in the wonderful fantasy-world of so much popular fiction was sane, practical, and truthful.

Thackeray had pretended that *Vanity Fair* was a novel without a hero, even though it obviously had a heroine, however bad. But in *A Hazard of New Fortunes* and to some extent in *April Hopes, The Minister's Charge,* and *The Quality of Mercy,* Howells succeeded in making novels in which no one person was preeminent. These novels asserted that the essential thing about our lives is the way we are associated, and attempted to counter the exaggerated and dreamy egotism that had been a genre quality of the novel. Henry James was overwhelmed by the richness of *A Hazard of New Fortunes,* yet he thought it lacked form and style. In spite of everything there is to be said for the novel, James may have been right. While *Hazard* does have certain formal principles of order, it also lacks a primitive story unity, which is purposely withheld. What makes the novel all the more significant is its close engagement with the modern world and the egalitarianism implied in its following several independent but linked careers. Howells was our ultimate democratic writer: he refused to tell us what to think about his characters' lives in his own voice; he tried to consider each of them as important as the others; and he managed to enter into almost every one in a magnificent way.

The fact that our first great realist also happens to be our most democratic writer shows that realism was not just a negative force combating the narcissistic ego, or the mystification of marriage, or the falsity of the period's ideal gender roles. The positive side of American realism was its vision of democratic action.[12] Howells was able to achieve what he did partly because he emerged from a people living in a roughly democratic system under conditions of relative ease—a people with some power to direct their own lives. It was because of this power that realism turned to the causal and material world and insisted on the primacy of what ordinary people, living under recognizable pressures, *try to do.* Realism never tells us what is to be done, but it assumes, fundamentally, that choice, regardless of the difficulties, exists.

Because realism reflected a limited but genuine sense of individual power to act in the world, realism occupied, historically and logically, a middle position between mid-Victorian women's fiction, with its powerful wonder-working heroines, and the modernist tradition as represented by James Joyce. What differentiates these three groups of fiction from one another is their varying use of the kind of projected activity we call daydreaming. In Susan Warner and Augusta J. Evans, the daydream was able to triumph over harsh social necessity. In Joyce on the other hand the world triumphs over the daydream in such a way that the most the daydreamer can possibly achieve is a moment of insight into his folly and the world's darkness.[13] "Araby" and "The Dead" end, not in action, but in moments of stunned, immobile understanding in which the protagonist perceives the utter vanity of his dreams. It is because the Joycean epiphany precludes all relevant action that *The Dubliners* and *A Portrait of the Artist as a Young Man* are not, in spite of all their exact historical and psychological detail, finally realistic. Realism minus the potentially effective human will is no longer realism.

The evidence of this claim is to be seen in Joyce's career, with its steady drift from realism toward allegory. Why was Joyce's climactic work a timeless dream (entirely different from daydream) at a wake? Because decent political activity had been excluded from his fiction from the beginning of his career. Joyce the exile became an allegorist for the same fundamental reason Boethius and many others have turned to this form. Unlike realism, the literature of writers with some democratic freedom, allegory is the literature of exiles, prisoners, captives, or others who have no room to act in their society. While realism pays close attention to the facts of the contemporary social scene, corrects some of the current stereotypes, and tries to represent the causal flow of events, allegory offers a timeless scene, a universe of static types and symbols rather than causal change, a view of behavior that sees the actor or hero as the matrix for competing absolutes or abstract types, and facts that require interpretation rather than recognition followed by action. Allegory is the product of mind living under absolutism and hence projects an implacable world of abstract types—precisely the type of world projected by the violated will. Allegory is one of many human artifacts expressing a sense of individual powerlessness.[14] The reason why *The Consolations of Philosophy* begins when the hero is thrown in prison is identical with the reason why *Pilgrim's Progress* begins at the point when the hero learns that his city is to be destroyed and that he can do nothing about it except seek another country. It is the same reason why so many medieval allegories begin as dream, consolation, vision, or escape for the soul that is doomed, helpless, or consumed by hopeless love. The reason is that in allegory, unlike realism, the individual is in chains.

Realism attacked abstract types because abstract types are the mind-forged manacles immobilizing the human will. In 1882 Thomas Sergeant Perry defended Howells' kind of fiction in the way that seems most fitting and true: "Just as the scientific spirit digs the ground from beneath superstition, so does its fellow-worker, realism, tend to prick the bubble of abstract types. Realism is the tool of the democratic spirit, the modern spirit by means of which the truth is elicited."[15] It is not hard to understand why abstract types should seem implacable to a cultivated mandarin living at a time when the *res publica* gets weaker and bullies get stronger, or to a Puritan overwhelmed by an arbitrary sovereign deity and endowed with a depraved will incapable of doing good. It is also possible to understand (though my own sympathies are strained) why early twentieth-century expatriates who felt swamped by the rise of the "vulgar" common man should prefer forms of literature that deny the possibility or importance of ethical-political activity. But I cannot sympathize at all with writers and intellectuals of the post-World War II era who live in the Western democracies (speaking loosely) and yet declare that realism is dead. Realism is far too important to let die, for if it does we do.

Part II

MALE AND FEMALE HUMOR

CHAPTER TWELVE

Easygoing Men and Dressy Ladies

Penelope Lapham in *The Rise of Silas Lapham* (1885) is the first humorous romantic female lead in a novel by an American man. The one character who considers this humorist marriageable is the man who loves her, Tom Corey. Everyone else, including Penelope herself, assumes that Tom prefers her sister Irene, a beautiful blonde who, as of chapter 7, hasn't heard of George Eliot. Not until Tom proposes does it become clear that he loves Penelope, who has not only read *Middlemarch* but shares Howells' view of Eliot's narrative technique: "I wish she would let you find out a little about the people for yourself."[1]

Penelope is sane, shrewd, unfashionable, and not pretty; she has the horse sense of the legendary self-taught, self-reliant American man; and in contrast to her sister, the pattern of femininity, she has an odd and active sense of humor. A few critics have dismissed the "subplot" of *Silas Lapham* as an unrealistic contrivance.[2] And except for Henry James, nobody has considered the character of Penelope to be a major achievement.[3] But this self-made girl is a triumph of American realistic art and as important a creation as any of Howells' and James's many American girls. Penelope is an authentic person, but one who was required by everything in her culture to make herself invisible; "'You never thought of me!' cried the girl, with a bitterness that reached her mother's heart. 'I was nobody! I couldn't feel! No one could care for me!'" (p. 226).

To seize the full significance of Penelope, we must try to come to terms with the long-standing tradition in the United States that women have, and ought to have, a basic incapacity for humor or wit. In 1842 a writer for *Graham's Magazine* issued a magisterial statement of this rule:

> Women have sprightliness, cleverness, smartness, though but little wit. There is a body and substance in true wit, with a reflectiveness rarely found apart from a masculine intellect. . . . We know of no one writer of the other sex, that has a high character for humor. . . . The female character does not admit of it.[4]

In 1871, when Basil March jokes about a collision on a steamboat voyage, "the ladies, perhaps from a deficient sense of humor, listened with undisguised displeasure."[5] In 1874 Robert Barnwell Roosevelt wrote that female humorlessness was universal: "There is one peculiarity about the female character which seems to be universal with the sex: they are unable to appreciate a joke, especially where that joke bears a little against themselves."[6] In 1885 Kate Sanborn attacked this widespread masculine opinion:

> There is a reason for our apparent lack of humor. . . . Women do not find it politic to cultivate or express their wit. No man likes to have his story capped by a better and fresher from a lady's lips. What woman does not risk being called sarcastic and hateful if she throws back the merry dart, or indulges in a little sharp-shooting. No, no, it's dangerous— if not fatal.
>   "Though you're bright, and though you're pretty,
>   They'll not love you if you're witty."[7]

In 1895 an interviewer in Auckland, New Zealand, asked Mark Twain if "any American woman [had] developed any capacity for dealing with American humour":

> "The only woman I know of," was the reply, "was a writer who wrote, possibly as far back as the '40's, 'The Widow Bedott Papers.' These were written by a girl of twenty. The book was a good one, and it lived for say 15 years, or possibly 20 years, and it is a good long life for a book."[8]

In 1902 a man ridiculed the anecdotes and practical jokes that were cultivated exclusively by men:

> The domain of humor is not infrequently subdivided on other than national lines. If there is any distinction of sex upon which man prides himself, it is his superior sense of humor. . . . There is a certain sort of

verbal nonsense, as there are forms of the practical joke, which induces a masculine hysteria while it commands only tolerance from the other sex.[9]

And in 1976 two women editors introduced a collection of women's humor, *Titters*, by saying exactly the same thing:

> More than one woman has actually been heard to announce, when confronted by some floundering male attempt to amuse, such as making-believe his shoe is a telephone and trying to contact the Coast on it, "I just don't think that's funny. But then, I have no sense of humor"—a statement that usually goes unchallenged. Women aren't supposed to be funny, particularly.[10]

The voluminous critical literature on American humor has yet to come to terms with the American habit of regarding humor as in some way masculine.[11] Of course, one does not have to look twice to see that American humor has been basically that. Where are the women among the Southwestern humorists before the Civil War, the "literary comedians" of the 1860s, and the comedians of the silent movies? Both the hoary joke cycles and the places where they were presumably kept in circulation—saloons, smoking cars, barber-shops—were exclusively masculine. True, we have had many women humorists and comedians, some of whom, such as Marietta Holley, may have rivaled Mark Twain in popularity.[12] But in the classic period of American humor, the 1860s, when Artemus Ward could be seen on stage, when Samuel L. Clemens turned into Mark Twain, and when we actually had an angular Western humorist for President, humor, like politics, was a club for men only. In fact, our first book about American humor, *Why We Laugh*, was by a politician who filled his pages with humor from the state and national legislatures, as if the government, too, was more than anything else a place where men could talk and laugh.[13]

One can sense why humor was a gender quality by glancing at the "boy books" of the 1870s and 1880s. In *The Story of a Bad Boy* (1870), *Tom Sawyer* (1876), and *Peck's Bad Boy and His Pa* (1883), the distinguishing mark of the boy is the tireless enterprise he devotes to practical jokes. The victim of his jokes is the adult order of things, often a kind motherly woman such as Aunt Polly or Aunt Sally (and much earlier, Mrs. Partington, tormented by Ike). In Mark Twain the bad boy is likely to grow up to be a success, and in *Peck's Bad Boy* the young practical joker is the capitalist in training: "Of course all boys are not full of tricks, but the best of them are. That is, those who are the readiest to play innocent jokes, and who are continually looking for chances to make Rome howl, are the most apt to turn out to be first-class business men."[14]

The bad boy had the enterprising spirit that would bring success in business, yet he had so little stake in civilization that he could joyfully assault it—make Rome howl. He represented a juvenilizing of the rough old tricksters of Southwestern humor. But instead of belonging to a bygone Southwestern frontier, he had a promising future in the city and was destined to grow up into the capitalist, secret mover of events and the most practical joker of them all. The bad boy's adventures brought into the open the secret life of the American man. The bad boy tradition continued into the twentieth century in children's books, Sunday comics, comic books, and animated cartoons. In *Billy Whiskers' Kids* (1903) by Frances Trego Montgomery, the boy goat, Night, is black while his sister, Day, is white. Night dreams up naughty tricks, flirts with a pretty kid, and torments the Sultan in the book's climax. Day generally remains sweet and patient, except when she gets jealous.[15] In *Little Nemo* (1906–1909), the brilliant cartoon by Winsor McCay about the dream life of a little boy, there is a bad boy named Flip, who is a natural spoiler and breaker of rules. Flip is fat and smokes a cigar; his face is ape-like. The only important girl in Little Nemo's dreams is a good and beautiful princess, who frequently reminds the dreamer to respect the fantastically elaborate procedures in her father's kingdom, Slumberland.

There was not a body of mischief-loving "girl books" in the Gilded Age, but there was *Little Women* (1868), whose theme, as the epigraph from *Pilgrim's Progress* points out, is moral discipline and serious preparation for adulthood and marriage. The practical joker in the book is a boy, Laurie, who victimizes a girl, Meg, by hoaxing her with a series of love letters purportedly from Mr. Brooke. Of course, one of the little women does have a sense of humor, but Jo is the exception that proves the rule—that humor was a masculine trait. If she makes the other girls laugh, she also whistles, uses slang, cuts her hair, has a standing quarrel with Amy (the most feminine of the four sisters), goes by a boy's name, runs a race with Laurie, and again and again shows how much she would like to be a man.

Over a half century after the boy books and *Little Women,* the Marx Brothers developed some of their funniest routines by using a matronly woman as their straight man, so to speak. Of course there was also Zeppo, but he became the romantic lead while Margaret Dumont served as the butt of humor. Dumont was the butt because she was a lady, or in other words, because she couldn't join in the fun, bend at the waist, or speak in a natural or vernacular way. Her lifted chin and stiff bosom were the outward signs of her genteel inflexibility toward life. Tall and awesome, she was always cast as a kind of comic heavy, the model of propriety, and the three madcaps who assaulted her were later versions of Tom Sawyer and the other boy practical jokers of the nineteenth century. American humor has been the literature (and cinema) of bad boys defying a civilization seen as feminine.

One of the basic explanations for the misogyny in male American humor is that women assumed control of public manners. The regrettable masculine disposition to utter oaths, for instance, led Adeline D. T. Whitney to confide an important truth about men to her gentle readers: "I am afraid that, as a general statement men are but men, too often; and that, lest they might be worse, it behooves somebody to look after them pretty carefully."[16] The opening chapters of the *Adventures of Huckleberry Finn* show how carefully two women try to look after Huck. These chapters give a perfect symbolic representation of the opposition in male and female roles. Huck's father takes him away to a cabin in the woods where the two males laze around all day; Huck's mothers—Widow Douglas and Miss Watson, the legally appointed guardians—try to civilize him.

It was just because women represented the approved control that Mark Twain, like many other men, both worshipped and laughed at good women. It may at first be paradoxical but it finally makes sense that the two books our best humorist was proudest of—*Adventures of Huckleberry Finn* and *Joan of Arc*—were so different: the explanation is that both were about saints. Maybe Ann Stephens was not so far off the mark after all in *Esther: A Story of the Oregon Trail* (1862) when she insisted: "It is a truth that your daring Western frontiersman makes a refined woman his idol—a creature to work for, fight for, and die for, if need be, without a murmur." This sentiment leads Kirk Waltermyer, the nature's nobleman type in the book, to affirm a sentiment so absurd that it would appear to represent the opposite pole from the sanity of humor: "All the herds on the perarer [prairie] are not worth a single curl of her har."[17] Yet even Mark Twain entertained this sort of absolute veneration from time to time for angelic womanhood. The only painting he fell for in *Innocents Abroad* was, alas, an Immaculate Conception by Murillo—a painting that projects the virgin against the night sky, her feet resting on a crescent moon. This perfect maid, far above all sublunary contamination, was, Mark Twain wrote, "the only young and really beautiful Virgin that was ever painted by one of the old masters, some of us think."[18] Mark Twain was not the only sucker. In De Forest's *Kate Beaumont*, at the moment when Frank proposes to Kate, she reminds him of "Murillo's Immaculate Virgin showing through hazes of aureoles."[19] The opening scene of Henry James's novel about a practical and humorous American shows Christopher Newman gazing at another of Murillo's Immaculate Conceptions in the Louvre. And W. D. Howells' Faulkner, a "'practical' politician" and "an unscrupulous manager of caucuses and conventions," not only worshipped Murillo's immaculate young woman but "made a complete collection of all the engravings of this Madonna."[20] The practical man worshipped the virgin no less than he made fun of her. He couldn't help worshipping her because she had charge of the idealism, purity, and refinement to which he felt he ought to devote his life, but didn't. And he couldn't help laughing at the unearthly virgin because it was she after all who inspired so many absurdities—*St. Elmo*, the saccharine death poetry, the purification movements such as prohibition, and much much more.

The difference in clothes worn by men and women were an obvious index of their opposing social roles. Looking back on the 1850s from the early twentieth century, Howells wrote:

> The women dressed beautifully, to my fond young taste; they floated in airy hoops; they wore Spanish hats with drooping feathers in them, and were as silken balloons walking in the streets where men were apt to go in unblacked boots and sloven coats and trousers. The West has, of course, brushed up since, but in that easy-going day the Western man did not much trouble himself with new fashions or new clothes.[21]

This passage suggests that some of the reasons why women dressed up had little or nothing to do with men. Frances E. Willard confirms this suspicion in her book of advice, *How to Win: A Book for Girls* (1887). Here she cites with approval a Boston lawyer "who declares that women do not dress so much to please men, but to escape the criticism or excite the envy of each other. I am afraid we must admit that this is nearer the truth than we like to confess."[22] If Willard was right, it would explain to some extent a male tendency, generally concealed, to ridicule women's fancy clothes. In Joseph Kirkland's realistic novel about pioneer life in Illinois, *Zury, the Meanest Man in Spring County*, Anne's fine Eastern dress makes the men laugh. In Beadle's *Dime Pocket Joke Book*, we find this revealing item among the "Hints to Young Gentlemen": "Don't submit to be crowded off the pavement into a muddy gutter by two advancing balloons of silk and whalebone. Haven't your newly blacked boots as good a claim to respect as their skirts?"[23]

Of course, one of the worst things a man could do would be to wear anything but the familiar uniform. When Zury goes into politics, his old friend Anstey takes a deep breath and reveals a horrible fact: "The' 'llaow [they allow] ye're a-puttin' on scollops."[24] Scollops are fancy trimmings: what Anstey means is that Zury is beginning to act better than his fellow men, and Anstey says this by means of a metaphor taken from women's fashions. The clearest denunciation of a man's feminizing himself through fashionable clothes is in Ann Stephens' able satire of urban artificiality in the 1840s, *High Life in New York*. The narrator of this work is an outspoken democratic hayseed named Jonathan Slick, who hails from Weathersfield, Connecticut. When Jonathan first meets his city relative, John, he writes back to his father:

> I rally believe you wouldn't know the critter, he's altered so. . . . I tell you what, his clothes must cost him a few. . . . You could a seen your face in his boots, and his hair was parted on the top of his head, and hung down on the sides of his face and all over his coat collar, till he looked more like a woman in men's clothes than any thing else. I thought I should a haw-hawed out a larfin, all I could do, though it made me kinder wrathy to see a feller make such an eternal coot of himself.[25]

All in all, there were many strong pressures that caused "the newspaper sex,"[26] as Howells once referred to men in 1870, to dress like clodhoppers and the novel-reading sex to look like a vision from an opium dream. This divergence was a central aspect of the cultural situation in force at the time the literary comedians evolved a new kind of humor in the late 1850s and early 60s. Almost to a man, these humorists began by putting on the mask of the slovenly, vernacular male. In an age when literacy was the prerequisite for gentility, characteristically male speech could not be printed, and fiction was written largely by and for women, the humorist was known for his inability to spell. The proprieties which the ladies superintended were too much for him. He was a throwback to an older, rougher ideal of masculinity. Like Bill Arp, who was modeled on an actual "unlettered countryman,"[27] he was often a homespun village philosopher. Artemus Ward, the best and most influential of the sixties' comic characters, was a traveling sideshowman from the good old days—"be4 steembotes was goin round bustin their bilers & sendin peple higher nor a kite. Them was happy days when peple was more intelligent & wax figger's & livin wild beests wasn't scoffed at."[28] Artemus Ward could be mean to animals, as when he whipped his kangaroo for fifteen minutes after it bit the hand of a customer, and he was always full of insular, red-neck intolerance for Mormons, Shakers, women's rights, Oberlin College, and free love communities. A part-time farmer from Baldinsville, Indiana, Artemus Ward was a lazy Northern Democrat who would just as soon let the South secede.

Much rougher than Artemus Ward was Petroleum Vesuvius Nasby, created by David Ross Locke just before the Civil War. His first and middle names refer to effluents from underground that were often associated with hellfire. This man from the underground was a Copperhead during the war and a no-account spoilsman under Andrew Johnson. According to a contemporary, Nasby represented "the whisky-drinking, corner-grocery [i.e., crossroads store] statesmen who have always infested the country."[29] His "boyhood wuz spent in the pursoot uv knollege and muskrats, mostly the latter."[30] He once spent thirty days in jail after robbing a grocery store. On leaving jail, his vision and purpose were clear. He would always persecute niggers, he took a pledge never to drink water, and he was determined to find a profession that would allow him to steal without being hauled up for it. In due time he was appointed postmaster of Confederate X Roads in Kentucky. Thomas Nast's portrait (*Struggles*, p. 305) of

Nasby enjoying the perquisites of office shows the archetypal slovenly male: with his big paunch, scruffy beard, and cigar, Nasby is leaning back in his chair and resting his feet on the desk next to his bottle.

This picture was not of Nasby alone, or of the familiar office seeker who could be stopped only by civil service reform, but of the generic easygoing American man. The signature of this man was his fondness for leaning back and putting his boots up where they weren't supposed to be. A popular poem said that the American man

> Finds not in the wide world a pleasure so sweet
> As to sit near the window and tilt up his feet,
> Puff away at the Cuba, whose flavor just suits,
> And gaze at the world 'twixt the toes of his boots.
>   (*Why We Laugh*, p. 48)

In Mary Jane Holmes's bestseller, *Lena Rivers* (1859), whenever the bluff and prankish John Jr. begins "to grow crusty," he is seen "elevating his feet to the top of the mantel."[31] In a poorly told anecdote in Beadle's *Dime Pocket Joke Book, No. 1*, a group of people in Southampton try to guess the nationality of a gentleman in the coffee-room:

> "He's an Englishman," said one, "I know it by his head." "He's a Scotchman," said another, "I know it by his complexion." "He's a German," said another, "I know it by his beard." Another thought he looked like a Spaniard. Here the conversation rested, but soon one of them spoke: "I have it," said he, "he's an American; he's got his legs on the table."[32]

Putting one's legs on the table was not merely a conspicuous way of taking one's ease. It was also a crude act of defiance. Howells probably understood this, as one senses in the contrast he draws between Venetian and American loafers: "The lasagnone is a loafer, as an Italian can be a loafer, without the admixture of ruffianism, which blemishes most loafers of northern race."[33]

This loafing ruffianism was associated with laughing groups of men, and women's fiction often glanced in fear and disgust at such groups. In Susan Warner's second novel, *Queechy* (1852), Fleda has to travel alone on the train. She hates to hear "the muttered oath, the more than muttered jest, the various laughs that tell so much of head or heart emptiness,—the shadowy but sure tokens of that in human nature which one would not realize and which one strives to forget."[34] In *The Wide, Wide World* the heroine goes to a store where she is waited on by a young man, a Mr. Saunders, whose bold eyes and "slovenly exterior" strike her "most unpleasantly." Before long he tries to browbeat her into making a hasty purchase. Significantly, Saunders first appears by coming out "from among a little group of clerks, with whom he had been indulging in a few jokes by way of relief from the tedium of business."[35] For this sensitive and genteel girl, the band of jokers is the enemy. In *The Lamplighter*, the heroine similarly feels an antipathy to a lazy and humorous gentleman whose "indolent air of ease and confidence" seems "very offensive."[36] The woman writer who took the dimmest view of joking may have been Rebecca Harding Davis. In *Margret Howth*, Huff the book-keeper tells Holmes a story he has been keeping all day:

> He liked to tell a story to Holmes; he could see into a joke; it did a man good to hear a fellow laugh like that. Holmes did laugh, for the story was a good one, and stood a moment, then went in, leaving the old fellow chuckling over his desk. Huff did not know how, lately, after every laugh, this man felt a vague scorn of himself, as if jokes and laughter belonged to a self that ought to have been dead long ago.[37]

It is easy to understand why Warner, Cummins, and Davis felt a repugnance for male humor. And it is also easy to see that they didn't understand it. That ill-dressed, cigar-smoking man who gazed at the world through the toes of his boots was an offense in their nostrils. Part-king, but also part-tramp, crude, loafing, easygoing, insolent, he had the essential American masculinity. Walt Whitman tried to capture his spirit in "Song of Myself," and James's Christopher Newman embodies his Platonic Idea and sometimes takes on his features. But perhaps neither Whitman nor James did him as well as the actor Joseph Jefferson. According to George William Curtis, writing in 1871, Jefferson's interpretation of Rip Van Winkle was "the most familiar and famous rôle in the American theater to-day." Jefferson's interpretation of the "good-natured, drunken idler" who was chased by his wife from the house ("which is hers"[38]) was so popular that the actor played Rip Van Winkle for the rest of his life, offstage as well as on. At a time when being a lady sometimes meant being a corseted artificial sentimentalist, the relaxed, ill-dressed, loafing man supplied the literary comedians with the mask that formed the basis of their humor. The prevailing view of American humor is that it developed out of a kind of border warfare between two cultures, vernacular and refined.[39] I am proposing an additional dialectic—between male and female. The social basis of American humor may have been the staggering difference in our ideal gender roles. What the humorist did was to play the ideal male type—the lazy unregenerate man who defied cultural norms perceived as feminine, not by saying "Don't tread on me" or "No" in thunder, but by relaxing, taking it easy.

Beadle's *Dime Pocket Joke Book* had an anecdote about masculine laziness that went as follows:

THE UNIVERSAL PASSION.—A foreigner, who had mixed among many nations, was asked if he had observed any particular quality in our species that might be considered universal. He replied, "Me tink dat all men *love lazy.*" (p. 19)

Not only did American men love to be lazy more than they loved ladies, but they chose the former partly to spite the latter. Without knowing it, the well-traveled foreigner had identified the local passion of American men.

CHAPTER THIRTEEN

Taking Down the Big One:
From Frontier Boaster to Deadpan Loser to Boy

Of course, the ideal of lazy masculinity is very different from the official ideal—the ambitious, enterprising businessman. Unlike Christopher Newman and Silas Lapham, who made their money after the war, the sloppy male, as impersonated by the humorists, was not at all up-to-date. He derived from a bygone, pre-Civil War era, like the sleepy old forty-niner who tells the story of Jim Smiley's celebrated frog. He gained his identity in the past—the Gold Rush, the traveling sideshow business, old steamboating times on the Mississippi—and was himself as much an anachronism as the old flush times he remembered. As Nasby, he was the blustering exponent of the losing side in the Civil War, and in countless other humorous pieces he was ignorant and countrified. The sloppy male was a failure, a loser, not at all a "live man." His deadpan speech, with its melancholy earnestness and inability to see the joke, was the telltale sign of his failure to keep up. This deadpan mask, slow-witted and queer, was the inverse of the look-alive go-getter a man was supposed to be. There must have been many men who had strong mixed feelings about this loser, men whose way of life had been transformed (like Rip Van Winkle's) into a quaint irrelevancy. Men were changed, or shoved aside, by the new disciplines of war, industry, urbanization. "Future shock," the necessary shadow of technological change, was undoubtedly much more of a shock in the 1860s than now, for at that time there was still a traditional agrarian world to be destroyed. When the literary comedians put on the mask of a drawling failure, they embodied all the old pleasant ways which men were required to renounce and suppress if they wanted to respect themselves. Men found the mask of the literary comedians a howling joke because it reanimated the self they had to leave behind them. The source of American humor was an unregenerate, but defeated, masculinity.

To understand the pain in the guffaw, the male psychic needs out of which laughter arose, we must return, briefly, to the frontier. One of the most important and persistent effects of the frontier was to relax the social contract by allowing frontiersmen to revert to the life of a hunter. The sophisticated French republican, Crèvecoeur, writing shortly before the Revolutionary War, considered frontiersmen an unhappy instance of cultural regression:

> By living in or near the woods, their actions are regulated by the wildness of the neighbourhood. The deer often come to eat their grain, the wolves to destroy their sheep, the bears to kill their hogs, the foxes to catch their poultry. This surrounding hostility immediately puts the gun into their hands; they watch these animals, they kill some; and thus by defending their property, they soon become professed hunters; this is the progress; once hunters, farewell to the plough. The chase renders them ferocious, gloomy, and unsociable.[1]

Many other observers, such as William Byrd of Westover, complained about the laziness of settlers on or near the frontier. But these cultivated men—Crèvecoeur with his physiocratic ideology based on the independent landholder, Byrd with his investments in land and aristocratic values—were hardly in a good position to appreciate the siren song that drifted out of the forested wilderness and caught the ears of so many American men. What that song promised was free land, abundant game, no taxes, no oppression—the illusion, in other words, of total independence. The frontier would be the place where you would be left alone to do just what you wanted. The appeal of this siren song was very deep. Primatologists, paleo-archaeologists, and anthropologists are converging on a more detailed view of how humans survived for at least one million years by means of hunting and gathering—men doing most of the hunting, women most of the gathering.[2] In late eighteenth- and early nineteenth-century America, the civilized overlay grew sufficiently thin that the conditions were met for European colonials to come out of culture in a very odd way, to acquire a new kind of self-knowledge. Our peculiar American masculinity originated in a discovery made again and again on the moving frontier by men who had begun life thinking of themselves as Europeans or colonials or Americans—the discovery that they were more wild than domestic, that civilized folks had been laboring under some pretty fancy mistakes about the nature of mankind. The frontier allowed the heady pleasure of a reversion to a savage state and released an enormous amount of masculine aggression.

I believe that one of the things that happened to many trappers, hunters, and casual wanderers and homesteaders was that they rediscovered those aboriginal, species-specific human traits that a mere 10,000 years of civilized life had not been able to expunge. Yet it would be naive to conclude that frontiersmen managed to become true savages. True savages grow up in particular cultures along with other members of a band. Because there is no such thing as a primitive human apart from any particular culture, there can be no such thing as a complete reversion to a savage state. This seems to me to be the basic illusion in the myth that is the subject of Richard Slotkin's stimulating book *Regeneration through Violence*.[3] Slotkin argues that John Filson's 1784 narrative of the life of Daniel Boone was the definitive American myth. This narrative told the story of a civilized man who turned into an archetypal hunter and settler. For Slotkin, the key element was violent combat. When Daniel Boone entered the wilderness, he joined an Indian in mortal combat, killing the Indian. But in the very act of doing so, he submitted to the wilderness order and acquired an Indian identity. One may accept the idea that frontier violence entered deeply into American masculinity, and yet remain skeptical of Slotkin's myth and symbol formulations. The question is this: how can you become an Indian in any sense without growing up in or living with a tribe? Many American men no doubt thought of themselves as in some way Indian. But that was an illusion.

There were a number of other illusions about the frontier, one of the biggest being that it was in some way the Land of Cockayne, a place where one could at last find the good life without having to work very hard. From the very beginning, in other words, the idea of the frontier was exceedingly cloudy, and this cloudiness has persisted down to our own time. Some people seem to believe that the first backwoodsmen habitually spoke in half-horse, half-alligator braggodocio. Others, such as Charlton Laird, accept Charles Dickens' version of Western life in 1842:

> There never was a race of people who so completely gave the lie to history as these giants, or whom all the chroniclers have so libelled.

Instead of roaring and ravaging about the world, constantly catering for their cannibal larders, and perpetually going to market in an unlawful manner, they are the meekest people in any man's acquaintance: rather inclining to milk and vegetable diet, and bearing anything for a quiet life.[4]

A partial solution to the fearfully contradictory evidence is to recognize that the frontier was enveloped from the beginning by a rich cluster of lies, illusions, myths, and golden dreams, and that practically everybody who went there did so very self-consciously, with certain very definite and strongly held opinions.

One of the primary reasons for insisting on the haze of illusions surrounding the frontier—and in particular on its siren song of ease and independence—is to reach an understanding of one of the oddest of native American products, tall talk. This term was used to designate several different, though equally hyperbolic, kinds of speech or writing—the use of preposterous Latinate language ("if 'taint, I hope I may be teetotaciously exfluncted"), the telling of a farfetched story, or the uttering of an absurd brag. Tall talk seems to have originated in conjunction with a certain stereotype, the Kentuckian, a person who lived only to drink, gamble, boast, and fight. It was the Kentuckian Dickens actually hoped to see. Walter Blair has found an early description of this creature, of two of them in fact, from an 1810 travel book:

> One said, "I am a man; I am a horse; I am a team. I can whip any man *in all Kentucky*, by G-d." The other replied, "I am an alligator, half man, half horse; can whip any man *on the Mississippi*, by G-d." The first one again, "I am a man; have the best horse, best dog, best gun, and the handsomest wife in all Kentucky, by G-d." The other, "I am a Mississippi snapping turtle: have bear's claws, alligator's teeth, and the devil's tail; can whip *any man*, by G-d." This was too much for the first, and at it they went like two bulls.[5]

The behavior exhibited in this scene is so interesting that it is easy to understand why Dickens made a point of looking for instances of it. It was this kind of braggadocio, exaggerated to the point of becoming fantastic and suicidal, that high-toned Europeans first learned to think of as "American humor." Christian Schultz, Jr., the traveler who brought home this particular gem, apparently presented it as fact.

But the anecdote was not factual, it was literary.[6] Only if this is understood can our earliest American humor come into focus. Like most of the pieces belonging to later Southwestern humor, this anecdote was originally told by someone very different from the two characters who end up fighting like bulls. Essentially, the piece is a burlesque of the raw independence of men on the frontier. The kind of tall talk the two men exchange has a simple social meaning—it makes them look more impressive—taller—than they really are. Each man is using speech to make himself look big, and one of the reasons each man does this is that he is affirming that archetypal and indomitable savage masculinity that was supposed to be attainable on the frontier. Their ritual boasts are the comic expression of the male ideal of total self-reliance and personal supremacy. Furthermore, each man recognizes that the other's boast is a challenge to combat that cannot go unanswered. Each man *must* answer the challenge. If he does not, it means he is admitting the lie on which he has staked his life—the lie that he has in some way managed to escape human limitations, relative status, mortality.[7] Yet the authors of pieces like this one were not jeering at or in any way satirizing the combatants. Men living in a culture that called forth enormous respect for displays of courage, good marksmanship, political oratory, and shrewd Yankee trading could hardly bring themselves to belittle any form of challenging male prowess. Yet they could not get rid of their sense of the unreality of the masculine ideal. So they laughed. It was by means of a humorous burlesque of the fool within that men stayed sane.

Male behavior in the first half-century of the Republic often exhibited the same weird combination of enormous inflation and enormous comic deflation. Several poets tried to write heavy Miltonic epics about our national independence, but the only good long poems to emerge from our revolutionary political history were mock-epics, *M'Fingal* and *The Hasty Pudding*.[8] Aside from Charles Brockden Brown's novels, our first long fiction with a native flavor was the debunking *Modern Chivalry* by Hugh Henry Brackenridge. Strangest of all is the song that by all rights is the real national anthem, "Yankee Doodle." This song was written by an Englishman in derision of colonial Americans, who then took it as their own marching song. This combination of revolutionary assertiveness and humorous self-deflation was deeply imbedded in the American character. It appears everywhere in *Walden*, even on the title page, which gives a polite printed form of the rooster's crow that backwoodsmen theoretically uttered: "I do not propose to write an ode to dejection, but to brag as lustily as chanticleer in the morning, standing on his roost, if only to wake my neighbors up." For a man to crow like a rooster was to utter a defiant challenge—and also to play the fool. It makes sense that American humor became the distinctive nineteenth-century literary genre for men.

The backwoods boaster was inevitably associated with a wild place that had not yet been tamed, but the men who wrote about him were inevitably associated with newspapers or law offices or army forts or the stage. In 1840 a Florida newspaper gave a brief account of a bragging speech by a backwoodsman named Little Billy. In this account, tall talk as a burlesque mode of speech has begun to crystallize into one of the narrative forms characteristic of South-western humor (1830–1855).

> As we were passing by the court-house, a real "screamer from the Nob," about six feet four in height, commenced the following tirade: "This is *me*, and no mistake! Billy Earthquake, Esq., commonly called Little Billy, all the way from the No'th Fork of Muddy Run! I'm a small specimen, as you see, a remote circumstance, a mere yearling; but cuss me if I ain't of the true imported breed, and can whip any man in this section of the country. Whoop! won't *nobody* come out and fight me? . . .
>
> "Maybe you don't know who Little Billy is? I'll tell you. I'm a poor man, it's a fact, and smell like a wet dog; but I can't be run over. I'm the identical individual that grinned a whole menagerie out of countenance, and made the ribbed-nose baboon hang down his head and blush. W-h-o-o-p! I'm the chap that towed the Broad-horn up Salt River, where the snags were so thick that the fish couldn't swim without rubbing their scales off!—fact, and if any denies it, just let 'em make their will! Cock-a-doodle-doo!"[9]

Little Billy's tall tale about towing a boat up a river is not intended to amuse or distract a group of idlers, let alone readers, but to make somebody stand up and fight. And unless the bystander pretends to swallow every word, he'll have to risk getting hurt. But of course there are no bystanders, only a silent courthouse. Little Billy is out of place, or out of time, and partly because of that, comic. He aims his challenge at the courthouse, the symbol of the law's arrival on the frontier and the sign of his own obsolescence. Frustrated by the refusal of anyone to answer him like a man, Little Billy stalks out of town, "walking off in disgust." He may not know it, but he has just lost the main event.

The fact that so incredibly many of the early tall talk anecdotes consist of a burlesque of male belligerence constitutes a weighty piece of evidence for viewing early nineteenth-century American humor as a very important masculine social institution. It of course was also a literary institution, and in the light of later writers like Mark Twain and William Faulkner, a very influential and valuable one. But because it emerged out of concrete historic circumstances, it is difficult not to yield to the temptation to wonder to what extent the burlesque boast mirrored actual behavior. Unable to resist temptation, I see at least five ways in which the chest-thumping wild man reflected male behavior.

First, I think this humorous figure bespeaks the centrality of bluffing in male encounters in that period. One of Augustus Baldwin Longstreet's sketches is narrated by a man who hears dreadful boasts and signs of battle in the woods. On investigating, he finds that it is only a boy playing at being a man: "I was jist seein' how I could 'a' fout."[10] Beadle's second *Book of Fun* (1860) reprinted an amusing story, "Bears in Arkansas," told by a hunter who happened to be standing near a bear tree when a small bear walked up to leave his mark. According to the narrator, bears mark trees because "it's a great satisfaction to an old he bar to have the highest mark on the tree." To his surprise, the narrator sees the young bear carry a "big clunk" up to the tree and by standing on it leave a mark "a foot above the highest."[11] These two anecdotes neatly point out the element of deception involved in ordinary masculine bluffing.

Another way the half-horse, half-alligator reflects the men who enjoyed laughing at this type is that it articulated their own sense of suppressed but latent animality. Here, we get a first-rate piece of evidence from *Huckleberry Finn*, where a roomful of men derive enormous enjoyment out of the spectacle of the Royal Nonesuch. Another novel in which a man impersonates a beast in order to amuse an audience, a mixed one in this instance, is *Kate Beaumont* by John William De Forest. A church fair organized to raise money for a steeple entertains the crowd with a howling gyascutus: "He ran at the shins of his keeper; he stood five feet eight in his boots, and pawed the kerosene-lit air; he howled in his virile fashion until the blood of small urchins curdled with horror." This almost uncontrollable beast is indeed remarkably virile. Later, after the impersonator takes off the costume and joins the audience, his sister says: "How could you make such a guy of yourself! But, really, it *was* funny."[12]

To make a guy of oneself—this phrase originally meant to make an object of ridicule of oneself. The dictionaries of American English do not cite De Forest's passage, which seems to me extremely suggestive in the way it brings together *guy* and *gyascutus*. De Forest may have seen a connection between these words. Could the connection be etymological? Could the casual American word for boy or man be identical in its origins with the word for a mythical virile beast?

But the gyascutus was not entirely mythical, and sometimes he got loose from his keeper. There is abundant evidence that it was anything but unusual for American men to go on a rampage when they drank too much. It is well to remember that drunkenness is shaped by culture as much as loving or fighting. Mark Twain gave a chilling portrait of a violent drunk in the *Adventures of Huckleberry Finn*, where Pap very nearly kills his own son. But this episode was not purely realistic; the satiric quality of Pap's speech suffices to prove that Mark Twain was doing much more than simply reporting behavior. Silas Lapham's drunkenness is much more realistic. Significantly, what Lapham does, before his wife finally succeeds in dragging him home, is to utter a challenging brag: "Ten years ago he, Silas Lapham, had come to Boston a little worse off than nothing at all, for he was in debt for half the money that he had bought out his partner with, and here he was now worth a million, and meeting you gentlemen like one of you."[13] One of the magnificent aspects of this novel is the way Howells reveals a wild, chest-thumping brother hidden under the outer layers of personality. But the most revealing portrait of the inner gyascutus is, once again, in De Forest's *Kate Beaumont*, in the character of the gentlemanly Randolph Armitage:

> "It seemed so absurd that any human being could become demented enough to beat and belabor inanimate things till he gasped with fatigue ... The man was more like a crazy monkey than like a human being. His pranks surpass all description."

This is his wife's description of Randolph, and we see it verified:

> "You bear a hand somewhere else," screamed Randolph, all at once
> beside himself with an insane rage, approaching to *delirium tremens*. "You
> bear a hand out of this house. You leave. It's my house."[14]

The master passion expressing itself in this drunk man seems to be
a rage at the temerity of someone's invading his castle. Was this
raging territoriality the passion of which our early American humor
was a (relatively) polite masquerade? After all, the hope of getting
free land of one's own was precisely what drew many men to the
frontier.

Although it would be naive to read those early half-horse, half-
alligator boasts as literal reporting of actual events, art surely influenced life in the last century as much as it seems to do today, and
many men may have playfully or self-consciously squared off in the
approved fashion. Even the cowboy who rides into town to shoot 'em
up was not simply relieving his pent-up feelings but following an old,
half-obligatory scenario. There is a passage in A. J. Sowell's *Rangers
and Pioneers in Texas* that suggests the ritual element in this kind of
male violence:

> Occasionally in some Western village you will hear a voice ring out on
> the night air in words something like these: "Wild and wooly," "Hard
> to curry," "Raised a pet but gone wild," "Walked the Chisholm Trail
> backwards," "Fought Indians and killed buffalo," "Hide out, little ones,"
> and then you may expect a few shots from a revolver. It is a cowboy out
> on a little spree, but likely he will not hurt anyone, as some friend who
> is sober generally comes to him, relieves him of his pistol, and all is soon
> quiet again.[15]

Finally, the ring-tailed roarer to some extent really did reflect a
kind of criminal bullying that emerged on the frontier. Here and
there men terrorized entire neighborhoods, though they generally
acted in consort with their brothers or cronies or gangs of outlaws.
A case in point is the Sullivan family in the Piney Woods section of
southern Mississippi known as Sullivan's Hollow. One of the Sullivans
once made a couple of passing strangers dance and whoop with him,
until he found out that one of them was related by marriage. Another
once got in a fight and had his abdominal wall slashed so badly his

intestines spilled out on the sand. He washed them in a creek and had himself sewed up. Then, "some said, he went out into the yard, climbed upon a stump, flapped his arms like a rooster's wings, and crowed."[16] In time the Sullivans spread elsewhere, one of them becoming notorious throughout the East Lawrence highlands of Kansas for his rough practical joking.

But it is time to return to literary history and attempt to sketch the literary evolution through the nineteenth century of the backwoods boaster and his characteristic form of speech, tall talk. Bearing in mind that this boaster was a burlesque of an ideal male gender role— the self-reliant, world-defying man—one sees a certain inevitability in the sequence of development.

1) 1800–1830. The ringtailed roarer and his boast. This early stage looks more like folklore than it really was. It shows up in travel books, newspapers, and the occasional literary character such as Nimrod Wildfire in James K. Paulding's *The Lion of the West* (1830).

2) Southwestern Humor. This phase ran from 1830 to 1855. Most of the pieces were sketches published in newspapers, books, and a New York magazine with a national circulation, *The Spirit of the Times*. The authors of many sketches never identified themselves. Known authors were generally professional men—lawyers, newspapermen, doctors, actors, artists, and army officers.[17] These writers frequently introduced their low-life humor by using a cultivated and ironic bystander, narrator, or narrative voice.

3) Literary Comedians of the 1860s. This phase began just before the Civil War, when Charles Farrar Browne took the persona of Artemus Ward and David Ross Locke that of Petroleum V. Nasby. Their humor not only circulated through newspapers but, miraculously, came to life on the stage. Samuel L. Clemens turned into Mark Twain and made paying audiences of gold miners laugh. The literary comedians wrote books, yet they were also public figures and were closely associated with their comic masks.

4) Boy Books. This phase came and went in the 1870s and 80s. What happens in the boy books is that a young practical joker, or more often a gang of mischievous and enterprising boys, torments a stable adult order.

These successive phases were four very widespread trends, each of which became an easily recognized mode in its time, gained a certain fashionable quality, and, except for the first phase, attracted many writers. Of course, there were numerous humorists who didn't fit into these modes, especially the Down East humorists, and there were some phases that would persist well into the twentieth century in the Mountain West. The reason for stacking these four phases in their order of development is to reveal the degeneration of an ideal type—the burlesque form of the mythic autonomous male. In the initial phase, he was already funny but still seen as bigger than life, a tall Kentuckian or six-foot-four Little Billy. In Southwestern humor he was still a boasting hunter or rowdy, but his adventures were more artistic and often framed by a far more civilized storyteller. With the literary comedians, the confident fighter turned into a humorless and incompetent oldtimer, a frontiersman collapsed into a hayseed. Finally, in *Tom Sawyer* and the other boy books, the central character was not even a man but simply a mischievous boy. Each phase of nineteenth-century American humor focused on a certain male type, and these types were the successively degenerate sons of Daniel Boone, the archetypal macho hero. Their decreasing stature, power, and wildness reveal what was happening to the ideal male self that was brought to birth by the vision of an apparently unlimited wilderness. Some cultures have made great epics out of defeat. We preferred to go the American way, laughing, with a great big guffaw. It is tempting to see in this shrinking devolution nothing but the harmful effects of industrialization and urbanization. That view, however, overlooks the falsity in the idealized male view of the frontier—the illusion that there one might finally achieve an archaic and self-reliant way of life. Even more, such a view overlooks the unreality of the whole idea of self-reliance or total autonomy.

Thus, the humor of the literary comedians represents an inevitable stage in a long socio-literary process. The harmless, easygoing old duffer who got center stage in so much humor of the 1860s and early 70s is what six-foot-four Little Billy inevitably turned into, after the courthouse was built and nobody would fight with him anymore. The literary comedians created the new ineffective type by actively impersonating him. Except for George Washington Harris, the Southwestern humorists had carefully distinguished between themselves and the backwoods ruffian, who was so rude and threatening they had to keep him at arm's length.[18] One of the ways they did this was by framing his rough assertiveness in an artificial prose that was warranted to be safely civilized. But the humorists of the 1860s were able to take the risk of dissolving this distinction because the old bully had passed his prime. Thus, they transformed themselves into Artemus Ward, Petroleum V. Nasby, Bill Arp, Mark Twain, founding their mask in every case upon a man who was a countrified survival from the past, an oldtimer who hadn't been able to adjust to the present. This man was a loser, a failure, and that was why men laughed at him.

The connection between failure and funniness is apparent in a trick of speech used by most of the literary comedians—their drawl. Of course, the drawl reflected a rural origin at a time when everyone knew the future lay in the city, but more than that the drawl revealed a leisurely and unfashionable spirit, one that would not be hurried or bothered. It was the sign of a man caught in the backwaters and content to stay there. It was a token of social or professional failure. In its countrified slowness, drawling was the oral equivalent to leaning back in your chair and propping your feet on the table. Drawling meant that you weren't going to worry about a thing and also that you weren't ever going to get ahead.

The most famous trademark of the comedians of the sixties, their deadpan delivery, was also a token of failure. Deadpan is not blankness of expression so much as a humorlessness charged with helpless sorrow. Artemus Ward spoke with "the melancholy earnest manner of a man completely unconscious that there is anything grotesque in what he says."[19] One of Mark Twain's first listeners recollected "his slow deliberate drawl, the anxious and perturbed expression of his visage, the apparently painful effort with which he framed his sentences, and, above all, the surprise that spread over his face when the audience roared with delight."[20] W. D. Howells' best American humorist, a Wyoming rancher in *Doctor Breen's Practice*, speaks "lifelessly," with "no gleam of insinuation in his melancholy eye." When he finishes a monologue, he gives "a sort of weary sigh, as if oppressed by experience." He utters his boasts "with a wan, lack-lustre irony, as if he were burlesquing the conventional Western brag and enjoying the mystifications of his listener."[21] And there it is: the literary comedians were not bragging like Little Billy but doing something sadder and more civilized. The deadpan comedian spoke with the sad sincerity of a man who had failed to get ahead and would never understand why. In Orpheus C. Kerr's Civil War letters, a solemn incompetent named Bob tried to fight a duel:

"Gaul darn ye!" screamed Samyule, turning purple in the face, "you've gone and shot all the rim of my cap off."

"I couldn't help it," says Bob, looking into the barrel of his pistol with great intensity of gaze."[22]

The whole deadpan mode is summed up in that great intensity of gaze—Bob's sober melancholy absorption in his own failure. What a far cry he is from a comic superman like Little Billy!

Suddenly men were more interested in victims and losers than in the confidence men and Yankee peddlers that had always been stock characters on the American scene. In Mark Twain's *Roughing It* we learn about a greenhorn who buys a bad horse, a "genuine Mexican plug."[23] About the seller, we learn nothing. Similarly, "The Great Jumping Frog of Calaveras County" tells us about the dupe, Jim Smiley, but not the anonymous trickster who fills the bullfrog full of shot. In a country where the ability to drive a shrewd bargain had been a classic test of manhood, men in the sixties seemed to be most interested in those who failed this ritual confrontation.

In Southwestern humor the distinctive way of talking was the extravagant spread-eagle boast of the proverbial scrappy frontiersman. Men laughed at this, but a generation later, when the literary comedians spoke with the born loser's flat literalism, they laughed a lot harder. Machismo had been trampled on in a vital spot. The old violent and self-sufficient masculine ideal had suffered a devaluation. The frontier was farther away than ever now, and men were beginning to suspect it would never come back. The Combine was consolidating its power. The 1860s, the decade of war and rapid industrialization, exacted a terrible cost from the men who made it all hum. As they moved from farms and small towns to the army, the factory, the city, they had to conform to a new masculine ethos, put on a new identity. Now they had to look sharp, get up and go, keep in step with large impersonal systems, acquire a new and mechanical sense of time.[24]

The fourth phase in the life of the incredible shrinking American man arrived in the 1870s and 80s, in an outpouring of boy books. In most of these books, the boy lived in an old-fashioned place, relatively untouched by urbanization or industrialization. He was "bad," though often only in play, like Tom Sawyer and his gang pretending to be marauders. The boy never had to work, he often skipped school, and his most distinctive act was the practical joke. In *The Story of a Bad Boy* he set off the town cannons or pushed an old carriage into the Fourth of July bonfire; in *Tom Sawyer* he fooled the town into thinking he was dead and then strode down the church aisle at his own funeral. The butt of his jokes was the community, the whole adult order of things, particularly its pieties and annual rituals, which he assaulted for the same reason that Little Billy assaulted the courthouse. The boy waged a careless, undeclared war against civilization and its discontents. He ran off to the river or the woods whenever he could—the very places that were once wilderness—and the games he played there imitated the exploits of a prior generation of men, the frontiersmen. The boy, in fact, was the remains of the man who had once found a new identity, or rather, a few pieces of a very, very old identity, in the wilderness.

CHAPTER FOURTEEN

Petticoat Humor

Women in nineteenth-century American literature are often dedicated and humorless; they do not know how to take it easy. In "Paul Blecker" Rebecca Harding Davis wrote, "I chose a bilious, morbid woman to talk to you of, because American women are bilious and morbid."[1] Olive Chancellor, who is said by James in *The Bostonians* to be typical (though he evades saying what she is typical of), is also bilious and morbid, "a woman without laughter."[2] Even Isabel Archer, who is much healthier than Olive, takes herself too seriously to see the unintended joke in her opinion of Henrietta Stackpole:

> "I am immensely struck with her; not so much for herself as what stands behind her."
> "Ah, you mean the back view of her," Ralph suggested.
> "What she says is true," his cousin answered; "you will never be serious."[3]

Like many heroines of the seventies and eighties, Isabel belongs to a type which H. H. Boyesen called "the aspiring woman." Boyesen encountered aspiring women all over the United States, but he found them most often in New England. The one trait they all had in common was that they were "bent upon improving themselves, in season and out of season."[4] An aspiring woman once asked Boyesen to explain Spinoza's *Ethics* while dancing with him. Elizabeth Stuart Phelps, the author of *The Gates Ajar* and *The Story of Avis*, was an aspiring woman. Surely, in her case as in that of many other women, there was a connection between "her high-minded constancy to her difficult ideals" and "the baffling, almost crushing, hindrance of ill-health."[5]

"Take it easy"—an expression formerly used by men more than

women in America—sums up our unspoken masculine ethos. Men living by this ethos tend to shrug off cultural responsibilities, leaving their women to assume them. Not surprisingly, some of the dominant feminine types in the nineteenth century—the aspiring woman, the girl who aims to be genteel, the mother—all have a committed, clutching character that does not permit laughter. The genteel girl in particular has her mind fixed with deathly concentration on propriety, her own appearance, pleasing others. In *Little Women* Amy is the fine lady among the four sisters. Before she and Jo set out on their social round, Amy makes her wayward sister dress properly and prompts her how to act at each visit. Naturally, Jo rebels and scandalizes Amy. In this novel the woman with a sense of humor has bad manners; elsewhere she comes from the West or lacks respectability. Mrs. Headway, who makes a splash in London society as a woman humorist in James's "The Siege of London," has all three of these disabilities. Though she scrambles into the British aristocracy, her native element appears to be the fabulous trans-Mississippi demimonde. Mrs. Headway takes it easy, sexually, like the humorous Mrs. Larue in De Forest's novel, *Miss Ravenel's Conversion from Secession to Loyalty.*

A sense of humor is not quite consistent with respectability. In *The Lady's Guide to Perfect Gentility* women were warned "Against Sarcastic Remarks" in a paragraph so titled.[6] Fanny Fern attacked this prohibition in a mock review: "When we take up a woman's book, we expect to find gentleness, timidity, and that lovely reliance on the patronage of . . . (the male) sex which constitutes a woman's greatest charm—we do not desire to see a woman wielding the scimiter blade of sarcasm."[7] In "Little Orphant Annie," the well-known poem by James Whitcomb Riley in which a bad boy and girl are snatched up by the "Gobble-uns," the girl is a disrespectful comedian:

> An' one time a little girl 'ud allus laugh an' grin,
> An' make fun of ever' one, an' all her blood-an'-kin.[8]

In *The Wide, Wide World*, the one humorous girl, Nancy Vawse, is bad and mischievous and wickedly annoys the convalescent heroine. Significantly, it is Nancy who raises a laugh on a male guest: "Mayn't the gentlemen take care of their own things in the stoop, or must the young ladies wait upon them too?"[9]

Nancy Vawse is a lowdown country girl with no aspirations. The opposite kind of country girl, the kind that aspires to gentility, was a familiar butt of humor. Ann Stephens ridiculed this type in *High Life in New York,* where the citified wife from rural Connecticut

> don't do nothing on arth natral, and as she did when she was a gal in Connecticut. Instead of standing up straight, and speaking to her com[p]any as if she was glad to see them, she stood with one foot stuck out and her hands jest crossed afore her, as if she couldn't but jest stand alone.[10]

Years later another woman writer laughed at a country gal named Ardelia Tutt who wanted to be a poet. "She wuz soft in her complexion, her lips, her cheeks, her hands, and as I mistrusted at that first minute, and found out afterwards, soft in her head too."[11]

A type that often seemed as humorless as the aspiring woman and the genteel girl was the mother. In the three families that produced James, Howells, and Mark Twain, the father had a strong sense of humor not shared by his wife. As Howells recalled in old age, his mother "had little humor of her own." Once, when her husband told her of a dying man's last words—"I have made my peace with God; you may call in the doctors"—her loyal son doubted "if she relished the involuntary satire as he did; his humor, which made life easy for him, could not always have been a comfort to her." Another time, when the mother asked Howells' older brother how the cow got out of the garden, she fell for his tall tale: the cow "pulled out the peg with her teeth and put it under her fore leg and just walked through the gate."[12] In Howells' novel about a family from the same state where he grew up, Ohio, the mother's life seems to revolve wholly around her daughter's troubles, and that may be why Mrs. Kenton "did not often make jokes."[13]

The classic treatment of the humorless mother is Mark Twain's not very funny sketch, "Experience of the McWilliamses with Membranous Croup," where Mrs. McWilliams is sure her child has diphtheria after it coughs once or twice. Frantic, she keeps her husband up all night, moving the crib from one room to another, adjusting the register, fetching the quilt, and keeping the fire going. The next morning the doctor comes and the child coughs up a splinter lodged in its throat. The husband has the ironic last word, and Mark Twain himself adds an ironic postscript: "Very few married men have such an experience as McWilliams', and so the author of this book thought that maybe the novelty of it would give it a passing interest to the reader."[14] Although McWilliams is the repository of common sense in the family, he nowhere takes the initiative in caring for his child. He is the passive victim of his wife, who has the child wholly in her custody but lacks the competence to carry out her responsibility. The husband does have the competence. We know that because he has warned his wife not to let the child chew a pine stick. But the child is her business and not his, and he submits to her impractical, irrational, panicky rule. He salvages his self-respect, however, by addressing her in an ironic way—precisely as Dr. Sloper speaks to his sentimental sister, Mrs. Penniman, in *Washington Square*, assaulting her with his sarcasm even while putting his only child in her care.

Mark Twain wrote two other McWilliams sketches, "The Mc-Williamses and the Burglar Alarm" and "Mrs. McWilliams and the Lightning." In the last of these domestic sketches, the wife's absurd fear exposes her husband to the laughter of his friends. Howells wrote Mark Twain that the piece was "uncommon good." Perhaps the McWilliams couple was modeled after the Clemenses, just as Basil and Isabel March were versions of William and Elinor Howells. After reading *Their Silver Wedding Journey*, Mark Twain decided that Isabel March was a portrait of *his* wife. Both writers often felt oppressed by the strictness and irrationality of their wives and to some extent struck back with irony. After a second look at *A Modern Instance*, Mark Twain wrote his friend: "And your sarcasms on women & people—durn it I always take them for compliments, on the first reading."[15] Howells' farces (but not his novels) often ridiculed women. In "The Mouse-Trap" (1886), a roomful of elegant ladies huddle on chairs and piano stool because a mouse is thought to be present. They escape only by making a mad screaming rush out the door. Significantly, in the opening scene of this farce one of these silly ladies attacks her husband for opposing women's suffrage. In much of their second-rate work, Howells and Mark Twain followed the usual male ploy: they acceded to the wife's crazy rigidity and then laughed up their sleeve at her.

Was this laughter a cruel misogyny? I don't think so. Only if one tries to understand the peculiar sense of oppression felt by men can one understand the reason why they loved to joke about petticoat tyranny, or mothers-in-law, or female garrulity. The mother-in-law jokes emerged from men's perception of the powerful nineteenth-century bond between women.[16] Of course, there was an obvious conventional aspect to these jokes. Still, there were probably many husbands who were surprised at the strength of their wife's attachment to her mother. Similarly, the jokes about women's talk reflect the assumption that women are naturally more cultivated than men and may be expected to assume social leadership. As for petticoat humor, the historic matrix out of which it arose was nothing less than the doctrine of women's sphere. In a world where men were cast as barbarians and women as nursery or parlor supervisors, it is hard not to suspect that many women took their role seriously, took advantage of the power it gave them, and began calling the shots with great self-confidence. Furthermore, the male barbarians would naturally have felt oppressed in the nursery or parlor, for if woman's place was in the home, the home could easily become her castle instead of her husband's. Only by slinking away with dog and gun could Rip Van Winkle loaf and invite his soul. The irony of McWilliams, Sloper, Mark Twain, Howells, and, much later, George Burns (the Gracie Allen George Burns, with his conspicuously male prop, a cigar), was their substitute for taking to the woods. Petticoat humor, like the male vices of smoke and drink, was the husband's revenge on his humorless, irrational, and exacting woman.

One of the strangest ironies in the nineteenth-century male–female dialectic was this: that even while women were felt to have greater reserves of sensitivity, intuition, and tact, and men were often assigned the role of all-around klutz, it was in fact the men who acquired more social experience in a wide range of institutions and occupations. I would imagine that many nineteenth-century men were aware of this irony, but I have found only one writer who had the nerve to speak up. "Does any woman realize," asked Oliver Bell Bunce, "how much tact men are found to exhibit in order to successfully keep their place in life?" The fact that Bunce put these words into the mouth of a crotchety old bachelor named Mr. Bluff suggests the extent to which he was challenging current doctrine. Bluff at least did not mince words: "In that tact which teaches us when to hold our tongues and when to speak, what to see and what not to see, I suspect that the masculine part of the community may claim some little preëminence."[17] The view that bachelor Bluff assailed has persisted down to the present. In *The Psychology of Sex Differences*, Eleanor Emmons Maccoby and Carol Nagy Jacklin suggest "that the social judgment skills of men and boys have been seriously underrated."[18] Surely one of the great trials for nineteenth-century men was the difficulty of getting along with a yoke-mate whose assumption of superior moral and cultural authority served to justify the sort of bossiness no man could ever get away with at work.

Petticoat humor appealed to all classes of men. It pervades an 1870 satiric essay by Bunce, "Some Notions about Domestic Bliss," where the narrator, a bachelor, pities his friend Appleby, whose wife's

> presence, her individuality, her temper, her ideas, her wishes, her inches, surround and multiply upon him on all sides. Appleby has no room in his own house, and a very small corner in the outside world, so completely does Mrs. Appleby fill the boundaries of Mr. Appleby's sphere, and crush him into diminutiveness.[19]

Talk about a room of one's own! Beadle's inexpensive and popular joke books were even fuller of this sort of humor, though expressed in a more vernacular form. In Beadle's 1860 *Illustrated Book of Fun,* there was a story about a man whose wife forced him to change their residence once a year. Once, when he began to remonstrate, his wife told him in no uncertain terms "that that was the way her blessed-and-now-gone-to-glory mother did when she was alive" and indignantly demanded if she wouldn't "be allowed to worship the memory of the only mother she ever had."[20] One of the best stories of all, found in the same collection, concerns a bridegroom whose newly wedded wife locks him out of the bridal chamber when she finds out he is a Democrat. Because of the significance of wedding night jokes in the petticoat tradition, and also the rarity of the Beadle joke books, I quote the whole story:

> The wedding was over, the guests had departed, and the happy pair had retired to their chamber, and were snugly ensconced in bed, when Jack, in the course of a quiet conversation with his wife, unwittingly alluded to his favorite subject, by casually speaking of himself as being a democrat.
>
> "What!" exclaimed she, turning sharply and suddenly toward him; "are you a democrat."
>
> "Yes, madam," replied Jack, delighted with the idea of having a

patient listener to his long-restrained oratory—"Yes, madam, I am a democrat, a real Jeffersonian democrat, attached to the great progressive party, a regular out and outer, doubly dyed and twisted in the wool."

"Just double and twist yourself out of this bed, then," interrupted his wife; "I am a whig, I am, and will never sleep with any man professing the doctrine you do!"

Jack was speechless from absolute amazement. That the very wife of his bosom should prove a traitor, was horrible! she must be jesting. He remonstrated—but in vain; tried persuasion—'twas useless; entreaty—'twas no go. She was in sober earnest, and the alternative left him was a prompt renunciation of his heresy or a separate bed in another room. Jack didn't hesitate. As he was closing the door, his wife screamed after him—

"I say, my dear, when you repent your heresy and your past errors, just knock at my door, and perhaps I'll let you in."

The door was violently slammed, and Jack proceeded wrathfully in quest of another apartment.

In the morning she met him as if nothing had happened; but whenever Jack ventured to refer to the previous night, there was a "laughing devil" in her eye, which bespoke her power and extinguished hope. A second time he repaired to his lonely couch, and a second time he called upon his pride to support him in the struggle, which he now found was getting desperate. He ventured curses "loud but not long," on the waywardness and caprice of the sex in general, and at his own wife in particular—wondering how much longer she would hold out—whether she suffered as acutely as he did, and tried hard to delude himself into the belief that she loved him too much to prolong the estrangement, and would come to him in the morning—perhaps that very night, and sue for reconciliation. But then came the recollection of that inflexible countenance, of that unbending will, and of that laughing, unpitying eye—and he felt convinced that he was hoping against hope, and despairing, he turned to the wall for oblivion from the wretchedness of his own thoughts. The second day was a repetition of the first; no allusion was made to the forbidden subject on either side. There was a look of quiet happiness and cheerfulness about the wife that puzzled Jack sorely, and he felt that all idea of forcing her into a surrender, must be abandoned. A third night he was alone with his thoughts. His reflections were more serious and impassioned than the night previous. What they were, was known only to himself, but they seemed to result in something decided, for about midnight, three distinct raps were made at his wife's door. No answer, and the signal was repeated in a louder tone; still all was silent, and a third time the door shook with violent attacks from the outside.

"Who's there?" cried the voice of his wife, as if just aroused from a deep
sleep. "It's me, my dear, and perhaps a little the best whig you ever did
see." The revolution, in his opinion, was radical and permanent.[21]

I don't laugh at the punch line, if that's what it is, but I still think this
is a classic American joke. The politics of it are symptomatic: the
man is a giddy kind of democrat; his wife is naturally conservative.[22]
The man learns to his surprise that the woman has the upper hand.
What gives her the upper hand, of course, is that she dispenses the
sexual goodies and has the greater self-control. How significant that
the Wedding Night constituted at one and the same time the terminus
of the bestselling women's novels of the 1850s and the inspiration
for this and many more male jokes. It looks as if men and women
approached the night to remember in strangely different ways. In
the women's novels, the single heroine reaches it only after a long
and hard course in self-denial and service to others. The novels do
not even hint what happens when the candle is blown out. But after
this hiatus, the story is taken up by the cycle of male wedding night
jokes, in which the wife is seen as cold, dictatorial, and invincible.
This contradiction in the prospective and retrospective views is
pleasant to contemplate. Someone or other must have gone through
one kind of hell.

The most sustained satire on the irrationality of progressive
"middle-class" wives, especially those who joined some of the reform
movements in the decade following the Civil War, was Robert
Barnwell Roosevelt's conservative book, *Progressive Petticoats: or,
Dressed to Death. An Autobiography of a Married Man* (1874). The first-
person narrator is named Peter Gill and comes from an Old Dutch
family. He gives us his idea of the cultural differences between men
and women early in the book:

> [Woman] is not only different by nature, but has been brought up in
> a very different school. He [man], in his coarser nature, has worked,
> plodded, toiled, submitted, suffered, striven, been knocked about and
> kicked and cuffed through life. She, with her more refined organization,
> has been admired, protected, petted, indulged, worshipped, obeyed,—
> has been kept from the world, shielded from trial, supplied with what
> she needed, and covered with the eider down of affection against the
> cold blasts of trial and exposure.

Peter Gill accepts these differences as right and natural and insists that he gets along well with his wife. He tells us that she is looking over his shoulder as he writes. He is proud of letting her "have her own way in everything."

But it soon becomes apparent that all is not well with this cozy, loving pair. *Progressive Petticoats* is a satire on women's fads, and we learn how Mrs. Gill takes up one panacea after another—the water-cure, graham-flour, a diet of beans as prescribed by Dio Lewis, a special scalp treatment to prevent loss of hair, deep-breathing, and the substitution of suspenders for corsets. In the water-cure phase, she makes her husband sit in a "sitz-bath" for the regulation ten minutes and then administers a "cold pour." Inspired by Elizabeth Cady Stanton and Susan B. Anthony, Mrs. Gill decides that "there is need of improvement in our sex" and sets out "to be orderly." She tries to channel her wild erratic energy by establishing a rigid household system that calls for mottos and account books. Once her husband injudiciously speaks his mind, "Oh, do leave that stupid account-book till another day." His wife promptly becomes ill for several days, and he has to do the shopping. The husband learns his lesson, and when his wife takes off her corset and puts on her "breechlettes" and goes leaping around the room—"No more weak backs for me; no more lying on the sofa reading novels!"—he only lies low. This couple seems to be a nineteenth-century version of Lucille Ball and Desi Arnaz as portrayed on the early *I Love Lucy* shows. Mrs. Gill talks a mile a minute, regularly free-associates, and rarely lets her husband get a word in edgewise. Once, when he makes the mistake of interrupting, she at once assumes her most dignified manner: "How often must I tell you that it is extremely impolite to interrupt a person who is speaking?" *Progressive Petticoats* is an amusing book, a notable contribution to the petticoat humor tradition. Its rendering of Mrs. Gill's giddy, true-believer devotion to each and every fad that comes down the pike is a fine thing in its way. But one wonders about the narrator. It is hard to believe him when he insists he loves the child he is married to. His rigid opposition to everything that might help her grow up—"women's rights, the demand for votes"[23]—suggests an iron-willed *parti pris* underneath his self-proclaimed appreciation of her.

Except for Roosevelt's *Progressive Petticoats,* most of the petticoat tyranny humor gives a pretty sketchy image of the domineering woman. The one significant exception, and the fullest nineteenth-century characterization of woman as silly tyrant, is to be found in *The Widow Bedott Papers*, published anonymously from 1846 to 1850. These papers were written by a woman, Frances M. Whitcher, who had to pay a big penalty for her sense of humor:

> I assure you that it has never been my lot to have many friends. And I will tell you what I believe to be the secret of it: I received at my birth, the undesirable gift of a remarkably strong sense of the ridiculous. I can scarcely remember the time when the neighbors were not afraid that I would "make fun of them." For indulging in this propensity, I was scolded at home, and wept over and prayed with, by certain well-meaning old maids in the neighborhood; but all to no purpose.[24]

The female created by Whitcher has some of the qualities of these old maids. Bedott is loquacious, strong-willed, irascible, and ignorant, full of intrigue and gossip, and always dead serious. Like Emmeline Grangerford and the Sweet Singer of Michigan, she has a habit of writing long wretched poems. She sends Parson Potter a cheese with a poem on it:

> Teach him for to proclaim
>   Salvation to the folks,
> No occasion give for any blame
> Nor wicked people's jokes. (p. 26)

No widow was ever more determined to marry than the Widow Bedott. When she finally snags Parson Sniffles (thereby rising a notch from her first husband, a deacon), she unmasks her lust for status and vulgar display:

> Them Scripter pieces that Sister Myers has got hangin' in her front parlor . . . strikes me as wonderful interestin', especially the one that represents Pharoh's daughter a findin' Moses in the bulrushes. Her parasol and the artificials in her bunnit is jest as natral as life. And Moses, he looks so cunnin' a lyin' there asleep, with his little coral necklace and bracelets on. (p. 224)

Joseph C. Neal thought that the *Bedott Papers* were "the best Yankee dialect stories that had yet appeared." He knew of "a lady who for several days after reading one of them, was continually, and often at moments the most inopportune, bursting into fits of violent laughter."[25]

Around 1870 David Ross Locke, the humorist who had created Nasby, made a play out of the *Bedott Papers*. As he couldn't find an actress willing to take the comic lead, the play did not reach the stage until Locke happened to see a skillful actor burlesquing an eccentric woman. "It was the most marvelous thing," Locke said, "that I ever saw."[26] The impersonator, Neil Burgess, jumped at the chance to do Bedott. The play opened in 1879 in Providence. Over the next three or four years the Widow became almost as popular a stage character as the figure who represented her opposite and born enemy, Rip Van Winkle.

The text of *The Widow Bedott* has not survived. This is unfortunate, as the author had spoken out in favor of woman suffrage as early as 1868, and in his poem "Hannah Jane" he told the story of a wife who grows old and dull as she works at home for a husband who enjoys a successful public career. One would like to know how a man with such strong feminist sympathies treated the most famous petticoat tyrant of the day. To get an idea of the play, we must rely on reviews, playbills, posters, and the like.[27] A plot summary in the New York *Mirror* indicates that the romantic subplot centered on the Widow's daughter, Melissa, who loves and secretly marries Tom in spite of her mother's determination that Melissa marry money. But the real action involved the Widow and Elder Sniffles. She begins by looking down on Sniffles as a Baptist but changes her tune on learning that he's a widower. He in turn becomes interested in the Widow because of her apparent wealth. In the second act there is a comic courtship scene where Sniffles mistakes the Widow for a burglar and hoots at her, whereupon she "improves the opportunity to faint in his arms." In the third act they become engaged and the heroine makes "arrangements for the entire renovation of the parsonage in accordance with her remarkable taste." They marry, and the fourth act shows their return to the parsonage and its new adornments— pictures of Pharoah's daughter finding Moses, and Venus and Cupid in "pantalettes." Sniffles hands the Widow the bill for the redecoration. She refuses to pay, and he finds out his new wife is not the woman he supposed. The situation is saved by the announcement that Parson Sniffles has been called to the ministry in Oregon. He hopes "the savages may relieve him of his wife."[28]

According to the anonymous author of this plot summary, not much of the dialogue was "taken directly" from the *Papers*. Yet the reviewer felt that "the style has been imitated so exactly that the closest scrutiny is necessary to detect where the original left off and the dramatist began." He quoted one of the Widow's lines—"I believe in election and damnation—election for myself and damnation for most other people."[29] Of course, the thing one is most curious about is the quality of Burgess' impersonation. Surviving comment suggests that Burgess was a first-rate imitator of "spinsters" and "shrewd, kindly country women."[30] George C. D. Odell saw him in the play's New York premiere in 1879. Several decades later the veteran playgoer vividly remembered Burgess:

> I still see him as Widow Bedott in the kitchen, making pies, straightening out the affairs of the neighbourhood, and personifying, in spite of his sex, the attributes of a managing woman. He was not the least bit effeminate, not at all like the usual female impersonator of minstrelsy or of variety, and yet he was Widow Bedott to the life, and with little suggestion of burlesque.[31]

The reviewer for the Providence *Journal* was equally impressed with Burgess' mastery of feminine speech: "there is a peculiar rapidity and impulsiveness to his utterance, which is exceedingly appropriate."[32] The reviewer for the New York *Mirror* stressed Burgess' consummate femininity: "there is not a movement, gesture, motion or action that is not thoroughly and perfectly feminine . . . he never oversteps the proprieties."[33] This last remark was probably intended to reassure people who might have considered Burgess the usual sort of burlesque female impersonator. Another review in the *Mirror* made the same point: "The chief credit for the success of the piece is due to the effort of Neil Burgess, who plays the 'heroine' . . . with an unction and an absence of any approach to vulgarity quite remarkable."[34] It seems right to conclude that the success of *The Widow Bedott* represented an invasion of the legitimate theatre by the variety stage, and that what made the invasion successful was Neil Burgess' high-quality impersonation of a major humorous type.

As the comic embodiment of women's sphere, the petticoat tyrant lent herself to many uses. George William Curtis used her to satirize phony highbrow taste in *The Potiphar Papers*.[35] Mrs. Potiphar has such a slavish respect for European and High Church fashions that she's a sucker for anything that smells aristocratic: she tries to dress a Yankee servant in livery, makes her husband build a palatial mansion, and sponsors an elegant ball that turns into a drunken rout. In her devotion to meretricious displays, Mrs. Potiphar closely resembles both the Widow Bedott and the wife in John William De Forest's novel *Honest John Vane*.[36] This woman spends so much on fashionable luxuries that her husband, an honest but slenderly endowed congressman, accepts bribes to pay her debts. De Forest and Curtis used the tradition of petticoat tyranny for social and political satire. Many other writers used it to portray the husband as underdog or sad sack. A good instance is the sketch, "'Tis Only My Husband," by Joseph C. Neal, author of the Irvingesque *Charcoal Sketches*.[37] Mrs. Pumpilion, the wife in this sketch, is one of the most savage ladies in the nineteenth century. Soon after the wedding, Mrs. Pumpilion sets out in cold blood to teach her husband never to go fishing again with Funny Joe Mungoozle, the wit of the "free and easies." Her weapons are violence, hysterics, and an all-night lecture. Within twenty-four hours she achieves a perfect sovereignty over her man, who is transformed into the same silent, humble spouse we meet, a century later, in Thurber. What is interesting in Neal's sketch is the instinctive enmity between the wife and the easygoing funny man: Mrs. Pumpilion sees that she must destroy her husband's friendship with this person. A sketch published in *Putnam's Magazine* in 1857, "The Husband's Friend," deals with the same sort of enmity.[38] Here, the husband's friend, named Savory, is the jolliest member, and the only bachelor, in a convivial male club. The name of the club, Ringdoves, signifies the husbands' domestic subjection. Significantly, every single wife blames her husband's late hours on Savory. The point of the sketch is the ingenuity with which the inoffensive Savory manages to get back into the wives' good graces. In *Prue and I*, by Curtis again, there is brief mention of a Jonathan Bud who, after marriage,

> makes no more hilarious remarks. He never bursts into a room. He does not ask us to dinner. He says that Mrs. Bud does not like smoking. Mrs. Bud has nerves and babies. She has a way of saying, "Mr. Bud!" which destroys conversation, and casts a gloom upon society.[39]

Howells had an ear that was unsurpassed for detecting the differences between literary convention and real life. In the Niagara chapter of *Their Wedding Journey* he produced the most finely honed variation on the theme of petticoat tyranny that I am aware of. When this chapter was first serialized, a writer for the *Nation* at once noticed and commented on the traditional quality of the humor:

> A principal characteristic of Mr. Howells's humor is its rare delicacy and subtlety. But in this October instalment of 'Their Wedding Journey,' some of the topics humorously treated—as the illogicality of woman, for instance—are not very far sought, nor treated so very differently from what is common when such topics are up for discussion.[40]

My own opinion is that Howells treated this topic in a fascinatingly original way. In a first-rate article on Howells, Thomas Sergeant Perry praised his humor by singling out the episode where Isabel refuses to cross the bridge.[41] Howells himself was proud of both this episode and the one in which Basil and Isabel happen to overhear Fanny, Richard, and Kitty trying to decide whether to change hotels. When he edited *Mark Twain's Library of Humor* in 1884, he inserted these and two other scenes from *Their Wedding Journey*. What is more, Howells not only collected Neal's sketch, "'Tis Only My Husband," for the *Library of Humor*, but probably, in the original version, juxtaposed it with his own eavesdropping scene from *Their Wedding Journey*.[42]

The significance of this juxtaposition becomes clear when one reviews this scene, which was titled "Trying to Understand a Woman" in the *Library of Humor*. Basil and Isabel have not been able to keep from overhearing three strangers, who rapidly assume the contours of familiar types—a sensible, long-suffering husband, an unreasonable and bossy wife, and a single girl. The wife, named Fanny, is nervous and upset because the hotel is empty and there will be no young men for the girl in her charge:

> "Come, now, Fanny," said the gentleman, who was but too clearly her husband . . . , "you know you insisted, against all I could say or do, upon coming to this house; I implored you to go to the other, and now you blame me for bringing you here."
> "So I do. If you'd let me have my own way without opposition about coming here, I dare say I should have gone to the other place."

The husband suggests they take Kitty to Quebec, and Fanny contemptuously says:

> "I wonder you ask, Richard, when you know she's only come for the night, and has nothing with her but a few cuffs and collars! I certainly never heard of anything so absurd before!"
>
> The absurdity of the idea then seemed to cast its charm upon her; for, after a silence, "I could lend her some things," she said, musingly. "But don't speak of it to-night, please. It's *too* ridiculous. Kitty!" she called out, and, as the young lady drew near, she continued, "How would you like to go to Quebec with us?"
>
> "O Fanny!" cried Kitty, with rapture; and then, with dismay, "How *can* I!"
>
> "Why, very well, I think. You've got this dress, and your traveling-suit, and I can lend you whatever you want. Come!" she added joyously, "let's go up to your room, and talk it over!"

The Marches overhear the whole transaction. Basil expects Isabel to share his amusement at the wife's inconsequential treatment of her husband, but to his surprise Isabel doesn't see that there is anything to laugh at. Basil explains, and as he does so he begins to speak "with heat at being forced to make what he thought a needless explanation." "'Oh!' said Isabel, after a moment's reflection, '*That!* Did you think it so very odd?'" With this, Basil realizes that his wife and the other man's wife are uncomfortably alike: "I supposed I had the pleasure of my wife's acquaintance. It seems I have been flattering myself."[43] The gap between the newly married couple stands revealed, and the question is: will Isabel be the proverbial bossy and unreasonable wife that Fanny has become?

The gap between Basil and Isabel opens wider and threatens to bring about a quarrel in the second episode collected in the *Library of Humor*—the amusing scene where Isabel is so consumed by a sudden irrational fear that she refuses to walk back across a bridge to the mainland. Her husband pleads with her and then loses his patience:

> "Isabel," he cried, "I'm ashamed of you!"
>
> "Don't say anything you'll be sorry for afterwards, Basil," she replied, with the forbearance of those who have reason and justice on their side.

A victim of her own silly fear, an embarrassment to her husband, Isabel still speaks with a perfect sense of rectitude. It looks bad—yet there is definitely a slyly humorous note in her warning. Then it appears that the hotel strangers—Fanny, Richard, and Kitty—are approaching. Isabel at once steels herself, takes her husband's arm, and walks back across the bridge. Mystified, her husband asks why she was so eager to avoid Fanny and company. "Why, dearest!" Isabel replies, "Don't you understand? That Mrs. Richard—whoever she is—is so much like *me*."[44]

Doesn't this settle the question whether this marriage can be saved? No petticoat tyrant could have delivered that last speech. The essence of the tyrannical wife was her rigid and unquestioning self-right-eousness. Authorized by divine right of woman's sphere, empowered by the blessed assurance that she had a higher moral sense than her husband and a superior intuition and tact, the petticoat tyrant had a maddening complacency that nothing could penetrate. Fanny has this complacency, but Isabel finally does not. Paradoxically, in the very act of acknowledging her resemblance to her irrational sister, Isabel achieves the self-consciousness that makes her human, and possible to live with. Howells' humor may be based on the traditional topic of woman's capriciousness, but he exhibits more understanding of the woman than is customary in nineteenth-century male humor.

Furthermore, even in Isabel's worst moments, she exhibits an interesting comic play-acting. Elsewhere in *Their Wedding Journey*, Isabel will at times merge into the outlines of the petticoat tyrant, as when she precipitates the first quarrel and then forces Basil to make all the apologies and concessions. Then there is the time when Basil wonders whether he should declare Isabel's purchases at customs. Isabel tells him "in terms that I am proud to record in honor of American womanhood: 'You mustn't fib about it, Basil' (heroically); 'I couldn't respect you if you did' (tenderly); 'but' (with decision) '*you must slip out of it some way!*'" On the surface she is laying down a perfectly unreasonable law to her husband, yet she does it with a strange comic elan. As her husband says to her in the end, Fanny Ellison "is a good deal like you, but with the sense of humor left out. You've only enough to save you."[45]

The Marches were the representative Howells couple, and they reappeared in nine novels and short stories. Howells never portrayed Isabel with the broad brush strokes Neal used for Mrs. Pumpilion, and as Isabel grew older, she mellowed considerably. She, Mrs. Corey, Mrs. Elmore, Mrs. Pasmer, Mrs. Mavering, and Howells' other irrational petticoat tyrants derived from the tradition represented by Neal's sketch. If Howells did in fact place Neal's tyrant side by side with his own more realistic version in *Mark Twain's Library of Humor*, it was to pay homage to a predecessor in masculine humor and also to invite his readers to check whether he himself hadn't represented the unreasonable wife more richly, more realistically, than Neal and all the other boys. Howells' rendering of Isabel was a breakthrough in two different respects: he began with a stereotype and then proceeded to bring it to life; and he suggested that, although women (and men) may enter marriage by playing stereotyped roles that derive from the culture at large, the marriage will "take" and the couple will work out a way to live together only if those roles are deeply compromised.

CHAPTER FIFTEEN

Funny Women

Julia Newberry, whose family fortune would later endow the Newberry Library, kept a diary from 1869 to 1871. She disapproved of a girl who "had evidently a great deal of book-knowledge, but seems lacking in what young girls almost always possess, namely, fun, humour, sarcasm & enthusiasm."[1] H. H. Boyesen agreed that upper-class American women had a great deal of humor. In fact they had too much: "What can be more distressing to a man, who has outgrown his first, callow youth, than the perpetual chaff and banter in which he is expected to indulge in his intercourse with ladies?"[2] In 1872, writing to his talented younger sister, Annie, who was attempting to break into journalism, W. D. Howells warned her against the kind of women's humor that fatigued Boyesen. Howells praised one of Annie's pieces for avoiding "violence or smartness, two points in which women are apt to sin in writing." But he still warned her about the "high young-lady-falsetto, in your tone."[3] Thus, Newberry, Boyesen, and Howells not only deny that young girls and ladies lacked a sense of humor, but they tell us that many of them were in fact funny. What are we to make of the contradiction between this claim and the rich evidence, cited in previous chapters, that American women lacked humor?

"How *could* women not have a sense of humor," someone, a woman, once said to me, "if they have to live with men?" In 1851 Henry Clay Lewis published a sketch, "The Curious Widow," about a woman who gets the last laugh. The widow, a landlady, has three lively young medical students who decide to play a practical joke on her. Aware of her curiosity about their things, they remove a deformed face from a Negro cadaver and wrap it up in folds of material. The young men hide and watch her unwrap the grotesque face. She looks at it, then laughs, so wildly that she is thought to be hysterical. As the boys come out from hiding and a crowd collects, the widow catches herself, puts on "an expression of the most supreme contempt," and coldly says, "Excuse me, gentlemen . . . I was just *smiling aloud* to think what fools these students made of themselves when they tried to scare me with a dead nigger's face when I had slept with a drunken husband for twenty years!"[4] This episode neatly scotches the opinion that a woman cannot have a sense of humor, particularly since those who are fool enough to count on it are still wet behind the ears.

The curious widow speaks in that authentic female American voice that is full of bitterness, fatigue, and native wit. One hears the same voice speak out in one of Howells' acerbic rural New England housewives: "'I hear,' said Mrs. Bolton, 'that them women come up here for *rest*. I don't know what they want to rest *from*; but if it's from doin' nothin' all winter long, I guess they go back to the city poot' near's tired's they come.'"[5] In the movie *Alice Doesn't Live Here Any More*, one hears a brassier version of the same voice in the middle-aged waitress played by Diane Ladd, who tells someone he can kiss her where the sun don't shine. One of the best instances of this voice is in a mid-nineteenth-century article by Fanny Fern that attacked men's views on women.

> Another writer thinks that women don't "smile" enough when their husbands come into the house; and that many a man misses having his shirt or drawers taken from the bureau and laid on a chair all ready to jump into at some particular day or hour, as he was accustomed when he lived with some pattern sister or immaculate aunt at home. This preys on his manly intellect, and makes life the curse it is to him.[6]

There are two basic reasons for the tradition that women are devoid of a sense of humor. The first is that, as I have tried to show in the two preceding chapters of this section, a great deal of American humor arose from specifically masculine concerns. The large body of petticoat tyrant jokes grew out of men's difficulties in getting along with women. Frontier and southwestern humor, the humor of the literary comedians of the 1860s, and the humorous boy books of the following two decades all dealt in various ways with the ideal male gender role of the totally independent man. These forms of humor were evolving phases of a single masculine joke, and they reflected basic conditions of male social life and also, perhaps, an inborn male aggressiveness. Certain kinds of humor, in other words, *were* for men only. But it would be a big mistake to think that humor per se was.

The second reason why both men and women have tended to make this mistake is even more important than the first one. The social roles assigned women in the nineteenth century led them to assume responsibility for the care of others, embody the finer feelings and discriminations, function as vicars of Christ in a coarse, ungodly world, and aspire to a high, self-sacrificial way of living. These imperatives forbade laughter. W. D. Howells succinctly explained why women enjoyed Mark Twain's humor less than men: "As most women are more the subjects of convention than men, his humor is not for most women."[7] Even the physical behavior that accompanies laughter was off limits for women. According to a gag in a Beadle joke book, "a woman can laugh too much. It's a fact; for only a comb can always afford to show its teeth."[8] Because women were not supposed to display their open mouths in laughter, a servant girl in one of Harriet Beecher Stowe's stories pulls her apron over her head to indulge the laugh she can't suppress. Indeed, it was precisely because women felt they should suppress their sense of humor that they occasionally exhibited a bizarre form of behavior that has since disappeared—hysterics. Hysterics is sick laughter, a ghastly simulacrum of a healthy physical and emotional release. It is well to remember, though, that most women did not get hysterical.

Several women writers—Grace Greenwood, Fanny Fern, Elizabeth Stuart Phelps, Adeline D. T. Whitney, Louisa May Alcott, Rebecca Clarke—were funniest in the stories they wrote for children.[9] There is a good reason for this. Girlhood, often seen as the golden age before long dresses or corsets, was the free time. Here is how Frances Willard wrote of her coming under the bonds of womanhood:

> This is my seventeenth birthday and the oath of my martyrdom. Mother insists that I shall have my hair done up woman fashion, and my dress made to trail like hers. She says she shall never forgive herself for letting me run wild so long. . . . My back-hair is twisted up like a corkscrew. I carry eighteen hairpins; my head aches; my feet are entangled in the skirt of my new gown. I can never jump over a fence again so long as I live.[10]

Is it any wonder in the light of a passage like this that laughter was often associated with the naturalness of girlhood? Catherine Beecher, an extremely serious person who did not exhibit a noticeable sense of humor, included "a strong love of the ludicrous" among the traits of her "*natural* character, as developed in childhood and youth."[11] In an 1895 interview, Mark Twain was reported as remembering only one woman humorist in America, Frances M. Whitcher, and as saying that her one book, *The Widow Bedott Papers*, was "written by a girl of twenty."[12] Actually most of these papers were written when the author was married and over thirty. The fact that Mark Twain apparently juvenilized the author is one more indication of the fact that girlhood was *thought* to be the time when females were humorous.

Appropriately, several popular women novelists tended to give their more uninhibited young heroines a conspicuous sense of humor. The most important of these writers was Mary Jane Holmes, whose second novel, *The English Orphans*, was praised for its "comic vein" in the *North American Review*.[13] The good girls in Holmes's fiction were merry and impulsive and had the "fun, humour, sarcasm & enthusiasm" that Julia Newberry thought "young girls almost always possess." Nellie Douglass in *'Lena Rivers* has a "loud, ringing laugh" that startles the proud and proper Mrs. Livingston.[14] Carrie Livingston, the designing young lady in the novel, has no humor at all. This contrast between the uninhibited heroine and the ambitious, hypocritical rival was the central feature of Holmes' first novel, *Tempest and Sunshine*. Julia, the Tempest of the title, is selfish and ladylike and her mind is always running on men. She deceives her sister Fanny's admirer into believing that Fanny has a bad character. Fanny, or Sunshine, is set down as a sweet, gentle, careless, accident-prone girl whom everybody likes. Instead of waiting to open a gate, Fanny hurdles it. At the table, she drops her fork while trying to learn to eat with it instead of her knife. When Dr. Lacey, her future husband, suggests she learn the feminine skill of piano-playing, Fanny replies: "I am taking lessons, . . . but I make awkward work, for my fingers are all thumbs, as you might know by my dropping that four-tined pitchfork this morning!" The awkwardness, the barnyard reference, the comic inflation all brand Fanny as rather unladylike. Dr. Lacey laughs at her, calls her "an original little piece," and likes her all the more.[15]

A more complete portrait of a humorous girl is to be found in a novel published in the mid-sixties, *The Gayworthys* by Adeline D. T. Whitney. In this book Joanna is contrasted to her subdued, religious sister who has "Madonna hair and quiet look," her fashionable and rather shallow cousin from the city, and a variety of other feminine types. When we first see Joanna in action, she is entertaining a circle of girls her own age. She has "a little positive emphatic way of her own of uttering droll or absurdly extravagant things, that made everybody else laugh with her." Anxious about a misunderstanding with a young man, she seems "a little more queer, and animated, and hyperbolical than usual." She ridicules a famous shortcake recipe and makes fun of the dress of her fashionable aunt from the city. In fact, like Frances Whitcher, author of the *Bedott Papers*, Joanna has an irresistible impulse to satirize feminine extravagance. She makes fun of the neatness and complacency of a neighbor who prides herself on her perfect housekeeping. She predicts that Stacy Lawton, a pretty flirt, is going to get religion when a handsome young minister arrives. She even pokes fun at the conspicuous long-suffering of a woman who apparently "believes Providence keeps a special rod in pickle for her, and doesn't do much else of importance but discipline and pity her." An older woman predicts that it won't be long before Joanna loses her sense of humor. Joanna does become less ebullient, but she remains "odd, quick, trenchant, and emphatic, as of old; full of little merry sarcasms and abruptnesses; you would think her life lay in looking on at life." Unfortunately, we're assured that she has a breaking heart inside.[16]

Another very important humorous type was the wise old woman—the shrewd old maid, old aunt, or grandmother. It may seem odd at first sight that the "queer" or "original" girl should share a trait with a type two generations removed from her. But the oddity vanishes if we recall how the old woman was often seen in the nineteenth century—as a feminine type *preceding* the age of modern refinement. The reason that the natural girl and the grandmother both had a sense of humor was that neither had yet been inhibited by femininity. A passage in praise of Grace Greenwood's humor makes the connection clear:

> She would laugh in the face of a sentimental young gentleman till he wished her at the other side of the world . . . In an age when to think is to run the risk of scepticism, and to feel is to invite sentimentalism, it is charming to meet a girl who is not ashamed to laugh and cry, and scold and joke, and love and worship, as her grandmother did before her.[17]

The finest of these old-fashioned women is Aunt Patty in Caroline Lee Hentz's 1846 novel, *Aunt Patty's Scrap Bag*. This book became part of Peterson's Library of Humorous American Works and was illustrated by the incomparable Darley. Unfortunately, the book is not worth reading for its story, a tale of brotherly jealousy in which the older brother, a misanthrope, kills the younger. Even worse, Aunt Patty hardly figures in the story after the opening chapters. She illustrates the transition between the older sort of humor character, with pleasant eccentricities, and the later humorist as comedienne. Aunt Patty has an exceedingly homely face that gives "one an idea of extreme goodness." She has warts and moles, a big nose, and takes snuff. Her right hand is withered. She interprets dreams and passes on old sayings: "You must never look after a person as long as you can see them . . . ; it is a sure sign that you will never see them again." She is said to have "all the disinterestedness and simplicity of a child," yet she has at the same time some sharp views of her own: "I wouldn't ask a man to have me if he was made of diamonds, and cased in gold. It is a sin and a shame, and a disgrace to the whole sex. If the truth were told, it is the way half the women get married, I do believe."[18]

The most fascinating aspect of Aunt Patty is the way she uses the sense of touch and sight to retrieve a huge body of legend, history, and local gossip. "One of her darling hobbies"—here she is close to the eighteenth-century humor characters—"was to collect pieces of calico, muslin, and silk, samples of the dresses of all her friends and acquaintances, and every once in a while she would open her scrap-bag, and review her treasures, telling the names of the individuals who wore such and such frocks, and relating many choice anecdotes." When the man of the family leaves on a long journey, she gives him a bag in which to collect pieces "of the dresses of all the ladies with whom he became acquainted." Like a quilt made of old dresses and shirts, the scrapbag is nothing less than the old woman's sensuous archives. When a girl brings out at random a piece of "ministerial-looking calico" with "broad shaded stripes, of an iron-gray colour," the past suddenly revives: "'Ah!' said Aunt Patty—the chords of memory wakened to music at the sight." Recollecting the time she first saw old Parson Broomfield wearing a coat of that cloth, she tells of the time when she was a little girl and the minister publicly noticed her. Someone asks whether the minister preached in the calico, and

Aunt Patty says:

"Oh! no, child—all in solemn black, except his white linen bands. He always looked like a saint on Sunday, walking in the church so slow and stately, yet bowing on the right and left, to the old, white-headed men, that waited for him as for the consolation of Israel. Oh! he was a blessed man, and he is in glory now. Here," added she, taking a piece of spotless linen from a white folded paper, ["]is a remnant of the good man's shroud. I saw him when he was laid out, with his hands folded on his breast, and his Bible resting above them."[19]

Aunt Patty does not speak in dialect. The book was written before local color existed.

There were many other kindly and humorous old maids and grandmas in women's fiction. The best character in Harriet Beecher Stowe's *The Pearl of Orr's Island* is old Miss Roxy, who "popped out observations on life and things, with a droll, hard quaintness that took one's breath a little."[20] In *The Lamplighter* there is a flowery old spinster who is seen with a good deal of affection. "It is true, time is inexorable," says the old lady, "but I cling to life, Miss Gertrude, I cling to life, and may marry yet."[21] Elizabeth Stuart Phelps invented several amusing old women with a vernacular humor that is pungent and aggressive. One of the best is Mrs. Butterwell, a salty, middle-aged Maine innkeeper's wife in a novel chiefly about a woman physician, *Doctor Zay* At times Mrs. Butterwell is a genuine local color person; frequently she becomes a spokeswoman for her author's strong views. Like Phelps herself, Mrs. Butterwell wants nothing to do with Calvinism, and when her husband grows despondent from a liver complaint, she tricks him into getting well by taking away his Bible and slipping him a copy of Mark Twain's *Innocents Abroad*. Mrs. Butterwell is full of scorn for dependent women:

Don't you know there are women that can't get through this valley without men folks, in some shape or 'nother? If there ain't one round, they're as miserable as a peacock deprived of society that appreciates spread-feathers. You know the kind I mean: if it ain't a husband, it's a flirtation; if she can't flirt, she adores her minister. I always said I did n't blame 'em, ministers and doctors and all those privileges, for walkin' right on over women's necks. It isn't in human nature to take the trouble to step off the thing that's under foot.[22]

There is a telling difference between Mrs. Butterwell's humor and that of the Southwestern humorists or literary comedians. The men were funny because they were playing the fool in one way or another. But Mrs. Butterwell's humor is a function of her sagacity. She is a wise woman who has acquired a good deal of bitter and practical knowledge, and she utters it in a manner that is wry instead of foolish or self-parodying. Her voice is very close to that of the popular newspaper columnists, Gail Hamilton and Fanny Fern. Like these writers, Mrs. Butterwell is funny because of her superior and pungent insight. In view of this, it is worth noting that the real heroine, Doctor Zay, is an extremely noble, hardworking, and competent professional, with little humor. She takes care of an injured upper-class Boston male who must stay inside and on his back, and who quickly develops flagrant symptoms of nineteenth-century femininity, becoming tearful, hysterical, and absurdly dependent on his physician. What the novel does is transfer power from male to female, but without exactly reversing the usual gender roles. Instead, the female becomes the strong, silent, humorless type, a successful "aspiring woman." Doctor Zay is a later version of Aunt Winifred, the wise woman in *The Gates Ajar* who reveals to suffering mortals the consolations of heaven. Doctor Zay, Aunt Winifred, and Avis are all illustrations of woman's superior spirituality. In Mrs. Butterwell, this superiority takes a vernacular form and emerges as a particular kind of feminine humor.

Mrs. Butterwell appears to have close affiliations with the most important wise old woman in nineteenth-century American literature, Samantha Allen. This character, also known as Josiah Allen's Wife, was created by Marietta Holley, who wrote fifteen books about her, always with Samantha as narrator, between 1873 and 1914. Some of the Samantha books were published by subscription by Elisha Bliss, Mark Twain's first publisher, and they apparently enjoyed large sales. Today they are virtually unknown.[23] Their author was friends with Frances E. Willard, head of the Woman's Christian Temperance Union, and Susan B. Anthony. To some extent Holley used Samantha in order to influence public opinion. Although Samantha was rich in down-home detail, she by no means represents a realistic or local color portrait. Her speech has too many features—malapropisms, well-articulated sermons, transcendent allegories—that point to other, more didactic literary traditions. Yet she is an original character and the pivotal figure in nineteenth-century female humor, for she was the great nineteenth-century superwoman—a sort of populist super-woman who wore domestic homespun and spoke vernacular humor.

Unlike modern feminism, which derives much of its strength from a rejection of the home, Marietta Holley made domesticity the basis of women's liberation. Samantha is first of all an expert wife, mother, and housekeeper, with a generalized competence that puts her in a different class from both Mrs. McWilliams and the masks of male humorists. Samantha is full of contempt for ineffective and senti-mental women like the Widder Doodle, who allowed her late husband to enslave her:

> Truly, if anybody don't know anything, you can't git any sense out of 'em. You might jest as well go to reckonin' up a hull row of orts, expectin' to have 'em amount to sunthin'. Ort times ort is ort, and nothin' else; and ort from ort leaves nothin' every time, and nothin to carry; and you may add up ort after ort, all day, and you wont have nothin' but a ort to fall back on. And so with the Widder Doddle, you may pump her mind till the day of pancakes, (as a profane poet observes,) and you wont git anything but a ort out of it,—speakin' in a 'rithmatic way.[24]

Samantha Allen is surrounded by fools, male and female, whom she suffers as best she can, but when pushed too far her deep womanly nature breaks forth in an inspired outburst. As a wise domestic manager, she hands out a great deal of advice on matters close to home. More important, she gives many blockbusting sermons on the big social and political questions of the day. Domesticity and mother wit may be the source of her wisdom, but each of her books is based on an excursion away from home and village. She invariably goes where the action is. In 1876 she goes to the Philadelphia Centennial, where she meets President Grant and earnestly tells him what's happening:

> Why Ulyssess, I couldn't begin to tell all the horrers and evils of war, not if I should stand here and talk to you till the year 1900; for it can't be told not by mortal tongue. It is a language writ in broken hearts, and despair, and want, and agony, and madness, and crime, and death, and it takes them to read it.[25]

Here, I believe, we see one of the reasons why the Samantha Allen books disappeared from view so rapidly. They are extremely preachy.

Furthermore, the author doesn't seem to understand that there is something preposterous in Samantha's buttonholing President Grant in this way. Evidently Samantha has a spiritual authority that allows her to get away with a harangue that would not be civil for a man. The trouble with much of the humor of Marietta Holley and Elizabeth Stuart Phelps was that it rested on an assumed superiority—the superiority of a higher culture, or of an unflawed heart, or of a more spiritual insight.[26] Neither author approached George Eliot's achievement in creating Mrs. Poyser in *Adam Bede*. "Populist" characters like Mrs. Butterwell and Samantha Allen have a vernacular power that finally seems a little factitious. They may speak as the natives speak, but something has been faked. They don't seem to feel the inner ease, the relaxed dignity that laughter requires. They don't take it easy.

Like the Widow Bedott, Samantha Allen was made the basis of a successful play, *Vim, or a Visit to Puffy Farm*, which opened in 1878 and appeared at intervals throughout the 1880s. Once again, the lead role was taken by Neil Burgess. Unfortunately, I have not been able to find a promptbook of the play or even to identify the author. Two programs bill the play as by the author of *Widow Bedott*—David Ross Locke.[27] This attribution is dubious. Another program implies that Neil Burgess was the author.[28] No program or review so much as mentions Marietta Holley. Samantha was renamed Tryphena Puffy, and her husband's character was greatly modified. In Holley's books, he had a narrow-minded asperity, but in the play he apparently became the familiar "down-trodden" husband and was played by an actor "whose oddity and demureness provoked much mirth." Other important charaters were Betsey Sonnett "an elderly spinster, given to poetry and matrimony," Deacon Simon Milkweed with his ten uniformed children, and Mattie Somers "the sunbeam of the farm."[29] The play probably lacked a tightly woven plot. One program identified the acts as follows:

ACT I   Puffy Farm
ACT II   Mattie's Birthday
ACT III   The Pic-nic and Josiah's Nightmare.
            The Village Choir.
            The Pic-Nic Dance.
            The Drive Home on the Revolving Stage.[30]

Act II probably led up to the comic climax that was featured in a large multi-colored poster. This scene apparently took place in the kitchen of the Puffy farm. A plucked chicken is shown flying in through an open window, and a man standing outside is shooting in. A young woman with her back to the window is surprised, and her red curls are flying up. Tryphena (Neil Burgess), wearing a green dress, is standing by the stove and has just spilled something on it, and a man is falling out of the china closet.³¹ Act III was virtually a series of variety acts, featuring a real horse on a moving stage (or else in front of a moving panorama), songs and dances, and most important, "the materialization of Josiah Puffy's nightmare."³² In this nightmare, the characters assumed various circus roles that burlesqued themselves. Tryphena Puffy became Mademoiselle Trypheni Pufferino (an aerial artist?) and her "down-trodden" husband became a clown.³³

Clearly, *Vim* was more of a farce than the books it was based on. Neil Burgess turned the central pair of characters, Tryphena and Josiah, into more emphatic caricatures of the wise old woman and the clodhopper husband. Howells thoroughly enjoyed the play. He considered Burgess' impersonation "of a bustling Yankee house-keeper" to be "deliciously true," and he also gave high marks to the "slow, taciturn, evasive husband, who had his own deliberate way in spite of all her volubility, energy, and rapidity." Howells remembered the play as a triumph of realistic humor:

When Mr. Burgess begins to talk, you want him to go on forever; every most satisfying accent makes you hunger for more. All of us know Tryphena Puffy; we remember her from childhood, or we have summer-boarded with her, or our lot is still cast with her in the country; we instantly recognize the type, and if Mr. Burgess will allow us to spend the evening in her company we can ask nothing better of him. When she sits down with her knitting and begins to rock, and asks, "Who'd you see at the post-office?—anybody 't I know?" it is enough. The drama can do no more, and in fact it does very little more than show this phase and that of her peremptory, kindly, shrewd, trusting nature.³⁴

When Howells assembled *Mark Twain's Library of Humor,* he included an excerpt from one of the Samantha Allen books.³⁵ Yet the evidence suggests that Howells thought much more of Neil Burgess' play than

Marietta Holley's book. The main reason for this may have been that the play eliminated the didacticism of Holley's books and desacralized the Spiritual Superwoman. In other words, Burgess took the one important humorous character that functioned as an auxiliary to a decidedly self-righteous women's movement and transmuted her into a type associated with local color and petticoat humor. Not until she was impersonated by a man could Samantha take it easy and become "homicidally funny."[36]

Julia Newberry, H. H. Boyesen, and Howells all assure us that the funny girl and the wise old woman were not simply stock types but bore some connection to actual types of women. Even more alive, I suspect, was a third category—the bright, witty lady. "Brightness," wrote the author of *Progressive Petticoats*, "seems to be a gift of a large part of the sex."[37] In Howells' novel, *The Lady of the Aroostook*, upper-class women in Boston are reported to "say witty things" with a "responsive quickness."[38]

The first discussion of the nature of polite female humor is to be found in the pages of a New York periodical, *The Critic and Good Literature*, which staged a brief debate on women's sense of humor in 1884. Significantly, the relevant articles came out a few months before Howells sat down to write *The Rise of Silas Lapham*. The debate was touched off by a sentence in Richard Grant White's "The Fate of Mansfield Humphreys": "There was in her soul a sense of delicacy mingled with that rarest of qualities in woman, a sense of humor."[39] White was at once caught up by Joseph B. Gilder, an editor of the *Critic* who wrote under the pseudonym "The Lounger":

> When a novelist sets out to portray an uncommonly fine type of heroine, he invariably adds to her other intellectual and moral graces the above-mentioned "rarest of qualities." I may be over-sanguine, but I anticipate that some sagacious genius will discover that woman as well as man has been endowed with this excellent gift from the gods.[40]

The next issue of the *Critic* ran an article by Alice Wellington Rollins, "Woman's Sense of Humor," which corrected the Lounger by pointing out that "our finest heroines,—Romola, Dorothea, Maggie Tulliver, Isabel Archer, the Lady of the Aroostook, Anne, Shirley—have none of them a particle of humor." Yet, Rollins argued, women were actually far more humorous than men, particularly in the drawing room, where "the delicious things said by bright women" were "unnoted except at the moment because they are sure to be followed by something brighter still." It was hard to describe women's humor, which was "too intellectually keen to be merely nonsense or fun, yet too delicately amusing to be actual wit."[41] In a second article, Rollins contrasted the quiet subtleties of women to "the boisterous shouts of laughter issuing from the 'den,'" where the men sit "smoking" and listening to "good stories" or to "some one professional wit."[42]

The discussions of women's humor in *The Critic* had at least one major consequence. They inspired Kate Sanborn to edit the first American edition of women humorists. According to Sanborn's memoirs, she had "a monomania . . . to prove that women possess both wit and humor,"[43] and in the summer of 1885 she hastily assembled *The Wit of Women*. The pieces in this collection appear to fall into two broad categories. The first of these consists of dialect and local color humor and may be designated by Sanborn's punning term, "Samples" (ch. IV). As the pun suggests, she associates dialect humor with old-time needlecraft and seems to regard it as a delightful pastime for ladies of leisure to cultivate. She introduces one particular sketch as "a quaint bit of satire from a bright Boston woman." It would appear that there is a parallel between the ladies who composed dialect and local color humor and the professional men in the 1830s and 40s who wrote Southwestern humor about crude frontier types. In each case highbrows amused themselves by taking off democratic lowbrows.[44] Sanborn considers the second category of women's humor—conversational wit, puns, light verse—as the more important: "I have reserved for the close numerous instances of woman's facility at badinage and repartee. It is there, after all, that she shines perennial and preeminent." In a way, Sanborn succeeds in making her case, as the epigrams are the best part of her book:

> A lady was discussing the relative merits and demerits of the two sexes with a gentleman of her acquaintance. After much badinage on one side and the other, he said: "Well, you never yet heard of casting seven devils out of a man." "No," was the quick retort, "*they've got 'em yet!*"[45]

The defect in *The Wit of Women* is the embattled earnestness with which it attempts to document women's humor. The wit and humor in Sanborn's compilation seem to issue from a strident self-confidence, a strong sense of superiority. In the seven devils joke the woman is not at all a fool. She knows where she stands and she holds her ground. As Alice Rollins wrote in one of her articles on women's humor, "whenever in the pages of our brilliant contemporary *Life* [a humor magazine], it becomes necessary to 'sit upon' a dude, to 'take down' an Anglo-maniac, or to snub the British aristocracy, *a young woman is usually chosen* to demolish the victim with her wit."[46] The humor of the literary comedians has an entirely different structure, for the persona is necessarily a fool and the laughter he touches off has elements of derision and pity directed at himself. He is a comic scapegoat who bears the suppressed nature or the forgotten past of the men who read or listen to him. The seven demons are out in the open, the petroleum gushes forth, Vesuvius erupts; and the masculine laughter that results registers a life-giving release—a momentary integration of the contradictory segments of the self. But feminine wit operates from a position of strength, or apparent strength—a refusal to let down the defenses. Instead of employing the studied incompetence that Mark Twain was to recommend in "How to Tell a Story," feminine wit uses the bright weapons of civilized discourse. Where masculine humor leads up to an explosion of laughter, feminine humor has more varied and less raucous effects. For men there is an ecstatic release of tension; for women, a continuation of it. And so it happened that women produced a mandarin humor that has been forgotten, and the uncouth barbarians produced "American humor."

It was this witty feminine badinage that H. H. Boyesen objected to. Henry James felt the same way about it. In reviewing Louisa Alcott's *Eight Cousins*, he wrote that the heroine's "conversation is salted with the feminine humor of the period. When she falls from her horse, she announces that 'her feelings are hurt, but her bones are all safe.'"[47] James made the same point about the heroine of Julia Constance Fletcher's *Mirage*, who was "very gracefully sketched, though the author is to a certain extent guilty of the regrettable tendency, common among American writers of fiction, of making her utter those 'smart' comicalities which are the note of the 'lady-correspondents' of certain journals."[48] In his phrase, "'smart' comicalities," I believe James touches on the brittle and poised defensiveness of much ladylike wit.

The queer or original girl, the wise old woman, and the bright lady were three major humorous types of women in fiction, folklore, and actual life. The first two types represented one general strategy allowing women to express their native humor—the strategy of playing a role seen as antecedent to repressive Victorian decorum. These types were funny-peculiar as well as funny-ha ha.[49] The third type, the bright lady, expressed her funniness precisely by cultivating this decorum and the elegant badinage of polite conversation. This kind of wit or humor became exclusively feminine and was characterized by its quick responsiveness and well-bred censoriousness. Appropriately, the witty lady often tended to put down snobs, boors, or other uncivilized men. She was funny in only one way—ha, ha.

But there was another alternative for the funny girl in the nineteenth century, and it may have been the most appealing one of all. She could be *really* peculiar: she could become a boy.

CHAPTER SIXTEEN

Funny Tomboys

Masculinization was in some ways a very attractive option for nineteenth-century girls. The turning point in Elizabeth Cady Stanton's *Reminiscences* came, according to Ernest Earnest, after her brother died. As she tried to comfort her father, he said, "Oh, my daughter, I wish you were a boy." Elizabeth hugged him and answered, "I will try to be all my brother was."[1] When Fanny Fern watched the ice skaters in Central Park, she said to herself:

> Coats and trousers have the best of it *everywhere* . . . Away went coat and trousers, like a feather before the wind; free, and untrammeled by dry-goods, and independent of any chance somerset; while the poor, skirt-hampered women glided circumspectly after their much-needed health and robustness, with that awful omnipresent sense of *the proprieties*, (and—horror of horrors—a tumble!).[2]

In *The Country of the Pointed Firs*, old Mrs. Fosdick who grew up in a sailing family remembers the time when she had to stop behaving as a boy:

> "Mother made my new skirt long because I was growing, and I poked about the deck after that, real discouraged, feeling the hem at my heels every minute, and as if youth was past and gone. I liked the trousers best; I used to climb the riggin' with 'em and frighten mother till she said an' vowed she'd never take me to sea again."[3]

Mrs. Fosdick is an active and sophisticated old woman, a survivor who has outlasted eight brothers and sisters.

The tomboy became a major type in the 1860s. Nowadays she is remembered only in the person of Jo March from *Little Women*. But there were many other tomboys, and one of them, like Jo, even had a boy's name—Harvey, in Anne Moncure Crane Seemüller's novel *Opportunity* (1867). Sylvia Yule, the heroine of Alcott's one serious adult novel, *Moods* (1864), was a tomboy. Beginning in 1866, Elizabeth Stuart Phelps wrote four novels about a lively girl with the significant name of Gypsy, "an outdoor girl who could row and skate and swim, play ball, make kites, coast and race and chop wood, and, greatest change of all, her brother Tom could say, 'I don't believe Gypsy cries four times a year . . . with all her faults there's none of your girl's nonsense about her.'"[4] It was in the late 1860s that a Western heroine first dressed as a man in one of Beadle's dime novels—Eulalie Moreau in Frederick Whittaker's *The Mustang-Hunters; or, The Beautiful Amazon of the Hidden Valley*.[5] In 1867 the Anglo-French woman writer, Ouida, invented the jaunty cross-dressing, camp-following Cigarette in *Under Two Flags*. These fictional tomboys were closely affiliated with certain burlesque roles played by actresses of the time. The hoyden who sported a cigar, the impersonation of male Greek gods by women, a wild parodying of sex roles in general all became central features of the burlesque theater in the 1860s.

Burlesque at that time was something of a leg show but had not begun to turn into a striptease. Burlesques still had the marginal respectability that allowed W. D. Howells to go and see and then describe them in a tantalizing but still informative chapter of *Suburban Sketches*. In both literature and theater, the war decade witnessed a strange new female breakthrough. This breakthrough must have been fed by many sources—the turmoil accompanying war, women's dissatisfactions, a new tendency to isolate the self-reliance that had been compromised by opposing qualities in the popular 1850s heroines. But the main literary source, I suspect, was one of the five or so most popular novels of the nineteenth century, a work so little known today that it is not even available at the New York Public Library (their one copy has been missing for several years)—*The Hidden Hand* by Mrs. Emma D. E. N. Southworth.

This novel was published three separate times—1859, 1868–69, 1883—in a weekly story-paper, the *New York Ledger*, before it finally appeared as a book.[6] (It was in 1884 that Howells got to work on *The Rise of Silas Lapham*.) This odd publishing history partly explains how the novel has managed to slip so completely through the nets of official literary history. But literary history has always thrown a rather coarse net and would easily miss a work that was so popular it was not only a bestseller in the United States but was translated into the major European languages and at least one of the minor ones, Icelandic. I must report that, like millions of other people before me, I enjoyed reading *The Hidden Hand*: I did not get disgusted very often, I remained interested in the story, I laughed out loud a couple of times, and it gradually dawned on me as I moved through the novel that the author had not only grasped something solid and important but had found a way to put it across in an aesthetic form. I cannot give a full account of *The Hidden Hand* in this study, where I must limit myself to sketching its single most interesting aspect and the explanation for the book's tremendous popularity—the fact that the heroine is a reckless, mischievous tomboy with the most pronounced sense of humor I am aware of in a nineteenth-century fictional heroine.

Southworth makes it clear early in her novel that the cross-gender traits of her heroine are her most salient qualities. Orphaned in New York, Capitola is not able to earn a living or protect herself from boys and men until she thinks of the expedient of wearing a male disguise. She acquires a cap and boy's clothes and gaily supports herself for a year by hawking newspapers. But she forgets to cut her hair, and one day a policeman who is watching her realizes she is a girl and hauls her in. Fortunately, a crusty old Virginia gentleman, who has been looking for Capitola, witnesses her trial and protects her from the strong arm of the law. He takes her back to his plantation, and the novel proper begins.

How does Capitola adjust to civilized life and a new role as girl? She doesn't give an inch. Street-wise and self-sufficient, she is unimpressed by her guardian, Old Hurricane, who up to now has not met the person he could not intimidate. Neither is Capitola impressed with her new life of ease: "I wish I was back in the Bowery! Something was always happening *there*! One day a fire, next day a fight, another day a fire and a fight together."[7] The author, of course, could not allow Capitola to use rough language; yet I do not know of another nineteenth-century heroine who gets away with language like this: "Walk with a little springy sway and swagger, as if you *didn't care a damson* for anybody" (p. 379; italics mine). The language as well as the swagger indicates the extent to which Capitola has adopted a certain masculine manner. Significantly, in this sentence she is

advising a very feminine girl how to carry off a masculine impersonation. Seventy years later, this "springy sway and swagger," in
company with a monotone and tough-guy sneer, would become the
trademark of another extremely popular female comic and male
impersonator, Mae West.

Religion was the great female institution in the nineteenth century.
How will Capitola respond to the pressures of the church? A good
minister sets out to bring the wayward girl into the fold. He begins
by professing "how deeply he compassionated her lot in never having
possessed the advantage of a mother's teaching." Capitola is apparently sober and contrite and sighs heavily: "Oh, sir, if I had only
known you before!" The minister becomes uneasy and begs the girl
to unburden her mind. "Oh, sir, I'm afraid to tell you! you'd hate
and despise me!" Finally, she risks telling:

> "And—and—I hope you will forgive me, sir! but—*but he was so
> handsome I couldn't help liking him!*"
> "Miss Black!" cried the horrified pastor.

What, he insists on knowing, was the name of the "base deceiver."
But he is not a base deceiver, insists Capitola. She likes him, she met
him while walking in the forest, and he is now hidden in her closet.
"Wretched girl!" intones the minister, "better you'd never been born
than ever so to have received a man!" "Man!" returns Capitola, with
flashing eyes, "I'd like to know what you mean by *that*" (pp. 223–226).
It turns out that Capitola has all along been speaking of a poodle,
though not quite as innocently as she pretends.

Not only has Capitola "sold" the reverend, but she has lampooned
his unctuous concern over the fate worse than death. To punish this
flouting of religion, Old Hurricane decides to keep Capitola home
from the fair: "You have no reverence, no docility, no propriety, and
I mean to bring you to a sense of your position by depriving you of
some of your indulgences!" Cap reminds the old man that he is not
her father or legal guardian. She even boasts of her orphan-status:
"The same fate that made me *desolate* made me *free!*" Old Hurricane
threatens her:

> "I have broken haughtier spirits than yours in my life. Would you
> know how?"

"Yes," said Capitola, indifferently. . . .
"Stoop and I will whisper the mystery."
Capitola bent her graceful head to hear.
"With the rod!" hissed Old Hurricane, maliciously.

Capitola jumps up blushing and faces him with "glittering" eyes.

"If ever you should have the misfortune to forget your manhood so
far as to strike me. . . ."
"Oh, you perilous witch, what then?" cried Old Hurricane, in dismay.
"Why then," said Capitola, speaking in a low, deep, and measured
tone, and keeping her gaze fixed upon his astonished face, "the—first—
time—I—should—find—you—asleep—I—would—take—a—razor—
and—"
"Cut my throat! I feel you would you terrible termagant!" shuddered
Old Hurricane.
"Shave your beard off smick, smack, smoove!" said Cap, bounding off
and laughing merrily as she ran out of the room. (pp. 227–230)

In spite of the unfortunate whimsy in Cap's last speech, I am still
amused by her pranks at the expense of her minister and her
guardian. In each one the girl plays a practical joke on an authoritative
man by making him fear something unspeakably bad. In the end,
she reveals that there is nothing to fear after all, though in revealing
this she lets the man know that he has been taken in by her teasing
bluff. Neither man can lay a hand on her, and she ends up the victor.

But what about love and marriage? Will Capitola make fun of that
too? Is nothing sacred? One of the most amusing scenes occurs when
the villainous Craven Le Noir proposes marriage. As he begins his
spiel, Capitola looks up "with surprise and interest." She is so ignorant
about "technical love-making" that she "did not exactly know what
was coming next." Craven pretends to pour out his heart in an ardent
yet humble declaration.

"Well, I declare!" said Cap, when he had finished his speech and was
waiting in breathless impatience for her answer, "this is what is called a
declaration of love and a proposal for marriage, is it?—It is downright
sentimental, I suppose, if I had only the sense to appreciate it."

Her apparently naive irreverence seems to lock Craven all the more securely within the rigid imperatives of his masquerade:

> "Cruel girl! how you mock me!" cried Craven, rising from his knees
> and sitting beside her.
> "No, I don't; I'm in solemn earnest! I say it is first rate! Do it again!
> I like it!" (p. 439)

In this and several other scenes, I think it is not too extravagant to
say that Capitola is nothing less than the female Huckleberry Finn.
These two characters are our great nineteenth-century comic orphans, female and male, whose scantily socialized points of view
expose the absurdities of civilization and its masquerades. Mark
Twain's orphan is undoubtedly the superior of the two. Yet Southworth's book is also a work of art. It is worth remembering that Mark
Twain got an incalculable boost from his friend W. D. Howells. The
one respectable literary friend and power-broker Mrs. Emma D. E.
N. Southworth knew was John Greenleaf Whittier, and he wasn't
worth so very much. Whittier made Southworth freeze her imagination by trying to legitimize it: he directed her in her writing of the
novel she would always be proudest of, *Ishmael*, a dull didactic
fictionalizing of the life of William Wirt. Yet Southworth was able to
do one thing that Mark Twain could not. She created a funny girl,
and not only that but embedded her in a burlesque melodrama that
made a coherent statement about the prison of femininity.

The histories of burlesque theater in America generally regard
Lydia Thompson and her British Blondes as the seminal influence
on American burlesque.[8] This company was formed in London for
the specific purpose of touring the United States. The Blondes were
established actresses in London. Their most influential production
in the New World was a travesty of the story of Ixion, who was
invited to visit Olympus, promptly lay siege to Juno, and was punished
for his temerity by being affixed to a wheel in Hades. The title given
the piece by Lydia Thompson's company was *Ixion; or, The Man at the
Wheel*. Lydia herself took the part of Ixion, and Jupiter was played
by Ada Harland (who later married Brander Matthews). The role of
Minerva, played no doubt as an old maid and bluestocking, was taken
by a man. Everything was done for laughs—except that Lydia and
the other actresses wore white tights and what Bernard Sobel has

called "a semblance of skirts, a foot in length, of thinnest mull with countless flounces."⁹

The historians of burlesque do not seem to be aware that the greatest American realist described his impressions of the form as it existed in its peak years, 1868 and 1869. It is true that Howells, in describing the British Blondes, did not wish to give too much away:

> Of their beauty and their *abandon*, the historical gossiper, whom I descry far down the future, waiting to refer to me as "A scandalous writer of the period," shall learn very little to his purpose of warming his sketch with a color from mine. But I hope I may describe these ladies as very pretty, very blonde, and very unscrupulously clever, and still disappoint the historical gossiper.¹⁰

Howells apparently knew that someone like me would come along one day, eager for information. He couldn't have guessed, however, that I would live in a time when the sight of a woman's legs had lost almost all shock value, and so he prevented his pen from transmitting the truth and beauty revealed to mortal eye. On the other hand, he had a great deal to say about matters of more concern here, such as the comic effect of cross-dressing: "It was also an indispensable condition of the burlesque's success, that the characters should be reversed in their representation,—that the men's *rôles* should be played by women, and that at least one female part should be done by a man" (p. 234). Howells emphasized, however, that the female impersonator was the most comical role:

> It must be owned that the fun all came from this character, the ladies being too much occupied with the more serious business of bewitching us with their pretty figures to be very amusing; whereas this wholesome man and brother, with his blonde wig, his *panier*, his dainty feminine simperings and languishings, his falsetto tones, and his general air of extreme fashion, was always exceedingly droll. He was the saving grace of these stupid plays; and I cannot help thinking that the *cancan*, as danced, in "Ivanhoe," by Isaac of York and the masculine Rebecca, was a moral spectacle; it was the *cancan* made forever absurd and harmless. (pp. 234–235)

Most interesting is Howells' extremely disapproving report of a concluding scene, probably in *Ixion*, that represented Hades. Extravaganzas and minstrel and variety shows all relied on breakdowns and the obligatory walk-around. Combining this "great final scene"[11] with a sketchy plot ending up in "the infernal world" makes for some interesting possibilities. As Howells dryly said, "the ladies gave the dances of the country [i.e., Hell] with a happy conception of the deportment of lost souls." Each one plunged "into the mysteries of her dance with a kind of infuriate grace and a fierce delight very curious to look upon." As the excitement rose, "those not dancing responded to the sentiment of the music by singing shrill glees in tune with it, clapping their hands, and patting Juba, as the act is called,—a peculiarly graceful and modest thing in woman." The "frenzy" conjured up a "Vision of Sin," and Howells suddenly experienced a weird displacement: "The spectator found now himself and now the scene incredible, and indeed they were hardly conceivable in relation to each other" (pp. 236–237). Howells' vertigo is more understandable if we recall that he saw the show in Boston.

Is there extant a more evocative description of the effect of burlesque at its best, before it began specializing in ritual undressing and simulations of sexual orgasm? In any case, one of Howells' points is that burlesque was alive and well before the advent of Lydia Thompson's Blondes. He traces one line of American burlesque theater to the opera bouffe, in particular *La Belle Hélène*. Best of all, he describes in some detail an unpretentious, non-mythological burlesque, *Three Fast Men*,[12] which he saw before the Blondes disembarked. This show's gimmick was to have three women try to scare their men back into the path of virtue by adopting male attire and behaving in a conspicuously dissolute way. One actress, for instance, appeared "now as a sailor with the hornpipe of his calling, now as an organ-grinder, and now as a dissolute young gentleman." The piece ended with the usual raucous medley of songs and dances, the most memorable of which, for Howells, was a girl's pensive rendition of "The Maiden's Prayer," which was "vehemently applauded." Called back for an encore, the girl "runs out upon the stage, strikes up a rowdy, rowdy air, dances a shocking little dance, and vanishes from the dismayed vision" (pp. 228–230).

In this play, I suspect, we are in the presence of a non-gallic Anglo-American burlesque, full of razzmatazz, shocking irreverence, and, yes, a moral lesson. What is most salient in *Three Fast Men* is the feminine impersonation of men. As Howells suggests, this feature was altogether different from the traditional male impersonation of women, which was essentially a joke. The female imitation of men probably had a more complicated appeal. There would have been elements of piquancy and comic bravura in the spectacle of a woman daring to act like a man. The bravura would be all the more appealing in a period when the gender roles were so opposed and stylized that Howells could feel it was slightly improper for a woman to tap her feet in time to the music ("patting Juba"). In other words, the female impersonation of males did not make a statement about males, but about females. That bit in which an actress sang a sentimental air and followed it up with a puckish routine for encore suggests that the basic appeal of a burlesque like *Three Fast Men* lay in the audacious scouting of true womanhood.

Now, if we recall the importance of romps and tomboys in women's fiction of the 1860s it would appear that the scouting of proper femininity on the stage represented a major symbolic breakthrough for women. This breakthrough preceded the arrival of Lydia Thompson and her British Blondes in 1869. What this company actually did was to exploit the breakthrough for the purposes of a leg show. Modern burlesque—female self-display for male enjoyment—did indeed begin to emerge with the Blondes. But the earlier burlesque represented something more protean and creative, and bore a relation to feminine ideals and fantasies. This earlier burlesque seems to have lasted not much more than a decade.[13]

Two theater events made the original breakthrough possible. The first of these took place in the Far West in the early sixties, when actresses elbowed their way into forms of entertainment that had been dominated by men—variety and minstrel shows. According to Constance Rourke's fine study of the variety stage in early California, Lotta Crabtree was the first woman to do comic breakdowns and minstrel routines. She learned her trade touring the California mining camps, the seedbed of so much American humor, and she got top billing in the San Francisco music halls at a time when variety, according to Rourke, was "a highly masculine theater, and attracted mainly an audience of men." By the end of the sixties she was a well-known star in the East. "Broad comedy for women was still rebellion,"[14] and so Lotta Crabtree developed a striking comic mode precisely by breaking the rules; she smoked cigars, showed her stockings, and specialized in hoyden (not siren) roles. She hit the big time at the moment that the funny tomboyish alter ego of Louisa May Alcott became famous.

The second source of burlesque roles for women was nothing else than the stage version of *The Hidden Hand*. A dramatization of the novel opened at the Bowery Theatre in July 1859, with Fanny Herring in the role of Capitola.[15] The play soon moved to more respectable headquarters, at the National Theatre, where it began a long stage life lasting several decades. It is said there were forty separate dramatizations. This may be, but I have seen only two different promptbooks.[16] In any case, there is abundant evidence that the play became an all-time favorite. The version written by Robert Jones stresses the breezy nonchalance of the lead role. Capitola first appears dressed as a boy. She speaks a slangy or colloquial language, as in the scene where she disguises herself as Clara (a very feminine girl), walks up to the altar with the villain, and then breaks off the wedding ceremony at the last possible minute: "No! not if he were the last man and I the last woman on the face of the earth, and the human race were about to become extinct, and the angel Gabriel came down from above to ask it of me as a personal favor." When the bridegroom and his father demand to know the meaning of this, Capitola answers, "It means, your worships' excellencies, that—you—can't—come it! it's no go! this chicken won't fight."[17] Jones also kept the scene where Capitola challenges Craven to a duel, an action that leads the villainous stuffed-shirt to say: "The idea of a girl challenging a gentleman! Why, the world's becoming so completely changed that I shouldn't wonder if the women usurped our positions in it."[18] This speech catches the basic appeal of the play and novel—the exciting spectacle of an intrepid girl's casually assuming and getting away with all the old male prerogatives.

To what extent did the breakthrough in female burlesque reflect current developments in the lives of contemporary women? Without pretending to settle the question, I would like to sketch a possible answer. In *Modern Women, and What Is Said of Them* (1868), Eliza Lynn Linton moaned the loss of standards: "We used to think we knew to a shade what was womanly and what was unwomanly. . . . if this exactness of interpretation belonged to past times, the utmost confusion prevails at present. . . . Men and tradition say one thing, certain women say another thing."[19] This book, published in England under the title *The Girl of the Period*, constituted the most bitter contemporary denunciation of women, picturing them as virtual whores, brassy, meretricious, domineering. Both Howells and James reviewed the book and considered it a piece of trash. Howells denounced it for its "air of brutality and of savage excess."²⁰ James saw it as the most vulgar sensationalism and offered what he hoped was a true picture of the modern "young girl of fashion":

> The most [i.e., worst] that you can say of her is that she is charming, with a *quasi*-corrupt arbitrary charm. She has, moreover, great composure and impenetrability of aspect. She practises a sort of half-cynical indifference to the beholder (we speak of the extreme cases). Accustomed to walk alone in the streets of a great city, and to be looked at by all sorts of people, she has acquired an unshrinking directness of gaze. She is the least bit *hard*.²¹

I think that James's picture probably came much closer to the truth about the new sort of audacity than Eliza Linton's. One of the first appearances in fiction of this new manner was the minor character Ella Wynkar in *Rutledge*, one of the four top bestsellers of 1860 in the United States. The well-bred yet saucy heroine of this novel tries not to behave like Ella, who "lacked Josephine's nice French tact and polish, and was very American and very New York in her rather 'loud' style, and very high-colored mode of expressing herself."²² This new type was worlds apart from the phony demureness of the wife satirized twenty years earlier in Ann Stephens' *High Life in New York*. What we see in all the fictional tomboys and stage cross-dressing, I suggest, is a symbolic representation of a newly emerging ideal gender role that was conspicuously unmannerly, outspoken, and challenging.

In the 1870s this new audacity coalesced in the form of the famous fictional type, the American Girl. Significantly, the heroine of James's first novel, Nora in *Watch and Ward*, would pass through a striking tomboy phase on the way to womanhood. As a girl Nora wears ragged dresses, gets sunburned, grows "more hardy and lively, more inquisitive, more active." Hubert says of her: "I can't think of her as a girl . . . ; she seems to me a boy. She climbs trees, she scales fences, she keeps rabbits, she straddles upon your old mare, bare-backed. . . . She's growing up a hoyden." She does not become a hoyden because Roger, her guardian, sends her away to school. The first time he visits her there he sees that she has "reached that charming girlish moment when the broad freedom of childhood begins to be faintly tempered by the sense of sex."[23] Two things happen at this moment: Roger begins to dream of marrying her and she herself develops "the sense of sex" that is so inconsistent with her free life as a child. The basic fact about the American Girl is that she used to be a romp, hoyden, or tomboy—a boy, in another word—and she cannot or will not accede to the conditions of adult femininity. There is a basic contradiction in her gender.

Capitola and the burlesque actresses represented a new and unprecedented breakthrough for women, a gaudy and euphoric liberation. But it was like the liberation that accompanied acid and rock a century later—more fantasy than real. It took place in novels or on the stage, two play-worlds where, according to ancient agreement, anything goes. The most negative portrait of the new American Girl who emerged from all that ferment was to be the disorderly Maud Matchin in John Hay's 1883 novel, *The Bread-Winners*, a character who, as we are explicitly told, had been a tomboy in girlhood.[24] The most tragic study of the American Girl would be Daisy Miller, a character whose remarkable independence turns into vulnerability because of her striking "puerility"—her childish vanity, her eager desire for male company and attention, and her fatal ignorance of how the world turns. And the most sympathetic treatment would be in W. D. Howells' great novel, *The Rise of Silas Lapham*, where Penelope would be so absorbed in her roles of humorist, tease, and family entertainer that Tom Corey's proposal, and her own sudden discovery of "the sense of sex," would cause a deep personal crisis of the sort one might as well call a nervous breakdown.

CHAPTER SEVENTEEN

Penelope Lapham in *The Rise of Silas Lapham*

The subplot of *The Rise of Silas Lapham* gives a perfect aesthetic form to the invisibility of the independent, humorous girl. Nobody imagines that Tom could possibly prefer Penelope to her beautiful sister. The tired old device of mistaken courtship acquires a rich contemporary meaning.

Nowhere outside the novel itself—neither in his prospectus, his "Savings Bank" Diary, or his correspondence—did Howells suggest that Penelope would be humorous.[1] The articles on women's sense of humor that appeared in the *Critic* shortly before Howells began writing *Silas Lapham* may have led him to make the female lead a humorist. It happens that the editors of the *Critic*, Jeannette and Joseph B. Gilder, were sister and brother of the editor of the *Century*, which serialized Howells' novel. But quite apart from the possibility of direct influence, it is clear that as Howells got to work on the novel in the summer of 1884, the question of women's humor was in the air. During the next summer Kate Sanborn would compile her anthology, *The Wit of Women*; just one year earlier, *The Hidden Hand* had appeared for the third and last time in the *New York Ledger*. Most important of all, Howells' work on *Mark Twain's Library of Humor* in the months before he began *Silas Lapham* had given him a detailed and crystalline overview of American humor.[2]

What kind of humorist is Penelope? It seems clear that she does not have the civilized feminine wit that had been so highly praised in the *Critic* articles and in *The Wit of Women*.[3] In fact, we are explicitly told (p. 134) that Penelope does not make epigrams. Rather, she seems to follow the advice Howells gave Annie in 1872: "keep the tone low, and let the reader do all the laughing."[4] Instead of scattering bright replies in high-toned drawing rooms, she entertains her family at home, often as a monologist. Sitting on the veranda at the Nantasket cottage, she holds Tom Corey and Irene spellbound with her "drolling" and "funning." As these unusual words suggest, her humor hardly conforms to standards of good breeding and propriety. In fact, Penelope has the manner of a vernacular male storyteller. She speaks slowly, with a "drawl" (p. 37), and her face has an "arch, lazy look" (p. 218). She sits "leaning forward lazily and running on, as the phrase is" (p. 133). To Corey, "her talk was very unliterary, and its effect seemed hardly conscious" (p. 133). She may not prop her feet on the rail, but in her improprieties of posture, bearing, and diction she clearly bears the distinctive marks of the proverbial male humorist.

Penelope is a male impersonator, yet her act is anything but a self-conscious or artificial pose. Her humor is part and parcel of an easygoing temperament that will not be hassled. When the strenuous Mrs. Corey decides she must invite the Laphams to dinner, Penelope wisely avoids the pointless ordeal and stays home. She feels oppressed by the decorum Mrs. Corey imposes. Her imagination has a kind of Wild West freedom, a feeling for improvisation and roughing it. Tired of all the talk about her father's new house, Penelope thinks "it would be a sort of relief to go and live in tents for a while" (p. 57). She enjoys Lapham's uncouth bragging, and she also enjoys mimicking and making fun of him. She has a wonderful gift for parodying the formulas of politeness and reducing them to nonsense. Thus, when Tom expresses his regret that Penelope missed the dinner, she slyly trips him up:

> "We all missed you very much."
> "Oh, thank you! I'm afraid you wouldn't have missed me if I had been there."
> "Oh, yes, we should," said Corey, "I assure you."
> They looked at each other. (p. 216)

Here Penelope does the same sort of job on Tom Corey as Ferris does on nervous Mrs. Vervain in *A Foregone Conclusion*:

> "I'm *so* pleased!" said Mrs. Vervain, rising when Ferris said that he must go. . . .
> "Thank you, Mrs. Vervain; I could have gone before, if I'd thought you would have liked it," answered the painter.[5]

As the contrast between these two exchanges suggests, there is less animus in Penelope than in Ferris, who gets genuinely irritated with Mrs. Vervain. Yet both Penelope and Ferris are doing essentially the same thing—burlesquing polite manners. This would be a male activity in a culture that makes etiquette feminine.

Given the masculine qualities of Penelope's humor, it is fitting that in one exchange with her father she actually threatens to become a man, and a lazy one at that. Her father says:

> "Now, I suppose that fellow belongs to two or three clubs, and hangs around 'em all day, lookin' out the window,—I've seen 'em,—instead of tryin' to hunt up something to do for an honest livin'."
>
> "If I was a young man," Penelope struck in, "I would belong to twenty clubs, if I could find them, and I would hang around them all, and look out the window till I dropped."
>
> "Oh, you would, would you?" demanded her father, delighted with her defiance, and twisting his fat head around over his shoulder to look at her. "Well, you wouldn't do it on *my* money, if you were a son of *mine*, young lady."
>
> "Oh, you wait and see," retorted the girl. (p. 58)

Like Capitola, Penelope sasses back the bullheaded old man who assumes authority over her. Unlike Southworth's heroine, however, Penelope evinces no sexual or generational bitterness. She does not make her father fear that she may cut his throat, does not show any real desire to become a boy. When she threatens to turn into the idle son who squanders the old man's money, she is giving free rein to her protean independence. Of course, there is a serious layer here: she is taking down her father for complacently sounding off on "honest livin'." Also, she is sticking up for her sister by defending the man she's presumed to be interested in (and Irene thanks Penelope for this loyalty later on). But basically, Penelope's "Oh, you wait and see" is an expression of a contented femininity that feels no pressure whatever: she feels free to do and become whatever she wants. Also, she is well aware how much her defiance pleases her father. Similarly, she flashes her wit at Tom on purpose to fascinate and attract him, and eventually she realizes this: "I know now that I tried to make him think that I was pretty and—funny" (p. 229). Her funniness *is* her beauty and the basis of her charm. Ideal femininity, as embodied by Irene, proves much less sexy than the vagrant, individual humor of a free spirit.

Penelope is a tomboy who does not dislike being female. The heroines closest to her would seem to be those of Mary Jane Holmes, with their untrammeled and slightly wayward manners. Penelope also resembles a character in Adeline D. T. Whitney's *The Gayworthys*, Joanna, who entertains others with monologues poking fun at conventional matters. But Penelope is even more original or queer than these heroines from the 1850s and 60s: "She had a slow, quaint way of talking, that seemed a pleasant personal modification of some ancestral Yankee drawl, and her voice was low and cozy, and so far from being nasal that it was a little hoarse" (p. 37). Like any successful performer, Penelope is like nobody else. She seems to be partly a throwback to an older, preindustrial New England; there is an archaic Yankee quality about her, slow but trenchant. (Her first name is so "old-fashioned" that it has often been "mocked"—p. 255). Yet she does not have a nasal voice, nor does she speak in dialect. The adjectives that describe her voice—low, cozy, and hoarse—suggest the throaty, even sexy, quality of Adah Isaacs Menken's voice.

Is it any surprise that the man who falls in love with Penelope does not happen to "get on" with "cultivated" (p. 170) Bostonians? Tom is fascinated by Penelope's humor and finds it impossible to describe:

> She never says anything that you can remember; nothing in flashes or ripples; nothing the least literary. But it's a sort of droll way of looking at things; or a droll medium through which things present themselves. I don't know. She tells what she's seen, and mimics a little. (p. 100)

This humor, which the young man here struggles to convey to his mother, is obviously anything but verbal or formulaic. The quality that seems to appeal most of all to Tom is the droll representational aspect. *Things* seem to present themselves in a new way in Penelope's speech and manner, which constitute a sort of medium, a magic mirror whose surface is so revealing and whose pantomimic working so impenetrable. It looks as if Penelope has the same master passions as the realistic novelist who invented her: she wants to see and then make others see. She educates herself, as did Howells, by reading and attending lectures and looking out the window. She is an observer on a "self-guided search for self-improvement" (p. 26) and she resents it when in *Middlemarch* George Eliot instructs the reader what to think about the characters: "I wish she would let you find out a little about the people for yourself" (p. 88). The fact that Penelope does not attend a fashionable school or move in good society confers on her the freedom to make sense of the world. Her humor is thus to some extent a function of her parents' social isolation in modern Boston and her own totally unconscious alienation. It is because she is on the sidelines that she gets high on reality and then on miming it for the amusement of others.

The one person in the novel who actively dislikes this free spirit is Mrs. Corey. The antagonism between her and Penelope goes much deeper than the clash of personality. Mrs. Corey is the feminine ruling class. She is a sober, responsible, devious manipulator. Like Margaret Dumont in the Marx Brothers films, she has a commonplace mind and expects a rigid adherence to the rules. When the hapless Mrs. Lapham has to confess that Penelope has not come to dinner, Mrs. Corey makes her suffer by publicly branding her with a letter which is almost as painful as Hester Prynne's "A"; "Mrs. Corey emitted a very small 'O!'—very small, very cold—which began to grow larger and hotter and to burn into Mrs. Lapham's soul" (p. 190). Mrs. Corey has taken upon herself the burden of regulating society. Her husband, who carries no burdens whatever, regards a formal dinner as an occasion for witty conversation. He is an inactive man who does not work and has no place in the world of men, staying at home while his wife goes out. He seems to bear the stigma of the subject husband, as he addresses his wife only in tones of irony. Mrs. Corey tolerates his wit and even tries to smile, but she cannot abide Penelope's humor, which seems rude and disrespectful to her. Like the bad girl in "Little Orphant Annie," Penelope is "pert," a "thoroughly disagreeable young woman" who "says things to puzzle you and put you out" (p. 169). Mrs. Corey refers to her as "the plain sister" (p. 99), as "little and dark" (p. 170). There is no social contract between the two women; they are necessarily enemies; and when the younger one takes away the older one's son by marrying him, it is abject defeat for an old-fashioned foot-bound mandarin.[6]

The differences between Irene and Penelope derive from an inner conflict in the Lapham family and the vernacular culture they represent. Both parents encourage the doll-like femininity of Irene and parade her before others as the warrant of their genteel social value. But they are also proud of Penelope's humor, wide reading, independence, and toughness. Lapham is "delighted with her defiance" of the values he thinks he believes in. The contrast between the two girls reflects his inner confusion. He wants a mansion on the water side of Beacon Street, and in his parlor at Nankeen Square he has installed "a white marble group of several figures, expressing an Italian conception of Lincoln Freeing the Slaves,—a Latin negro and his wife,—with our Eagle flapping his wings in approval, at Lincoln's feet" (p. 215). As we see, the most showy and spurious excesses of the post-Civil War period have invaded Silas Lapham's home. The source of his wealth—paint, which he advertises by painting the landscape—shows that he himself has helped make it a Gilded Age,[7] a cheaply colored "Chromo-civilization" in E. L. Godkin's famous phrase. And yet Lapham is also an aboriginal, freedom-loving, plainspoken Yankee with big fists and an ancestral honesty and simplicity. The terrible marble group is about liberation, after all, and Lapham himself had volunteered in the Civil War. Poor pretty Irene is the product of his phony values, and Penelope the product of the old and real ones. Irene conforms to a "gilded" standard of femininity and effaces her own individuality. But her plain dark sister is free to develop her mind, her pantomimic skill, and her odd way of talking because she is a total failure at conforming to the ideal gender role. Similarly, Lapham saves himself only by failing in business. In a civilization that goes wrong by "gilding" nature, humor and integrity are both incompatible with success.

But Penelope is the offspring of her mother as well as her father. Persis—Howells had used this name in *The Lady of the Aroostook* for the wife of the bluff New England captain—comes from Vermont and has the true native gumption, but she has been softened by life in Boston. She no longer has anything to do with Silas' work. In his crisis she abandons him. The jealousy that overcomes her is a symptom of the growing separation between husband and wife. Fortunately the chasm closes; Silas and Persis reach an understanding after their last bitter quarrel; and they return to the old place in the country. This return to the land has an entirely different meaning here from what it had in *A Modern Instance*. In the earlier novel Marcia's return is part of an unqualified defeat, but the Laphams' return puts them back in touch with an honest way of life. Silas puts on his comfortable old clothes again and seems "more the Colonel in those hills than he could ever have been on the Back Bay" (p. 363). And Persis can at least resume the character revealed by her spunky arguments with her husband and the name he affectionately gives her.

"Pert"—the word Mrs. Corey applies to Penelope's sassy quickness—happens, not by accident, to be identical with Mrs. Lapham's nickname. The word merits more than passing attention. To be pert was to be humorously self-assertive and cheeky in a feminine way. Neither a pert girl nor a pert woman could ever be a proper lady. Howells himself spoke for genteel decorum when he ridiculed a statue of the madonna in *Venetian Life* for its "pert smile."[8] Yet there was a strong tendency in vernacular American culture to approve of pertness in women. Often spelled *peart*, the word was applied to women in a complimentary way by many different kinds of speakers, rich and poor, Southern or Northern, black or white, male or female. In Albion Tourgee's *Bricks without Straw* a North Carolina planter says to one of his female slaves, "I'm very well, thank ye, Lorency, an' glad to see you looking so peart."[9] In Mary Jane Holmes's *Tempest and Sunshine* a black auntie in Kentucky praises Fanny, a white girl, by saying she "allus was peart like and forrud."[10] In Sarah Orne Jewett's first book, *Deephaven*, the narrator joins in the laughter at a story told by the energetic Mrs. Bonny and then writes: "One might have ventured to call her 'peart,' I think."[11] In *Silas Lapham* Howells returned to the popular rural valuation of the lighthearted gutsy equality of which pertness was the expression. More than that, Howells revealed the continuity between the humor that defines Penelope and the country spunk and sauciness of her mother. Yet he did not make Penelope a country hoyden but an odd amalgam of old New England and big city anonymity and alienation. Just as Jewett's narrator, who was also from Boston, had to distance herself from "peart" by means of quotation marks, Howells would show that Penelope's inheritance of her mother's pertness would be in grave disharmony with modern urban life.

If wealth, the move from country to city, and the historic changes of the Gilded Age have deposited a terrible contradiction in the older Laphams, these forces practically destroy Penelope. The crisis begins at the moment when Tom Corey's declaration of love brings Penelope's girlhood to an end. Just before this moment Penelope seems as rational as ever. Her opinion of the popular novel *Tears, Idle Tears* is as level-headed as any of her ideas. She sees the hollowness of the heroine's self-sacrificial refusal to marry the man she loves just because he happened to love another woman first: "But it *wasn't* self-sacrifice," says Penelope, "or not self-sacrifice alone. She was sacrificing him too; and for someone who couldn't appreciate him half as much as she could." Tom calls this popular novel "a famous book with ladies" and says, "they break their hearts over it" (p. 217). Is Penelope one of these ladies or is she still the laughing girl? She answers this question herself in admitting that she has not only read the book more than once but has cried over it. Evidently, Penelope is not so exclusively the bystander as she has appeared. In fact, like the man in the prison chant, she has a long chain on and from now on will feel its drag and attempt to behave in precisely the same manner as the heroine of the silly novel she couldn't help crying over. After Corey's proposal Penelope speaks like a tragedy queen: "Life has got to go on. It does when there's a death in the house, and this is only a little worse" (p. 230). She exacts a lofty promise from Tom, then gives him a despairing embrace. Craziest of all, she insists that even though she and Tom want each other, it is impossible for them to marry—because of Irene.

Penelope's trouble goes very deep. In giving way to the feeling that self-denial is better than happiness, she is doing more than succumbing to popular sentimentality as embodied in *Tears, Idle Tears*. Her heart has been corrupted by her culture. Her lofty renunciation is nothing less than a misguided attempt to be feminine in the approved way. The reason Howells preached against self-sacrifice in so many novels was that self-sacrifice was the essence of femininity, which defined woman as being-for-others and not being-for-herself.[12] Irene sitting at the Corey dinner, a beautiful and silent mannequin, is being-for-others. Penelope, defined by her perception, her comic sensibility, is being-for-herself. Self-sacrifice, the ultimate form of being-for-others, has a persistent and dangerous appeal for Howells' heroines—Helen Harkness, Imogene Graham, Alice Pasmer, Hermia Faulkner. If these ladies are so rigid, irrational, and solemn, it is because they lack that confidence in their inner value that allows men to take it easy. Self-sacrifice is both the ultimate expression of their sense of worthlessness and an attempt to influence—to control—the real world *in some way*. In passing from girlhood to womanhood, Penelope has to overcome the temptation to throw herself away. She has to stifle the false inner voice that tells her she cannot respect herself unless she destroys herself.

Tom's love makes Penelope conscious for the first time in her life of "the sense of sex"[13] and her own reciprocal feelings; yet the sense of sex also dictates self-denial. And if this double bind were not enough, Penelope has another serious problem. The fact that up to now she has been a kind of male impersonator means that, her femaleness notwithstanding, her public self has basically been masculine. The sudden necessity to define a public feminine role destroys her self-confidence and brings about a temporary breakdown.[14] For a period of weeks or months, she rarely leaves the house. She has a "wan face." In her mother's words, she "just sits in her room and mopes" (p. 259). She even gives up reading. When she tries to write a note to Tom, her inability to assume a public role or style leads her to tear up one draft after another. Her mother says: "A girl that could be so sensible for her sister, and always say and do just the right thing, and then when it comes to herself to be such a *disgusting* simpleton!" (p. 304). With her usual shrewdness, Mrs. Lapham senses that Penelope has always projected her own femininity onto Irene. Now that Pen must be her own woman, she can't help falling apart.

Fortunately, Penelope fights back, regains her old sanity, and marries the man she wants. But it is clear that there is no place for her in Bostonian society. After she has spent a week with the Coreys she is glad to leave for Mexico City. Not even Bromfield Corey could appreciate her humor. Howells' last word on Penelope is a dry speculation that "our manners and customs go for more in life than our qualities" (p. 361). What this means apparently is that society cannot accommodate Penelope, no matter how fine her individual qualities may be. Howells condemns society for excluding her and suggests that we "pay too much" for "civilization." And then he hedges and speaks for the Coreys:

> But it will not be possible to persuade those who have the difference in their favor that this is so. They may be right; and at any rate the blank misgiving, the recurring sense of disappointment to which the young people's departure left the Coreys is to be considered. That was the end of their son and brother for them; they felt that; and they were not mean or unamiable people. (p. 361)

This important passage reveals one of many major differences between *Silas Lapham* and the novel that was serialized simultaneously in the *Century, Adventures of Huckleberry Finn*. Huck is the orphan saint whose ingenuousness exposes the absurdity or evil of society. But *Silas Lapham* is a more urbane novel, and does not accord any one character, either Penelope or her father, the kind of moral authority Huck enjoys. There is something to be said, after all, for the Coreys. The character of Penelope may represent the sort of freshness that society inevitably stifles; yet for all this Howells refuses finally to side with her against the Coreys (or with the Coreys against her). To fail to see this, as one critic has failed,[15] is to miss the basic point about Howells' novels: they seek to represent the totality of contemporary society, imperfect as it is, and not to transcend it. Francis Hackett grasped this point in writing about *The Rise of Silas Lapham* in 1918: "It is the main achievement of this novel that it drives us to realize the inexorable necessity and the equally inexorable cruelty of exclusiveness, social and sexual, in direct proportion as we have imagination."[16]

One of the basic reasons why Howells was a great realistic writer was that he did not indulge the transcendent allegiances that permit such sweeping dismissals of society as one finds in Thoreau or Mark Twain. As a man, Howells belonged to the contemporary world. The novel in which the hero finds virtue only by renouncing his Back Bay social ambitions and returning to the ancestral home in the country actually helped pay for Howells' own new mansion on Beacon Street. Even as Howells decided to make his female lead an unconventional vernacular humorist, and then audaciously married her to a Brahmin scion, he was anticipating the Boston debut of his daughter Winifred. Still, I see no sufficient reason for judging Howells a hypocrite in these instances. Like any member of a changing society, he was full of contradictions. Yet he succeeded in holding on to his basic decency and his broad sympathy for various categories of people. One of the remarkable aspects of the composition of *Silas Lapham* is that an author fastidious enough to flesh out Bromfield Corey could give such a profound and sympathetic portrait of a vernacular rebel like Penelope. It was, however, precisely this sort of personal amplitude that enabled Howells at one and the same time to dream up a wonderfully pert and perverse humorist and move toward a more complete representation of the American scene than any novelist before him.

Howells' own sense of humor had always had a remarkable catholicity. In "A Day's Pleasure," he felt a combination of enjoyment and respect, mixed with fear, for the drunken wit of a ribald old sailor.[17] In "A Pedestrian Tour," he was amused by a group of tattooed stable-grooms working for a circus who "talk nothing and joke nothing but horse." In a sense Howells was one of these men: "Their life seems such a low, ignorant, happy life, that the secret nomad lurking in every respectable and stationary personality stirs within me and struggles to strike hands of fellowship with them. They lead a sort of pastoral existence in our age of railroads."[18] Yet Howells felt an even stronger loyalty to the traditions of blueblood wit as represented by Oliver Wendell Holmes, Sr., George William Curtis, and James Russell Lowell. In 1882 the man who devoted his life to a literary genre patronized largely by women wrote that Artemus Ward and Petroleum V. Nasby rather disgusted him: "American humorists formerly chose the wrong in public matters: they were on the side of slavery, of drunkenness, and of irreligion; the friends of civilization were their prey; their spirit was thoroughly vulgar and base."[19] No wonder so many of the enemies of civilization in Howells' fiction, the vulgar and base men like Bartley Hubbard in *A Modern Instance*, Dickerson in *The Coast of Bohemia*, and Bittridge in *The Kentons*, are careless scoffers who take nothing seriously. The joker was wild in Howells' imagination, wild in the same sense as in the traditional deck of cards: he was powerful and threatening because he was independent of suit, caste, order, and every civilized rule. He was one and the same with the ring-tailed roarer created by civilized men who observed or thought about the frontier. But wild power can be a source of good as well as evil. Late in life, Howells still couldn't choose between two printers he knew in his adolescence, a conscientious young journeyman "who wished to hold me in the leash of his moral convictions," or a "merrymaker" and "companion in laughter" named Sim Haggett.[20] Looking backward, Howells saw that "there was a moment, baleful or hopeful as the reader may decide, when . . . it appeared as if we almost expected to be saved by humor."[21] It was because of the joker's great power for good that Howells considered Mark Twain the greatest American writer—of course, not the Mark Twain who lampooned New England's finest at the Whittier birthday dinner, but the Mark Twain who was at heart manly and noble and never wrote a coarse thing, and who appealed to Howells to censor him whenever he *did* write a coarse thing. Mark Twain was "the Lincoln of our literature," in Howells' telling phrase, because he was the great leader who subdued our rebel American humor.

Finally, Penelope is not a person but a fragment of her creator, who admitted late in life that a writer's characters "all come out of himself."[22] She was to some extent Howells' comic mask, just as Artemus Ward and Petroleum V. Nasby were the easygoing alter egos of more exacting and successful men and not real men themselves. Those countrified, old-fashioned losers who made men laugh were as out of place in America as Penelope Lapham. They represented a submerged self in their creators and audiences, a self that was sent under in proportion as traditional rural life was destroyed. The American humorist was by definition insincere, not even trying to integrate his odd mask with the rest of himself. Howells was not spared the male schizophrenia that was epidemic in the nineteenth century. In the character of Penelope, he dredged up an alternative self that spoke with an "ancestral Yankee drawl," and then he sent her into southern exile. Penelope represented a way of seeing, thinking, and talking that was a very important part of the enormously complex and successful person who created her. But she was only a part, and in the end it was impossible for Howells, like all the other upward bound men, to heal his schizophrenia. There was no prevention. Laughter was the only medicine.

Part III

W. D. HOWELLS AND
AMERICAN MASCULINITY

CHAPTER EIGHTEEN

The Male Risk

To be male rather than female is to encounter greater dangers from conception through birth to death. More men than women go to prison, get injured in fights, have automobile accidents, get drafted and sent to war, fight fires, apprehend fleeing criminals, tell official lies in front of TV cameras and hostile reporters, wake up in fear from nightmares of rapid automatic gunfire, practice sword-thrusts or drives to the goal or brilliant touchdowns in daydreams.[1]

It is no exaggeration to say that the struggle begins at conception. A male has one X and one Y chromosome, while a female has two X chromosomes. The significant fact is that the X chromosome has many more genes than the Y chromosome. Thus, a male is more likely than is a female to show the effects of a harmful recessive gene. If a female has a bad gene, she will not be affected (though her progeny may) if it is overridden by a dominant gene on her other X chromosome. A male lacks this safety factor.[2]

As a growing boy or young man, the male faces many more trials of strength than does the female. And unless he lives in an advanced industrial system or has a privileged place in a preindustrial one, he must exert his strength again and again to earn his livelihood. The hardest fieldwork, the heaviest lifting, has always been his job. Even today, moving ninety-four pound sacks of cement remains a job for men, provided there isn't a forklift around.

But the biggest problem that boys and men must solve is not muscular but social. In many cultures femininity is something a female is born with, a natural endowment she may struggle against or not, as it happens. But masculinity has an uncertain and ambiguous status. It is something to be acquired through a struggle, a painful initiation, or a long and sometimes humiliating apprenticeship. To be male is to be fundamentally unsure about one's status and hence to struggle to win the cocky certainty known as masculinity. When it is won, it is signified by subtle tokens of posture, dress, speech that cannot be counterfeited. Robert J. Stoller, has written with great insight on the problem of masculine identity:

> There are special problems in a boy developing his masculinity that are not present in the development of femininity in little girls. In contrast to Freud's position that masculinity is the natural state and femininity at best a successful modification of it, . . . I . . . feel that the boy's relationship to his mother makes the development of feminine qualities more likely. . . . The boy . . . must manage to break free from the pull of his mother's femaleness and femininity, a task that is so frequently uncomplete, to judge by the amount of effeminacy, passivity, or forced hypermasculinity one sees.[3]

Stoller might not accept this rather bald formulation of his views, but it seems to me that he is basically saying that boys, like girls, begin life as females but must then struggle to remake themselves into something considerably different—men.

Of course there are certain differences between the sexes that are not a consequence of culture in any way—sexual organs, skeletal, muscular, and hormonal features. Boys are naturally more aggressive than girls. Boys—and here the evidence backs up the folklore—are more apt than girls to disobey adult authority and do what other boys think best.[4] But in other respects boys resemble girls more than they resemble men: boys do not have a low voice, they don't have to shave, and they live at home with their mothers. In the first half of the last century, American boys still wore the traditional European unisex clothing for young children—a long dress.[5] When boys were fitted for trousers, sometimes not until the age of five, it was a momentous public transition. Now nobody would ever mistake them for a girl for the rest of their life. Another transition came when they stopped wearing short jackets in adolescence. Fanny Fern was particularly envious of males at this juncture, for it was the time when females had to begin wearing long skirts: "[A boy's] whole future life will be license after jacketdom, as decreed by society and the laws; while a severe woman-discipline surely awaits the most frolicsome girl, beginning from the moment when she first learns what her heart is made of, till death stills its yearnings."[6] Up to a point, boys and girls went to school together. Then those boys who went to college left home for an all-male institution that had close links with certain all-male professions. Until after the Civil War higher education for girls was a joke.

In dozens of different ways, the basic pattern in nineteenth-century America was that girls and boys started out doing the same things but gradually diverged until they ended up in the radically unequal domains of woman's sphere and man's world. Woman's sphere was the natural realm—home, family, food. These were the ancient givens of human life. Man's world was the new and artificial realm of inventions and industry, credit and law, and all the diversified careers these new institutions required. The basic story of male life lay in its escape from the natural realm to the new urban and industrial culture. Today women have also joined the new culture. But there was a moment in the mid-nineteenth century when one gender was traditional and the other modern. At that moment Fanny Fern wrote, "I often see in the papers advertisements of 'shirts made—to order,' but I never saw an advertisement of a corresponding female garment made that way."[7] Men were in the machine age, women still at home in a craft culture.

Yet nineteenth-century masculinity was not simply a product of industrialism. Among many preindustrial, even preagricultural, peoples, men spend a lot of time in a men's hut, which may be off limits to women, and participate in activities, both productive and ritualistic, that are defined as exclusively male. Such peoples often have male initiation rites that are conducted by senior men and from which women are excluded. In the Gahuku tribes of highland New Guinea, the long and complicated initiation rites for boys that Kenneth F. Read observed required all the men and boys to gather by the river on a certain day. After various displays of self-torment and bravado and other activities, the men and initiated boys ran back uphill to the village. Read noticed that the men seemed anxious. They kept looking around and in back of themselves. Suddenly they ran into an ambush. The village women attacked, apparently in earnest, throwing stones and pieces of wood and causing minor injuries. Read comments:

> These graphic rituals of opposition spoke of deep-seated divisions in Gahuku life, not only the formal, ceremonial structure of male and female relationships, but also the avowed notions of superiority and a

schism that often revealed itself in open antagonism. . . . The fury of the present assault convinced me that the ritual expression of hostility and separation teetered on the edge of virtual disaster.[8]

What the Gahuku women were attempting to do was to break up the ceremony and recapture the boys. This female interference in male initiation ceremonies has a remarkable structural parallel in nineteenth-century America, where there was also a rigid separation between male and female spheres. In these two divided cultures initiation for boys brought out into the open the antagonism between male and female interests. American women also fought a hard and not always losing battle to keep their sons, rather than surrender them to the ancient enemy, the fathers. Many popular nineteenth-century women's novels represented this battle from the mother's point of view, and in many of these novels the mother succeeded in holding on to her boy. In *The Hidden Hand* Mrs. Emma D. E. N. Southworth drew an arresting picture of the ideal relationship between mother and son in the scene were Traverse returns home after a day's work elsewhere:

> [Traverse] came joyously forward to his mother, clasping his arm around her neck, saluting her on both cheeks, and then, laughingly claiming his childish privilege of kissing "the pretty little black mole on her throat."
> "Will you never have outgrown your babyhood, Traverse?" asked his mother, smiling at his affectionate ardor.
> "Yes, dear little mother! in everything but the privilege of fondling you!"[9]

Of course, the American mother won this victory by using different weapons from the Gahuku women. The American mother did not fight with sticks and stones. She fought with words, in the form of children's fiction, gospel songs, prayers, and direct and earnest adjuration. "Jesus Loves Me," one of the first religious songs learned by many Protestant boys and girls, was written by Anna Warner— the sister of the author of *The Wide, Wide World*. If we can judge from a fascinating episode in *The Lamplighter* (1854), these religious charms often worked quite well. In this novel the youth who will eventually marry the heroine becomes a man by going out to India to work for a mercantile firm. During Willie Sullivan's absence, his mother abruptly fails. She is distressed by the knowledge that she will never see her son before she dies. Then she has a dream in which she seems to be "sailing rapidly through the air." She sees a city below her, spots Willie, and hovers above him as he enters an elegant club where a group of fallen men invite him to have a drink. On the point of accepting, he is saved by her touch on his shoulder. Later, he is tempted by a fashionable young siren. This time, the spirit of his mother doesn't fool around. She seizes him bodily and ascends with him into the air, and as she does so her "manly son" becomes in her "encircling arms a child again."[10] When Mrs. Sullivan wakes up, she is happy and peaceful. She no longer regrets dying without one last moment with her boy. She knows that after death her spirit will still be a mighty guide to him. Then she dies and sure enough, when Willie finally returns to the United States, it turns out that he is still pure and very eager to marry his boyhood sweetheart. The mother has managed to prevent her boy from joining the corrupt male world by going into a kind of trance that enables her to invoke an ultimate spiritual power.

Given this sort of pressure, it isn't surprising that many American men and boys have been exceedingly anxious about their masculinity. A case in point is Hemingway, the great macho writer whose first novel was narrated by a man who had lost his balls in the Great War. Even better instances can be found in our comic strips and animated cartoons. When animal characters began to replace humans, there was a decrease in social reference and a great enlargement in the possibilities of graphic caricature. But even in the Bugs Bunny and Porky Pig cartoons, there are strong vestiges of standard male stereotypes and the basic male dilemma in the United States. Porky Pig is a version of Little Lord Fauntleroy: he wears a caricature of a little boy's jacket, stutters, tries to be good and make others be good, and he is generally victimized. Who prefers this sissy over the outlaw rabbit who always wins? In name, if not in habitat, Bugs is the stock urban ruffian. Furthermore, when Mel Blanc created his speech, he imitated the familiar stereotype of tough guy talk from the Bronx or Brooklyn. The Bugs Bunny cartoons recreated the basic male American opposition between the lovable bad boy and the stuffy good boy. Bugs has hundreds of antecedents in comic strips and popular plays and vaudeville and burlesque routines. He was closely related to Flip, the sneering, cigar-sporting city kid in Winsor McCay's great *Little Nemo* strip. According to a recent history of comic strips, the most important type in early Sunday comics (1896–1916) was the "demon child."[11] The hero of the very first comic strip of all, R. F.

Outcault's *Yellow Kid*, talked in Bowery and dealt in comic mayhem. Other demon children, all masculine, were Rudolph Dirk's Katzenjammer Kids, Outcault's Buster Brown, Winsor McCay's Little Sammy Sneeze, Tad Dorgan's Johnny Wise, James Swinnerton's Jimmy, Lyonel Feininger's Kin-der-Kids. Probably the most important antecedent of these funny demon boys was Chimmie Fadden, the tough Bowery newsboy whose exploits appeared in the New York *Sun* and were first collected in 1895. And of course there were the influential bad boys from the 1870s and 80s: Tom Sawyer, the hero of Aldrich's *The Story of a Bad Boy*, and Peck's Bad Boy. Even earlier, looming out of the dim mid-century background, stands the scrappy figure of Mose the Fire B'hoy, the belligerent Bowery roustabout who was so popular on stage in the 1850s.[12]

Why was the bad boy such a significant comic type in American culture? In his brilliant review of *Adventures of Huckleberry Finn*, Thomas Sergeant Perry saw Huck as "an incarnation of the better side of the ruffianism that is the result of the independence of Americans."[13] But there was another important source of "ruffianism" besides independence, as we see in Mark Twain's "The Story of the Bad Little Boy." This piece contrasts the rough little lawbreaker who gets away with murder and the mild, school-loving boy who gets thrashed for a theft he never committed. The lawbreaker was a rebel, and what he was rebelling against was an effete, domestic, Sunday School civilization—a female civilization. The opposition between the good little boy and the bad little boy was so important in American culture because it reflected a basic fact of life for boys growing up in a country where the male world and the female world were so different they constituted two separate nations: the boy was torn between two incompatible ways of life. Beginning as an appendage of his mother, he had somehow or other to make a place for himself in a world where you had to fight to prove yourself.

One of the biggest masculine fears in the last century was the fear of not somehow being able to win a place among other men and boys. This fear underlies the many American stories about men who end up in solitary hell—"Wakefield," "Bartleby the Scrivener," "Free Joe and the Rest of the World," "The Man without a Country." This fear also explains two curiously exaggerated responses in Howells' novels—the guilt deposited in Silas Lapham for unloading Rogers from the paint firm, and Hawberk's recourse to opium after Royal Langbrith unloads *him*. To be driven out of a business one has helped build up was a fateful and ultimate kind of event for Howells, mainly because it meant losing one's hard-won place. And yet, paradoxically, it was two ambitionless and isolated males—Leatherstocking and Huckleberry Finn—who became our most important fictive characters. Just as Mark Twain canonized Tom Blankenship, Howells gave a special place in his account of his childhood, *A Boy's Town*, to a born outsider whom he identified only as a "kindly earth-spirit."[14]

There is a striking difference between the women's bestselling novels of the 1850s and the later books that deal in some way or other with boy life. To be orphaned, for a girl, is, in the early novels, to suffer the ultimate pain, something so terrible that it does not need to be explained why the orphan heroine should devote herself for the entire narrative to reconstituting a domestic life. But in the boy books, the heroes voluntarily run away from home, preferring to take their chances in the world. Christopher Newman in *The American* and Huckleberry Finn in Mark Twain's novel illustrate the basic male dream—being entirely on one's own, autonomy. Ellen Montgomery in *The Wide, Wide World* is ripped from her mother's arms in a brutal caesarian separation, but Huck Finn lights out for the territory so the Widow Douglas won't "sivilize" him. There is a total difference here in the ideal forms of male and female maturation. In Joseph Kirkland's novel *Zury* (1887), a sadder but wiser mother admits: "No man who is ever going to come to anything is ruled by family affection."[15]

In actual fact, many boys surely found it a hard thing to run away from home, to break the promises made to their mothers, to get on in the wide, wide world. For many reasons, it was not easy to negotiate the transition from the domestic to the secular sphere. Some of the sex-role literature of the last decade seems to assume that the basic way a boy acquires his adult gender role is modeling himself on his father. But the many boy books that were written by Americans in the Gilded Age suggest that the father had very little influence on his son's developing masculinity. Indeed, in *Peck's Bad Boy and His Pa*, the boy victimizes his father rather than imitates him. It was not the father that enabled the boy to escape women's sphere and define his own masculinity. The most important institution that enabled boys to do so was composed of other boys, not adults. This institution was the outlaw gang—the comitatus that commanded the ultimate loyalty of boys.

CHAPTER NINETEEN

That Old Gang of Mine

In 1864 Mrs. Emma D. E. N. Southworth worked out an answer to the question—How does a boy grow up to be a successful yet good man?—in her topselling two-volume novel, *Ishmael*. The hero of this book is called Ishmael because he is illegitimate, a fact of which he is deeply ashamed. Growing up in poverty, he is determined to better himself. He eventually succeeds as a lawyer by studying very hard. One night, when the beautiful Claudia returns from an evening at the President's in Washington, she finds Ishmael burning the midnight oil:

> The whole face of the house was closed and darkened except one little light that burned in a small front window at the very top of the house.
> It was Ishmael's lamp; and, as plainly as if she had been in the room, Claudia in imagination saw the pale young face bent studiously over the volume lying open before him.[1]

When Ishmael first goes before the bar, it is to defend a woman whose husband aims to take away her children after having deserted her. Ishmael not only succeeds in defending her against this male aggressor, but refuses to allow her to pay him. Later he saves Claudia from her evil husband.

Ishmael was the sort of novel that men found hard to take. Its hero, a product of female aspirations, was a pure Galahad devoting his life to female vengeance against the male world. As a boy, Ishmael is insufferably good; as an ambitious young man, he gets ahead by adopting the strategy of the feminine novelist who locks the attic door, writes out her heart, or at least her vengeful fantasies, and wins fame and fortune by selling these fantasies to other women. Men could not abide a book like *Ishmael* because they knew that a man had to learn how things worked in order to get ahead, and even more important, had to *know* what kind of creatures were his bosses, fellow workers, employees. Only a person excluded from the work-aday life could solace herself with the daydream that a bookish prig would be able to rise and conquer a dog-eat-dog world. *Ishmael* was intolerable because it said that the best way for a boy to grow up was never in any way to say or do anything that would not be correct for a woman.

It was books like this that led Thomas Bailey Aldrich and Mark Twain and a number of other male writers to write the bad-boy books that became so popular in the 1870s. These books imply that the best way for a boy to grow up into a good man is to challenge the stultifying adult order, run wild with a gang of boys, and explore the world on his own. The best-known boy books are *Tom Sawyer* (1876) and *Huckleberry Finn* (1885). As one sees in the first few chapters of the latter book, the outlaw gang of boys functions as an alternative to the established community. The gang meets in a cave away from town in the middle of the night, and it has its own inflexible code of rules. An aggressive secret society, it preys on Sunday Schools and ruling women, though apparently without doing any lasting damage. The gang leader is mischievous and enterprising, and he proves himself a future leader of men by his prowess in dreaming up elaborate practical jokes. He is the inventor as malicious social engineer.

Mark Twain was less interested in the nature of the gang than in the figures of the gang leader and the total outsider. To understand the gang itself, we must go to works like Thomas Bailey Aldrich's *The Story of a Bad Boy* (1870), Hamlin Garland's *Boy Life on the Prairie* (1899), and Howells' *A Boy's Town* (1890) and *The Flight of Pony Baker* (1902).

Tom Bailey, the hero of Aldrich's book, starts out in New Orleans, where his tormenting a slave shows that he has yet to acquire a true boy's republicanism. When he moves to New England, the first boy he sees offers to "lick" him "for two cents."[2] The next boys he happens to see are fighting behind a barn. Evidently, New England lacks the artificial distinctions that helped spoil Tom in New Orleans. He has to fend for himself in Rivermouth, his new home, where he finds himself a total outsider. It is not long, however, before he joins a group of close companions.

It is at this point that Tom begins to turn into a proper boy. He is accepted as a member of the Rivermouth Centipedes, a genuine "secret society" (p. 100). In the initiation ceremony Tom is blindfolded and his hands are tied. An unknown voice warns him "that it was not yet too late to retreat if I felt myself physically too weak to undergo the necessary tortures" (p. 101). A pistol goes off near his ear. He walks up a precarious plank. Someone reads the code of bylaws to him and explains the penalties he will suffer if he should ever "reveal any of the secrets of the society" (p. 103), and then he falls into a barrel. In this initiation ceremony Tom has to face unknown dangers by blindly trusting the boys to guide him through. Thus, once he becomes a Centipede, he belongs to a group much more loyal to one another than to anyone else in town. After their most glorious coup—setting off a number of old cannons in the middle of the night—they all maintain a perfect silence. The climax of the book comes when the South End and North End boys fight for possession of a certain snow fort. Aldrich actually draws a military diagram in order to show how the opposing forces are disposed. Miniature territorial warfare, practical jokes played on adult society, secret formal gangs—these seem to be the things that little boys are made of. And not just little boys, either, for the gang members grow up to be successful men living in faraway places. The permanent outsider, by contrast, a bully and talebearer named Conway, becomes a cheating shopkeeper and never leaves the village. If one intends to become a manly success in the big outside world, it looks as if one must first be a member of the boyhood gang.

One of the aims of *The Story of a Bad Boy* was to give a sympathetic representation of male aggression. To some extent, the book was about the socialization of future elders and leaders: it is no accident that one gang member grows up to be a judge, another a wine merchant in California, another a consul in Shanghai, while the ostracized boy joins the petty bourgeoisie and never leaves town. The Rivermouth Centipedes (one body with many legs) is a boyhood version of the aggressive business organizations that would be responsible in the Gilded Age for the under-the-table railroad rebates, political bribery and lobbying, and secret business compacts of the kind Dreiser wrote about in *The Financier*. Yet the secret male organization also reaches back to more primitive ways of life as well. There is a remarkable parallel to Aldrich's gang in a Pawnee Indian story about a secret society, "The Mischievous Society of Boys."[3] The mischievous boys in this story violate a cardinal rule by meeting in a lodge whose owners have died. There they establish their own circumcision ritual and frighten other villagers. They conduct a successful raid on another tribe, return with horses and greatly increased prestige, and eventually marry and become fully accredited members of the tribe. In this story just as in *The Story of a Bad Boy*, membership in the outlaw gang leads directly to approved forms of manhood in a society that places a high value on the aggressive male.

In its day *The Story of a Bad Boy* was a very important book. It countered the feminine or Sunday School version of boyhood with a masculine version that came closer to the truth without sacrificing respectability. It also countered the lies told by Horatio Alger, Harry Castlemon, and Oliver Optic in their stories about the appallingly brave and upright chaps who so often bear the first name of Frank.[4] A number of other bad-boy books appeared in the 1870s, the most important being *Tom Sawyer*. Other contributions were *Being a Boy* (1877) by Charles Dudley Warner and *Donald's School-Days* (1879) by General Oliver Otis Howard. In 1879 Lee and Shepard tried to capitalize on the trend by bringing out a new issue of Benjamin P. Shillaber's *Ike Partington; or, the Adventures of a Human Boy and His Friends*. Ike, as Horace Scudder noted in his review, "was a youngster who sported mischievously about an American Mrs. Malaprop." The book seemed rather pale to Scudder, who was "not quite sure that the real boy is always playing little pranks" and wondered whether there was "quite as much need as there once was of entering a protest against the conventional boy of the story books."[5]

Howells was editor of the *Atlantic* when this review appeared. He too was well aware that the prankish boy had himself become a stereotype. In time he would become a kind of cult object. A generation earlier, in the 1850s, the pure orphaned girl had been the great spiritual authority. She was the heroine of dozens of bestselling novels, and in one strange book, *The Prince of the House of David* by Joseph H. Ingraham, she became nothing less than Jesus H. Christ's most influential apostle. In this historical novel Adina gives an eyewitness account of His life through a series of letters to her skeptical father. Happily, having been on the spot, Adina is in a position to tell the *full* story and thus flesh out the evangelists' brief and inadequate sketches.[6] But after the tide had turned in the 1870s and 80s, it was the boy's turn to be the mouthpiece of various theses, gospels, panaceas, and myths. Of all these boys, Huck Finn, the boy-tramp who becomes a vehicle for a brilliant analysis of human folly, seems to be the only one who still speaks with authority—precisely because he makes no claims for himself. Nobody remembers William H. Harvey's *Coin's Financial School* (1894), a bestselling monetarist tract where a bright boy confounds the spokesmen for wealthy Eastern gold interests. Nobody reads Frank A. Munsey's story of a precocious businessman, *The Boy Broker* (1897). It looks as if Tom Sawyer evolved, at least in one direction, into the sort of stereotype that was all too useful for men propagandizing for political or business interests. Perhaps this development had been foreshadowed by Aldrich's hint that membership in the gang of boys led to membership in the ruling gang of men.

Hamlin Garland's and W. D. Howells' accounts of boyhood had nothing to do with the spirit of capitalism. In fact, their books may well represent a partial reaction against the prank-playing stereotype. Whatever the precise inspiration, *Boy Life on the Prairie* and *A Boy's Town* would be the best realistic accounts of boyhood to emerge from rural nineteenth-century life. Both books were autobiographical, yet sought to give a general account of boyhood in the West. Howells wrote: "For convenience, I shall call this boy, my boy; but I hope he might have been almost anybody's boy; and I mean him sometimes for a boy in general, as well as a boy in particular."[7] Garland aimed "to depict boy life, not boys; the characterization is incidental." He insisted that while many of the events did not happen to him, "they were the experiences of other boys, and might have been mine. They are all typical of the time and place."[8]

Garland begins *Boy Life on the Prairies* at the moment Lincoln Stewart arrives at the family homestead in northern Iowa and ends the narrative with Lincoln's going away to school. In between, Garland follows the seasonal cycle of farm work and provides chapters on other topics and all the while tells the story of Lincoln's maturation. The single most important activity in his life seems to be work, to the limit of his capacity. Work meant survival, the acquisition of traditional skills, the attainment of manhood. When Lincoln tied his first sheaf of wheat, "right there he became a man" (p. 248). He is even prouder when he makes his first haystack in the approved way, bigger at the top than the bottom. He and the other men frequently race at their work. At all times they take pride in their endurance. At work or play, one of the most important principles in Lincoln's life is that of the contest. Not at all a belligerent boy, he nonetheless takes a great interest in the legendary fight between Lime Gilman and Steve Nagle, or in the battle of the bulls. The fights are generally unavoidable: when the boys go to town for the Fourth of July, they can't help joining combat with the bullying town boys. Physical struggle, whether in work or in fight, is an essential aspect of boy life on the prairies, and along with struggle goes a good deal of belittling banter.

Another essential aspect is Lincoln's camaraderie with three "inseparable" (p. 299) companions—Owen Stewart, Milton Jennings, and Rance Knapp. The last of these, introduced on a galloping horse, becomes Lincoln's hero and ideal. Milton is the weakest boy; "only his love of horses and his fairly good horsemanship saved Milton from being called 'a girl-boy'" (p. 100). None of the boys are well characterized. Although these boys do not really constitute a gang, they necessarily stick together against all outsiders. The best time they ever have together occurs when they travel westward and spend a week camping by a lake. During the first night, as Lincoln watches the smoke rise from the campfire, "it seemed gloriously like the stories he had read, and the dreams he had had of being free from care and free from toil, far in the wilderness" (p. 230). One of these stories might well have been Captain Mayne Reid's *The Boy Hunters; or, Adventures in Search of a White Buffalo*. Whatever the source, Lincoln's imagination has been highly colored by literature, and Garland himself insists on a rather self-conscious primitivism: "To a boy like Lincoln or Rance, that evening was worth the whole journey, that strange, delicious hour in the deepening darkness, when everything seemed of some sweet, remembered far-off world and time—they were living as their savage ancestry lived, they were getting close to nature's self" (p. 231).

That boy life is savage would be the basic idea in Howells' incomparable work *A Boy's Town*. But Howells was less liable than Garland to confuse his reading and daydreaming with the way things really were. Garland's book is full of invaluable memories and vignettes and episodes, but Howells' book has a value beyond historical authenticity: it is the culminating work of art on what it once meant to be a boy.

Long before he ever thought of writing the book, Howells made a trial run at celebrating the wild and rebellious aspect of boyhood. At the age of twenty-one, ten years before Aldrich's novel appeared, Howells wrote an affectionate sketch of a boy ruffian for the *Ohio State Journal* called "Bobby: Study of a Boy." Bobby is a twelve-year-old "stoga-booted young rogue." Formerly he was the favorite of his aunts and uncles. Now only his grandmother can put up with him. He interrupts his father at meals. He is rude to the girl he used to walk home from school with. He nurses a certain plan of assaulting the teacher, "Old Smith," in case he should ever try to punish him. He is happiest of all outdoors: "In the summer, he spends a great part of each day in the water, in the fall he goes on nutting and wild grape excursions, and roams about the grand old woods, dreaming wild and blissful dreams of the savage life he would like to live." At the end of the sketch the youthful writer contended, "in defiance of his relatives," that Bobby had "a great and a good heart."9

"Bobby" anticipates *A Boy's Town* in many interesting ways, most conspicuously in making a case for the boy savage. But there are differences. Bobby is really more an adolescent than a boy, and he does not seem to have any companions. The sketch is in fact a kind of genre piece, a study of the characteristics of a familiar type. The book Howells would write thirty-two years later would focus on a boy in all the complexity of his relations to other boys, his parents, the many features of his town, and the imposing institutions of boy society. With his wonderful capacity for resisting the pretenses embedded in passing literary fashions, Howells neither defended nor attacked the boy savage, or portrayed him as essentially independent of his home, or pretended that his life was free and happy and devoid of conflict. "My boy," as he refers to the chief figure of his memoirs of his life in Hamilton, Ohio, would have many problems and anxieties. He is afraid the constables will catch him after joining the other boys in building a fire in the streets. Like his companions, he is terrified when Old Griffin catches them swimming inside the corporation line and threatens to drag them naked through the town. Indeed, Howells' emphasis on the nightmarish side of childhood has misled his biographers, who have read *A Boy's Town* as psychological, not social, portraiture and ignored the conventions Howells was opposing.[10] Like Mark Twain and E. W. Howe, who also wrote about Western boyhood in the 1880s, Howells was to some extent countering the growing mythology that made the early Midwest look like the paradise of boys. And Howells had another, even more important reason for giving plenty of attention to fears and superstitions: the central idea in *A Boy's Town*, worked out in a dozen different ways, is that boyhood in the life of a man corresponds to savagery in the history of the human race. Howells had used this idea in characterizing Bobby's roaming the woods. He again had recourse to it in *Suburban Sketches*: "The first men were homeless wanderers; the patriarchs dwelt in tents, and shifted their place to follow the pasturage, without a sigh; and for children—the pre-historic, the antique people, of our day—moving is a rapture."[11] But it was not until *A Boy's Town* that Howells gave his sustained attention to "the pre-historic, the antique" aspects of childhood. To be a boy, he now saw, was to inhabit a raw, danger-haunted world, and this threatening insecurity partly explains what he now considered the most important institution in the life of boys—their forming an invisible, separate society.

This society is not something boys fabricate, as Tom Sawyer fabricates a gang of play-robbers, but a pre-existing code that all boys have to learn and obey. They come under the code in their early childhood, give it their complete loyalty, and then grow out of it after passing the code on to other younger boys. As Howells wrote:

> Everywhere and always the world of boys is outside of the laws that govern grown-up communities, and it has its unwritten usages, which are handed down from old to young, and perpetuated on the same level of years, and are lived into and lived out of, but are binding, through all personal vicissitudes, upon the great body of boys between six and twelve years old. (p. 67)

Like the mischievous society of boys in the Pawnee story, the world of boys that Howells remembered was outside adult law and custom, and in fact was hardly noticed by grown-ups. Unlike the Pawnee boys, however, or the Rivermouth Centipedes, or for that matter Tom Sawyer's gang, Howells' society is not exclusive. He believed that it could be found everywhere, and that no boy could avoid it. The basic reason for its universality, in Howells' view, was that it was a relic institution from "the far-off savages" (p. 67).

Howells' chapter on the laws of the society of boys is one of the best things he ever wrote. "The first great law" (p. 68), he said, was that no matter what any other boy did to you, you had to seek justice by fighting him yourself. If he was too big to fight, you had to endure the wrong. Under no circumstances could you appeal to "the teacher or your mother" (p. 68) for help.[12] Another law was that every new boy had to establish himself by fighting. Even today, this law is not totally in abeyance. But how many men can remember the fine print as well as Howells could? "When you moved away from a neighborhood you did not lose all your rights in it; you did not have to fight when you went back to see the boys, or anything; but if one of them met you in your new precincts you might have to try conclusions with him" (p. 68).

No boy could be seen playing with a girl in public, for fear he might become known as a "girl-boy." When a boy's mother had company he had to go hide in the wood-shed or the barn or some place away from home. When he wanted another boy to come out and play, he "called him with a peculiar cry, something like 'E-oo-we, e-oo-we!' and threw stones at trees, or anything, till he came out" (p. 75).

The boys virtually formed a complete society, with seasonal rituals and a tough, arbitrary, inflexible, and barbaric system of rules. No boy who cared to be respected by other boys (and nobody else counted) could afford to slight these rules. It is striking how often they required the boys to ignore girls, mothers, and homes. Probably the reason why boys had to call out their friends by throwing stones rather than knocking at the door was that houses were the head-quarters of female control.[13] Mothers had to be avoided for the same reason: "The mother represented the family sovereignty; the father was seldom seen, and he counted for little or nothing among the outside boys. It was the mother who could say whether a boy might go fishing or in swimming, and she was held a good mother or not according as she habitually said yes or no" (p. 75). The worst mothers of all were those "who would make a boy put on a collar when they had company" (p. 76).

To some extent Howells exaggerated the prevailing differences between boy life and girl life in 1840s Ohio. Because of the peculiar views of his mother, his childhood home was not at all typical, Mrs. Howells drawing "a sharp line between the duties of her boys and girls in the tradition of her Pennsylvania origin. Indoor work was for girls, and outdoor for boys."[14] Further, Howells deliberately ignored girlhood institutions and heightened the freedom of boyhood, providing little information about the chores ordinarily assigned to boys or about his own work in his father's printshop or in pursuit of delinquent subscribers to his father's newspaper. In spite of these qualifications, however, Howells' general picture of boyhood life is too circumstantial, consistent, and candid to be doubted. The basic fact about this life was that boys more or less ran wild, spending much of the day in rivers, canals, ponds, and woods, living in an open-air culture entirely their own while romping in what was left of the wilderness. While the girls became integrated in the adult order from an early age, the boys left home and earned a public place in a non-domestic society that was simultaneously free of external control and extremely exacting internally. There is a remarkable congruence between the picture Howells draws and the modern view of childhood gender-differences in hunting and gathering societies. According to Donald Symons, "girls can begin to make a significant economic contribution much earlier in life than boys can, so while boys play at hunting and fighting, girls assist their mothers in gathering, infant care, and other domestic tasks."[15] Howells' account of boyhood life reveals nothing less than a reversion, possible for a brief moment in nineteenth-century America, to the conditions of savage life. That, of course, was precisely Howells' point: boys' town was a relict form of human savagery.

Unfortunately for Howells and his boyhood comrades, in nineteenth-century America hunting, fighting, and gang-life could not lead to approved forms of manhood. To be a boy was to have to negotiate some terrible gaps in growing up. Girls slowly turned into women, but boys struggled through radical discontinuities. From their mother's bosom boys had to fight their way into the vestigial savagery perpetuated in the ancient society of boys, and then, unlike Aldrich's junior capitalists, most of them had to abandon *that* in order to become men. Howells had to face an additional discontinuity. When his family moved to another town, the boy "found himself deathly homesick" (p. 239). A few months later he went back for a short visit to his old home. At first he could not find very many of his old friends. Those he found greeted him "with a kind of surprise." He felt in them a "refusal, or reluctance" (p. 244). After school let out, he found some more boys, "but none of them knew just what to do with him. The place that he had once had in their lives was filled; he was an outsider, who might be suffered among them, but he was no longer of them" (p. 245). The ancient comitatus had become an alien world. Thus, insofar as *A Boy's Town* is a narrative, it does not tell about initiation but about a kind of dropping out.

But there was an even greater conflict in Howells: *all along*, he had been something of an alien in boys' town. He may have been regarded as a full member in good standing, but he could never forget—and here is where Howells' account seems most truthful and penetrating— his loyalty to his mother and father and *their* code. He became painfully aware of this inner division after moving away:

> Then he began to be very homesick, and to be torn with the torment of a divided love. His mother, whom he loved so dearly, so tenderly, was here, and wherever she was, that was home; and yet home was yonder, far off, at the end of those forty inexorable miles, where he had left his life-long mates. (p. 242)

This torment had been present all along. Will had been taught by his mother not to lie, but like the other boys he had to deny going swimming. "The home instruction was all against fighting" (p. 69)— but it was impossible to live peacefully in boys' town. When all the children decided to persecute an inoffensive new teacher, Will joined in, even though the man had treated him kindly. Once, when Will was fishing in a canal, the teacher came up to him and made a friendly overture. Will, loyal to the boyhood code, refused to speak. Another time, the code obliged him to punish a rather timid boy for some offense or other. Will hit him on the face, as he was supposed to, and felt sick about it afterwards, "like a brutal ruffian" (p. 74). Again and again, Will obeyed the dictates of the savage society of boys only to realize how cruel or mean he was. In fact, Howells never told the worst, for, as he admitted, "it is only in some of its milder manners and customs that the boy's world can be studied" (p. 68). In *Years of My Youth*, published a quarter century after *A Boy's Town*, Howells hinted at the compulsions he felt when he was "a boy struggling tooth and nail for my place among other boys." In declaring that "no man, unless he puts on the mask of fiction, can show his real face or the will behind it,"[16] he confessed that he had not told all in his autobiography. At the cost of a great deal of guilt and anxiety, Howells in his boyhood had struggled with the torment of living in two incompatible worlds. There was no way he could reconcile his dual membership in women's sphere as embodied by his home and the prehistoric society that survived as boys' town. This was one of the inevitable contradictions in growing up male. Unlike almost all other writers, Howells tried not to deny it. The boy, he insisted, "would like to please his father and mother, but he dreads the other boys and what they will say; and so the light of home fades from his ignorant soul, and leaves him in the outer darkness of the street" (p. 213).

Howells' most arresting story of the terror a boy feels at finding himself in this "outer darkness" is in his second book about boyhood, *The Flight of Pony Baker*.[17] One of the basic ideas in this book is that a boy must make a show of running away from home in order to retain the respect of other boys. Unhappily, Pony Baker, although he plays with the other boys, happens to love his mother and is afraid to leave her. Three times he tries and fails to run away. The third time his friend, Jim Leonard, tells a circus roustabout that Pony is an orphan and wants to join the circus.[18] "Parents living?" asks the man. Pony is so afraid he can barely say "yes." "Well, that's right," says the circus man, "When we take an orphan, we want to have his parents living, so that we can go and ask them what sort of a boy he is" (p. 149). Stringing Pony along, the man tells him to wait on his front steps for the circus procession at "about one o'clock in the morning" (p. 151).

At supper that evening, Pony feels so miserable he can hardly eat. He goes up to his room long before it's time to go to bed. Worried about him, his mother asks him if he's still angry at her for something she did earlier. "Oh no," he says, and embraces her and cries. he feels he will never see her again. Although he tries to stay awake into the night, he dozes off. Suddenly, he hears the circus and "knew that the procession was coming for him" (p. 161). He tried to dress, though for some reason his jacket had only one sleeve. Slipping downstairs with his bundle, he went out on the front steps and saw nobody coming down the street but the magician, who wore "a tall, peaked hat, like a witch." This frightening figure

> took up the whole street, he was so wide in the black glazed gown that hung from his arms when he stretched them out, for he seemed to be groping along that way, with his wand in one hand, like a blind man.

He kept saying in a kind of deep, shaking voice: "It's all glory; it's all glory," and the sound of those words froze Pony's blood. He tried to get back into the house again, so that the magician should not find him, but when he felt for the door-knob there was no door there anywhere; nothing but a smooth wall. (p. 162)

It is a dream, of course, a nightmare that shows how the little boy really sees the horror of having to leave home. The magician comes from the big adult world outside the small town. He speaks for the glamor, the glory of this world, and he is outsized in comparison to the tiny street. He wears the costume that shows he has mastered the arts of the circus and other mysterious adult institutions. But at the same time there's something wrong with him. He seems to be blind; he gropes; he wears black; he is utterly terrifying. If *that* is what it means to leave home and rise to fame and glory, Pony wants back inside. But he is trapped in "the outer darkness of the street."

Howells' mother apparently held on to her second son very hard. After he and Elinor were married and living in Venice, he had to reassure his mother in a letter—

And now, mother, in regard to my absence: I know how it grieves you; and why you should feel it peculiarly, for I remember how hard it used to be for me to leave home, and you doubtless remember that, too, and contrast it with my present willingness to be away. But when you think, dear mother, you cannot believe that I love you less, but only that being now a man I judge more clearly of evils and bear them better.

After her death a few years later Howells wrote Joseph, his older brother: "How do we appear now to mother?—It all comes to this at last, whatever I begin to talk or think of." Two days later he wrote his father:

I wish that my work were always such as could please her now where she is. But neither this nor my life is so,—I feel it with shame and despair. It seems the worse for me not to be all I can be, because I feel so deeply the idleness of the worldly success I most strive for.

The intensity of his guilt, however, proves his mother's influence. He had written Joseph that it was "odd . . . we got little or no harm out of that Hamilton life which was moral death to so many of our mates."[19] But it does not seem odd at all when one remembers the parents. Evidently Howells was not left alone in the outer darkness of the street after all.

Or was he? This was to be his fundamental uncertainty. He would one day try to resolve it once and for all, when Tolstoy's Christian pacifism would permit him to reaffirm the German pietistic pacifism he had got from his mother. Tolstoy taught him how to find the doorknob and go through the smooth wall and get back in the old house. But there was a price to be paid.

CHAPTER TWENTY

Ambition vs. Selflessness

Howells was not the only boy whose youthful dreams were haunted by the promise of glory. Pony's dream about a giant wizard stalking the street of a small town and chanting, "It's all glory," is reminiscent of the only dream Henry James paid attention to in his memoirs. This dream took place in the Galerie d'Apollon, which, in James's image, formed "a prodigious tube or tunnel through which I inhaled little by little, that is again and again, a general sense of *glory*."[1] Young Sam Clemens yearned for the same thing when he watched the steamboats or enviously beheld John RoBards return "in unimaginable glory" from a trip to the California gold fields. Sam got his own taste of glory when he helped a traveling hypnotist confound a staunch local skeptic.[2] Evidently, our three greatest writers of the Gilded Age all reveled in dreams of glory when they were boys. One of the explanations for this interesting coincidence may be that ambition had an incredibly inflated value in the 1850s and 60s.

Among farmers and small-town tradesmen, one of the most important indices of proper masculinity had traditionally been shrewd judgment, variously called smartness, gumption, or 'cuteness' (from acuteness). In Sarah Orne Jewett's story, "The Hiltons' Holiday," a farmer living on land cleared by his father and himself says of a boy who died long ago, "Poor little John, for all he was so young he had a great deal o' judgment; he'd ha' made a likely man."[3] In this older agrarian world, you proved yourself a likely man by demonstrating your skill, intelligence, and competitiveness among your neighbors. Ambition, an essential attribute, generally had a local reference. But in the modern world, with its much bigger business systems, communications networks, and cities, success came to mean something rather different—the power to dominate the lives, the minds, the *imaginations*, of millions of others. In a world where you could be made restless by reading of somebody's grand coup in a city you had never even seen, the greatest kind of power was that of making millions of other readers feel the same dissatisfaction or envy eating at you. The new way of proving one's masculinity was to fight one's way to the top so that the whole world could see that you were number one. Kingship became the number one male American fantasy in the Gilded Age.

There is plenty of evidence for believing that this fantasy was widespread. Today no one would give a second thought to the use of *king* to designate a captain of industry. In fact the word is obsolescent; nobody ever calls Colonel Sanders the Southern fried chicken king. But kings were everywhere in nineteenth-century America. The first instance of this usage in the *Dictionary of American English* dates from 1846:

> How would she strive, in fitting verse, to sing
> The wondrous Progress of the Printing King?

In 1862 someone was said to be "called the 'Strawberry King' . . . [because of] unquestionable pre-eminence in this branch of fruit culture."[4] No doubt the usage had been around for some time if strawberries, even, had found their liege lord. But regardless of the exact date of origin, by the Gilded Age the usage had become standard. In *The Rise of Silas Lapham*, Bromfield Corey adopts it with an ironic twist in telling his wife that their son has gone to ask Lapham for a job: "He left me yesterday afternoon to go and offer his allegiance to the Mineral Paint King."[5]

I suspect many American men took kingship much more seriously than Bromfield Corey. It is well to remember that the town houses the Vanderbilts erected on Fifth Avenue in the 1870s were imitation castles. As we see in the *Adventures of Huckleberry Finn*, there was a stock joke about men who dreamed or pretended that they were the long lost son of Louis the Sixteenth. The megalomania which led one to fancy one was Napoleon became stereotyped. Even Henry James felt its effects: after a series of strokes partly destroyed his brain, he dictated letters in the name of Napoleon. Many European travelers in the United States were struck by Americans' fascination with the European aristocracy. Mark Twain and Henry James were

by no means the only Americans to write about American claimants
who thought of themselves as the rightful inheritors of entailed
estates in England. Why did it become commonplace to call the
Gilded-Age millionaires robber *barons*? Why did lucky goldminers
become *nabobs*? Why did San Francisco have a *nob hill*? For the same
reason that boys played, and play, king of the mountain, tramps
became kings of the road, a home-run hitter was dubbed the Sultan
of Swat, a jazzman and an actor the Duke. F. Scott Fitzgerald, in-
fected with the fantasy more than most men, had literal daydreams
of being king. If his fiction isn't sufficient to prove this, there is his
autobiographical "Author's House," which recalls "my first childish
love of myself, my belief that I would never die like other people,
and that I wasn't the son of my parents but a son of a king, a king
who ruled the whole world."[6]

This is not the place to explore all the sources of the male dream
of sitting on top of the world. Certainly, our romantic historians
contributed more than their share to this dream. According to Ann
Douglas, "Sparks, Prescott, Motley, Bancroft, Parkman, and their
followers were writing what Nietzsche would call 'monument' history:
the commemoration and celebration of significant masculine achievement."[7] But it is hard not to suspect that the main source must have
been the well-publicized spectacle of successful go-getters like Gould
and Rockefeller, and also the undeniable truth that huge chunks of
the new world were ready to be grabbed. Business itself was dominated by the push for total mastery. The words "acme" and "ace"
were often used as names of businesses, not just because they would
come near the beginning of the directory or could serve to conceal
the actual owner, but because they meant *No. 1. Ace* in fact, became
a very important word in the masculine vocabulary. You could
indicate your casual respect for another man by calling him "ace."
Or you might praise a good raconteur as an "ace storyteller."

Howells became our ace novelist in the 1870s and 1880s, and he
later acquired an unfortunate title based on his middle name, Dean.
He achieved what he dreamed of in his adolescence, when he had
"a selfish ideal of my own glory."[8] Yet if he achieved his ambition,
he could not, especially in the 1880s and after, help belittling the
drive that took him to the top. In his old age, he came to admire his
father for not trying to get ahead: "I think now that he was wise not
to care for the advancement which most of us have our hearts set

upon, and that it was one of his finest qualities that he was content with a lot in life where he was not exempt from work with his hands."9

Most interesting of all, as Howells looked backwards he saw that his literary ambition had actually blinded him to the social world around him: "My ambition was my barrier from the living world around me; I could not beat my way from it into that; it kept me absent and hampered me in the vain effort to be part of the reality I have always tried to portray."10

Howells had the humility to understand that ambition was the great American daydream—that it was like any other daydream that becomes too pleasant to be relinquished. Ambition enabled men to repudiate the present for the sake of future glory. Thus, Howells often punctured ambition for the same reason he attacked so many popular myths and slogans in American life. His best work corrected—not censored—dreams. An important passage from his essay, "I Talk of Dreams," displays the natural antagonism between critical thinking and daydream (and also draws an interesting distinction between daydream and sleep dreaming):

> [The critical faculty] seems absent, too, in what we call day-dreaming, or that sort of dramatizing action which perhaps goes on perpetually in the mind, or some minds. But this day-dreaming is not otherwise any more like night-dreaming than [artistic] invention is; for the man is never more actively and consciously a man, and never has a greater will to be fine and high and grand than in his day-dreams, while in his night-dreams he is quite willing to be a miscreant of any worst sort.11

Night dreaming, like a boy's town, is a vestige of prehistoric savagery; daydreams are a form of fantasied transcendence; the two merge in the actual careers of certain powerfully egotistic and destructive American capitalists, such as Howells' Royal Langbrith. What many twentieth-century writers have dignified as the "American Dream," Howells saw as a perverted yet basic male fantasy. Astonishingly, Howells' brilliant understanding of the links between the male psyche and American history and culture have been almost completely ignored.

One of Howells' finest accounts of male daydreams, and of the ways in which they connect up with the nuts and bolts of the publishing industry, is *The World of Chance* (1893). This book tells of the selling of a bestseller, a third-rate psychological thriller with the title *A Modern Romeo*. The author, Percy Ray, is a talented writer living the usual half-conscious life. As he walks to a newspaper office looking for work, "he painted his future as critic of the journal with minute detail; he had died chief owner and had his statue erected to his memory in Park Square before he crossed that space." This is a standard sort of daydream: it is about glory, not pleasure; it gives the insignificant young man a magnified image of himself as seen through the eyes of others. The daydream is so intense it completely distracts the daydreamer as he walks across the square. Yet he remains sane. So intense are his daydreams, however, that he himself wonders—

> "why we never expect our day-dreams to come true?"
> "Perhaps because they're never bad ones—because we know we're just making them," said Mrs. Denton.
> "It must be that! But, do we always make them? Sometimes my daydreams seem to make themselves, and they keep on doing it so long that they tire me to death. They're perfect daymares."[12]

Is it the daydreamer who makes the daydream? Ray does not answer this excellent question, but Howells, in a dozen or so novels, does, and the answer he comes up with is precisely what we would expect of a writer with such a profound social vision. We can't help having our daydreams, he says, because they are the internal aspect of our crazy civilization.

One of the most important institutions feeding our fantasy life, in Howells' fiction, is the publishing industry. In *The Minister's Charge* a young man helps some people get out of a burning residential hotel. Reporting on the event, the newspapers exaggerate the rescuer's risk in order to satisfy and stimulate "the popular love of the heroic."[13] The popular romance, in Howells' view, also has an incalculable influence, chiefly on women but also on young and insecure men. In *The Kentons*, for instance, an adolescent named Boyne has read and been impressed by *Hector Folleyne*, a "heroical" romance in which a European crown princess falls in love with an American lad "very little older than Boyne himself."[14] A malicious joker named Trannel claims that the novel was actually based on his own romantic involvement with a royal person, and he convinces Boyne that the young Queen of Holland has fallen in love with him after seeing him from a distance. When the Queen's carriage comes to a halt during a procession, Boyne is persuaded that she is inviting him to step forward. He does so, and the police, nervous about anarchists, promptly haul him away. Boyne is victimized not only by Trannel but by the publishing industry's crass exploitation of mass fantasies.

But the most important source of male fantasy, in Howells' novels, is the glorification of business. This glorification finds expression in the daily press, as we see in the opening chapter of *The Rise of Silas Lapham*, where Bartley Hubbard transforms the businessman's generally honest answers into the going clichés:

> Simple, clear, bold, and straightforward in mind and action, Colonel Silas Lapham, with a prompt comprehensiveness and a never-failing business sagacity, is, in the best sense of that much-abused term, one of nature's noblemen, in the last half of his five eleven and a half. His life affords an example of single-minded application and unwavering perseverance which our young business men would do well to emulate.[15]

The reason why this pap was provided by a cheap press was that the self-made Adam was the great male god. As George Towle wrote in *American Society* in 1870, "The pushing self-made man is perhaps most of all honoured, respected, and aided; and few there are who do not refer with pride to their early days of hardship and indomitable perseverance."[16]

The novel in which Howells gave his most careful attention to the destructive consequences of the glorification of the self-made man was *The Son of Royal Langbrith*. The character named in the title had been a very successful crook in his lifetime. The novel concerns his son, James, who ignorantly worships his father's memory. Hoping to honor the "royal" family heritage, James forces a commemorative statue of the old robber baron on his reluctant townsmen. In so doing James actually carries out what was, for Percy Ray in *The World of Chance*, only a daydream. James's favorite fantasy is that he is a grand and benevolent seigneur. Others see him very differently. His fellow students at Harvard regarded him as an ass. A businessman says of him: "If his mother hadn't babied him up so, and kept him in cotton all his life, I could have worked him into the business before this, and now I could leave it in his hands."[17] His mother isn't entirely responsible, for, as Howells shows, she herself is trapped by the falsifications that come with her wealth. Howells' greatest achievement in the novel is to demonstrate the idea that Hawthorne only fiddled around with in *The House of the Seven Gables*—that ill-gotten wealth wreaks its own vengeance: James Langbrith grows up to be an insufferably pompous and condescending dreamer because he can't be told how much his daddy cheated and what a pig he was.

But of course it is not just the myths about business that are destructive. Business itself, in Howells' view, destroys. Business destroys calm, trust, native human helpfulness (which Howells calls altruism), and all stable ways of life. Business destroys fraternity. In *A Hazard of New Fortunes* (1890), which tells of an attempt to establish a cooperative magazine, the financial angel, Dryfoos, threatens to withdraw his support unless Lindau, an old 1848 socialist, is removed from the staff. In *The Quality of Mercy* (1892), a defalcating treasurer runs away to Quebec and for a time lives entirely alone. The isolated Northern vacancy in which he sinks represents the true direction of his career. In *The World of Chance* (1893) Percy Ray's preoccupation with the "chance" his novel may become a bestseller distances him from the best single woman he is likely to know. When he finally proposes, chiefly out of a peculiar sense of obligation, she no longer loves him. The name of this young woman who is missed by the young man on the make is, not by accident, Peace.

Business destroys peace in Howells' fiction for a very simple reason: business is the war of each against all. In the mid-1880s, Howells gave a very favorable picture of the American businessman in the person of Silas Lapham. This man is a magnificent, vulgar, thick-necked, ham-handed success, a good man in every sense including the ethical. But, ominously, he is able to prove his goodness only by giving up all his wealth. Two things are worth noting: 1) Howells' unworldly definition of success, of rising, requires that his hero give up his wealth, prestige, and place in the city, and that he shrink into an old man in the country with a pathetic dream of a comeback. 2) It does not seem probable that a Gilded Age millionaire would observe the old preindustrial code of the gentleman and thus refrain from defrauding the investors Rogers digs up. In writing *Silas Lapham*, Howells brought forward a fictive millionaire so richly and lovingly imagined that only Dreiser could improve on him. But Howells was able to create Lapham only by accepting a precondition that Dreiser would not have to concede—making believe that the new plutocracy had the old decency. Thus Howells was at pains to exhibit Lapham's generosity in taking care of the shiftless daughter of his old war buddy. Ten years later, in an essay on New York City, Howells would reverse himself on this point and admit that the self-made man did not often help the indigent.[18]

But in 1884 Howells was still unwilling to accept what he couldn't help knowing—that capitalism was profoundly destructive. At the peak of his capacity and career, Howells had to believe that the men who were making it in America—and making it in a way that left whole industries and categories of natural resources associated with single names—would still remember the public interest. He saw that the whole irreversible transformation of this country that took place in the Gilded Age was partly fueled by male fantasies of power and conquest, but he could not grasp the huge uncontrollable drift of technological progress. He wrote campaign biographies of Abraham Lincoln and Rutherford B. Hayes. He hoped that voting the straight Republican ticket was still another way of fighting slavery.[19] But in trying to embody his faith in *The Rise of Silas Lapham*, Howells had, apparently, a nervous breakdown. "The bottom fell out,"[20] as he confessed ten years later. When he recovered, his social and economic views became quickly radicalized. He wrote a public appeal to the Governor of Illinois for clemency for the Haymarket anarchists. He fell under the spell of Tolstoy. He and Elinor decided, briefly, that they no longer cared "for the world's life, and would like to be settled somewhere very humbly and simply, where we could be socially identified with the principles of progress and sympathy for the struggling mass."[21]

After Silas Lapham all Howells' rich, self-made men turned noticeably crafty and tyrannical. The public face of America grew more ugly in his fiction. He took his readers to a black ghetto, a flophouse, a mill town in New England. He dared to tackle New York City, which he portrayed not as a human community but as a grab-bag of races, classes, and characters and as an intersection of forces amplified beyond the ability of humans to comprehend or withstand. In a well-known passage of *A Hazard of New Fortunes*, he saw the city streets as the visible result of "the fierce struggle for survival." Their visual appearance was a demonstration of "the chaos to which the individual selfishness must always lead."[22] In his essay, "New York Streets," the advertising placards covering the facades of buildings are not eyesores so much as tokens of the hidden war: it is as if the signs are all yelling at one another. The elevated railroads represent a successful corporate raid on the public domain. Everyone lives in the thick of an "economic warfare . . . as unconsciously as people lived in feudal cities, while the nobles fought out their private quarrels in the midst of them." The most stunning instance of this warfare is an empty city lot:

> I did not think any piece of our mother earth could have been made to look so brutal and desolate amidst the habitations of men. But every spear of grass had been torn from it; the hardened and barren soil was furrowed like a haggard face, and it was all strewn with clubs and stones, as if it had been a savage battleground.[23]

In the 1960s the radical imagination tended to picture American capitalism as a "system," an "establishment"—an image that justified a great deal of paranoia. Howells saw capitalism as the reverse of order or agreement—an atavistic reversion to a savage state of warfare in which fierce masculine egos fought for supremacy.

The savage battleground was too much for Howells. Like many other Americans in the late 1880s and early 90s, he became very interested in the cause of altruistic socialism. In January 1888 he wrote Hamlin Garland: "I am reading and thinking about questions that carry me beyond myself and my miserable literary idolatries of the past; perhaps you'll find that I've been writing about them. I am still the slave of selfishness, but I no longer am content to be so."[24]

Several years later, after his thought had matured, he wrote a romance that is often, and incorrectly, classified with the many utopias published in the 1890s. *A Traveller from Altruria* does, it is true, posit a perfect alternative society founded on the principle of altruism. But instead of attempting the impossible and showing us how Altruria works, Howells invokes it as an ideal standard in order to reveal the actual class lines Americans refused to see. As a work of critical realism, *A Traveller from Altruria* is first-rate. But it has the defect that vitiates so many radical critiques of American society. This defect does not involve Howells' insistence that people are naturally altruistic if they are only given the chance. Howells was right on this point. Helpfulness is as natural to us as aggression. In fact, altruism is not specifically a human quality at all; many animals exhibit it, as sociobiological investigations have found; it is precisely *because* we are animals that we often voluntarily give one another a hand. No, the basic defect in *A Traveller from Altruria*, and in all of Howells' economic novels from *Annie Kilburn* to *The World of Chance*, is his doctrine that the cause of all the trouble is the ego.

The sanctity of egolessness has been a feature in American radicalism since at least as early as the time of John Woolman (whose journal Howells greatly admired). At all times this principle has been cloaked with one religious system or another. In the nineteenth century a sort of transcendental surrender replaced Woolman's passivity before the Inner Light. In our day egolessness draws its artillery from Zen or Tao.[25] The main effect of such religious window-dressing is to garner an invincible piety and respect for the principle of selflessness.

But there is something absurd and self-defeating in the notion that the human ego is so bad that any spontaneous expression of it must be suspect. For Ginsberg to convert to egolessness was probably essential therapy. For Howells to convert was a disaster. Early and late, one of his sanest themes had been the specious attraction of self-sacrificial celibacy. In *Their Wedding Journey* he gave close attention to the Soeurs Grises of Montreal and the "self-sacrifice" this order required of its members: "The two young girls at the head were very pretty, and all the pale faces had a corpse-like peace.... Would it be yet more cruel if every year two girls so young and fair were self-doomed to renew the likeness of that youthful death?"[26] In *The Undiscovered Country* Howells pictured the Shaker commune as a pure and selfless, yet life-denying, coed farming convent. When James read the novel he wrote Howells that he had described the Shakers "too un ironically & as if you were a Shaker yourself. (Perhaps you are—unbeknown to your correspondents & contributors!!— & that this is the secret of the book!)"[27]

This was a shrewd guess. Underneath Howells' commitment to marriage, the world, what he would later call "complicity," he found it hard to forget his early love—purity. Thus, he disowned purity again and again. *Indian Summer* (1886), for instance, traced the embarrassments that result when an ardent girl throws herself at a middle-aged man in order to compensate him for being jilted by another woman twenty years earlier. In *April Hopes* (1887) Howells showed how Puritan ethics lead to "nervous" tyranny in Mrs. Mavering and a repulsive sort of petticoat tyranny in Alice Pasmer. But even as Howells finished this novel, he became so appalled by the social disorders of the capitalist world of chance that he returned to his old flame, which he had spent so much of his career repudiating. Three years after writing about the unhealthy Alice Pasmer, who is inspired by her dreams of perfection to think of joining an Anglican sisterhood, Howells wrote about another idealistic girl, Margaret Vance, who actually joins a celibate sisterhood in order to do the good she has always been frustrated from accomplishing. Apparently, Margaret's selfless devotion is the best available remedy for all the poverty, disorder, and injustice in *A Hazard of New Fortunes*. Near the end of the novel, when Basil and Isabel March happen to see her on the street, "she smiled joyfully, almost gayly, on seeing them, and though she hurried by with the sister who accompanied her, and did not stay to speak, they felt that the peace that passeth understanding had looked at them from her eyes." Basil thinks "she is at rest, there can't be any doubt of that." Isabel is more dubious. She remembers Margaret's talk with Conrad Dryfoos before he got shot in his ineffective attempt to intervene in the streetcar strike. Clearly, Isabel has in mind the destructive consequences of Margaret's idealism. But Basil will hear nothing of this:

> "If she unwittingly sent him to his death, she sent him to die for God's sake, for man's sake."
> "Yes—yes. But still—"
> "Well, we must trust that look of hers."[28]

If novels were pinball machines, there would be a very bright and noisy "TILT" at the end of *A Hazard of New Fortunes*. Howells had never permitted the virtuous claims of self-sacrifice to pass unexamined. Here, however, the character who is closest to being his spokesman closes the debate. "We must trust" that Margaret has found the one way to the peace that passeth understanding in the modern city. Everything finally rests on a passing glimpse of "that look of hers." We are not to question, not to try to find out what she is specifically doing, or whether she is helping anyone besides herself. It looks as if the spectacular social upheavals of the 1880s, which Howells interpreted as a result of unchecked egotism, scared him into accepting, or at least considering, the one form of self-denial he had always attacked—virginity.

Of course, Howells did not abandon realism in his economic novels. Mr. Homos from Altruria may be utterly sane and level-headed, a perfectly and implausibly uncomplicated man, but all of Howells' other social reformers who run a tilt at human selfishness are a little cracked and invariably ineffective. Rev. Peck in *Annie Kilburn* is notably rigid and humorless: he forgets to take care of his daughter and there is "a mystical, almost a fantastical, quality"[29] in his thought. Conrad Dryfoos in *A Hazard of New Fortunes* is partly an unfledged boy rebelling against a domineering father. Denton in *The World of Chance* is so obsessed with social injustice that he goes crazy. Convinced that there must be expiation, he decides to kill himself and his innocent sister-in-law, Peace. When he is prevented from hurting her, he kills himself. Yet—and this is the troublesome thing in Howells—all of these characters, even Denton, are animated by ideas that Howells himself espoused at one time or another. The idea that all men are bound together in complicity underlies Denton's hope that one person may die for many; and Howells himself had dramatized these views in *A Hazard of New Fortunes*, where Conrad is the sacrificial lamb. Howells' most articulate and sensible radical is David Hughes, an old Brook Farmer who has lived much of his life in a family commune (the sort of commune Howells' father attempted to establish with his brothers in 1850). Hughes claims to "abhor dreamers," decides the commune is guilty of "eremitism," and moves to New York to disseminate his views. He is for altruism and against egotism and competition. Like Bellamy in *Looking Backward* (1888), he looks forward to a form of state-monopoly. In criticizing the ugliness of New York City, he says:

> I hold that the average tasteless man has no right to realize his ideas of a house in the presence of a great multitude of his fellow-beings. It is an indecent exposure of his mind, and should not be permitted. All these structural forms about us, which with scarcely an exception are ugly and senseless, I regard as so many immoralities. . . . The city should build the city, and provide every denizen with a fit and beautiful habitation to work in and rest in.[30]

David Hughes gives a forceful statement of one kind of socialism. But what does he achieve? As his family gradually goes to pieces under the pressure of the chaotic metropolis, Hughes gets weaker and sicker. He manages to finish his book analysing the destructive effects of modern egotism, but he can't even get the book published. In his last moments, when he asks David Ray, the successful romancer, whether a publisher has accepted the book, his daughter breaks in before Ray can speak and tells the old man that his great work will soon see print. Thus, the old radical dies in the blessed illusion that his thought will live after him.

Howells is to be applauded for allowing his realism to triumph—for demonstrating the blind alley to which his own denunciation of egotism leads. But he is to be censured for espousing, or at least giving such careful consideration to, an absurdity in the first place. There is an impractical, self-cancelling aspect in his radicalism that makes nullities out of those who espouse it. But moving beyond censure, let us ask the important question: *why*, as Howells approached his fiftieth birthday, did he undertake an assault on selfishness after having argued against feminine self-sacrifice in so many novels? As a young boy, Howells, like Henry James, had been taught that selfishness was wrong, and that he should always side with the lower against the higher. Now, in the last half of the 1880s, having risen to the top, Howells was so consumed with guilt that his reading of Tolstoy[31] revived the ethical commitments he had partly abandoned in leaving home. In making his way in the world, he had necessarily disregarded the family teaching on equality and fraternity. The strategy by which he buttressed his choice in the 1870s and 1880s is revealing: he wrote about the folly of women who were tempted to immolate themselves. His women characters might be tempted by their reading of popular romances such as the fictive *Tears, Idle Tears*, or by their inheritance of New England "ethicism" or "Puritanism," or by the code that it was wrong for women to satisfy themselves. Whatever their temptation, their only salvation lay in selfish enjoyment. But Howells' crusade against irrational female self-abnegation had one fatal defect, as far as he was concerned—it didn't seem to apply to his men characters. Men, in Howells, are different from women in a significant way: they have more latent brutality and savagery. They don't need to be told to look out for themselves. As long as Howells lived the polite feminine belletristic life, all went well. Devoting himself to a genre patronized by women, writing narratives about delicate female perplexities and embarrassments, he himself remained feminine and was therefore able to do

what so many of his female characters are supposed to do—assert
himself, be selfish, be happy, work, get ahead. But the minute he left
the artificially delimited female sphere and stepped out into the
public world where so many vested interests were guarding their own
with such jealous attention and attempted to define himself as a man
among men, defying the Republicanism he had always defended, he
got into trouble. One of the first big signs of this trouble is the
contradictory ethical meausage in *Silas Lapham*, where the subplot
teaches the familiar lesson that Penelope should not sacrifice herself
even while the main plot hammers home the view that her father
must sacrifice *himself*. In some people, this double standard would
cause no difficulties. But for a person who lived on the boundary
between woman's sphere and man's world, who had not been able to
decide, finally, whether he wanted to be a good boy at home or a bad
boy with his peers, the double standard meant a painful uncertainty.
Small wonder that "the bottom dropped out" as Howells tried to
finish the novel.

The contradiction that rose to the surface in this novel reflected
the fundamental dilemma in growing up male in Howells' culture.
He had resolved the dilemma in adolescence by becoming "literary."
But this solution no longer worked once he committed himself to the
public world in the 1880s. Now Tolstoy began to speak to Howells
with an irresistible voice, and Howells became a disciple. He underwent "an experience for me somewhat comparable to the old-fashioned religious experience of people converted at revivals." Tolstoy,
he insisted, "shows that the selfish life, the individual, the personal
life, is always misery and despair."[32] Howells developed an unsatisfactory ethical system based on a concept—"complicity"—that stressed
one's inevitable guilt for social evils but said nothing about the
possibility of concrete social action. He felt that something must be
done even while insisting that the only possible doer, the selfish ego,
was wicked. The active and self-assertive men in his fiction were now
almost necessarily evil or at least unscrupulous; the good people were
all too liable to be one variety or other of fool. Worst of all, Howells
turned against his "miserable literary idolatries of the past." I am not
sure whether Howells would have accepted the diagnosis, but his
basic problem, bothering him ever since the time he found he had
to join the savage society of boys in violation of his mother's and
father's teaching, bothering him even more as he entered an adult

world with all its hypertrophied greed and ambition, was a deep, inexpugnable feeling that is was wrong, all wrong, to be masculine.

The most serious consequences of Howells' systematic attack on selfishness is, in my opinion, the lifeless quality that becomes more and more evident in his novels after *Silas Lapham*. This later fiction is pervaded with a constant self-checking or self-holding in the interests of general amenity. Henry James criticized this aspect in his review of a novel Howells published in 1898. James was oppressed by "the predestined beauty of behavior on the part of everyone concerned—kindness, patience, submission to boredom." All the characters seemed to have a "friendly wit" that served to "minimize shocks and strains." This wit

> muffles and softens, all round, the edges of *The Story of a Play*. The mutual indulgences of the whole thing fairly bathe the prospect in something like a suffusion of that "romantic" to which the author's theory of the novel offers so little hospitality. And that, for the moment, is an odd consummation.[33]

As James sensed, Howells' new ethic was working against his old realism.

CHAPTER TWENTY ONE

"The Best Men"

Nice guys finish last; gentlemen don't go into politics; represent-ative government has been subverted by big business. These notions first gained currency in the United States in the period following the Civil War. The 1873 novel from which this period got its name, the Gilded Age, dealt, fittingly enough, with the tricks by which lobbyists and other private interests managed to get their hands in the public till. An 1880 political novel, Henry Adams' *Democracy*, tried to show that democratic institutions had succumbed to corruption. In 1895 Mark Twain expressed the belief that a third party of "the best men" was the one thing that could save the republic. Recalling the 1884 election, when the liberal Republicans bolted the party in order to vote for Cleveland rather than Blaine, Mark Twain said:

> Once upon a time, about 14 years ago, we had a strong third party, and that party attracted some of the best men in the country to it. The Mugwumps, as they were called, went down in a subsequent Presidential election before the folly of the people, and it hasn't reappeared. But it's wanted badly enough. It seems to me that you've got right at the basis of things if you have that strong third party with the best men in it. It doesn't matter what their views are, so long as they are the best men.[1]

Opinions like this, Henry Adams' autobiography, and the undeniable growth of industry, bribery, and urban machine politics have all given rise to the familiar notion that it was in the Gilded Age that liberal gentlemen lost control of American politics.

The best treatment of liberal reformers in the Gilded Age, "*The Best Men*" by John G. Sproat, suggests that this view is seriously defective.[2] "The Best Men" were those who generally wanted lower tariffs, Civil Service reform in order to reduce patronage and the power of party organizations, and, by the early seventies, an end to Reconstruction. They often represented "aristocratic" interests and bitterly opposed the influence of big business on politics. They believed, like the author of *The Rise of Silas Lapham*, that honesty and decency were needed most of all. They tried to bring back into politics the virtues of the gentleman. They themselves often tried to embody good taste and uprightness. Generally, they failed, except in one respect—they succeeded so well in articulating their point of view and justifying their ineffectiveness that they saddled later generations with precisely the view of the Gilded Age that they themselves found so solacing— the times were so rough, vulgar, and unscrupulous that no good man could possibly rise to a position of influence.

In fact, it looks as if the best men were not so much kicked out as that they abdicated. There is a succinct expression of this deceptive abdication in Edith Wharton's novel, *The Age of Innocence*, which takes place in the 1870s:

> Everyone in polite circles knew that, in America, 'a gentleman couldn't go into politics.' But, since he could hardly put it in that way to Winsett, he answered evasively: "Look at the career of the honest man in American politics. They don't want us."

The evasive speaker here, Newland Archer, believes that "the country was in possession of the bosses and the emigrant, and decent people had to fall back on sport and culture."[3] This was a very convenient opinion if sport and culture happened to be what you wanted to fall back on.

The fact is, many would-be reformers came from an artificially fastidious social class and spoke for gentry interests. Geoffrey Blodgett's excellent account of the connections between "Reform Thought and the Genteel Tradition" points out that the reformers worked in "alienation from the party system."[4] There were undoubtedly many causes contributing to this alienation, and one of them was, not that politics took on a lower tone, but that gentlemen, from Jacksonian times on, took on a higher tone. "Till within twenty years," wrote Thomas Wentworth Higginson in 1881, "it has been the accepted theory, that civilized society lost in vigor what it gained in refinement."[5] Men were eager to give up colloquial speech and manners in order to approve themselves gentlemen. Then, when it appeared that cultivated men were not always taken seriously in caucus or saloon, it became commonplace to declare that, in politics, no gentlemen need apply.

The most important public medium for the best men was the *Nation*. Howells and Henry James were associated with this magazine at its beginning in 1865. Thomas Sergeant Perry reviewed and panned hundreds of current novels in its pages. In Geoffrey Blodgett's words, while the *Nation's* "subscription list always remained small, it connected widely scattered readers to a national community of thought." Blodgett writes:

> Godkin was less a national leader of public opinion than the intellectual strategist of the gentry's reluctant withdrawal from practical politics. His influence was perhaps more precisely captured by the civil service reformer Silas Burt, who thanked Godkin in 1899 for his clarity in reporting "the progressive political and civic degeneracy you have observed in this country since you made it your home."[6]

Howells came to understand that there was something essentially frivolous in the *Nation*, however well disguised. In 1877 he wrote Charles Dudley Warner: "That article of yours on The Nation was one of the truest—in fact the truest—thing ever said about that paper. Its writers are political satirists; I fancy they must often be amused to be taken seriously by people who look to them for some scheme of reform."[7]

Harriet Beecher Stowe once consoled Rebecca Harding Davis for a slashing review by writing that the *Nation* "has no sympathy with any deep & high moral movement—no pity for human infirmity. It is a sneering respectable middle aged sceptic who says I take my two glasses & my cigar daily."[8] The class, gender, and complacent inactivity of Stowe's personification reveal just what *The Nation* stood for.

The Nation partly answered a need many gentlemen felt for male clubs. When Melville wrote "The Paradise of Bachelors and the Tartarus of Maids," he had no trouble finding an all-female Hell in New England but he had to go to the London Inns of Court to find a sufficiently paradisiacal all-male club. According to Stow Persons, the first major club for writers, intellectuals, and professionals was the Boston Saturday Club, organized in 1855. One of the groups inspired by the Saturday Club was the conversation circle known as The Club, which dated from 1868 and numbered among its members William and Henry James, Henry Adams, Oliver Wendell Holmes, Jr., John Fiske, Thomas Sergeant Perry, and Howells. In New York the most formidable group was the Century Club, which was designed to further "the cultivation of a taste for letters and the arts and social enjoyment."9 Discussions at this club led to the establishment of the National Academy of Design, the Metropolitan Museum of Art, and the American Museum of Natural History. These clubs had a great influence on the cultural life of their cities. But the effort to establish a national academy patterned after the French Academy failed. And even more important, the conversation clubs had nothing to do with the nuts and bolts of city politics.

In the 1730s Benjamin Franklin and other craftsmen, businessmen, and writers established a secret lodge-like club in Philadelphia, devoted to conversation and self and civic improvement. According to Franklin's autobiography, this club had an enormous influence on public life. But in the last half of the nineteenth century, the elite conversation clubs were on the periphery of city politics and completely outside of national affairs. Where, wondered the liberal reformers, was the club that was running things? The answer they came up with—the saloon-clique—probably reflects their own alienation, or aloofness, at least as much as it reflects the actual state of affairs. Thus, in *Miss Ravenel's Conversion from Secession to Loyalty*, the saloon-clique is a sort of *deus ex machina* that serves to explain how politics get interjected into the military. Instead of promoting Carter, the professional soldier, the War Office gives way to civilian pressure and promotes Gazaway, a cowardly New York politician who makes his saloon his base of operations. The outstanding example of a novel reflecting the "best men's" paranoid sense of being out of the club is John Hay's anti-labor novel *The Bread-Winners*. Its hero is a model patrician; its villains are criminals who seize on labor agitation as an avenue to plunder. The source of the trouble is a radical working-man's club called The Bread-Winners. John Hay was a friend of Henry James; he later became Secretary of State when another reform-oriented patrician, Theodore Roosevelt, became President. Hay, DeForest, Godkin, Henry Adams, and other best men were not, in fact, liberals or conservatives but patricians opposed to both the masses and the new plutocrats. To espouse the modernist denigration of "mass culture," I submit, is to espouse a version of their patrician ideology.10

One of the most interesting aspects of the isolation of the best men is the fact that they were often seen as lacking virility. "Party spokesmen," according to Blodgett, "dismissed them as 'political hermaphrodites,' 'eunuchs,' 'man-milliners,' and 'miss-Nancys.'"[11] He attributes this name-calling to their exclusion from the two political parties and the anti-intellectualism that Richard Hofstadter has explored. But there is another reason why the gentlemen reformers were ridiculed as sissies: some of them *were* sissies. Anti-intellectualism exists, of course, but so does a matching condition that shows up all too often in the nineteenth century—anti-physicalism. This anti-physicalism was extremely common in New England in the mid-nineteenth century. In "The Custom-House," Hawthorne was both fascinated and repelled by the old Inspector, a complacent old codger who was "so earthy and sensuous"[12] that it seemed impossible he could have a soul. In "The Artist of the Beautiful" the basic contrast was between a gross man and a delicate man, and it is more than clear which side Hawthorne was on. Both *The Scarlet Letter* and *The Blithedale Romance* reveal an enmity between an active go-getter (Chillingworth, Hollingsworth) and an excessively refined and passive man (Rev. Dimmesdale, Miles Coverdale). One of the central concerns of *The Scarlet Letter* is the double life of the refined man, secretly much more gross than he dares admit. One main reason why Hawthorne became the American writer generally agreed to be our one undoubted classic in the three decades after his death in 1864 is that he gave full expression to the unhappy position—the hypocrisy, self-doubt, or marginality—of the cultivated man. To some extent, the man who was so often noted for being shy, withdrawn, and weird made it respectable to be a sissy.

One of the basic facts about highbrow American culture at mid-century is that it was remarkably effete. A writer who chose not to give his name complained about this in 1856:

France, England, Germany, Sweden, but most of all our own country, has furnished forth an army of women in the walks of literature.... Her literature has been more sensuous than intellectual. More than this, we are confident that the magnetism produced by her out-given heart-throbs has warmed into vitality a vast number of womanly men who, without manly force, or manly vigor of intellect, have given way to unmanly mawkishness and morbid complainings, Laura Matilda pretti-nesses and sentimentalisms, quite to the shame of manhood.... Our literature is growing rather fine than forceful, more elegant than original. . . . We are tired of the whole school of mosaic workers like Longfellow, and imitators like Bayard Taylor, and [George William] Curtis, and [Richard Henry] Stoddard.[13]

Howells and James were much more forceful and cogent than these earlier male writers. Yet there is an undeniable similarity between the two groups, and this similarity is uncomfortably apparent in Howells' defense of American realists:

It is the difference of the American novelist's ideals from those of the English novelist that gives him his advantage, and seems to promise him the future. The love of the passionate and the heroic, as the Englishman has it, is such a crude and unwholesome thing, so deaf and blind to all the most delicate and important facts of art and life, so insensible to the subtle values in either. . . . There can be little question that many refinements of thought and spirit which every American is sensible of in the fiction of this continent, are necessarily lost upon our good kin beyond seas.[14]

Basil Ransom's diatribe in *The Bostonians*, which takes place in the 1870s, thus applies not only to James and Howells, and their age, but to a large segment of American culture extending over at least two generations: "The whole generation is womanised; the masculine tone is passing out of the world; it's a feminine, a nervous, hysterical, chattering, canting age, an age of hollow phrases and false delicacy and exaggerated solicitudes and coddled sensibilities."[15]

There were, of course, many levels in the effeminate culture Ransom assailed. But the upper tiers, into which James and Howells successfully made their way in the late 1860s and early 70s, were perhaps the most effeminate of all. In the eyes of Thomas Wentworth Higginson, a former abolitionist and now an early supporter of female suffrage, this cultivated effeminacy represented a real danger. "No," he wrote in 1870, "it does not seem to me that the obstacle to a new birth of literature and art in America lies in the Puritan tradition, but rather in the timid and faithless spirit that lurks in the circles of culture."[16]

A timid spirit lurks everywhere in the early writing of James and Howells. James's "Travelling Companions," which appeared in the *Atlantic* the same year as Higginson's denunciation, is a case in point.

In the opening sentence James's first-person narrator establishes his refinement by denying the truth Mark Twain had announced the year before in *Innocents Abroad*—the truth that Leonardo's Last Supper was irreparably damaged. Clearly distrusting the evidence of his eyes and, like Curtis, Mitchell, and many others, preferring the "ideal" to the actual, James's man writes: "The most strictly impressive picture of Italy is incontestably the Last Supper of Leonardo at Milan. . . . The mind finds a rare delight in filling each of its vacant spaces, effacing its rank defilement, and repairing, as far as possible, its sad disorder." This glib denial that the painting has been practically destroyed reveals the narrator's unsubstantiality, which becomes more and more salient as the story unravels. When he sees a Crucifixion by Tintoretto, he is moved only by the artistry. His traveling companion, Charlotte Evans, more solid than this frothy aesthete, cares only for the subject. Sober, strong, and independent, Charlotte does not get upset when she and the narrator must spend the night in Padua. She weeps over paintings, only smiles at the narrator's unconvincing protestations of love. She is said to be "an example of woman active, not of woman passive." The resolution of this interesting story, in which the male lead is too gauzy to get the attention of the female lead, seems as juvenile as *Watch and Ward*, which was written about the same time. Charlotte's father dies; she goes to pieces and exhibits a "gentle weakness and dependence;"[17] simultaneously, the narrator begins to feel a genuine love for her. Thus, Charlotte becomes a true woman by collapsing; the narrator becomes a man by developing an honest feeling for a weak woman. So ends the predicament of a grown man who suspects he is a mouse. James never collected the story.

Howells' *Suburban Sketches* often displays the same airiness as "Travelling Companions." The narrator of these sketches, whether identified as the Contributor, the "aesthetic observer," or Frank, often represents the same kind of delicate sensibility evident in James's story. In "A Day's Pleasure" this person compulsively embroiders every plain circumstance. When practical Aunt Melissa decides not to go to the beach after all because it's too late and "it wouldn't be good for the child," Frank promptly spouts:

> I always find that, after working up to an object with great effort, it's surpassingly sweet to leave it unaccomplished at last. Then it remains

forever in the region of the ideal, amongst the songs that never were sung, the pictures that never were painted. . . .[18]

Ironic or not, there is something pretty fishy about this happy babbler who claims to enjoy all interrupted pleasures. Fortunately, Howells managed to get a handle on the nervous mentality that preens itself on being egoless and aesthetic. Fifteen years later he would have an older, wiser middle-aged man reflect: "If he had been a younger man he would have anxiously considered this [visiting Mrs. Bowen any day of the week] indulgence and denied himself, but after forty a man denies himself no reasonable and harmless indulgence."[19] The year when Howells himself stopped being this kind of man was perhaps 1879, when he wrote *The Lady of the Aroostook*. Like James's "Travelling Companions," this story tells how a plain, serious girl makes a man out of a vaporing aesthete. Howells' novel characterizes the young man, Stanihope, with a verve and richly detailed inventiveness that James could not begin to match in his own satirical portrait of a Boston aesthete, Louis Leverett in "A Bundle of Letters." At one point, when Staniford is spinning one of his fancies for his friend Dunham, he abruptly finds he has nothing more to say and wobbles like crazy: "Suggest some new topic, Dunham; talk of something else, for heaven's sake!"[20] This neatly catches the glib, slightly hysterical loquacity that had run wild in Howells' own voice a few years earlier.

One of the most important truths about Howells is that his success in getting control of his own effeminacy enabled him to make several penetrating studies of the effeminate aspect of genteel masculine culture. One of the finest of these studies is the novella *A Fearful Responsibility* (1881), which explores the anxieties of a very unmanly college professor who goes to Venice when the Civil War breaks out. Owen Elmore (a Welsh name like Howells') is mortified that everyone takes for granted his unfitness for war, but also relieved at being able to escape it. Unhappily, his troubles follow him. In Venice he and his wife reluctantly assume responsibility for an American girl, Lily, who, without being properly introduced, has struck up an acquaintance with a tall, spectacularly handsome Austrian officer—a man who represents the profession Elmore has fled. When the officer proposes and the girl, eager to accept, asks the Elmores what she should do, the professor coerces her into rejecting the offer. Lily gets two other proposals from much less attractive men—a chauvinistic Englishman, a slight and boyish Dane—but she has no interest in these men. She appears to undergo a striking loss of vitality. Then she leaves, and a decade later Elmore hears that she has married a painter in Omaha. At the end he is left anxiously wondering whether, in trying to live up to the fearful responsibility of looking out for the girl in Europe, he did the right thing in thwarting Lily's romance.

A Fearful Responsibility deals with the same things as *Daisy Miller*—a chilling masculine failure, a possible aborting of love. Lily is of course no match for James's marvellous portrait of Daisy. But Winterbourne is no match for Elmore. Howells' novella is a subtle fable about masculinity denied: a sickly coward elbows aside a bold warrior; the men and women dwindle away in scruples, worries, and doubts; a young virgin languishes for ten years, or at least worries about whether she should be languishing. But the story is more than a fable because of the realistic exploration of the unsatisfactory accommodation between the professor and his wife. Elmore is notably pompous and boring, perhaps in an attempt to salvage a measure of dignity. But his "dreamy withdrawal" from life renders him vacant and fatally imperceptive: when a suitor brings Lily a turtle and flowers, Elmore supposes that the gifts are for himself. His wife taunts him for his learned ignorance. At times she intimidates him with an explosive scorn. Her loving ways—kissing him on top of his head—are of the kind that reduce him to a boy's stature. Yet, it is noteworthy that his wife refuses to gather up the reins in her own hands. She forces Elmore to assume responsibility for all the difficult decisions, and then she dumps on him afterwards:

> "Well, Owen," she said, "you've done it now."
> "Done what?" he demanded.
> "Oh, nothing, perhaps!" she answered, while she got on her things for the walk with unusual gayety; and, with the consciousness of unknown guilt depressing him, he followed the ladies upon their errand, subdued, distraught, but gradually forgetting his sin. . . .[21]

The professor is a timid and exceedingly stuffy man; his wife is a blocked and infantile woman; and there is nothing they know how to do together but pick and worry. In this novella Eros is so sick he is probably beyond recovery.

Howells' most masterful study of the unmanly man may be Don Ippolito, the Venetian priest in *A Foregone Conclusion* (1875). Henry James considered this strange character, a non-believing mechanically-gifted Venetian priest who falls in love with an American girl, to be Howells' finest masculine figure to date.[22] Don Ippolito looks at first like a person who should have been an inventor. When he approaches Ferris, the American consul, it is to present his latest contrivance—a cannon with a hidden charge that causes the weapon to blow up when the enemy captures and tries to use it. Like many actual men who nurse an idea of a new invention, however, Don Ippolito is more of a dreamer than an inventor. Ferris points out the obvious disadvantage of the self-exploding cannon—the heat of firing will detonate the hidden charge for friendly and enemy forces alike. The priest's apartment is full of models of his other inventions— a gadget for taking one's own photograph, collapsible furniture, a movable bridge, a perpetual motion machine. All these inventions seem to have "some fatal defect: they were aspirations toward the impossible, or realizations of the trivial and superfluous" (p. 51). The priest even has a piano and a melodeon placed at right angles to each other so that he can play them simultaneously, one hand on each. As this bizarre skill suggests, Don Ippolito uses his mechanical skill for grotesquely impractical purposes. He is a realist's version of Hawthorne's artist of the beautiful.

A Foregone Conclusion is among other things a penetrating study of male impracticality. Don Ippolito's ingenuity has never found a proper outlet because he was consigned as a boy to a priesthood that finds its most perfect expression in the Corpus Christi procession—a gaudy and hierarchical masquerade. Don Ippolito is utterly thwarted by the byzantine hierarchy that defines his place in the world. It doesn't help matters that he has lost his faith. But the most fatal aspect of his membership in the priesthood is that it has prevented him from testing his fantasies and thus encountering reality. Locked up in an airless church, the tragic man dreams of America as a "new world of freedom and justice" (p. 211), yet his old acceptance of "life-long defeat" (p. 209) shows that he lacks precisely the willingness to take a risk that is the indispensable prerequisite for democratic life. Life in a stultifying hierarchy has both aroused the desire for freedom and prevented the priest from acquiring the independent manhood American life requires. Like Owen Elmore the college professor, Don Ippolito the priest suffers from an incurable malaise because he has not succeeded in becoming a man.

In fact, there are dozens of passages in *A Foregone Conclusion* that make Don Ippolito look positively feminine. At one point he paces up and down "with his sliding step, like some tall, gaunt, unhappy girl" (p. 192). Another time he sits "in the womanish attitude priests get from their drapery" (p. 133). Ferris says that a priest is "more helpless than a woman, even" (p. 157). When Don Ippolito cries, Mrs. Vervain says:

> "But, shedding tears, now: it's dreadful in a man, isn't it? I wish Don Ippolito wouldn't do that. It makes one creep. I can't feel that it's manly; can you?"

Don Ippolito himself admits in effect to not being a man. Florida Vervain says to him:

> "But surely you can somehow help yourself. Are men, that seem so strong and able, just as powerless as women, after all, when it comes to real trouble? Is a man"—
>
> "I cannot answer. I am only a priest," said Don Ippolito coldly, letting his eyes drop to the gown that fell about him like a woman's skirt. (p. 146)

The tragic story Howells told in *A Foregone Conclusion* was the foregone defeat such a man would suffer if he were suddenly aroused to take the long-postponed risk and try to prove himself a man at last. Florida Vervain, the idealistic American girl who sees how unhappy Don Ippolito is, cannot begin to sense the constraints that encompass him. Thus, she ardently supports him as he begins to consider renouncing the priesthood. She has "a heavenly scorn of everything but the end to be achieved" and inspires him to aim for "the pure ideal" (p. 174). The priest unfortunately has no idea how ignorant she is when (like Hester Prynne to Arthur Dimmesdale in the forest) she says, "Leave Venice! There are other places. Think how inventors succeed in America" (p. 175). Worse, mistaking her sympathy and idealism for personal interest, Don Ippolito imagines that she returns the love he feels for her. Emboldened, he makes plans to leave the priesthood, marry Florida, support himself with his inventions in the United States. But his pathetic dreams collapse when he tells Florida how much he loves her and asks her to marry him, and she recoils in disgust—"*You? A priest!*" (p. 212). Even worse, perhaps, she mothers him: "She flung her arms about his neck, and pulled his head down upon her heart, and held it tight there, weeping and moaning over him as over some hapless, harmless thing that she had unpurposely bruised or killed" (p. 215). Thus, the priest's last-ditch attempt to break out of prison only confirms the fact that he is still a helpless baby.

Don Ippolito is one of the strangest romantic leads in an American novel. But his oddity is not gratuitous. If, like Melville's or Haw-thorne's many isolated men, he is "the albino of his species" (p. 82), he is disfigured in a way that mesmerizes the attention of more normal men. Once, Don Ippolito tells Ferris and the Vervains about one of his adventures when he was a young priest. For one evening, he and a friend took off their clerical attire and wore "citizen's" clothes. "For a whole night," he says,

> "we walked about the streets in that dress, meeting the students, as they strolled singing through the moonlight; we went to the theatre and to the caffè,—we smoked cigars, all the time laughing and trembling to think of the tonsure under our hats. But in the morning we had to put on the stockings and the talare and the nicchio again."

After he finishes this story, "every one was silent as if something shocking had been said." The person who is shocked most of all is Ferris, who is reminded "of some girl's adventure in men's clothes." In fact Ferris becomes very nervous: "He was in terror lest Mrs. Vervain should be going to say it was like that; she was going to say something; he made haste to forestall her, and turn the talk on other things" (p. 79).

Why would this story make Ferris so nervous? For precisely the same reason that Henry James found the whole character of Don Ippolito "a real creation,—a most vivid, complete, and appealing one." James, like Ferris, was stirred by the exhibition of a man who was not quite a man and painfully conscious of his shortcoming. James wrote:

> The poor caged youth, straining to the end of his chain, pacing round his narrow circle, gazing at the unattainable outer world, bruising himself

in the effort to reach it and falling back to hide himself and die unpitied,—is a figure which haunts the imagination and claims a permanent place in one's melancholy memories.[23]

James's image of the cage was entirely his own, as was the juvenilizing of the priest in the word "youth." Don Ippolito's name derived from Hippolytus,[24] the young man who spurned Phaedra's love and was killed for it. Still, Howells by no means presented the priest as a youth—though Edel's biography makes it clear that Henry James still felt like one when he wrote this review, at the age of thirty-one. The reason Don Ippolito haunted James's imagination was that James saw himself in the priest. In view of this, it is fascinating to observe that when James alluded to the priest eleven years later, he described him as "a kind of maidenly figure."[25]

With the exception of Don Ippolito, priests or Protestant clergymen did not appeal to James's imagination. Howells, however, invented a score or so of them, and in almost every case he presented them as effeminate or timorous or remarkably idealistic refugees from the rough male world. In *The Quality of Mercy* (1892), for instance, a Catholic priest has "beautiful, innocent eyes like a girl's," and when he smiles, "the innocence of his face was more than girlish, it was childlike."[26] In *The Shadow of a Dream* (1890), James Nevil is pure, upright, and weak. Much weaker is Conrad Dryfoos in *A Hazard of New Fortunes* and Ben Halleck in *A Modern Instance*. Howells did invent some strong and forceful ministers, it is true—Peck in *Annie Kilburn*, Sewell in *Silas Lapham* and *The Minister's Charge*. But for the most part Howells' ministers have a noticeable weakness, and what is more, arrive at a sense of themselves and their calling after passing through a stronger man's shadow. It is in a sense Bartley Hubbard that sends Ben Halleck into the ministry. Similarly, Conrad Dryfoos wants to be a minister because he has such a dictatorial old goat of a father. And in *The Landlord at Lion's Head*, the little boy whom Jeff Durgin terrorizes with his dog grows up, fittingly, with a strong calling to be an Episcopalian clergyman. The ministry, in Howells, looks very much like an idealistic alternative for young men scared by the brutal initiation rituals of American masculinity.

There is a profound historical truth in Howells' treatment of effeminate or weak clergymen. As Ann Douglas has shown, the clergy, the old intellectual elite, underwent a distinct feminization in the first half of the nineteenth century:

> Cut off at every point from his masculine heritage, whether economic, political, or intellectual, the liberal minister was pushed into a position increasingly resembling the evolving feminine one. Who else was barred with him from the larger world of masculine concerns, who else was confined with him to a claustrophobic private world of over-responsive sensibility, who else but the American lady? . . . . Harriet Martineau reported that the commercial classes treated the clergy disdainfully as powerless, ill-informed "people halfway between men and women."[27]

In retrospect it is clear that the clergy were not the only male professionals who were feminized. Professors, poets, and romancers also suffered, or chose, the same kind of peripheralization. Howells observed and recorded this process from the 1850s on. His first friend, "the most original spirit" he ever knew, shared Howells' interest in reading Cervantes and learning foreign languages. "The usual thing," wrote Howells in old age, would have been for this boy "to read law and crowd forward in political life, but my friend despised this common ideal." It was a sign of the new dispensation in the feminine fifties that this boy wanted to become a professor. Significantly, Howells stressed his femininity: "I can see my friend's strange face now, very regular, very fine, and smooth as a girl's."[28] Howells was himself caught up in the same pervasive historical changes as this boy. But as I have argued from many different angles, Howells to some extent succeeded in reaching, and then communicating, an objective understanding of contemporary history. His realism enabled him to resist, and give an artistic representation of, the processes that exiled Henry James, excluded Henry Adams from the seats of power, and embittered E. L. Godkin. While these gentlemen all decided in one way or another that the best men had been defeated by democratic vulgarity and mediocrity, Howells saw the deeper truth: an aristocratic fastidiousness that refused to question itself was every bit as responsible for the tone of public life as the mushrooming plutocracy. The "best men," as Howells' fiction showed again and again, had a fatal weakness.

Part IV

THE GENTLEMAN OF SHALOTT:
HENRY JAMES AND
AMERICAN MASCULINITY

CHAPTER TWENTY-TWO

The Plot with a Secret

Henry James's best fiction deals with solitary people trying to find out about something that is hidden. Winterbourne wants to know if Daisy Miller is innocent or not. The editor of "The Aspern Papers" searches for the documentary evidence of an old love affair. The narrator of "The Figure in the Carpet" develops an obsessive interest in the hidden pattern of a great novelist's work. John Marcher wastes a lifetime wondering what the beast in the jungle will prove to be. Spencer Brydon pursues his "alter ego," the man he would have become if he had remained in America. The short stories and novellas that are felt to be James's best often tell of an unmarried person, a man, who looks for secret knowledge with idle—or passionately busy—curiosity.

Winding through James's fictional landscape is a strange blank wall whose lack of feature somehow indicates an absorbing secret on the other side. In "The Ghostly Rental," the longer the narrator looks at the outside of a deserted colonial house, "the intenser seemed the secret that it held."[1] In *The American* the narrator speaks of "those gray and silent streets of the Faubourg St. Germain, whose houses present to the outer world a face as impassive and as suggestive of the concentration of privacy within as the blank walls of Eastern seraglios."[2] The narrator of "A Passionate Pilgrim" sees the college walls at Oxford in the same curious way: "The plain Gothic of the long street-fronts of the colleges—blessed seraglios of culture and leisure—irritate the fancy like the blank harem-walls of Eastern towns" (*Tales*, 2:290). It may not be farfetched for James to associate an aristocratic section of the Left Bank with Eastern harems, but why would the all-male Oxford colleges remind him of them?

The tantalizing blank wall is not an accidental image in the fiction of a man who writes about single men looking for a secret. Many of James's novels have the kind of plot that represents the way things would probably happen in a world of deceptive facades—the plot based on a secret. This plot, hackneyed in James's time and not quite obsolete in ours, operates in a very conventional way in his earlier novels, particularly the three international novels at the beginning of the New York edition. Thus, the denouement of *Roderick Hudson* (1876) begins at the point where Christina Light discovers that she is Giacosa's illegitimate daughter. This is the formal secret of the novel, and it leads Christina to marry Casamassima and jilt Roderick Hudson, who then becomes helpless and apathetic. In *The American* Christopher Newman finds out from Valentin that the Bellegardes have a dark family secret; and from Mrs. Bread he learns the full story of the late marquis' murder. Claire de Cintré senses this melodramatic family skeleton and flees to a convent. But the practical self-made American must deal with the secret in other ways, as the final chapters show. In *The Portrait of a Lady* it is a woman who has a secret to learn—the secret of Pansy's birth, told by Osmond's sister. With this revelation, Isabel realizes precisely how she has been betrayed by those she trusted, and manipulated in the very choices she thought were freely made. In these three novels the secret is a fact about the past, a dark fact telling of crime or illicit sexuality in respectable people. In each case those who know the secret are Europeans or expatriate Americans grouped in families, sexual liaisons, or other alliances. Those who don't know the secret are single Americans—Roderick Hudson, Christopher Newman, Isabel Archer.

Perhaps the secret-plot seems formulaic and subliterary, the stock-in-trade of cheap romance, melodrama, or detective fiction. But James, the first great modernist in English, not only used the secret-plot in his best work, early and late, but with a continuing refinement. In his first two international novels the formal secret has the slightly factitious quality of an obligatory convention. But in the three international novels that conclude the New York Edition, the secret-plot is used with a sincerity and rigor found in no other nineteenth-century novelist after Jane Austen.

In *The Ambassadors* the formal secret is the fact that Chad is having an ordinary affair with Madame de Vionnet. Strether is anxious to know the full truth but afraid to find out. He struggles to sort out the truth from the lies (Little Bilham's "virtuous attachment") and his own mistakes. He deals with a number of distressing revelations along the way, as when Chad declares that his "relations" with Mme. de Vionnet are "awfully good." Strether's drive to grasp the nature of these "relations" comes to a temporary halt in Book Sixth when he holds to the theory that they must be platonic: he now understands, he insists, "what a relation with such a woman—what such a high fine friendship—may be. It can't be vulgar or coarse."[3] But when Strether sees the couple floating down a river in Book Eleventh, he discovers that "high fine" things can also be "vulgar or coarse" and tries to face up to this truth. In *The Wings of the Dove* the formal secret, kept from the American, Milly Theale, is Kate Croy and Merton Densher's clandestine engagement, and also the grim conspiracy that requires Densher to make up to Milly in order to get a grip on her wealth. Milly is not the only innocent figure in the book. Densher, who lacks a "talent for life," is extremely slow to grasp why Kate keeps urging him to see Milly. Densher, with five of the novel's ten "books" from his point of view, and Milly, with three, are the two innocent characters, and what they mainly do is to acquire dreadful secret knowledge. In *The Golden Bowl* the formal secret is again a sexual liaison, this time between Charlotte Stant and Prince Amerigo. The first half of the novel shows how the liaison develops, and the second half, almost entirely from Maggie's point of view, shows how the American, once again, slowly uncovers the truth and then acts to recover her husband. Book Fourth, the longest of the novel's six "books," painstakingly traces Maggie's growth in awareness. She begins by imaginatively walking around a pagoda concealing Charlotte and the Prince, and ends by realizing "the horror of the thing hideously *behind*, behind so much trusted, so much pretended, nobleness, cleverness, tenderness."[4]

The secret-plot is part and parcel of the generative core of James's fiction, along with the concealment imagery, a narrative texture based on the activity of finding something out, and an archetypal pattern of life for James's many innocents who taste the bitter fruit of the tree of knowledge. The secret-plot expresses the inner difference James saw between Europe and America, and it leads to his obsession with limited point of view: his greatest interest was the process of vision, revision, and discovery in an inexperienced American or in some other kind of innocent. The shared "European" knowledge the innocent discovers almost always turns out to be about sex—sex seen as something low, furtive, and manipulative. Frequently, the innocent discovers the harsh truth about human bestiality only through the most refined sort of ratiocination, and he then remains uncontaminated by it. Christopher Newman, Isabel Archer, and Milly Theale all refuse to take vengeance. In the end, after being forced to understand the coarse, cruel world, they withdraw. Except for Maggie, who manages to repossess her husband without seeming to act in a selfish way, they all renounce the world and the right to be happy in it, the right to live for themselves.

In James's hands, the secret-plot turned into an artifice for dramatizing the relationship between the world and a certain sort of person, the Jamesian hero, whose distinguishing characteristic is that he remains a stranger to all human groups. He has never been initiated—he is a simple "American" baffled by "European" society. Sometimes he is curious, imagining seraglios behind the exclusive facades he cannot penetrate; at other times he attempts to repress the dark knowledge he can't help suspecting. In either case, when he finally learns the truth, his decision to renounce represents nothing less than an elemental withdrawal from the group he now sees he cannot live with, a dignified but final act of *escape*.

The fact that he renounces in the name of a high fine consistency, or because of a spoken pledge or a selfless standard that calls itself moral, has blinded too many readers to the nature of the act. It cannot be forgotten that the fictional societies in which James exiles his ultramoral heroes are so structured that their members must be fierce, ambitious, mercenary, exploitative, and heartless. Groups of men and women, in James, all follow the same basic rule—everyone uses, traps, feeds on everyone else in an ulterior way.[5] The finely conscious Jamesian hero is a spectator at a slave market. But even though he is supposed to be a good observer, he doesn't understand that it is a slave market until he learns that he himself has been bought and sold. His act of renunciation is an act of slave morality. Retreating to the privacy of his fine vibrations, the ultimate form of the private life defended so vigorously by James, he lives more exclusively than ever through his eyes, his imagination, his fine consciousness; and the fact that he does so tells us something about James and his fiction that cannot be ignored: the act of renunciatory escape which his novels and stories reenact is the characteristically autistic act of someone who must accept an ultimate defeat. Renunciatory escape is the James daydream, both painful and consoling, so deeply cherished he almost never put it to the test by considering it objectively.

James was so detached, so uninitiated, so alone, as he once admitted to Morton Fullerton,[6] that all human associations remained secret societies from his point of view. He never learned the things boys took for granted, never caught on to the language men actually spoke. Early in life he failed to earn masculinity in the ways that American boys and men had to earn it. He grew up a genderless man with a dark suspicion that all sexual roles and functions are sinister. His own social function was to write a body of fiction about sensitive, genderless minds, usually devoid of desire, who discover the secret shameful facts of life about a species essentially alien. Even those novels by James that do not tell the international story—*The Princess Casamassima, The Tragic Muse, The Spoils of Poynton, What Maisie Knew, The Awkward Age,* and the two unfinished novels, *The Sense of the Past* and *The Ivory Tower*—tell of a fine soul's aborted initiation into a coarse group.[7]

I will now argue that James's aborted masculine initiation, however useful in the ways I discussed in part 1, was finally a type of deformity, and that this deformity impaired his writing. The genre in which James mainly wrote, the novel—a genre he helped change once for all—had generally dealt with courtship, marriage, and the complex life of society. The traditional requirement for novelists had been a knowledge of men (and women) and manners; after James the traditional requirement has frequently appeared to be a thorough alienation from society,[8] James made the novel available for the interests and strategies of modernism mainly because he knew so little.

CHAPTER TWENTY-THREE

The Boy Who Could Not Become a Man

As a kid, Henry James never joined a gang of bad boys. Neither is there one recorded incident from his boyhood in which he did something bad, something he was later ashamed of. The picture one gets of him from his late memoirs, *A Small Boy and Others,* is completely different from his own picture of American boys and girls at large. Of the latter, James wrote: "It is sometimes affirmed by the observant foreigner . . . that American children are without a certain charm usually possessed by the youngsters of the Old World. The little girls are apt to be pert and shrill, the little boys to be aggressive and knowing."[1] Among James's fictional children, there is only one— Daisy Miller's obnoxious kid brother—who is aggressive and knowing. All the rest—Pansy Osmond, Dolcino, Morgan Moreen, Flora and Miles—seem, at least on the surface, incredibly cultivated. Like James himself, they are generally solitary, reasonable, and good.

James's one novel about childhood, *What Maisie Knew,* is not about "a rude little boy"[2] but a fantastically sensitive girl. James couldn't make the protagonist of this book a boy precisely because "boys are never so 'present'" (p. 143). Maisie is certainly "present," as she lives wholly among adults, never plays with other children, and takes no interest in the things children do together. When she hears "Mrs. Wix's original account of Sir Claude's affection," it all seems "as empty now as the chorus in a children's game."[3] *Any* children's game would probably seem empty to James's fictional children, who all have a denatured, rococo quality.[4] It is all too clear that not one of them has ever been able to get away from the rigid and killing adult order, let alone down to the old swimming hole. Two of the boys, Miles and Morgan, are so precocious they die of early coronaries. Daisy Miller's brother is prematurely wizened. Few of these little people seem to have the distinctively childish resources that are necessary to survive adult pressure. Howells grew up in the separate, savage world he called a boy's town. James's children haven't heard of this place.

There is, on the face of it, no reason to assume that James was at all like any of his fictional children. Yet the two autobiographical volumes he lived to complete—A Small Boy and Others and Notes of a Son and Brother—tell of a child rather similar to Maisie Farange. In these volumes James attempted to trace "the personal history . . . of an imagination,"5 to explain why he became a novelist. James's leading idea is that he developed an active imagination, a self-satisfying play of mind, by becoming an observer of life instead of a participant. As a small boy, he enjoyed nothing more than "the so far from showy practice of wondering and dawdling and gaping."6 Although he was at liberty to go where he wanted in New York, "the only form of riot or level ever known" to him was "that of the visiting mind" (Small Boy, p. 25). Practically everything that he remembered seemed to be a "scene," a spectacle from which he derived a thrill, a lesson, an insight, a speculation. "Observing" was how James solved the problem of how to live in a society where a boy could not be respected except by fighting. He escaped danger by becoming a visiting mind.

Many of James's critics seem to accept the idea that "seeing," in Ora Segal's words, "could be an authentic rather than merely a vicarious form of 'being'—a form more intense and more valuable than any other."7 I doubt that it is even possible to live wholly as an observer, let alone desirable to do so, and I will argue the matter in the following chapter. The point to be made here is that James did not voluntarily limit himself to "seeing." There was a time when he wanted to join the gang very badly, but was not allowed to. At the school he attended in New York when he was ten years old, he was full of admiration for the boys who were "the biggest, the fairest, the most worthy of freedom" (Small Boy, p. 227; italics mine). He once asked one of these "heroes" to show him how to do a trick, but the boy only taunted him for asking. James sat next to another boy, named Simpson, who "reeked, to my sense, with strange accomplishment— no single show of which but was accompanied in him by a smart protrusion of the lower lip, a crude complacency of power, that almost crushed me to sadness" (Small Boy, pp. 224–225). This protruded lower lip was the familiar badge (at least in the United States) of the small-time male tyrant and pack leader. Only by belonging to his pack was it possible for a boy to acquire knowledge and power. If James was "crushed," it was because he wasn't allowed, or able, to join. He remained uninitiated and lived with a

> dazzled, humiliated sense, through those years, of the common, the baffling, mastery, all round me, of a hundred handy arts and devices. Everyone did things and had things—everyone knew how, even when it was a question of the small animals, the dormice and grasshoppers, or the hoards of food and stationery, that they kept in their desks, just as they kept in their heads such secrets for how to do sums—those secrets that I must even then have foreseen I should even so late in life as this have failed to discover. (*Small Boy*, p. 223)

James could not learn the secret tricks for doing things. He was particularly mystified by the "ledgers, daybooks, double-entry, tall pages of figures, interspaces streaked with oblique ruled lines that weirdly 'balanced,' whatever that might mean" (*Small Boy*, p. 223). The mysteries of boyhood led directly to the mysteries of business.

One of the fundamental influences on Henry James as a boy was his parents' refusal to let him be like other American boys. His father was determined that his sons would be different:

> I have grown so discouraged about the education of my children here, and dread so those inevitable habits of extravagance and insubordination which appear to be characteristic of American youth, that I have come to the conclusion to retrace my steps to Europe, and keep them there a few years longer. My wife is completely of the same mind.[8]

Isn't this rather chilling, the father's determination that his boys grow up to live *exceptionally* within bounds and more tamely (the opposite of extravagantly and insubordinately) than other boys? And isn't it ominous that Henry James alone of the four boys was the good one, the "angel," of the family? It appears that one of the reasons Henry couldn't learn the secret arts all the other boys at school knew was that his parents (like Pansy's father and Dolcino's mother) leaned on him very hard. Even more important, young Henry *did not like* this treatment. In old age James dramatized his arrival in the Old World as an entering into the Promised Land. But there were times, in his teens, when, like Randolph Miller, he wanted to go home. At the age of seventeen he wrote from Bonn to his best friend Thomas Sergeant Perry: "I think that if we are to live in America it is about time we boys should take up our abode there; the more I see of this estrangement of American youngsters from the land of their birth, the less I believe in it."9 There is a note of suppressed desperation in this well-chiseled opinion. Henry knew that he was isolated at the time of life when it is so important to have friends. Later, he used six exclamation points to announce his family's impending return.

But wasn't there the James gang? Since his family enjoyed such a richly affectionate life together, wouldn't membership in that warm and brilliant group constitute a sufficient society for Henry? If I am not mistaken, Leon Edel has shown that the answer to this question must be no. Henry James, Sr., was visionary, erratic, and ineffective, and lacked a professional or public role in a country that defined men by the way they earned a living away from home. Edel has properly emphasized that James was embarrassed by his father's failure to achieve some kind of public identity. Even as an old man, he considered his father's frequent moves between Europe and America so anomalous that he tried to cover up a fifteen-month residence in Newport.10 Seeing his father as weak and unsettled, James takes his place among many American writers who, as Quentin Anderson has noted, "had either been let down by their fathers or acted as if they had."11 Not unexpectedly, James became a mama's boy—the type scorned most of all by American boys. Even when Henry was almost thirty years old, he still wrote back to Mary James to justify his travel expenses in Europe. His warm relationship with his mother was fine—but it didn't help him get on in the world of men.

The power vacuum left by the father was partly filled by the older brother, who, in Henry's word, "bullied" him (Letters, 2:316). William James was the worst older brother imaginable, so energetic and universally competent that Henry gave up ever trying to equal him. Henry felt that he himself had "an understanding indisputably weak and shy" (Notes, p. 4). He "feared and abhorred mathematics" (Notes, p. 3). But William had a positive vocation "for Science, physical Science, strenuous Science" (Notes, p. 122)—as if science, which is only a Latin word for knowledge, as Jacob Bronowski has said, was some sort of competitive sport. William was also a much better artist than Henry, who gave up painting after seeing William's skillful drawing of a cousin's nude body. The older brother's robust ability sent Henry retreating back into himself. As William went on to become a medical doctor and psychologist and finally a pragmatic— and popular—philosopher, Henry perfected a very private art that made a virtue out of obstructed points of view and impractical renunciations.[12]

Edel has made it clear that Henry's relationship with his older brother was one of the most important influences on him. Several of James's novels, especially *Roderick Hudson,* would deal with the great interest a subdued man takes in a virile, energetic one. The clearest representation of this relationship is to be found in James's first novel, *Watch and Ward,* where Roger Lawrence stands for Henry and Hubert Lawrence for William. Between these two fictional characters there is

> a large measure of healthy boyish levity which kept them from lingering long on delicate ground; but they felt at times that they belonged, by temperament, to irreconcilable camps. . . . Roger was of a loving turn of mind, and it cost him many a sigh that a certain glassy hardness of soul on his cousin's part was forever blunting the edge of his affection.

Why would this point be made unless the men, nominally cousins, were very close to begin with? Hubert is "so terribly clever and trenchant" compared to Roger, who allows "him a large precedence in the things of the mind."[13] One way to sum up the relationship is to say that Roger wants to love clever Hubert more than clever Hubert will stand.

But William was not the only brother Henry loved and despaired of following. Wilky, the son born after Henry, may have been at least as important. Wilky hated reading and for a time got on in the world in a way that Henry envied. When Henry would be "wondering how" to manage something or other, Wilky "solved the question simply *ambulando*"—with a "sociable stroll" (*Notes,* p. 33). When the James brothers lived with a German tutor in Bonn in 1860, Henry never got acquainted with the German schoolboys. All he knew was that they were "inordinately gothic." He used this formula as a "relation, or a substitute for a relation, with them." Wilky, who somehow knew all the secret handshakes, "tumbled straight into their confidence all round" (*Notes,* p. 34).

During the Civil War James lived with his parents in Newport and then moved in with William at Cambridge; Wilky volunteered, along with the youngest brother, Bob. The first time Henry saw Wilky with his military company, he saw with a shock that the younger brother's "state of juniority" had changed to "supremacies" (*Notes,* p. 372). Somehow, Wilky's "sociability" had given him mastery of "such mysteries, such engines, such arts" (*Notes,* p. 372) that Henry, who could never "'do things,'" could only "hang about" (*Notes,* p. 373) in envy. The closest he came to war was by reading Wilky's fine letters written from the front. Here one sees the basic pattern: James's family life did not so much initiate him into a group as encourage him to live in the "constant hum of borrowed experience" (*Notes,* p. 413). But to do this was to fail to grow up.

The Civil War gave young men a supreme opportunity to validate their male prowess. Many of the volunteer units, as is apparent in Mark Twain's account of the Marion Rangers, were essentially outlaw gangs for big boys.[14] As Howells recalled in his memoirs, volunteers from the country strode with linked arms through Columbus, Ohio, pushing everyone off the pavement.[15] Howells fled to a consulate in Venice but felt like a coward.[16] James, residing in New England, lived in a more distressing limbo. He had nothing to do that counted for anything, and the boy who had "dawdled and gaped" through childhood now, in imagination, "hung about with privileged Wilky" (*Notes,* p. 394), who was transforming himself into a man. As Leon Edel and Daniel Aaron have shown, James's Civil War stories reflect a deep feeling of ineffectiveness and humiliation.[17] Late in life, as James recalled the soldiers killed in the Civil War, he visualized them as "blandly ignoring us, looking through us or straight over us at something they partake of together but that we mayn't pretend to know" (*Notes,* p. 246). Henry James hadn't been initiated, and the spirits of the slaughtered combatants wouldn't deign to notice him. There was something important, known to Wilky and the others, which he hadn't found out. And the image by which he conveys his sense of ignorance and insignificance is identical with the one at the end of "The Aspern Papers," where the narrator, an essentially inactive man who devotes his life to a dead but very active poet, stares up helplessly at the statue of Colleoni:

> I only found myself staring at the triumphant captain as if he had an
> oracle on his lips. . . . But he continued to look far over my head, at the
> red immersion of another day—he had seen so many go down into the
> lagoon through the centuries—and if he were thinking of battles and
> stratagems they were of a different quality from any I had to tell him
> of. He could not direct me what to do, gaze up at him as I might.
> (*Complete Tales*, 6:378)

Given the crucial place in the story of this tableau—the parasitical
man looking up at the tall warrior, who ignores him—it seems fitting
that one of James's early novels dealt with a passive man's devotion
to an active and energetic one, a painter imagined as the romantic
conqueror that Jeffrey Aspern himself was. Many critics have disa-
greed as to what or who *Roderick Hudson* is really about. Perhaps one
reason for this is a general reluctance to recognize the homosexual,
or at least homophilic, content of the book.[18] The basic passion in
this novel is not the painter's love for Christina Light, or Mary
Garland's love for Roderick, but Rowland's love for Roderick. Of
course there is no suggestion in the novel that this love is in any way
genital. An allusion in a book review to Emperor Hadrian and
Antinous makes it clear that James was not so naive on this score as
readers may be tempted to think.[19] But there is no doubt that
Rowland loves Roderick (as well as Mary Garland) and that this love
explains the patron's unshakable devotion to the painter.

In the 1860s James was still unwilling to give up the hope of
becoming a man like other men. Accordingly, if he couldn't go to
war, he could at least enter a more refined and ceremonious form
of combat—the law. He entered Harvard Law School in 1862. This
decision was not really so odd, for he wanted more "data in the
American kind." He needed "an initiation . . . into some given thing"
(*Notes*, p. 304). Perhaps, by studying law, he would be able to crack
the secret code everyone else knew. He saw that his fellow students
devoted themselves to "the joy of associated adventure" and "the
ardour of battle" (*Notes*, p. 359) as if they were an elite warrior caste.
But James could not join the playful struggle. He merely watched.
In the end the other students were all transformed into "a troop of
actors . . . on that further side of footlights to which I never went
round" (*Notes*, p. 327). James was still only an observer.

Yet he wanted to be a man, and the strength of this desire is evident in his heated denunciations of effeminate or weak or excessively conscientious heroes in women's novels. Thus, in 1868 he would call the hero of Rebecca Harding Davis's *Dallas Galbraith* "worse than a woman's man—a woman's boy." This character, James wrote:

> would never in the world have sacrificed himself at the outset to the reputation of Laddoun. . . . He would have clung to the letter proving his innocence with a most unheroic but most manly tenacity. . . . He conducts himself on his return among his people, like—like nothing in trousers. . . . Instead of hovering about his paternal home like a hysterical school-girl, moaning over his coarseness and inelegance, he would have walked straight into the midst of it, with a very plain statement of his position and his wishes.[20]

How unJamesian this sounds! How hard this youthful reviewer would have been on the delicate hero of *The Princess Casamassima!* Yet in the 1870s James would often ridicule effeminate heroes. He was ironic about a man's failure to assert himself in a novel by Helen Hunt Jackson: "In spite of his artistic temperament, he bears his cross with the meekness of a Catholic saint of legend."[21] And in reviewing another woman's novel, *Mirage,* James generalized about the effeminacy of the heroes of American novels:

> Very noteworthy is the partiality of American story-tellers for aesthetic heroes. The usual English novelist, desiring to provide a heroine with an interesting and inspiring suitor, picks out a brilliant young man of affairs—a rising young statesman or a prospective commander-in-chief, a man of action, in short, of some kind. The American narrator, on the other hand, is prone, less gloriously, to select an artist, with a "sensitive mouth."[22]

It appears that James had two flatly contradictory attitudes to the ideal of the aggressive American man, whom he generally figured as a businessman. On the one hand he regarded the businessman in a way the beginning reader of James rapidly senses: the businessman was a crude and hamhanded philistine. Again and again James complained of the fact that American men were interested in nothing but business: the minute they got up in the morning, they were "hurled straight . . . upon an office or a store."[23] Indeed, James's fundamental objection to the American "social order (so far as it *was* an order)" was that "its main ideal" was "a 'strict attention to business'" (*Notes,* p. 116). Deeply buried under this scorn, however, was a very different attitude—an intense fascination verging on worship. One is reminded of what happens in *Watch and Ward,* where, at the beginning, hard Hubert spurns gentle Roger, and at the end, Hubert is made to seem a very shallow and unworthy sort of person. James wanted to love that man, *be that man,* but he wasn't allowed to.

One of the best pieces of evidence that James secretly admired the businessman is the novel he wrote at about the same time as two of the reviews I quoted just above—*The American.* Christopher Newman is the most glorified portrait of a Gilded Age millionaire that I know of. He may be uncultivated, but he is a superb and successful macho, and James loved him so much and identified with him so closely that he lost all distance once the plot thickened.[24] Other things were involved, especially James's distaste in 1875–76 for French manners and for the moralistic attitudes embodied by some of the plays of Dumas *fils.* Yet there is a lot of melodramatic and non-ironic heroism in *The American.* Newman is nothing less than the new American man, the ideal gender-role, and the fact that the warmest and most cultivated man in the novel, Valentin (with a name that means *love*), at once takes to Newman, seems very significant to me. For short and pudgy Valentin is in this respect another version of Roger Lawrence, who was also short and pudgy.[25] Both men feel the same kind of hero-worship for a stronger, more incisive man that Henry felt for his older brother William. The self-made man, after all, is the opposite of the sissy, the mother-made man. It is to be expected that the latter will have strong mixed feelings about the former.

Soon after writing *The American,* James turned to feminine topics and drew a distinctly unlikeable portrait of the businessman in the character of Caspar Goodwood. James's heroes of the 1880s would be mild and nonassertive Englishmen like Hyacinth Robinson and Nick Dormer. But in the late nineties, James's interest in the American businessman revived. According to Edith Wharton,

> He was acutely conscious of this limitation, and often bewailed to me his total inability to use the "material," financial and industrial, of modern American life. Wall Street, and everything connected with the big business world, remained an impenetrable mystery to him. . . .[26]

James himself would say the same thing in a way that suggests the degree to which he regarded "business" as a secret society: "the world of affairs . . . is as special and occult a one to the outsider as the world, say, of Arctic exploration—as impenetrable save as a result of special training." Here James implied a comparison between the businessman and the most romantic hero there was in the 1890s— the explorer. But James's favorite image for the businessman at this time is the most telling—the warrior:

> The typical American figure is above all that "business man" whom the novelist and the dramatist have scarce yet seriously touched. . . . He is often an obscure, but not less often an epic, hero, seamed all over with the wounds of the market and the dangers of the field, launched into action and passion by the immensity and complexity of the general struggle, a boundless ferocity of battle.[27]

If James saw the businessman as an epic hero, isn't that another way of saying that James saw him as the most manly kind of man there could be?

In Howells' *A Traveller from Altruria* (1894) a shrewd, authoritative banker says that the millionaire had become the great ideal type for most Americans.[28] This new ideal stirred the popular American imagination as never before with fantasies of wealth, power, imperial conquest, and other versions of megalomania. Henry James was also stirred—and repelled. The story in which he dramatized his contradictory attitudes toward business and the millionaire was "The Jolly Corner" (1908). The hero of this story, Spencer Brydon, is a James-like expatriate who has spent his life enjoying the refinements of the old world. One of the most important details in the story is that Spencer's father apparently wanted him to go into business. In leaving the United States, Spencer was "perverse" and disobedient, virtually defying his "father's curse" (*Tales*, 12:204). In other words, the cultivated expatriate felt a definite *obligation* to fight it out on Wall Street. He was *supposed* to be a millionaire. Now he wonders what he would have been like if he had done what good (i.e., bad) American boys ought to do.

When Brydon finally meets up with the person his father, or his culture, meant him to be, this person turns out to be a terrifying yet strangely two-dimensional aggressor, not an alter ego so much as a demon ego. Of course, we do not get a clear view of this demon ego. His only distinct feature is his two missing fingers, a detail that evokes the struggle for success in the New York business world. The reason the demon ego is mutilated is that business is a form of combat. The reason he has succeeded is that, as we see, he fights hard and well at close quarters. Brydon is more timid. Brydon relishes the pursuit of his demon ego only as long as he thinks of it as a big game hunt. The moment the hunted turns at bay, Brydon loses heart. Brydon does not like to fight, an aversion reflected in his decision thirty years ago to live abroad. The basic difference between him and his millionaire-self is in their attitudes toward fighting. That is because, in James's imagination, the proper spheres of male activity in America—business and law—were nothing less than versions of war. Wall Street was no doubt a more dangerous place than Harvard Law School, but both represented an arena for the structured male combat that James felt a weird obligation to join, but couldn't.

The missing fingers signify something else as well. In the earlier stages of industrialization there were many accidents resulting in the loss of limbs or digits. Cogs, gears, belts, spindles, and other mechanical contrivances were dangerous, and the owners of mills, "works," and other operations had little incentive to see that working conditions were safe. W. D. Howells recalled that "some boys left school to work in the mills, and when they could show the loss of a finger-joint from the machinery they were prized as heroes."[29] The alter ego's amputated fingers prove that he has not run away from the machine, as did Howells, James, and Henry Adams, who would stare, a little stupidly, at the spinning dynamo. The missing fingers are the initiatory mutilation, signifying that the New York self has endured the disfiguring pain that makes him a man. But for Brydon (and James) he does not become a hero so much as a demon.

In James's contradictory attitudes, the millionaire somehow combined the obligatory nature of the superego with the libido's fury. But the Freudian terminology can be discarded. Gender roles offer a more parsimonious explanation. Growing up in a culture that required boys to enter stylized forms of combat before they could be considered men, James failed for a variety of reasons to make the grade. His failure to become a man endowed him with the dream self that he would finally track down in "The Jolly Corner." By returning to the place where he began, Brydon-James worked up the nerve to look in the face the archetype of aggressive masculinity he had run away from so many years earlier.

One of the basic givens in Henry James's life was a deep and humiliating anguish at his failure ever to become a proper man. How revealing that the important thing in "The Jolly Corner" is not what Spencer Brydon has done in his thirty years abroad *but what he didn't do as a youth* and that he was *justified in not doing it.* The story rationalizes inactivity. Yet—and this is another basic given—James was terribly ambitious. On one of the rare occasions when he spoke of his ambition, he qualified it with the word *ferocious:*

> It is time I should rend the veil from the ferocious ambition which has always *couvé* beneath a tranquil exterior; which enabled me to support unrecorded physical misery in my younger years; and which is perfectly confident of accomplishing serious things! (*Letters,* 2:156)

There is even some evidence that James, at least in his late twenties, wished to become a husband and father. The evidence is in *Watch and Ward* and rests on the premise that Roger Lawrence is to some extent a self-portrait. (I think there is every reason to grant this premise: Roger is kind, generous, ineffective, and has the basic respect for the freedom of others that was so admirable in James. Also, "the desire to get the better of his diffidence had given him a somewhat ponderous formalism of manner, which many persons found extremely amusing.") The master passion in this man, who is so distinguished and so discounted, is to get married:

> From an early age his curiosity had chiefly taken the form of a timid but strenuous desire to fathom the depths of matrimony. . . . He had been born a marrying man, with a conscious desire for progeny. . . . he was serving a devout apprenticeship to the profession of husband and father.[30]

Of course, Roger is not the ordinary apprentice bridegroom. There is something just a little ripe about his curiosity to fathom the depths, just as there is something fishy in a novel that tells how a young man brings up his adopted ward to be his wife. No other book James ever wrote would be pervaded to an equal degree by a man's eagerness to lose his virginity. When Roger toys with the idea of compelling

Nora's affection, he uses an image of penetration:

> Roger caught himself wondering whether, at the worst, a little precursory love-making would do any harm. The ground might be gently tickled to receive his own sowing; the petals of the young girl's nature, playfully forced apart, would leave the golden heart of the flower but the more accessible to his own vertical rays.[31]

Watch and Ward is a desperately lustful book. The basic question it raises is whether the golden heart of the flower is going to be accessible to good, mild, honest, tasteful, tolerant Roger and his noble vertical rays or to those of Hubert or Fenton, the cheap, dishonest *men*. We see the importance of this question if we remember how Roger always yields to Hubert, always feels "like a small boy, like an old woman"[32] with Fenton. The desperately held daydream that James's first novel articulated was that the male who finds it hard to make his way in the world, compete with his fellows, and impress the girls (the novel begins when Isabel Morton turns down Roger's proposal of marriage), can win the best girl of all—and can do it, not by joining in the great struggling world but by staying at home and raising an orphan girl. As J. A. Ward has written, "Roger wants not to master life, but to combine adult experience—that of a father, a suitor, and a husband—with the security and ease he had known in childhood." The best reason for seeing Roger as a representation of James is that James let Roger get away with it: "In effect the novel tests Roger's experiment in evading life and finds it successful."[33]

Watch and Ward was a sissy's domestic fantasy. Roger got his heart's desire, but James had not yet solved his basic problem—how to find a possible male role. If I have read his work and life correctly, the way he resolved this problem was, strangely, to become feminine. It is in this context that his strange entanglement with Minny Temple comes clear. After Minny died, in March 1870, James was transfixed by the odd notion that death had changed her into a stable image *in his mind*. "The more I think of her," James rather heartlessly wrote, "the more perfectly satisfied I am to have her translated from this changing realm of fact to the steady realm of thought."[34] And how steady James's realm of thought proved to be! Ten years after dying, Minny would be reincarnated in the restless and ardent Isabel Archer—and, after another twenty years, in Milly Theale.

Why was James satisfied by Minny's death? Edel interprets the satisfaction mingled with his grief as another instance of "the eternal balance sheet of the love-death."[35] Love, for James, means that one partner feeds on the other. Thus, Edel argues, as James traveled by himself in Europe and learned how to stand on his own two feet and got well of his old complaint (identified by Edel as constipation), Minny had to die. But there is a serious error in Edel's interpretation. James didn't love Minny Temple. There undoubtedly was a bizarre equation in James's imagination between Minny and himself, but Edel has misread it.

To read the equation correctly, we need to isolate two distinct ideas about Minny that run through James's letters and memoirs. First there is the idea that Minny would continue to live: "Something tells me that there is somehow too much Minny to disappear for some time yet—more life than she has yet lived out."[36] Second, there is the idea that she embodied Henry's adolescence. As he wrote to William, Minny "*represented* . . . *Youth,* with which owing to my invalidism, I always felt in rather indirect relation" (*Letters,* 1:224; italics James's). Forty-five years later, James gave Minny the last and longest chapter of his memoirs of adolescence, because, he claimed, he and William had felt her death "as the end of our youth" (*Notes,* p. 515). James's basic feeling towards her was not love but a sense of identification. She came to represent in his mind his *own* past—the youthful, adolescent past he missed because of his "invalidism" and his isolation. James substituted *her* for his own past, and then went on from there. She became a steady image in his mind because he took her over. He had not been able to enter the aggressive male gangs that held the keys to power and knowledge and prepared boys for adulthood in a rough capitalist society, and so the only way he could manage was by a literal, if subtle, change of gender.

Why did James light on Milly for his alter ego? One basic reason is that they were both gender outcasts. Milly once wrote, "If by chance I say anything or ask a question that lies at all near my heart *my sisters* all tell me I am '*queer*' and that they 'wouldn't be me for anything'" (*Notes,* p. 494; italics mine). She admired William James and other virile men: "The men in society, in New York, this winter, are principally a lot of feeble-minded boys; but I was fortunate enough to escape them, as my partner for the German was a man of thirty-five, the solitary *man,* I believe, in the room" (*Notes,* pp.

455–456; italics hers). Henry James, Sr., once told her that she had too much "pride and conceit" (*Notes*, p. 510). The man she loved, John Chipman Gray, as good as told her that she was "intellectually so unsympathetic" (*Notes*, p. 503). She had strong religious doubts and was taken to hear Phillips Brooks in Philadelphia; but she rejected his easy liberalism. All in all, it appears that Minny Temple may have been as restless, slightly unfeminine, and high-spirited as Isabel Archer and some of James's other heroines. By writing about this nonconformist type, James wrote some of his best books. Minny had made "a transcendent protest against our acquiescence in its [the world's] grossness" (*Letters*, 1:219). At least this is how James interpreted her character, and he would carry on her protest for the remainder of his life. One and all, his fine consciousnesses discover the world's grossness and then refuse to acquiesce in it. "Doomed" but dominant Minny gave James his basic play-self.

As James grew older, his image of Minny became more distorted. Her final avatar, Milly Theale, is a passionately sympathetic observer, quite different from the earlier, more presumptuous Isabel Archer. Milly is her own fine consciousness, but in the earlier novel it is Ralph, not Isabel, who functions as the Jamesian observer. Near the end of life, in 1914, James declared that Minny's finest quality was her "sense for verity of character and play of life in others" (*Notes*, p. 461). But the person who wrote the letters reprinted by James in his memoirs was far from being a passive observer.

If Minny Temple helped provide James with a *modus vivendi*, Europe helped even more, as it promised to be the great good unbrutal place where he wouldn't have to endure the scornful horselaughs of men who despised nobody so much as they despised sissies. In *The Ambassadors* and other later works, James would associate a kind of superb masculinity with Europe. But in the 1870s Europe often seemed feminine to him, particularly as contrasted to the United States. In fact, the year James moved to Europe he wrote that America humbled itself before Europe like "Hercules at the feet of Omphale."[37] In his account of his adolescence he associated Europe with "the *ewig Weibliche* of literary allusion" (*Notes*, p. 518). When he visited England in 1869 he savored "the mildness of the critical air and the benignity of the social." England was *safe*— provided, of course, that one was "on the right side at least of the social line."[38] James never forgot a Mr. Lazarus Fox, a British retainer he encountered in 1869. The young traveler vastly preferred this man's feudal deference to the independent ruffianism of lower-class American men. In England a gentleman didn't have to fight for his place.

James's letters home in the later 1870s list his many London dinners and weekend visits and seek to convey an impression of great sociability. But he admitted to Henry Adams that these letters gave "an exaggerated impression of my social career" (*Letters*, 2:109). To Howells he wrote: "If I were to tell you whom I see; it would make a tolerably various list: but the people only pass before me panoramically, and I have no relations with them" (*Letters*, 2:107). To his old friend Grace Norton he wrote: "I have, however, formed no intimacies—not even any close acquaintances. I incline to believe that I have passed the age when one forms friendships; or that every one else has!" (*Letters*, 2:195). The idea that James made a social conquest of London is something of a distortion.

It took James many years to lose his "superstitious valuation" (*Letters*, 1:274) of England. By the middle eighties, in *The Princess Casamassima*, he saw London as a scene of implacable class struggle. In *The Tragic Muse* (1889) the engaging hero, Nick Dormer, drops out of a promising political career and becomes an artist. In *Guy Domville*, James's best play, the hero not only drops out of society but enters a monastery. But if Domville dropped out, James had not yet decided to do so when he stepped out on stage on opening night. At that moment he stood before the public as never before. Up to now he had been a "deeply hushed failure" (*Notes*, p. 4), observing others perform in the "footlights" he never dared cross. For the first time in his life he left his safe inner chamber; the key turned in the lock and turned once only; he stepped out into the bright lights. The horror was, the gallery hooted at him. It was the same old taunting voice. James saw once and for all and with terrible anguish that London was not the refuge he had dreamed. It too was coarse and brutal, like New York, and he fled inward, this time for life. That same night he wrote in his notebook:

I take up my *own* old pen again—the pen of all my old and unforgettable efforts and sacred struggles. To myself—today—I need say no more. Large & full & high the future still opens. It is now indeed that I may do the work of my life. And I will. X X X X X I have only to *face* my

problems. X X X X X But all that is of the ineffable—too deep & pure
for any utterance. Shrouded in sacred silence let it rest.[39]

Criticism of James has not grasped the implications of James's
abysmal failure as a dramatist. James *should* have succeeded. He had
everything going for him—a thorough acquaintance with both the
London and Paris stage, a brilliant gift for fictional architecture, a
sense for drama, a modest fame, and all the right connections in
publishing, theater, and among reviewers. He failed because he could
not create an action—a visible, physical *deed*—or write dialogue
representing one. He could not do these things because his failure
to achieve manhood in the culture where he passed his youth and
most of his boyhood left him unable, in his own life, to conceive and
carry out a physical, self-assertive act. His spectatorial attitude
reflected an inner passivity, a kind of motionlessness that made him
a very poor play writer. Simultaneously his inability to *do* was the
cause of his lifelong infatuation with the stage, which represented a
shortcut to glory and power for the ambition inside him. James's
realization on the opening night of *Guy Domville* that he could not
make it in the theater meant that he could triumph only in a world
of his own creation. That is the disquieting significance of his renewed
dedication to the novel, his "*own* old pen." From now on he would
take refuge from reality in what may be the first modernist novels
written in English. The fact that these novels issued from a "shrouded"
personal defeat, resting in "sacred silence," should cause us all to
heave uneasily in our sleep.

The striking differences between the novels James wrote before
1890 and after 1895 have been ably summarized by Philip M.
Weinstein.[40] The "contours of the external world" in the later fiction
are "less ample." There is "an even more reduced scope of activity:
sexual innuendo, intrigue, or intimacy is virtually at the center of
what is happening." Even more, one is often uncertain "what is going
on." Most important of all, "the perceiving mind . . . has begun to
engross the author's attention." Over and over James tells the story
of sensitive but uninitiated people—Fleda Vetch, Maisie Farange, the
governess at Bly, Nanda Brookenham, Lambert Strether, Milly
Theale, Maggie Verver, Ralph Pendrel—who try to live in a society
where it transpires that the others are bound together by coarse
common knowledge. James made stunningly beautiful fiction out of
this donnée, and Weinstein shows how he blended outer and inner

perspectives, comedy and pathos, irony and poignancy. This delicate balance is what saves James. In *The Sacred Fount* alone among James's novels, the central character seems to lose the sense that there is actually a world not penetrated by his own mind: "*I* alone was magnificently and absurdly aware—everyone else was benightedly out of it."[41] Here the unnamed narrator may have momentarily lost hold, like Decoud drifting away from society in *Nostromo*. But ordinarily, as when James exhorted the sculptor Hendrik Anderson to avoid "MEGALOMANIA," the "dread Delusion,"[42] he did not lose sight of the fearful limitations of the self in isolation. That is why his autobiography is so fine. A ruthless confession, it mingles tender sympathy for the unfledged self with a wonderful "objectivity" (*Notes*, p. 371) toward the freakish qualities in James that made him a writer.

When the Great War broke out in 1914, James, seventy-one years old, tried harder than at any point in his life to come out. It was the second big war to touch his life, and he fought on the home front with everything he had, visiting Belgian refugees and wounded Tommies and promoting a volunteer ambulance corps in France. Saul Rosenzweig has argued that James was attempting to lay the ghost of his ignominious Civil War record.[43] Now he hoped to prove himself a man at last. America's cowardly refusal to join the cause allowed James to turn the tables: this time *he* would be the warrior.

A year later, James suffered a series of strokes. With part of his brain destroyed by lack of oxygen, he rose to assert his dominance once and for all. He ceased to be the sissy whose life was focused on Wilky's letters from the front. Now he was the general in command, and he dictated in the person of Napoleon:

> Dear and most esteemed Brother and Sister,
>   I call your attention to the precious enclosed transcripts of plans and designs for the decoration of certain apartments of the palaces here, the Louvre and the Tuileries. . . .[44]

His lifelong balancing act having become too difficult for his now impaired mind, James was at last swamped by the humiliation of not growing up to be a man. Supine on his death-bed, "that queer monster, the artist,"[45] assumed one last disguise. He transformed himself into the supreme commander of the warring hordes of men who had terrified and laughed at him, and then he died.

CHAPTER TWENTY-FOUR

"Observing": The View from James's Room in the House of Fiction

"Observing," James's substitute for action, is the main activity and subject of his fiction. Practically everyone, even the seasoned Louis Auchincloss, accepts James's claim to be a good observer. I shall now argue that James was in fact a very poor observer—that his fiction, rather than offering any sort of knowledge of men and manners, offers the pleasures of escape from a reality seen as secretly coarse, brutal, sinister, and exploiting.

Is blind Tiresias, old man with withered dugs, the best observer of mankind? Maybe, but it must be remembered that the Greek Tiresias knew the pleasures of sex from both the male and female side. The modern Tiresias—the observer of T. S. Eliot's wasteland and his/her many parthenogenetic offspring—is a bystander who regards sexuality and most ordinary gender roles with profound loathing. How can this negative creature possibly understand what goes on among us?

Critics have not yet given careful thought to James's lifelong disdain for the ordinary. This disdain was most pronounced in his twenties, when, in reviewing *Our Mutual Friend,* James wrote that Dickens "reconciles us to what is commonplace"—and then added that the value of this service "is questionable." James considered Dickens "a great observer and a great humorist, but . . . nothing of a philosopher."[1] James's review of *The Belton Estate* saw the book's accurate social detail as a trivial sort of achievement:

Mr. Trollope is a good observer but he is literally nothing else. He is apparently as incapable of disengaging an idea as of drawing an inference. All his incidents are, if we may so express it, empirical. He has seen and heard every act and every speech that appears in his pages.[2]

When W. D. Howells reviewed James's first book, *The Passionate Pilgrim and Other Tales,* he ended by wondering whether James was excessively interested in "a certain kind of cultivated people" who "are often a little narrow in their sympathies and poverty-stricken in the simple emotions." In the same review Howells was critical of James's use of a narrator who could not "keep himself from seeming to patronize the simpler-hearted heroes, and from openly rising above them in a worldly way."[3] Howells was obviously wrong if he meant to outlaw the use of a limited narrator. But he was right on the mark in detecting James's weakness for narrowly cultivated types. Not long after reviewing James, Howells created a Boston snob, Miles Arbuton, who "had always shrunk from knowledge of things outside of a very narrow world."[1] In a letter to Howells James sharply objected to this character as "decidedly a shade too scurvy."[5]

Underneath all the manners, the style, the articulateness, the intimidating ponderousness, James was much more the daydreamer and theory-spinner than the sharp-eyed observer he often thought he wanted to be. In the early 1860s Henry visited his brother William in Cambridge. William wrote home to complain that Henry "could in no wise satisfy my craving for knowledge of family and friends—he didn't seem to have been on speaking terms with anyone for some time past, and could tell me nothing. . . . Never did I see a so-much uninterested creature in the affairs of those about him" (*Notes,* p. 151).

Henry himself admitted as much. In a telling passage of his memoirs, he wrote that his older brother's success at a certain point "had much, *had more than aught else,* to say to the charming silver haze just then wrapped about everything of which I was conscious" (*Notes,* pp. 15–16; italics mine). The causal sequence here is crucial: what the older brother's success does to the younger and unfledged brother is to make him close his eyes and dream—not open them and see. What's more, if Henry dropped out of the competition, he did so with an "ecstasy of resignation" (*Notes,* p. 13), retreating to a vague but pleasant inner space. Was this merely the narcissism of dreamy adolescence? One can answer yes only if one is prepared to concede that James never left adolescence, for the central choice his fiction dramatized was an ecstatic retreat from the world. First and last, James's fine consciousnesses would spend a great deal of time in silver and golden hazes.[6] The sense of things vaguely melting together was to remain a favorite Jamesian experience.

When James gazed at paintings, landscapes, Italy, things often seemed to swim together in a distinguished vagueness. Golden chalices gleamed in deep embrasures. Candlelight was reflected from gilded picture frames. Everything melted into rich brown tones. James invoked this swooning image of rich old things over and over. One of many examples is his memory of his visit in his early twenties to Charles Eliot Norton's library at Shady Hill—"where the winter sunshine touched serene bookshelves and arrayed pictures, the whole embrowned composition of objects in my view, with I knew not what golden light of promise, what assurance of things to come" (*Notes*, p. 405).

James wrote a great deal about painters and paintings, but I do not see how his art criticism can be called anything but dilettantism. In 1872, after visiting the Louvre with Norton, James prayed "*not* to grow in discrimination" (*Letters*, 1:300). He was put off by Fromentin's *Les Maitres d'autrefois*, which took a professional interest in "the technical side" of "the mysteries . . . by which the picture was made."[7] When James saw some of the "earliest" tourist photographs ever taken in Europe, he loved their "old-time mellowness and softness." More recent shots were "harsh in proportion" (*Letters*, 1:252). The photographs by Alvin Langdon Coburn that James allowed into the New York Edition have a gauzy and indistinct atmosphere. For James, a painting was improved if it hung in the "crepuscular London atmosphere." It was even better when, as in some of Bellini's canvases, art shed its "quiet radiance from the depths of some sombre sacristy."[8] The visual effect James liked best was "the tone of time." He *liked* poor lighting, faded colors, heavy layers of varnish. When Mark Twain complained about these things in *Innocents Abroad*, it was tantamount to confessing himself a boor. But who would be more likely to appreciate the original bright colors of the London National Gallery's cleaned and restored Bacchus and Ariadne by Titian, Henry James or Mark Twain? It's suggestive to note that one of Wilky's Civil War letters says that "Willy's artistic eye"—not Harry's—"would have enjoyed the sight" of a brigade's campfires (*Notes*, p. 386). Willy and Wilky had the painter's eye, not Harry, who may have tried to be one upon whom nothing was lost but inevitably confused seeing with activities that were essentially different.

There is a sobering instance of James's poor observation in "The Jolly Corner." Returning to New York, presumably near the beginning of the twentieth century, Spencer Brydon is stunned by "the differences, the newnesses, the queernesses, above all the bignesses" (*Tales*, 12:194). But where do we see any of this? Where does James *establish* New York's heartless modernity? It is necessary for him to do so; "The Jolly Corner" may be a kind of ghost story, but the quest for Brydon's New York self can have no meaning unless the story gives us a sense of what New York has become. I can find only one descriptive detail—the streetcars where people scramble "as the panic-stricken at sea scramble for the boats" (p. 196). This is the one vivid "modern" detail in the story. But streetcars, whether pulled by horses or engines, had been around for a long time. James himself had used the identical image thirty years earlier (in 1878) in describing a Boston horsecar: "When it reached a certain point the people . . . projected themselves upon it in a compact body—a movement suggesting the scramble for places in a life-boat at sea." Furthermore, in the novel from which this passage comes, *The Europeans,* the events take place "upwards of thirty years since."[9] And that's not all: one reason the crowded horsecar became a permanent prop in American life for James was that Howells had pointed out its significance in *Suburban Sketches* in 1872:

> When I see such a horse-car as I have sketched move away from its station, I feel that it is something not only emblematic and interpretative, but monumental; and I know that when art becomes truly national, the overloaded horse-car will be celebrated in painting and sculpture.[10]

James got so far as to see the horsecar as emblematic, and then it took its place among the newspapers, the hotel lobby, the lank male jaw, and a number of other easily retrievable symbols.

I do not see how it can be denied that James's profound solipsistic tendency hindered his powers of observation. In his memoirs he recalled John La Farge, an early mentor and "role model," as the ideal solipsistic artist: La Farge had "a nature essentially entire," which grasped "the truth of what would work for it most favourably should it but succeed in never yielding the first inch of any ground." He covered himself "from edge to edge with the defence of his serenity" (*Notes,* p. 99). La Farge also taught James that he could shield himself from the ridicule and aggression of American men by cultivating the artificiality of a European dandy. But this defence fatally limited James's range of perception, though not its intensity. When he and T. S. Perry became friends at Newport, James's "working . . . universe" was divided into "the wondrous esoteric quarter peopled just by us and our friend [La Farge] and our common references, and the vast remainder of the public at large, the public of the innumerably uninitiated even when apparently of the most associated" (*Notes,* p. 87). Here James approaches the unbalanced passage in *The Sacred Fount* where everyone but the narrator is "benightedly out of it."

It was precisely because of his solipsism that James lived in "the tension of perception" (*Letters,* 1:109). He became the Vigilant Writer, always Collecting Material. He had to be vigilant because he didn't pick things up the way people ordinarily do, unconsciously or at least without such specialized effort. His memoirs and the texture of his later novels suggest that his solipsism insulated him from others except in brief stunned glimpses that would then send him back upon himself. Most of the snatched glimpses and vignettes in his memoirs seem to point a far-reaching moral, and they are linked together by a raptly inward-gazing prose that spins out their significance at enormous length. The structure of James's memoirs is identical with that of his literary inspiration. When someone's anecdote gave James the "germ" for one of his fictions, he wanted to stop everything, shut the storyteller up, and pare the story down to its bare minimum, a brief glimpse of "clumsy Life . . . at her stupid work."[11] In his preface to *The American,* the same passage in which he admitted that this work was a romance also gave away his fondness for eliminating as much reality as possible from his fictions without tipping off the reader. In his fiction as in his memoirs, he would exhibit a few vivid grains of "clumsy Life" in the dense amber medium of his mature play of mind. His procedure was to begin with a little raw experience, then construct a substitute world full of the order, harmony, amenity, and rich reverberations he missed in reality.

There is a fascinating example of this procedure in the essay James wrote at the age of seventy on Mr. and Mrs. James T. Fields. Fields had once joked with Howells about the paradox of young Henry James writing such pessimistic stories with "his mother's milk scarce yet dry upon his lips." Howells told the story to James, and James was insulted. This happened in the 1860s. *Fifty years later* James recalled Fields's joke in connection with the "troubled face of my young relation with the *Atlantic*," and then devoted a paragraph to refuting Fields. After trying once again to dispel the rankling insult, James tried to feel "an anxious kindness for Mr. Fields."[12] In this episode we see one of the basic features of what can be reconstructed of James's inner life—the connection between his passionate inward reverie and his desire to regain a sense of dignity.

Many of James's fine consciousnesses lead the same sort of inner life. They are afraid of having to realize something bad, and they ransack each bit of experience (there are never very many of these bits) for the last possible reverberation. Thus, Strether's glimpse of Chad at the opera touches off an entire chapter of passionate rumination and inference. Strether is supposed to be a promising receptor of impressions, yet this one glimpse teaches him more than fifty-five years of direct experience. What's he been doing all this time? And how revealing that it is a glimpse of a demonstrably successful man that touches off this reverie—a man who had not yet grown up when Strether last saw him! It looks as if Strether is going through an experience not very different from Henry's dismay at seeing little Wilky metamorphosed into a man by the Civil War, or Roger Lawrence's feeling of inadequacy before his manly rivals, Hubert and George Fenton. And just as the manly rivals turn out to be cads in the end, meaning that Roger won't need to suffer from their superiority, so, in *The Ambassadors*, Chad, magnificent man of the world as he first appears, proves in the end to be rather cheap. In other words, the same self-consoling adolescent fantasy that operated in James's juvenile *Watch and Ward* reappears in a work of his personal and artistic maturity. And how striking that the fantasy (the unworldly and sensitive man will prove in the end to be the best man) is identical with the basic political daydream shared by "the best men," as John G. Sproat has called them—the aristocratic liberal reformers of the Gilded Age.

Admittedly *The Ambassadors* gives one an impression of a very tough, well-seasoned sensibility. But this impression is deceptive. The novel has a soft core. In fact it is because it is soft at the core that it has such a seasoned look. It is surprising that James's readers are not generally more canny about his claim to be one upon whom nothing is lost. There is in James's writing an endless oscillation between a desire to escape the wide, wide world and a desire to prove to the world that one has mastered it by one's own patented techniques of thought. There is an unbroken thread running from the Master's finest novels all the way back to little Henry's dawdling and gaping. James himself admitted this continuity at one point, when he recalled his habitual woolgathering in Bonn: "To feel a unity, a character and a tone in one's impressions, to feel them related and all harmoniously coloured, that *was* positively to face the aesthetic, the creative, even, quite wondrously, the critical life and almost on the spot to commence author" (*Notes*, p. 25). Here, in spite of the extravagant humor, we see just how uncritically James regarded the silver haze he so often sought. He had a fatal tendency to face the world with closed eyes and an ecstatic expression, endlessly digesting a few pieces of the abrasive world. And his celebrants have a fatal tendency to refer in passing to such wholly imaginary mental states as "full consciousness" and refute their rivals as not being adequately "responsive" to the Master.

James was obviously the "psychological novelist" par excellence. But what kind of psychology did he offer? In *The Passages of Thought*, Gordon O. Taylor sets out to show how James slowly moved to a representation of mental processes in his narratives. By the time he wrote *The Ambassadors*, he was able to render "Strether's mental state" as "most often one of partial bewilderment under the assault of impressions which he must sift and filter to fathom the situations from which they arise."[13] This is the mental state that William Veeder has considered in a more recent book. Veeder has gone farther than anyone else in attempting to describe the patterns in Jamesian mental "flow." He has spotted several patterns, among them these: 1) a vague initial "something" coming into focus, 2) negative-positive dialectic, and 3) alternation of literal and metaphorical statement. These various small-scale patterns in James boil down to one kind of mental process—search. And with each small-scale discovery, as we read through the narrative, "we are impelled on, to seek further definition in experience."[14] Precisely—what James's prose, especially his later prose, represents so fantastically well is the varied movements of the searching but still innocent mind. This is *all* the psychology James gives us. If one believes that "seeing," or rather, *trying* to "see," is the most "authentic" human activity, then one may want to concur with the high valuation of James. But if one does not accept this dubious premise, if one insists that great literature give a truthful account of human passions, or behavior, or social life, one will not bend one's knee in homage to such a strangely limited writer.

Part of the problem in reading James is to discern his complicated position with regard to the realistic novel. The essential points seem to me to be these:

1. As James's early reviews of Trollope and references to Flaubert reveal, he began his career with a strong commitment against realism. This commitment, probably derived from his father, has never been brought into clear focus by James's critics.

2. Up to about 1885, James, moving with large-scale cultural currents and reacting against women's fiction, moved towards realism.

3. All the while, James's interest in representing reality *as seen* by a cultivated mentality led him to qualify his realism. As James E. Miller says, "James's emphasis on the *personal* impression and point of view was indeed intentional and sufficiently strong to call into question the loose labeling of James as a member of the traditional nineteenth-century 'realistic school.'"[15]

4. In the mid 1880s James distanced himself from Howells' increasingly aggressive realism and debunking attitude toward highly refined types. James's picking up his "old pen" after 1895 represented not only a final repudiation of play-writing but a renewed dedication to his private and solipsistic tendencies.

For all but about a decade of his life James would have been displeased at being classified among the realists. Like many writers today, he saw the novel as radically discontinuous from ordinary life. Looking back on his boyhood, he believed that he got "the best" part of his education from reading the *Revue des Deux Mondes*, a magazine from which he derived "all that was finest in the furniture and the fittings of romance." Back issues accumulated in a closet where they came to form "an alternative sphere of habitation" (*Notes*, pp. 85–86). This phrase, I believe, sums up James's prevailing view of fiction, even to the point of including the essential image—fiction as one's other, secret *house*. James regarded literature as a separate (but well-furnished) reality. In maturity he would figure fiction as a house made up of innumerable rooms, from each of which a caged observer looks out through a window. This disturbing image implies an impassable barrier between the novelist and the world he observes, and it also implies a shut-in and unventilated way of life. James's own quarters in the house of fiction amounted to a well-appointed closet with an inadequate view, a room not very different from the various prisons inhabited by Isabel Archer—the closed-off library, the Palazzo Roccanero, the "house of suffocation" that her married life with Osmond amounts to.

James's failure does not lie in his refusal to give an objective representation of reality. No writer has an obligation to be a realist. Fantastic narratives can give as good an account of human passions as realistic ones. James's failure lay in his insistence in one way or another that the shut-in life is after all better than the open-air life, or worse, that the secret alternative sphere is all there is. Many readers of James have felt a strong need to protest against this silent valuation. In 1882 Horace Scudder had this to say about *The Portrait of a Lady:*

> This self-consistency is a separate thing from any consistency with the world of reality. The characters, the situations, the incidents, are all true to the law of their own being, but that law runs parallel with the law which governs life, instead of being identical with it. In Andersen's quaint story of the Emperor's New Clothes, a little child discovers the unreality of the gossamer dress, and his voice breaks in upon the illusion from the outer world. Something of the same separation from the story, of the same unconscious naturalness of feeling, prompts the criticism that, though these people walk, and sit, and talk, and behave, they are yet in an illusionary world of their own.[16]

Modern readers might want to protest that Scudder fails to allow for the freedom of art in this passage. But those who use this argument to reject Scudder's critique ought to be aware that they are automatically giving up the position that James's novels represent accurate observation. One can not have it both ways, valuing James as an observer of the human scene *and* as a distinguished post-realistic maker of autonomous objects of art. He cannot be both of these at the same time. And yet that is precisely the nature of the claim that I feel James is making whenever I read him.

No wonder James is so often compared to the Naked Emperor.

Alone from boyhood on, his face averted from reality, the Gentleman of Shalott, James was a lifelong weaver of a figure in a carpet. His fictive designs are characterized by extreme symmetry, coherence, internal ironies, and intricacy, and an unrelenting consecutiveness of action and conversation. Nothing simply happens and nobody ever lets anything drop. The great mind never sleeps. A treatment of personal liberation ends up as a marvelously patterned work of art. In fact *The Ambassadors* is as inferential a piece of narrative as Poe's stories about detective Dupin, that claustral sophisticate who solves the external world while smoking opium in his chamber. After Strether sees Chad at the opera, he figures (helped by Maria Gostrey) that someone must have reformed the young man. Only a woman could have brought about such a transformation. Therefore *cherchez la femme*. And behold, she appears in Book Fourth in the person of Madame de Vionnet, after Strether has been reasoning his way toward her for almost a third of the novel. Meanwhile, Strether has been living more strenuously and anxiously than ever before, always worrying about Chad and hardly ever relaxing and really enjoying Paris. It takes intense effort to find the group's secret when one is an outsider—or to build up a convincing simulacrum of life when one is too busy inside to see life for what it is. Deep within James and Strether (his son died in childhood) there seems to be a solipsistic child who fails to notice other people and creates an autonomous world of his own by repetitive patterns of sound and movement. Or is it rather a caged wolf treading back and forth, his gaze quickly sweeping the external world as his feet pivot in the same spot, his nose grazes the same bar?

In view of the fact that James's work had a strong antirealistic aspect, it is anomalous that ever since the James revival of the forties, he has been regarded as a profound commentator on American life.[17] Admittedly, as the titles of *The American* and *The Bostonians* indicate, James pretended to play this role. But *The American* gives an extremely unrealistic and melodramatic account of American (and French) life.[18] James knew as little about the title character as he knew about the Legitimists among French aristocrats in the second Empire. Of course, he had plenty of *ideas* about the French nobility, as he had been reading the romances of Octave Feuillet and Victor Cherbuliez in the *Revue des Deux Mondes* for many years, and he also knew that the practical, humorous, energetic businessman was an ideal American type. But the fact remains, he didn't know very much about either of them.

But so what, it might be objected: didn't James once praise "an English novelist, a woman of genius,"[19] who wrote about French Protestants after seeing a group of them through an open door? Didn't he say that a novelist can piece out the whole from a part? Of course, and James was that kind of novelist. But I see no reason to depart from the old wisdom that a writer should know something about the sort of people he writes about. Also, I see no reason to accept James's theory without testing it. The question is, can a writer become a major critic of a society without knowing much about it? If one tests James's theory by looking at *The American,* the answer seems to be no. Newman is abstract and theoretical. His sudden gratuitous revulsion from business is highly improbable, as is his conversion to cultural acquisition. In the mid-1870s James had a very weak grasp of the motives that led robber barons to try to buy up Europe. And worst of all for a story that focuses on love, it is hard to believe that Newman actually *wants* the diaphanous Claire de Cintré. In fact, only after Newman can no longer get her is James able to convince us that he loves her—a telling omission. And is this the language a representative American man, a New Man, would use in proposing?

> If you want brilliancy, everything in the way of brilliancy that money can give you, you shall have. And as regards anything you may give up, don't take for granted too much that its place cannot be filled. Leave that to me; I'll take care of you; I shall know what you need. Energy and ingenuity can arrange everything. I'm a strong man![20]

James himself admitted (*Letters,* 2:87) what this passage makes clear—that Newman's speech is wooden and bears no connection to vernacular American speech. Given this failure, how can it be claimed that *The American* is a classic work of realism? And why does the nineteenth-century novelist whose representation of American speech was so rich, varied, and accurate, reflecting class and regional differences,[21] always play second fiddle to James? Is it because modern criticism has no way of detecting the accurate or inaccurate representation of speech? Yet speech reflects character, to some extent *is* character. One of James's basic problems in *The American* was that Newman was an Olympian fantasy—the strong American man that James had failed to become. If one compares Newman to Silas Lapham, Howells' fine portrait of the self-made man, one sees that a novelist who knows something about his subject has an advantage over one who knows next to nothing and ends up projecting only his private fantasies on the unscored page.

But perhaps *The American* was only journey work, preparing the ground for James's more masterful representations of American life. Yet the American men in *The Portrait of a Lady* and *The Bostonians* remain as theoretical as Newman. How can sophisticated readers—particularly those who have learned to spot sex-role stereotyping in women characters—accept Caspar Goodwood? This stiff wooden businessman, who doesn't seem to exist apart from Isabel and who has nothing to do in life but pressure her, is a portrait of American masculinity as a dull, persistent force. Basil Ransom in *The Bostonians* is hardly more subtle. James modeled this virile, aggressive Southerner after Mississippi's Senator Lamar, whom he barely knew. In a letter to John Hay, James confessed that he had faked Ransom—"he remains a rather vague & artificial creation, & so far as he looks at all real, is only fait de chic."²² I agree. And I think that the reason why Ransom and Goodwood and James's other American men are so awful is that they reflect James's great anxiety over American masculinity. Goodwood's name would reappear in Bloodgood, a New York businessman in "A Round of Visits" who embezzles the savings of a Jamesian expatriate. Goodwood, Bloodgood, and Ransom are all contrasted with more aesthetic or effeminate men—Henry Burrage, Matthew Pardon, Ned Rosier—and easily resort to violence. In climactic scenes both Goodwood and Ransom use force on a woman. Isabel frustrates Goodwood, but Verena is actually pulled away in tears by Ransom. Both men are versions of *the man*, that potent figure looming over the narrator of "The Aspern Papers" when he gazes up at the statue of Colleoni, or when he catches distant echoes of Jeffrey Aspern's gallantry with the divine Juliana. It is this same potent figure that Spencer Brydon innocently pursues in "The Jolly Corner," and then desperately tries to escape. Brydon's unseeing hysteria—"But this brute, with his awful face—this brute's a black stranger" (*Tales*, 12:231)—reflects James's own fear, uneasiness, humiliation in the presence of male American aggression. James, too, was afraid to look, and that is one of the reasons why at least half a dozen of his contemporaries—Mark Twain, W. D. Howells, Joseph

Kirkland, Stephen Crane, Theodore Dreiser, and Jack London—wrote about American men with greater insight and understanding than James.

Hawthorne's complaint in his preface to *The Marble Faun* that it was almost impossible to write romances "about a country where there is no shadow, no antiquity, no mystery, no picturesque and gloomy wrong, nor anything but a common-place prosperity, in broad and simple daylight"[23] made a big impression on James. He regarded Hawthorne's American notebooks, with their thin and random observations, as "a practical commentary upon this somewhat ominous text." The notebooks revealed the thinness of American life, "the lightness of the diet to which his [Hawthorne's] observation was condemned."[24] But James drew the wrong inference, for there is abundant evidence, as James W. Tuttleton has pointed out,[25] that Hawthorne was a rather poor observer of social life. Hawthorne himself said as much in his Custom-House essay:

> The fault was mine. The page of life that was spread out before me seemed dull and commonplace, only because I had not fathomed its deeper import. A better book than I shall ever write was there; leaf after leaf presenting itself to me, just as it was written out by the reality of the flitting hour, and vanishing as fast as written, only because my brain wanted the insight and my hand the cunning to transcribe it."[26]

Like the other writers in our strange American Renaissance, Hawthorne tended to read the world as symbol and allegory. He lived in a period when metaphor and image flourished more than plot, the sentence and the paragraph were better crafted than the essay, and the short story attained a perfection unmatched by any kind of novel-length narrative. "Our classical writers," Daniel Aaron has concluded after surveying our Civil War literature, "simply did not know the land and people they spoke to and spoke for."[27] Hawthorne's lament about the dull homogeneity of American life would impress others besides James, most notably Lionel Trilling. But the lament is suspect because it comes from a poorly qualified witness.

One of James's most influential passages is his catalogue in *Hawthorne* of all the missing institutions in nineteenth-century America. The passage has been quoted so often that I don't care to reproduce it here. Essentially, James criticized the United States for lacking a polite society and various feudal vestiges. The only positive element James conceded America was its humor, and the concession was made in a patronizing tone:

> The American knows that a good deal remains; what it is that remains— that is his secret, his joke, as one may say. It would be cruel, in this terrible denudation, to deny him the consolation of his natural gift, that "American humour" of which of late years we have heard so much.[28]

The brittle condescension is a telltale sign of James's uneasiness and lack of rapport with American character. Still, there is a weird truthfulness in what he says. The joke *was* the secret. Humor, as I have argued in part 2, was a central male ritual in the nineteenth century. Many humorists got their laughs by wearing a mask that represented an ideal male type, the nonchalant, no-account, countrified loafer. American humor, written by men and circulating in male-dominated media—*The Spirit of the Times*, newspapers, the early variety stage—was in a very real sense the secret of American male society.

At the Custom-House the man Hawthorne "used to watch and study" with the most curiosity was the old Inspector, whose laugh "perpetually reëchoed" through the building.[29] One of Hawthorne's finest tales, "My Kinsman, Major Molineux," shows how a young man from the country gets initiated into the fallen American city by the act of laughing. Robert Dusenbery has made a suggestive analysis of Hawthorne's "merry company" of laughers.[30] Dusenbery shows that laughter in Hawthorne's tales is generally characteristic of "certain persons who are inwardly corrupt," and he then divides the laughers into five classes, running from innocence to evil:

1. Uncorrupted children whose mirth expresses a natural goodness.
2. Those who frequent taverns and city streets. (Although Dusenbery doesn't make the point, these would be mostly men.)
3. "Practical men of affairs" who laugh "at the pretensions of sensitive, artistic souls."
4. Faustian mockers of the world and of themselves, such as Ethan Brand.
5. Satanic persons, like the figure of Goodman Brown's grandfather.

Dusenbery's conclusion is that "the merry company laughs its way to hell; and laughter represents gradations of evil among men." The fact that these gradations also run from weakness to increasing mastery and power over others is surely not accidental and suggests a further conclusion: the five classes of laughers stand for the graded initiations in a malevolent secret society.[31] This secret order was in some ways coterminous with man's world in nineteenth-century America, and this casts further light on why Hawthorne and James were not amused.

James was never qualified to describe American men. He often proclaimed that Americans had little "division of *type, . . .* opposition and contrast" (*Notes,* p. 360). Believing in Tocqueville's myth of homogeneity and insulated by class pride, he never saw very much of American life. On the rare occasions when he descended into the "mysterious democracy," as someone calls it in *The Bostonians,* he found an exciting diversity. Once he visited an encampment of disabled soldiers at Portsmouth during the Civil War and spent several hours listening to their stories (and also emptying his pockets). For once James saw that American men were anything but featureless and dull: they had "colour and form, accent and quality." He was entranced by the "poetry of the esoteric vernacular" (*Notes,* pp. 314, 315). *Esoteric vernacular!* In 1898 James reviewed *Calamus:* "Whitman wrote to his friend of what they both saw and touched, enormities of the common, sordid occupations, dreary amusements, undesirable food; and the record remains, by a mysterious marvel, a thing positively delightful." How could ordinary life and language possibly be interesting? "The riddle," James wrote, "is a neat one for the sphinx of democracy to offer."[32] But the riddle was in the eye of the beholder. James might have been able to reach a reasoned judgment if he hadn't subscribed to the myth of American homogeneity. But James had to believe in this myth. From the beginning he wanted to belong, as people do, and he slowly discovered that he never would. And so he complained that all American men had to go into "business," and he failed to draw one convincing portrait of an American man.

CHAPTER TWENTY-FIVE

Who Made James the Modern American Master, and Why?

For the inner life of man, its essential traits and essential conflicts can be truly portrayed only in organic connection with social and historical factors.

> Lukács, *Studies in European Realism*, p. 8

> America is rediscovering its greatest novelist
> and to celebrate this fact we offer
> The Great Short Novels of
> HENRY JAMES
> Edited, with an introduction and comments
> by PHILIP RAHV
> (Dial Press advertisement in *Partisan Review*, Fall 1944)

The place to begin is George Santayana's original definition of the genteel tradition, which gives a brilliant formulation of the antithetical relationship between power and the alternative sphere:

The truth is that one-half of the American mind, that not occupied intensely in practical affairs, has remained, I will not say high-and-dry, but slightly becalmed; it has floated gently in the backwater, while, alongside, in invention and industry and social organization the other half of the mind was leaping down a sort of Niagara Rapids. This division may be found symbolized in American architecture: a neat reproduction of the colonial mansion—with some modern comforts introduced surreptitiously—stands beside the sky-scraper. The American Will inhabits the sky-scraper; the American Intellect inhabits the colonial mansion. The one is the sphere of the American man; the other, at least predominantly, of the American woman. The one is all aggressive enterprise; the other is all genteel tradition.[1]

Surprisingly, this famous passage turns out to be partly about man's world and woman's sphere in America. Yet the genteel tradition is not exclusively feminine. It includes the highminded alternative culture that women's fiction helped constitute in the last century, but it also includes "the best men" of the Gilded Age and certain other groups. The "becalmed" part of the American mind was partly a vestige from the past, partly a rigid counterculture, but mostly it was a consequence of powerlessness—the static shadow world that took shape after the triumph of the will. While men operate the levers of an expanding technology, pushing real masses here and there, women and a few men construct an arbitrary, non-natural, non-useful realm where the laws of nature need not apply. In the room the women come and go, talking of Michelangelo.

To insist that art is autonomous, or that Henry James be read only with reference to himself, is to deny the truth that Santayana perceived: there is an antithetical relation between aggressive male power armed with capital and technology, and the alternative sphere. James's patriarchal grandfather died one of the richest men in America; his son wrote books like *The Secret of Swedenborg* and worked out a private, ameliorative, and ecstatic metaphysical system that apparently left not one single convert. William James, inventor of the "cash value" philosophy, was the most practical philosopher in the United States since Benjamin Franklin, though not the most brilliant; his younger brother wrote "The Jolly Corner," which concludes with the hero contentedly resting in a woman's lap after finding out he did the right thing after all in leaving his native country. Henry James cannot be understood apart from American masculinity, its violent rites of passage, the Civil War, the rough and tumble of primitive capitalism, and female American culture in the 1860s and 1870s.

Yet it is essential to be as precise as possible in locating James—and his devotees—in society and history. James's slashing attacks on women's fiction in his early reviews and his hostile portraits of society matrons remind us that within the genteel tradition there were obviously many different cohorts and cultures. Certain features of James must be situated within the broad middle ground of the genteel tradition—his disdain for the ordinary, his conspicuous elegance, his alienation from man's world. Yet he went far beyond the bounds of standard literate speech in evolving the alternative language that his late prose very nearly amounts to. And his lifelong hatred of certain kinds of snobs and social procedures reminds us that he did not inhabit Santayana's "colonial mansion." Like many writers, James had his own alternative sphere, "a world elsewhere." Yet is is insufficient simply to locate him in a supposed tradition of alienated writers. For this supposed tradition would itself be a product of history.

Like Henry Adams, James is one of the few American writers who bridged two entities not often perceived to be related—the genteel tradition and modernism. In American culture, just as in British and European culture, there was a definite continuity running from one of these to the other. One should not be deceived by the ferocity of modernism's attack on the "genteel," for modernism was in essentials rather similar to its favorite adversary. Both defined themselves against a mainstream seen as coarse, powerful, dominant, and yet clearly inferior to themselves. The genteel tradition and modernism were each an outsiders' elite. In modernism, however, one was both farther outside and more elite, for, from a social point of view, modernism was a radically detribalized gentility.[2]

Hence the parallel between the modernists and the bestselling women writers of the 1850s. The central figure in every bestselling woman's novel of that decade (except *Uncle Tom's Cabin*) happened to be an orphan who found out the hard way that this world was not her home, and what is an orphan if not alienated? The fine alienated sensibility would be *the* central sensibility in James and a great number of modernists. And there is nothing surprising in this parallel: the isolato is inevitably the central character is any literature created by and for those who find themselves, in fundamental ways, excluded from the contemporary world. Herman Melville coined the word *isolato* in *Moby-Dick* to express the solitary aspect of the sailors on the Pequod, most of whom have different nationalities. A little before Melville was rescued from obscurity in the 1920s, Joyce, Kafka, Proust, T. S. Eliot, and others had begun to create a literature of the isolato. These authors were themselves exiles and solitaries, and the fictional societies they created had a radically alienating effect on the sensitive individual. Again and again they invoke the opposition between a Blazes Boylan and the impotent Bloom, Apenecks and Prufrocks, triumphant vulgarity and scared refinement, grouped insiders and the lonely outsider, power and powerlessness. At the center of modernist literature one encounters the same sort of person as in James's fiction and women's fiction—a superior but uninitiated self, a mandarin turned pariah. That is why many modernist apologies, such as José Ortega y Gasset's *The Dehumanization of Art,* manage to combine a very old kind of social elitism with a very new kind of isolation.[3]

One of the ways in which modernist writing reflects the same sort of powerless elitism as the fantasy literature of woman's sphere is the all but inevitable presence of the fallen aristocrat. In many women's novels, the heroine had an innate nobility that was so fine it did not need to be attested to by noble ancestry. She was just better, though generally nobody but the reader had the wit to understand, and thus the heroine had to suffer and work along with the ordinary ruck of people until Prince Charming came along and pulled her back up to her proper level. Prince Charming never shows up in James, Pound, Joyce, or Eliot, unless he's the one who makes the rain fall at the end of *The Wasteland.* Otherwise, things go not all that differently in modernist writing, which inevitably deals with the same displaced nobility. Ulysses is no longer a chief but an exiled Jew embedded in a densely textured modern city. Odysseus Pound listens to Tieresias's prophecy in Canto 1 and then sets off on his wanderings through chaotic fragments of history as he tries to return to the lost Mediterranean homeland. In Eliot's thought and verse, democracy has truly wasted the land; the ancient power-giving king lies helpless and the modern city stinks with decay. But why did Tom from St. Louis, or old Ez from Idaho, worry so much about fallen majesty? Oh, the noble homes of England! Underneath the irony and despair of modernism lies a genuinely sappy and not at all uncommon fantasy about the lives of the great.

Another thing many modernists had in common with both James and the women writers of the nineteenth century was a conspicuously defective sense of historical process in combination with a painful sense of historical pressure. In "Hugh Selwyn Mauberly" Pound summed up the causes of World War I:

> There died a myriad,
> And of the best, among them,
> For an old bitch gone in the teeth,
> For a botched civilization,

Charm, smiling at the good mouth,
Quick eyes gone under earth's lid,
For two gross of broken statues,
For a few thousand battered books.

Beautiful—but, as Stephen Spender has pointed out, World War I was not fought over old books and statues. Here, as in so much of Pound, there is a pervasive and low-key silliness that is hard—at first—to detect. In this instance, the silliness partly stems from an exaggerated sense of individual helplessness. In Pound, as in James, there is a thoroughgoing passivity, in spite of both men's fascination with American machos and/or Renaissance condottieri. As Spender again has pointed out, "the 'Voltairean I' of Shaw, Wells, and others acts upon events. The 'modern I' of Rimbaud, Joyce, Proust, Eliot's Prufrock is acted upon by events."[4] Admittedly, these writers might have insisted on this very point themselves. Much of their work represents a conscious exploration of their own ignorant and excluded state. But the question is this: isn't this ignorant, excluded state a *deformity*? It is easy to see how much it impaired women novelists in the middle of the nineteenth century. Nobody argues that their sequestration from man's world was on the whole a blessing. Everybody agrees that this sequestration conferred a sort of second-class status and reinforced the unreal and "sentimental" side of their writing. Why, then, is it so hard for us to see that an analogous sequestration has had an emptying effect on the modernists? The answer is, they are the makers of *our* escapist daydreams.

Modernism has a close affinity with solipsism. When Decoud drifts away in a launch in *Nostromo*, losing contact with society, he discovers the void that modern literature loves to explore. Whereupon he kills himself. Modernism, seeing that society prevents us from an encounter with *nil*, generally considers *nil* the more honest alternative. Lionel Trilling also saw that the idea "of escaping wholly from the societal bonds" was the "chief idea of modern literature," admired the idea with the usual reservations, and defended the teaching of modern literature to university students.[5] It is good to follow Decoud, though of course without killing oneself. But an error has crept into the argument. The fact that society prevents us from an encounter with *nil*, or self-derangement, or unreason, by no means implies that *nil*, or self-derangement, or unreason represents the real state of affairs. As usual, the less sweeping inference is to be preferred. In this case the proper inference is very simple: the fact that we do not function very well if we are removed from our social order or prevented from assuming a place in one means that *we are social animals*. Modernism, the expression of detribalization in an elite class, exemplifies that truth over and over. But modernism never comes to understand it, let alone do anything about it, for modernism cannot take seriously the social and historical milieu. Instead, modernism repetitiously drives forward to what Irving Howe once called, I don't know how seriously, "the one uniquely modern style of salvation: a salvation by, of, and for the self."[6] Howe did not explain how this sort of self-creation was possible or desirable, nor why he chose to call it "salvation" rather than, say, narcissism, or autism, or solipsism. Approached from within, all these things can, no doubt, look and feel pretty good. But when we see them in someone else they look very unattractive. Modernism, with its disdain for the tribe, is helpless here. Realism, a genuinely tribal literature, has more insight, for it knows that we are what we are because of complex social contracts and a long chain of events including our own prior choices.

There are many reasons why, in the twenty-five period from 1930 to 1955, Henry James was moved from a coterie studio to the hall of the immortals. As early as the 1890s many advanced young artists and writers had regarded him as "the Master." In old age he continued to attract a devout following, many of whom—Percy Lubbock, Desmond MacCarthy—would keep the altar trimmed after James's death. Later the Agrarians, Fugitives, and other Southern conservatives showed precisely the kind of interest in James's work that one would expect. In 1934 an issue of *Hound and Horn* was devoted to James. New Criticism, in some respects a new form of the Southern conservative tradition, exerted a decisive influence in persuading students and English professors to take James more seriously.[7] But the most influential group of all in getting James accepted as a major figure was, paradoxically, a circle of once-radical New York critics who maintained close contact with Marxist thought. The fundamental reason why James was proclaimed the great nineteenth-century American author is that the collapse of American radicalism in the late 1930s and early 1940s left the intellectuals who gathered around the *Partisan Review* in precisely the same limbo that has always engendered or promoted genteel culture under whatever name it goes by. The Partisan Reviewers loved James because his fiction supplied the ideal material prop—highbrow fantasy masquerading as realism—for mandarins on the margin of American political life.

In attempting to demonstrate the truth of this claim, there is no point in belaboring the obvious: that *The Partisan Review* was in fact a highbrow journal, that it was tremendously influential in reorganizing American culture, that practically all those associated with the journal, those Norman Podhoretz has called "the family,"[8] had been committed to Communism earlier in the thirties, or that practically everyone in "the family" had lost this faith by the early 1940s and was now committed to the great early twentieth-century modernist writers. What must be demonstrated, however, is that the element in modernist literature that drew the Partisan Reviewers most of all was its renunciation of society as such, and that this renunciation in James served to validate his greatness.

On the first point, it is clear that for both Lionel Trilling and Philip Rahv, modernism represented an advanced form of individualism, a more extreme self-determination apart from society. Trilling was unusually lucid on this point. The "end" of modern literature, he declared, "is not merely freedom from the middle class but freedom from society itself."[9] Rahv was not quite so candid. In his 1942 essay, "On the Decline of Naturalism," he expressed the widespread sense of crisis among intellectuals on the left that resulted in their loss of interest in the great social novelists like Theodore Dreiser: "Manifestly the failure of the political movement in the literature of the past decade has resulted in a revival of religio-esthetic attitudes. The young men of letters are once again watching their own image in the mirror and listening to inner promptings." Rahv's decisive language—"manifestly," "failure"—leaves no doubt that he regarded "the political movement" as dead. But where was he positioned in relation to the "religio-esthetic attitudes" of the young men? His diction suggests that he viewed them with condescension, but a later passage from the same essay offers a qualified endorsement of political and social withdrawal:

And from a social-historical point of view this much can be said, that naturalism cannot hope to survive the world of 19th century science and industry of which it is the product. For what is the crisis of reality in contemporary art if not at bottom the crisis of the dissolution of this familiar world.

Evidently, the young men are only being honest in responding as they do to "the crisis of reality." Hence Rahv insisted that any live artist must see that "reality itself" is to be brought "into question," must not deny "the ever-growing element of the problematical in modern life."[10]

The important themes in Rahv's writing in the early 1940s—the paralyzing effect of this new disease known as "the problematical," the superiority of the psychological perspective over the social or political perspective, the tyrannical aspect of most social movements, and the sanctity of the private life—all lent strong support to his fondness for James. In 1945 he brought out an edition of James's most ambitious and substantial novel about American life, *The Bostonians*. Rahv's was the first twentieth-century edition of this novel. He approved of its negative picture of "the hysteria of Feminism." Because he overlooked or did not know about the many close friendships between women in nineteenth-century America,[11] friendships that were passionate but probably for the most part non-genital, Rahv saw Olive Chancellor as a brilliant, pre-Freudian study of lesbianism. In his view, the novel's basic "criticism of American life" was that it did not leave the individual alone:

> "In this country the people have rights but the person has none." This concern with the status of the individual, with defending the integrity of the personality and its right to its own discriminations and its own experience, is the central thread that runs through all of James's fiction.

Although Basil Ransom forcibly deprives Verena of her own "discriminations" and "experience," Rahv insisted on "the author's apparent sympathy" with this Southern reactionary. And although Basil's ambitions lie wholly in the urban North, Rahv saw him as a precursor of the Southern agrarians. Even more weirdly, Rahv saw Basil as an early version of the most distinguished modernist of all, T. S. Eliot. What Basil had in common with these gentlemen is that his "criticism of modern civilization is rooted in traditionalist principles." *The Bostonians* was a great novel because it sent up a large effort of radical social reform.

For Trilling, as for Rahv, impacted radicalism led directly to a proclamation of *The Bostonians* as a masterly representation of the deathly anomie of American social life. Yet Trilling's case is far more instructive, largely because of the remarkable links among his account of the failure of Communism in America in *The Middle of the Journey*, his effort to discern the essential common feature in the modernist texts he taught at Columbia, and his defense of *The Bostonians* as a masterly representation of the life-denying qualities in nineteenth-century American radicalism.

The Middle of the Journey offers an unrivaled insight into the left-wing depoliticization that to a large extent caused the "James revival." Trilling began writing the novel in 1946. It was published the following year.[12] The events it recounts took place in the late thirties, when many American Communists were struggling with the problem of the show-trials. The novel's two central characters are all defined in terms of their relationship to the Communist Party. John Laskell, the leading character, experiences a major Dantesque conversion or deconversion in the middle of his journey of life: he abruptly loses his faith in the radical cause. There are several reasons for this sudden change. He has almost died from a serious illness. He has acquired a new sense of his biological and existential nature, rather like Rahv's young men looking for themselves in the mirror and heeding their "inner promptings." Even more important, he sees that the Stalinist ideology of his old friends, the Crooms, has an "abstract" quality that ignores human needs and easily justifies assassination as a political means. But most of all Laskell is stirred by the conservative fears of Gifford Maxim.

Maxim, the most spectacular character in the novel, had been a member of the inner and secret Communist Party, the *real* Party with direct links to Moscow. He had gone underground. Now that he has recanted and resurfaced, he is afraid he will be assassinated. Very few people take his fears seriously. But Laskell does. Laskell, although he can't accept Maxim's new religiosity, believes he may very well be in danger. The reason why Laskell believes this is that he now sees the cruel absolutism that is latent in the Crooms' radicalism. He believe that their kind would be capable of anything. Laskell abandons his radical commitments, not because he recognizes the intellectual flaws in Marxist-Leninism and not because of any kind of alternative social vision, but because of fear—his own fear of death and Maxim's fear of the Crooms' kind of absolutism. When Trilling began writing the novel, he had not yet conceived of the character of Gifford Maxim; apparently, Laskell's political detoxification was to be the primary focus. But in the novel as written, Maxim stands very close to the center. He and his fear justify everything the novel says about man and politics.

In view of Maxim's central role, it is essential to note that this character, as Trilling has admitted in the 1976 introduction to a reissue of the novel, was based on Whittaker Chambers. The fact that Trilling, like so many others, came under the influence of this gifted public hypnotist to some extent explains the completely unconvincing argument at the heart of *The Middle of the Journey*—the argument that the Crooms' kind of absolutism justifies Maxim's fear of assassination and Laskell's abandonment of social justice. This is precisely the argument that became the staple plot in the 1950s radio program, *I Was a Communist for the FBI*. All that is missing is that the Crooms get a message from the secretary of the local cell that *they* are to be the assassins.

Even more interesting is that Maxim is in precisely the same position as Basil Ransom in *The Bostonians*. Both are threatened by the Left—by radical feminist reform or by Marxist subversion—and both feel themselves in extreme jeopardy. Hence, when Trilling wrote his introduction to his 1953 edition of *The Bostonians,* he, like Rahv, was profoundly impressed by James's portrayal of Ransom. For Trilling, too, feminism was a dead movement—an old, stuffy, unfunny, unimportant, and more than anything else, antisexual crusade. So stultifying was this crusade, in fact, that it even threatened James the artist as he tried to work out his one big novel on American life. James triumphed by seeing that the right way to make feminism work in a novel was to focus on its repressive and antierotic side. In doing so James represented "the bitter total war of the sexes" that would appear in Strindberg and D. H. Lawrence. But although Trilling praised the novel for its rendering of the sexual war, what he was actually praising it for was that it supported Basil's version of male supremacy, and attacked feminism. The proof of Trilling's partisanship is to be seen in his ill-advised interpretation of Basil as not only a proto-Agrarian but a brilliant anticipation "of the collateral British line of romantic conservatives": "[Basil] is akin to Yeats,

Lawrence, and Eliot in that he experiences his cultural fears in the most personal way possible, translating them into sexual fear, the apprehension of the loss of manhood."[13]

Failing to notice the irony with which James at times treated Basil, obviously unaware of James's own candid assessment of the poor quality of characterization—"Basil Ransom is made up of wandering airs & chance impressions, & I fear that as the story goes on he doesn't become as solid as he ought to be. He remains a rather vague & artificial creation, & so far as he looks at all real, is only fait de chic"[14]—Trilling's strikingly poor judgment tells us less about the novel than about the reasons why he fell for Ransom. Trilling clearly identified with the figure of the embattled conservative threatened by radicals so committed to their political causes that they deny the "biological" and "conditioned" aspect of human life.

It was partly because James succeeded in justifying Basil's sexual fear that Trilling proclaimed *The Bostonians* a "remarkable" representation of "the American actuality," so remarkable that *nowhere in American literature* "had the nature of the American social existence ever been so brilliantly suggested." The other reason for the novel's greatness was its representation of "the peculiar tenuity of the fabric of American social life." In support of this claim, Trilling cited such evidence at Basil's social life in New York, where he had "no other companion than his little variety actress."[15] Thus, *The Bostonians* shows that even in nineteenth-century American society there prevailed the alienation so conspicuous in modernist literature. Hence James's greatness. Yet Trilling's opinion is suspect. He never brings forward evidence from outside the novel for the "peculiar tenuity" of American life, and he never evinces a solid grasp of nineteenth-century American society, history, or popular fiction. He mentions very few Howells novels in his extremely discursive essay on this writer.[16] I am frankly skeptical that Trilling had any firm basis for thinking there was a "peculiar tenuity" in American society in the 1870s, and I suspect he derived this idea from the going doctrine on social *anomie* and from James's complaint about the thinness of American life in *Hawthorne*. If I am right, Trilling's praise of *The Bostonians* is not only perfectly circular but shows that Trilling, like Rahv, read James in a way that was wholly uncritical. Apparently it did not occur to Trilling that James had no way of knowing what an ambitious lawyer from the sticks would do to get ahead in New York. Thus, a depoliticized critic helped exalt a depoliticized writer, neither of whom was sufficiently aware of his real place in history.

In *The Middle of the Journey* Laskell feels a moment of extreme panic when the Crooms fail to meet him at the railroad station. In the 1976 introduction, Trilling seemed to think this panic was not motivated. But the motive is perfectly clear. The unwell Laskell feels helpless and alone in a foreign country: two of the images in his mind involve individuals tortured in Mexico and China. Laskell's fear is essentially no different from the uneasiness felt by a member of an urban ethnic enclave when he ventures into the countryside. The combination of Trilling's artistic skill in representing this fear and his apparent unconsciousness of it reveals the extent to which he denied his own origins. Alfred Kazin has pointed out that "for Trilling I would always be 'too Jewish,' too full of my lower-class experience. He would always defend himself from the things he had left behind."[17] All this suggests a further consideration: is it possible that some of the lucubrations in *Partisan Review* and elsewhere about "mass society" partly emerged from a sense of the United States *as a foreign land?*

Notwithstanding Trilling's sweet and reasonable comprehensiveness, his reasons for appreciating *The Bostonians* seem as dubious as the case he makes for withdrawing from political life in *The Middle of the Journey*. In both instances, Trilling, rather like Dostoevsky in *The Possessed*, sees radicals as a kind of demon-ridden folk. There is clearly some truth in this view, as there is in Trilling's insistence that American radicals often exhibit an "imperious" refusal "to consent to the conditioned nature of human existence." He was surely on the mark in perceiving that this refusal occasionally serves to justify real tyranny and terror and more frequently leads to a short-circuiting of those democratic political processes that depend on "opinion, contingency, conflicts of interest and clashes of will and the compromises they lead to."[18] But it is one thing to denounce absolutist politics, quite another to abandon liberal reform. Laskell doesn't withdraw from radical politics alone; he quits politics, period. He may do so in the name of our "associated life," but that is surely window-dressing, given the fact that he ends up *out* of this same associated life.

The first third of *The Bostonians* is brilliant if distorted social fiction; the remainder of the novel is a letdown, as many readers have complained.[19] Rahv and Trilling performed a service in drawing a very interesting and virtually unread novel to the attention of modern readers. Yet these critics not only exaggerated James's achievement in the novel but praised it for the wrong reasons. They distorted James's hostile exposé of a social movement's tyrannical aspect into a denunciation of progressive reform. They were far too eager to identify with the aristocratic male lead, and they failed to notice how little real information James supplied about this character. They were far too hasty and uninformed in praising the novel's accuracy of representation of a large social scene. The reason they made these mistakes, giving their highest praise to *The Bostonians* and proclaiming James the great nineteenth-century American realist, was that the book authorized their escapist fantasies. The book said—to them— that the public life always seeks to destroy the private life (Olive tyrannizing Verena), and that the best an independent intellectual can hope to achieve in mass society is a well-armed, fully self-conscious withdrawal (Basil taking Verena and writing essays for a small-circulation review). Their mistake—reading *The Bostonians* and James's other novels as accurate social realism—validated an elitist political inactivity by grounding it in apparent social fact. James was the one pre-modern writer who showed that the modernists and not the naturalists were on the right track.

The balked former radicals who helped canonize James in the 1940s form an arresting historical parallel with the ineffective gentlemen reformers of the Gilded Age, "the best men" who gathered around E. L. Godkin at the *Nation* (see chapter 21). Each group had a small-circulation magazine that became very influential in cultivated or highbrow circles. Each group was led by stern intellectuals who severed, or originally lacked close ties to popular American life. Both groups saw this culture as by and large beneath criticism—though they criticized it extensively—and both applied their own special term to the contemptible democratic public. Only, what was *vulgar* in the Gilded Age became *mass* or *low-brow* or *middle-brow* in the *Partisan Review*. Strangest of all, the writer who expressed the essential fantasy of "the best men" happened to be identical with the writer who was rediscovered and placed in glory by the Partisan Reviewers.

But of course there is no strangeness at all in this coincidence. The social and political alienation that led to the rediscovery of James was not essentially different from the unachieved manhood that led James himself to work out the most distinguished "alternative sphere" in American literature. Those who read Santayana's definition of the genteel tradition as applying only to the nineteenth century or to an obsolete sort of social decorum miss the point. The genteel tradition is not only alive and well, but for many intellectuals and writers it is *still* all there is. The genteel tradition remains exactly the same sort of thing it has always been—a superior counterculture that defines itself against the ordinary, the practical, the material. It insists as it has always done on art as something separate, something vastly more distinguished.

Notes

1. A GENRE AND ITS ABSORBED AUDIENCE

1. David Masson, *British Novelists and Their Styles: Being a Critical Sketch of the History of British Prose Fiction* (Boston: Lothrop, 1875), p. 298.

2. "Censor" (pseudonym for Bunce), *Don't: A Manual of Mistakes & Improprieties More or Less Prevalent in Conduct & Speech* (London: Ward, Lock, n.d.), p. 59. Bunce was an editor at Appleton's. *Don't* appeared in 1883.

3. Quoted from an American magazine by James D. Hart, *The Popular Book: A History of America's Literary Taste* (New York: Oxford University Press, 1950), p. 91. On Howells and James, see *Criticism and Fiction* (New York: Hill and Wang, 1967), p. 149, and Leon Edel, ed., *The American Essays*, (New York: Vintage, 1956), pp. 203–204. In 1899, when Howells went to a reception at the English (literature) Club in Lincoln, Nebraska, he was met by women only; Robert Rowlette, "William D. Howells' 1899 Midwest Lecture Tour," *American Literary Realism* (1976), 9:3.

4. According to Frank Luther Mott, *Golden Multitudes: The Story of Best Sellers in the United States* (New York: Macmillan, 1947). See also Hart, *Popular Book*, p. 90, and Fred Lewis Pattee, *The Feminine Fifties* (New York: Appleton, 1940). For more recent views see Mary P. Ryan, *Womanhood in America, from Colonial Times to the Present* (New York: New Viewpoints, 1975), p. 143, and Ann Douglas, *The Feminization of American Culture* (New York: Avon, 1977), p. 72. See also Mary Kelley, "The Sentimentalists: Promise and Betrayal in the Home," *Signs* (Spring 1979), 4:434–446; Charles H. Sergel, "The Comparative Popularity of Authors," *The Critic* (1887), n.s. 8, p. 100.

5. Anna Warner, *Susan Warner ("Elizabeth Wetherell")* (New York: Putnam, 1909), pp. 135, 398, 91, 399, 89–90. The second quotation comes from Susan's journal. Edward Halsey Foster, *Susan and Anna Warner* (New York: Twayne, 1978), has a recent monograph stressing political and religious backgrounds. For bibliography, see Dorothy Hurlbut Sanderson, *They Wrote for a Living* (West Point, N.Y.: Constitution Island Association, 1976).

6. Noah Porter, *Books and Reading; or, What Books Shall I Read and How Shall I Read Them?* (New York: Scribner, 1870), pp. 229, 220.

7. Nina Baym, *Woman's Fiction: A Guide to Novels by and about Women in America, 1820–1870* (Ithaca: Cornell University Press, 1978).

8. Oliver Bell Bunce, *A Bachelor's Story* (New York: Townsend, 1860), p. 90. For a discussion of empathetic-identification, see Margaret Mead, "Evolutionary Implications of Learning by Empathy, Imitation, and Identification," *Continuities in Cultural Evolution* (New Haven: Yale University Press, 1964).

9. "They like the hero, and Mrs. Simpson cried over the last scene." This is the report that first indicates that *A Modern Romeo* is going to become a bestselling novel in Howells' study of the literary marketplace, *The World of Chance* (New York: Harper, 1893), p. 342.

2. FANTASY IN THE NOVEL

1. Ann Douglas, *The Feminization of American Culture* (New York: Avon, 1977), p. 9.

2. Marcia Westkott, "Dialectics of Fantasy," *Frontiers: A Journal of Women Studies* (Fall 1977), 2:1–7. For a theoretical Jungian approach, see Lee R. Edwards, "The Labors of Psyche: Toward a Theory of Female Heroism," *Critical Inquiry* (Autumn 1979), 6:33–49.

3. Lee Edwards, "Love and Work: Fantasies of Resolution," *Frontiers: A Journal of Women Studies.* (Fall 1977), 2:32.

4. Norman N. Holland, *The Dynamics of Literary Response* (New York: Oxford University Press, 1968), p. 31.

5. John G. Cawelti, *Adventure, Mystery, and Romance: Formula Stories as Art and Popular Culture* (Chicago: University of Chicago Press, 1976), pp. 29, 30, 34. See also Tzvetan Todorov, "The Typology of Detective Fiction," *The Poetics of Prose*, Richard Howard, trans. (Oxford: Blackwell, 1977), pp. 42–52.

6. Adeline D. T. Whitney, *The Gayworthys: A Story of Threads and Thrums* (Boston: Loring, 1865), p. 122. This vignette was intended to have a typical quality, the Gairs being a representative urban family and contrasted to the more earnest and individualized country Gayworthys. Henry James did a hatchet job on the novel at the age of 22—*North American Review* (October 1865), 101:619–622.

7. The studies of gender and society I am most indebted to are Margaret Mead, *Male and Female, a Study of the Sexes in a Changing World* (New York: Morrow, 1949); Robert J. Stoller, *Perversion: The Erotic Form of Hatred* (New York: Pantheon Books, 1975), and the same author's *Sex and Gender: On the Development of Masculinity and Femininity* (New York: Science House, 1968); and Eleanor Emmons Maccoby and Carol Nagy Jacklin, *The Psychology of Sex Differences* (Stanford: Stanford University Press, 1978). My basic theory of role-acquisition comes from L. Kohlberg, "A Cognitive-Developmental Analysis of Children's Sex-Role Concepts and Attitudes," in Eleanor Emmons Maccoby, ed., *The Development of Sex Differences* (Stanford: Stanford University Press, 1966). This theory says that children learn certain sex-roles, not through unconscious imitation or submission to heavy pressure, but by acquiring a *conception* of "sex-typed behavior" that "stems from organized rules the child has induced from what he has observed and what he has been

told." These rules are simple and involve "a limited set of features that are salient and describable from a child's point of view (e.g., hair styles and dress); the child's sex-role conceptions are cartoon-like" (*Psychology of Sex Differences,* pp. 364–366. This theory is not mechanistic, nor does it explain human development in terms of processes of which we are unaware. It has an obvious relevance to a conscious heroine-focused activity like novel-reading.

For modern, sexually oriented studies of female fantasies, see Nancy Friday, *My Secret Garden: Women's Sexual Fantasies* (New York: Trident, 1973), and Karen Shanor, *The Fantasy Files: A Study of the Sexual Fantasies of Contemporary Women* (New York: Dial, 1977).

8. Stoller, *Perversion,* pp. 63, 83; italics mine.

9. Joyce Berkman, "The Nurturant Fantasies of Olive Schreiner," *Frontiers* (Fall 1977), 2:11. James, a shrewder commentator on popular fiction and culture than he is generally given credit for, once described a father's attempt to make a sympathetic appeal to his daughter in these terms: "There was a passage during which, on a yellow silk sofa under one of the palms, he had her on his knee, stroking her hair, playfully holding her off while he showed his shining fangs and let her, with a vague, affectionate, helpless, pointless 'Dear old girl, dear little daughter,' inhale the fragrance of his cherished beard." This treatment promptly brought tears to the girl's eyes. See *What Maisie Knew* (London: Heinemann, 1898), p. 150.

10. Susan Warner, *Melbourne House* (New York: Robert Carter, 1864), 2:96. The illustration is in 1:229.

11. Susan Warner, *The Wide, Wide World* (Philadelphia: Lippincott, 1875), 2:327, 333.

3. LOVE INTEREST

1. *Graham's Magazine* (1854), 45:n.p.

2. Joseph Kirkland, *Zury: The Meanest Man in Spring County: A Novel of Western Life* (Urbana: University of Illinois Press, 1956), p. 303.

3. John Updike, "The Future of the Novel," *Picked-Up Pieces* (New York: Knopf, 1975), p. 19. At the turn of the century an aesthetic young man ventured the daring notion that "the novel of the future is going to be the novel without a love story." Frank Norris, *The Pit* (New York: Evergreen, 1956), p. 56.

4. Nina Baym, *Woman's Fiction: A Guide to Novels by and about Women in America, 1820–1870* (Ithaca: Cornell University Press, 1978), pp. 38–40. On husband hunting, in an 1877 novel an old-fashioned widow voices the requirements of propriety: "No *lady* will ever allow herself to become interested in a gentleman till he has positively sought her in marriage." This is the "first and great commandment, upon which all the law and prophets of womanhood hung." Elizabeth Stuart Phelps, *The Story of Avis* (Boston: Houghton Mifflin, 1905), p. 176. Doesn't this "commandment" largely explain why the heroines don't chase husbands? As for rescues, the heroines

of *The Wide, Wide World, Queechy, Beulah,* and *Faith Gartney's Girlhood* (four bestsellers) are all rescued by their future husbands, and the heroines of *The Lamplighter* and *'Lena Rivers* are rescued by their fathers. On happy endings, excluding *Uncle Tom's Cabin*, every single bestselling novel written by an American woman in the 1850s and 1860s (using Mott's estimated sales figures and criteria for determining bestsellers) had a happy ending. These fifteen books were *The Wide, Wide World, The Curse of Clifton, The Lamplighter, Tempest and Sunshine, 'Lena Rivers, Beulah, The Hidden Hand, Rutledge, Malaeska, The Fatal Marriage, Faith Gartney's Girlhood, Ishmael* and *Self-Raised* (a single novel though listed separately in Mott), *Hans Brinker or, The Silver Skates, St. Elmo,* and *Little Women.* See Frank Luther Mott, *Golden Multitudes: The Story of Best Sellers in the United States* (New York: Macmillan, 1947), pp. 307–309. On Baym's side, Mott offers no data to support his claims on minimum sales figures. By happy ending I mean the engagement or marriage of the heroine. (In *The Wide, Wide World* a future engagement is presumed.) An exception to all the happy endings was Evans' Civil War novel, *Macaria; or, the Altars of Sacrifice* (1864).

Elaine Showalter, *A Literature of Their Own: British Women Novelists from Brontë to Lessing* (Princeton: Princeton University Press, 1977), also overlooks the importance of heterosexual attraction in women's novels. In chapter 5, Showalter interprets the male heroes as "in large part projections of aspects of the women themselves" (p. 133). The good heroes reflected "female fantasies . . . more concerned with power and authority than with romance" (p. 136). The Rochester types "represent the passionate and angry qualities in their creators" (p. 143). This view seems unbalanced. It is one thing to perceive that women's heroes reflected women's perspectives and fantasies. It is an entirely different thing to imply that these heroes were not seen and read as masculine.

5. Augusta J. Evans, *St. Elmo* (New York: Carleton, 1868), pp. 338, 471. Also, when St. Elmo reads a false report of Edna's engagement, "his swarthy face paled" (p. 539).

6. Susan Warner, *Queechy* (New York: Putnam, 1852), 2:290–293. The vernacular word for love-interest in America is *romance*, with the accent on the first syllable at least as early as 1852 (*Queechy*, 1:89). Skillful writers strained to make the proposal scene subtle and indirect; see Howells' early poem, "Before the Gate," *Atlantic* (August 1869), 23:176.

7. In "The Origin of ·Genres," *New Literary History* (Autumn 1976), 8:159–170, Tzvetan Todorov suggests that many genres have a particular speech-act as their generative core. One of his examples is a kind of poem from the Luba culture in Zaire, that is based on the speech-act of inviting someone to dine. Todorov's essay implies that it is hopeless to consider genre apart from culture.

8. Catherine Beecher, "An Address to the Christian Women of America," in Gail Parker, ed., *The Oven Birds: American Women on Womanhood, 1820–1920.* (Garden City, N.Y.: Doubleday, 1972), p. 150. See also Kathryn Kish Sklar, *Catherine Beecher: A Study in American Domesticity* (New Haven: Yale University Press, 1973), pp. 155–163.

9. Augusta J. Evans, *Beulah* (New York: Derby and Jackson, 1860), 339–340. "No longer a mere self-willed girl, consulting only her own wishes and tastes, she had given another the right to guide and control her" (p. 340). For a good recent discussion of the domestic ideal, see Nancy F. Cott, "Domesticity," *The Bonds of Womanhood: 'Woman's Sphere' in New England, 1780–1835* (New Haven: Yale University Press, 1977), pp. 63—100.

10. George Henry Lewes, "The Lady Novelists," *Westminster Review* (1852), as reprinted in Elaine Showalter, ed., *Women's Liberation and Literature* (New York: Harcourt Brace Jovanovich, 1971), p. 175.

11.Mary P. Ryan, *Womanhood in America, from Colonial Times to the Present* (New York: New Viewpoints, 1975), p. 154.

12. See Bronislaw Malinowski, *Sex, Culture, and Myth* (New York: Harcourt, 1962), pp. 32–33; also M. F. Ashley Montagu, ed., *Marriage: Past and Present/ A Debate between Robert Briffault and Bronislaw Malinowski* (Boston: Porter Sargent, 1956).

13. Kirkland, *Zury,* ch. 10. The most popular literary retelling of the story was Longfellow's poem, "The Courtship of Miles Standish." Harriet Prescott Spofford retold it in "Priscilla," in *Three Heroines of New England Romance* (Boston: Little Brown, 1894). James Whitcomb Riley wrote a poem about a folk performance of the story, "John Alden and Percilly." Perhaps the classic nineteenth-century American treatment of the intangible barriers between a young man and woman who love each other was James Russell Lowell's interesting poem, "The Courtin'," where the young couple seem helpless to express their interest in one another until he abruptly kisses her. Then they are happy and tearful.

4. HOME SWEET HOME

1. William Wasserstrom, *Heiress of All the Ages: Sex and Sentiment in the Genteel Tradition* (Minneapolis: University of Minnesota Press, 1959), p. 12. The review was in the *American Journal of Psychology* (November 1890), 3:258–259.

2. See R. W. B. Lewis, *Edith Wharton: A Biography* (New York: Harper and Row, 1975), pp. 52–53.

3. It is not long before the Falkners have separate bedrooms. *Together* (Greenwich, Conn.: Fawcett, 1962), p. 52.

4. Carl N. Degler, "What Ought To Be and What Was: Women's Sexuality in the Nineteenth Century," *American Historical Review* (December 1974), 79:1467–90. At the beginning of the nineteenth century there was still a great deal of casual premarital promiscuity in New England. By the 1840s, this would be associated with the backwards rural life. The country bumpkin who serves as a vehicle for a satire in *High Life in New York* recalls: "I don't mean to say that Judy had any thing agin sparking in a reg'lar way, on Sunday nights in the east room, when the paper curtains was all down and the old folks had gone to bed. It cum kinder nateral to set up till two or three o'clock, and Judy warnt by no means old-maidish." Ann Stephens,

High Life in New York. By Jonathan Slick, Esq., of Weathersfield, Connecticut (New York: Edward Stephens, 1843), p. 12. It is significant that this sparking was OK even though it did not represent serious courtship. W. D. Howells would often glance with half-averted eye at couples making out in public, generally implying that they are lower class. Hamlin Garland, *Rose of Dutcher's Coolly* (1895) has an episode in which a woman schoolteacher in the country stimulates a sudden rise in promiscuity among her older pupils.

5. M. E. W. S., "New England Women," *Atlantic* (August 1878), 42:234. For two different variations on the view that the industrial revolution had an adverse effect on women's roles, see Mary P. Ryan, *Womanhood in America, from Colonial Times to the Present* (New York: New Viewpoints, 1975), pp. 83–191, and Ann Douglas, *The Feminization of American Culture* (New York: Avon, 1977), pp. 50–93. In a review of Rayna R. Reiter, ed., *Toward an Anthropology of Women*, in *American Journal of Sociology* (1977), 82:872, Sherry B. Ortner expresses the consensus of the writers in the book: "things changed for women with the rise of the state, generally for the worse." For a forceful statement of the opposing view, see Edward Shorter, "Women's Work: What Difference Did Capitalism Make?" *Theory and Society* (Winter 1976), 3:513–527. Shorter analyzes the sexual division of labor and the differences in sex roles among peasants in preindustrial France and demonstrates that capitalism in the first half of the nineteenth century enhanced women's status and freedom. Douglas' *Feminization of American Culture* seems to demonstrate the opposite point for the same period in the United States—however, it is well to remember that this book focuses on upper-middle-class women, who, unlike working women, experienced a loss of economic function with industrialization. Also, of course, preindustrial life in Europe and North America seems to have had some remarkable dissimilarities. Interestingly, W. D. Howells' mother (born in 1812 to an Irish father and Pennsylvania Dutch mother) "drew a sharp line between the duties of her boys and girls in the tradition of her Pennsylvania origin." Howells, *Years of My Youth* (Bloomington: Indiana University Press, 1975), p. 86.

6. Robert Frost, "Home Burial," *Collected Poems* (New York: Halcyon, 1939), pp. 69–73. See Richard Poirier, "Women at Home," *New York Review of Books* (September 29, 1977), 24:34–39.

7. Edward O. Wilson, *On Human Nature* (Cambridge: Harvard University Press, 1978).

8. Quoted from Martha Saxton, *Louisa May: A Modern Biography of Louisa May Alcott* (Boston: Houghton Mifflin, 1977), pp. 65–66.

9. Howells, *Annie Kilburn, Harper's Monthly* (July 1888), 77:270.

10. James *The American Scene* (Bloomington: Indiana University Press, 1968), pp. 345, 64–65, 164. Many novels offer a kind of confirmation. In Henry Blake Fuller's *With the Procession* (1895), the successful Chicago businessman, David Marshall, has nothing to do at home except read the newspaper, stare out the window, and pace up and down the sidewalk in front of the house (his wife won't let him smoke inside).

11. Mrs. S. A. Southworth, *The Inebriate's Hut; or, The First Fruits of the Maine Law* (Boston: Phillips, Sampson, 1854).

12. Charlotte Perkins Gilman, *The Home: Its Work and Influence* (Urbana: University of Illinois Press, 1972), pp. 293, 294. First published 1903. For a good account of Gilman's thought, see Carl N. Degler, "Charlotte Perkins Gilman on the Theory and Practice of Feminism," *American Quarterly* (Spring 1956), 8:21–39.

13. Oliver Bell Bunce, "A Further Notion or Two about Domestic Bliss," *Appleton's Journal of Literature, Science, and Art* (March 19, 1870), 3:328–329. This and the earlier article, "Some Notions about Domestic Bliss," (March 12, 1870), pp. 295–296, were collected as chapter 2 in Bunce, *Bachelor Bluff: His Opinions, Sentiments, and Disputations* (New York: Appleton, 1881). The bluff bachelor was the favored mask of Bunce, a polite, vigorous iconoclast.

14. William Henry Milburn, "An Hour's Talk about Woman," in *The Rifle, Axe, and Saddle-Bags, and Other Lectures* (New York: Derby and Jackson, 1857), pp. 189–191, 169.

15. Alexander Hamilton Sands, *Recreations of a Southern Barrister* (Philadelphia: Lippincott, 1859), p. 199.

16. Augusta J. Evans, *Beulah* (New York: Derby & Jackson, 1860), p. 454. Elsewhere, Dr. Asbury voices the author's extreme conservatism: "My wife is an exception, but the mass of married women, now-a-day, (sic) instead of being thorough housewives (as nature intended they should), are delicate, do-nothing, know-nothing fine ladies. They have no duties" (*Beulah*, p. 296).

My argument is that bad marriage was common, but I am not quantifying this assertion. Page Smith was reckless in claiming "there is substantial evidence that the vast majority of American marriages, at least in the larger cities of the East and Middle West in the nineteenth century, were minor disasters. *Daughters of the Promised Land* (Boston: Little, Brown, 1970), p. 131.

17. Milburn, *Rifle*, p. 191. See Kirk Jeffrey, "The Family as Utopian Retreat from the City," *Soundings* (Spring 1972), pp. 21–41.

18. Sands, *Recreations*, p. 196.

19. *Boston Quarterly Review* (October 1859), p. 492, and *Continental Monthly* (May 1864), p. 23, as quoted in Herman Lantz, Martin Schultz, and Mary O'Hara, "The Changing American Family from the Preindustrial to the Industrial Period: A Final Report," *American Sociological Review* (June 1977), 42:406–421. This study checked 6,559 magazine issues from 1850 to 1865 and found a much higher proportion of articles dealing with family conflict than in periods before 1850. Lantz *et al.* propose that the 1850–65 years were pivotal in the history of the modern family. For other studies of the nineteenth-century family, see Stow Persons, *The Decline of American Gentility* (New York: Columbia University Press, 1973), pp. 74–102; William J. Goode, *The Family* (Englewood Cliffs, N.J.: Prentice Hall, 1964); and especially Edward Shorter, *The Making of the Modern Family* (New York: Basic Books, 1975). For an attack on Christopher Lasch's *Haven in a Heartless World: The Family Besieged* (New York: Basic Books, 1977), see Adrienne Harris and Edward Shorter, "Besieging Lasch," *Theory and Society* (September 1978), 6:279–292. For an excellent study of the ways social structure causes inevitable marital conflict, see Robert Murphy, "Social Structure and Sex Antagonism,"

Southwestern Journal of Anthropology (1959), 15(1):89–98, and Charles and Cherry Lindholm, "Marriage as Warfare," *Natural History* (October 1979), 88:11–20. For a nineteenth-century American statement, see Eliza Bisbee Duffey, *The Relations of the Sexes* (New York: Estill, 1876).

20. Adeline D. T. Whitney, *Mother Goose for Grown Folks* (Boston: Houghton Mifflin, 1890). First published 1860.

21. Fanny Fern, *Caper-Sauce: A Volume of Chit-Chat about Men, Women, and Things* (New York: Carleton, 1872), p. 296. See particularly the essay in this volume titled "Sauce for the Gander."

22. Quoted from James Parton et al., *Eminent Women of the Age; Being Narratives of the Lives and Deeds of the Most Prominent Women of the Present Generation* (Hartford: Betts, 1868), pp. 210–212. Another early sharp-tongued women's advice columnist was Jane Swisshelm. For a brief excerpt from her *Letters to Country Girls* (New York: J. C. Riker, 1853), see Gerda Lerner, *The Female Experience: An American Documentary* (Indianapolis: Bobbs-Merrill, 1977), pp. 116–118.

23. H. Augusta Dodge, ed., *Gail Hamilton's Life in Letters* (Boston: Lee and Shepard, 1901), p. 434.

24. *Ibid.*, pp. 588–589. Apparently written April 25, 1867.

25. Fanny Fern, *Caper-Sauce*, p. 272.

26. *Ibid.*, pp. 12–13.

27. Jack London, *Martin Eden* (New York: Holt, Rinehart and Winston, 1956), p. 87.

28. W. D. Howells, *The Minister's Charge* (Boston: Ticknor, 1887), p. 204. Howells, *Criticism and Fiction* (New York: Hill and Wang, 1967), p. 94, wrote that novel-reading was "hardly more related to thought or the wholesome exercise of the mental faculties than opium-eating." Howells' Miss Cotton in *April Hopes* is a portrait of an unmarried woman who has constructed a "rose-coloured ideal world" from her reading of "genteel novels." *April Hopes* (New York: Harper, 1888), p. 174. One of the most direct assaults on girlish fantasies about marriage is in Marietta Holley, *Samantha among the Brethren* (New York: Funk and Wagnalls, 1892), pp. 31–47.

29. Ryan, *Womanhood in America*, p. 258. See also pp. 155–158.

30. Mrs. E. D. E. N. Southworth, *The Curse of Clifton* (Philadelphia: Peterson, 1852), p. 259.

31. Thomas Bailey Aldrich, *Majorie Daw and Other People* (Boston: Osgood, 1873), pp. 249, 248, 261. Howells considered this Aldrich's second-best story and collected it in *The Great Modern American Stories* (New York: Boni and Liveright, 1920).

32. Statistically, cohorts of American women born in 1860s and 70s had a significantly higher proportion of unmarried members than any other age group from 1835 to 1930. See Daniel Scott Smith, "Family Limitation, Sexual Control, and Domestic Feminism in Victorian America," in Mary S. Hartman and Lois Banner, eds., *Clio's Consciousness Raised: New Perspectives on the History of Women* (New York: Harper, 1974), p. 121. Helen Waite Papashvily, in *All the Happy Endings* (New York: Harper, 1956), focuses on the secret war between the sexes in "domestic" fiction of the period.

33. Charlotte Perkins Gilman, *Women and Economics: A Study of the Economic Relation Between Men and Women as a Factor in Social Evolution* (Boston: Small, Maynard, 1911), pp. 128–129. First published 1898.

34. Howells, *Criticism and Fiction*, p. 96; italics mine.

5. DOMESTIC BITTERNESS AS PRESENTED IN POPULAR WOMEN'S NOVELS

1. Mrs. Gaskell, "Preface," in Maria S. Cummins, *Mabel Vaughan* (Leipzig: Tauchnitz, 1857), p. vii.

2. *The Age of Innocence* (New York: Scribner, 1920), p. 45.

3. Susan Warner, *The Wide, Wide World* (Philadelphia: Lippincott, 1875), 1:67, 69.

4. *Queechy* (New York: Putnam, 1852), 2:187.

5. Quoted from *The Deserted Wife* by Helen Waite Papashvily, *All the Happy Endings* (New York: Harper, 1956), p. 116.

6. Augusta J. Evans, *Beulah* (New York: Derby & Jackson, 1860), p. 228.

7. Mrs. Adeline D. T. Whitney, *The Gayworthys: A Story of Threads and Thrums* (Boston: Loring, 1865), pp. 276, 236–237. Henry James detested the sailor for his scorn of the girl—*North American Review* (October 1865), 101:620–621.

8. *The Complete Poetical Works of John Greenleaf Whittier* (Boston: Houghton Mifflin, 1903), p. 63.

9. *Bret Harte's Writings: Poems* (Cambridge: Houghton, Mifflin, n.d.), p. 290. From "Mrs. Judge Jenkins."

10. Harriet Beecher Stowe et al., *Six of One by Half a Dozen of the Other/An Every Day Novel* (Boston: Roberts, 1872). In an earlier novel by Whitney, *Faith Gartney's Girlhood* (one of the two topselling books of 1863 by an American author), a wise middle-aged nurse declares, "It's an awful thing to tangle up and disarrange the plans of Providence. And more of it's done, I verily believe, in this matter of marrying, than any other way. It's like mismatching anything else,—gloves or stockings,—and wearing the wrong ones together. They don't fit; and more'n that, it spoils another pair." Adeline D. T. Whitney, *Faith Gartney's Girlhood* (Boston: Loring, 1863), p. 294. This idea—an unwise marriage often spoils a good match—is evident in Rebecca Harding Davis' contemporary story, "Paul Blecker,"—*Atlantic* (May, June 1863), vol. 11. Grey Gurney, who married the wrong man before she knew any better, says to the man she now loves, "There's thousands of young girls married as I was" (p. 592).

11. *Gayworthys*, pp. 62, 65. The reason the author flinches at the word *affinity* is that it was code for free love. Unhappy marriage was one of the big themes in women's fiction in the 1860s. According to Nina Baym, *Woman's Fiction: A Guide to Novels by and about Women in America, 1820–1870* (Ithaca: Cornell University Press, 1978), p. 206, Marion Harland's *Husbands and Homes* (1864) "shows a new emphasis on bad marriage rather than no marriage as the source of the deepest feminine misery. All six of the stories in the group are chronicles of married misery." Baym regards the generally

unhappy homes in earlier 1850s novels as a byproduct of the plot that told of a heroine's struggles and trials: "In accordance with the needs of plot, home life is presented, overwhelmingly, as unhappy. There are very few intact families in this literature, and those that are intact are unstable or locked into routines of misery" (pp. 26–27).

12. *The Titan* (New York: Dell, 1959), p. 79. The passage is presented as an exaggeration of attitudes prevalent in good Chicago society during the Gilded Age. Bromfield Corey gives a satiric sketch of the same attitudes as evident in Boston: "The women in America represent the aristocracy which exists everywhere else in both sexes. You are born to the patrician leisure; you have the accomplishments and the clothes and manners and ideals; and we men are a natural commonalty, born to business." Howells, *April Hopes* (New York: Harper, 1888), pp. 311–312.

6. JOHN WILLIAM DE FOREST VS. ELIZABETH STUART PHELPS

1. Elizabeth T. Spring, "Elizabeth Stuart Phelps," *Our Famous Women. An Authorized Record of the Lives and Deeds of Distinguished American Women of Our Times* (Hartford: Worthington, 1884), p. 566. For other studies of Phelps, see Mary Angela Bennett "Elizabeth Stuart Phelps," Ph. D. dissertation, University of Pennsylvania, 1939; Christine Stansell, "Elizabeth Stuart Phelps: A Study in Female Rebellion," *Massachussetts Review* (Winter-Spring 1972), 13:239–256.

For James's low opinion of Phelps's work, cf. his passing mention in his reviews of *Lothair* in *Atlantic* (August 1870), 26:251, and *Ezra Stiles Gannett* in *Nation* (April 1, 1875), 20:228. Howells faulted her for vagueness, obscurity, and "a certain feminine desire to get yet one sigh or one gasp more out of expression" in his review of her *Poetic Studies* in *Atlantic* (July 1875), 36:108–109. In a survey of short stories in the "Editor's Study," *Harper's Monthly* (February 1887), 74:485, Howells gave her story "In the Gray Goth" a left-handed compliment by calling it "very simple, powerful, and affecting, and of an unstrained human quality which the gifted author too seldom consents to give us."

For Phelps's low opinion of Howells and realism, see her *Chapters from a Life* (Boston: Houghton Mifflin, 1896), pp. 257–266.

Phelps is an example of what Diana Trilling has called the twentieth-century heroine of sensibility—that projection of "female self-love in which one counts how many more, and more acute, nerve-ends women have than men." "The Liberated Heroine," *Partisan Review* (1978), 45:514. It was the nineteenth century that saw the full efflorescence of this mentality.

2. Phelps, *Chapters from a Life*, pp. 94–109. Phelps's statement about the angel came from St. John and hence reveals her extreme self-exaltation. Worse, the whole idea was stolen from an earlier woman's novel: "'The angel said unto me Write, and I wrote.' It was with no irreverence that Harvey, then and ever after, quoted John's words as the only explanation she could

give to herself or others of her course in life." Anne Moncure Crane, *Opportunity. A Novel* (Boston: Ticknor and Fields, 1867), p. 198.

3. Elizabeth Stuart Phelps, *The Gates Ajar* (Cambridge: Harvard University Press, 1964), p. 104. For background, see Barbara Welter, "The Feminization of American Religion: 1800–1860," in Mary S. Hartman and Lois Banner, eds., *Clio's Consciousness Raised: New Perspectives on the History of Women* (New York: Harper, 1974), pp. 137–157, and Ann Douglas, *The Feminization of American Culture* (New York: Avon, 1977).

4. Thomas Beer thought that no great literature dealt with the Civil War "because of that spiritual censorship which strictly forbids the telling of truth about any American record until the material of such an essay is scattered and gone"—*Stephen Crane* (New York: Octagon, 1972), p. 43. For other theories of the dearth of good fiction about the war, see Daniel Aaron, *The Unwritten War* (New York: Knopf, 1973), pp. xiii–xix, 327–340. For a good brief survey of Civil War fiction, see Wayne Charles Miller, *An Armed America: Its Face in Fiction* (New York: New York University Press, 1970), ch. 3.

5. John William De Forest, *Miss Ravenel's Conversion from Secession to Loyalty* (Columbus, Ohio: Charles E. Merrill, 1969), p. 134. For discussions of the novel, see Gordon Haight, introduction to *Miss Ravenel's Conversion from Secession to Loyalty* (New York: Rinehart, 1955); Albert E. Stone, Jr., "Best Novel of the Civil War," *American Heritage* (June 1962), 13:84–88; Claude M. Simpson, Jr., "John W. De Forest, *Miss Ravenel's Conversion*," in Wallace Stegner, ed., *The American Novel from James Fenimore Cooper to William Faulkner* (New York: Basic Books, 1965), pp 35–46; E. R. Hagemann, "John William De Forest's 'Great American Novel,'" in Charles Alva Hoyt, ed., *Minor American Novelists* (Carbondale: Southern Illinois University Press, 1970), pp. 10–27.

6. Joseph Kirkland, *The Captain of Company K* (Ridgewood, N.J.: Gregg, 1968), p. 83. To some extent, De Forest romanticized combat. In 1886, after reading *War and Peace*, he wrote to Howells: "Let me tell you that nobody but he [Tolstoy] has written the whole truth about war and battle. *I* tried, and I told all I dared, and perhaps all I could. But there was one thing I did not dare tell, lest the world should infer that I was naturally a coward, and so could not know the feelings of a brave man. I actually did not dare state the extreme horror of battle, and the anguish with which the bravest soldiers struggle through it." Quoted from Edmund Wilson, *Patriotic Gore* (London: André Deutsch, 1962), p. 684.

7. James F. Light, *John William De Forest* (New York: Twayne, 1965), p. 123. For other discussions of the novel see W. D. Howells, "The Heroine of 'Kate Beaumont,'" *Heroines of Fiction* (New York: Harper, 1901), 2:152–163; Joseph Jay Rubin's informative introduction in *Kate Beaumont* (State College, Penn.: Bald Eagle Press, 1963), pp. 7–40; and Harvey M. Sessler, "A Test for Realism in De Forest's *Kate Beaumont*," *American Literary Realism* (Fall 1969), 2:274–276. My quotations come from the Bald Eagle Press edition.

8. Philip Edward Sullivan, in "John William De Forest: A Study of Realism and Romance in Selected Works" (Ph. D. dissertation, Southern California,

1966), sets down parallel passages from De Forest's fiction and journalism and "suggests that De Forest was at his best when he used journalistic accounts as a basis for his fiction, but that when he resorted to imaginative treatment of topical material, his fiction was less effective." See Billi Rogers, "John William De Forest," *American Literary Realism* (Summer 1975), 8:244–245.

9. Quoted from Wilson, *Patriotic Gore*, p. 697. Howells endorsed De Forest's view: "A certain scornful bluntness in dealing with the disguises in which women natures reveal themselves is perhaps at the root of that dislike which most women have felt for his fiction, and which in a nation of women readers has prevented it from ever winning a merited popularity." "The Heroine of 'Kate Beaumont,'" *Heroines of Fiction* (New York: Harper, 1901), 2:153. Howells admired and supported De Forest: see his reviews of *Miss Ravenel's Conversion, Kate Beaumont, The Wetherel Affair,* and *Honest John Vane.* A remark in the *Kate Beaumont* review ("As we said in speaking of 'Overland,' . . .") suggests Howells also wrote the review of this book. *Atlantic* (January 1872), 29:110, 111. The Gibson and Arms bibliography does not identify this review as by Howells.

Helen's Babies by John Habberton was one of three top bestsellers of 1876; *That Husband of Mine* by Mary Denison came out in 1877.

10. Elizabeth Stuart Phelps, *The Story of Avis* (Boston: Houghton Mifflin, n.d.), p. 446.

11. Stansell, "Elizabeth Stuart Phelps," p. 247.

12. "The Contributors' Club," *Atlantic* (February 1879), 43:258.

13. *Atlantic* (April 1878), 41:487. Thomas Sergeant Perry, "Recent Novels," *Nation* (March 21, 1878), 26:202, was also impressed by the novel. "There are bursts of truth, and of rarely expressed truth, which lift the book far above the mere record of conjugal infelicity." He thought it "a pity that the effect of the whole should be so much injured as it is by the unnaturalness of Ostrander, who has all the faults . . . of a married man. . . ." Perry felt that "under the guise of fiction the book is really a protest against marriage."

14. Cf. Avis' midnight vigil, pp. 325–326. The other novel of those years that dealt with broken marriage was Mary J. Holmes's *Daisy Thornton* (1878), one of the trashiest books I have read. Daisy marries her husband when she is only sixteen and interested in nothing but money and clothes. Her husband is too serious for her and she returns to her Indiana home, where her father arranges a quickie divorce. Her husband nearly dies when he hears the news. He recovers and remarries. Daisy, meanwhile, has gone to Europe and become a true woman. Hoping to remarry her husband, she hears instead that he has married another. Now Daisy nearly dies. After recovering, she devotes herself to philanthropy. Then her old husband's second wife dies of smallpox—in Daisy's arms—and the original couple remarry. Thus, the author proves that what God has joined no man may put asunder.

15. In Phelps's defense, one might recall the completely phony nature of other early American hallucinations in literature. Fitz Hugh Ludlow's *The Hasheesh Eater* (1857) has an embarrassing falsity that makes Avis' visions look like honest reporting: the moment Ludlow's tripper takes a few grains of hash, he sees a complete Eastern city.

16. Some of the books Phelps wrote after *Avis* sought the remedy for sexual hatred in platonic love. In *Friends: A Duet* (1881), there is, in Spring's words, "a wistful search for knowledge whether between men and women there cannot be . . . friendship without love and marriage . . .—affection without passion" (p. 578).

Phelps probably did *not* read the popular fifties novels. She mentioned reading Stowe and then boasted: "Poor novels and stories I did not read. I do not remember being forbidden them; but, by that parental art finer than denial, they were absent from my convenience" (Phelps, *Chapters from a Life*, pp. 91–92). But she identified herself all her life as one of those "women who think and feel, and who care for other women and are loyal to them" (*ibid.*, p. 15). Both for author and Avis, *Aurora Leigh* was the one great inspiration (*ibid.*, p. 65; *Avis*, ch. 4). In 1877 Phelps delivered a course of lectures at Boston University on "Representative Modern Fiction," apparently focussing on George Eliot (Spring, "Elizabeth Stuart Phelps," p. 570). Phelps began pushing for dress reform as early as 1869, "abjuring trains, and excessive trimmings, and tight waists" (*ibid.*, p. 576).

17. The main source of information is her husband's biography, Austin Phelps, "A Memorial of the Author," in *The Last Leaf from Sunny Side. By H. Trusta* (Boston: Phillips, Sampson, 1853). In *Chapters from a Life* Phelps drew a veil over her mother's memory. The mother wrote ten books (counting "The Angel over the Right Shoulder"). She was a descendant of Governor Winthrop. Her father was the big influence in her life, and some of her earliest memories were of his "severe self-discipline." As a child, she was obsessed by death. According to her husband, she suffered from a "*cerebral disease*" (italics his) that brought "severe and frequent headaches, . . . partial blindness, . . . temporary paralysis of portions of her body, and great prostration of the nervous system." She attended Jacob Abbott's Mount Vernon school in Boston, married in 1842, and lived in Boston until her husband's removal to Andover in 1848. Her most popular book, *The Sunny Side; or, the Country Minister's Wife*, was said, generously, to have "from three to five hundred thousand" readers (all quotes from "Memorial," pp. 7, 31, 32, 83).

18. Austin Phelps, "Memorial," pp. 9–10, 98.

19. *Ibid.*, p. 65. According to Nina Baym, the heroine of *The Sunny Side* is a superhuman wonder: "She must run a household, participate in numerous parish functions, be on call for frequent unexpected visits by women of the congregation, and absorb the tensions generated by a husband who is much in the house but so absorbed in his work that he hardly notices his wife from one day to the next." *Woman's Fiction: A Guide to Novels by and about Women in America, 1820–1870* (Ithaca: Cornell University Press, 1978), p. 247. Martha Hubbell's more truthful book, *The Shady Side* (1853), rejected the fixed cheerfulness of Mrs. Phelps's bestseller.

20. "Memorial," pp. 66, 67.

21. *The Angel over the Right Shoulder, or the Beginning of a New Year. By the Author of "Sunny Side"* (Andover, Mass.: Warren F. Draper, 1852), pp. 21–22. For another discussion, see Margaret M. Culley, "Vain Dreams: The Dream

Convention in Some Nineteenth-Century American Women's Fiction," *Frontiers* (Winter 1976), 1:94–102. The story was popular, with at least nine American editions.

22. Ursula Le Guin, *The Tombs of Atuan* (New York: Bantam, 1975).

23. Spring, "Elizabeth Stuart Phelps," p. 562. The name Mary Gray had come from "an intimate friend of her mother's" (p. 561).

24. "Memorial," p. 104. In lumping her two sons together and giving them both to the ministry, Mrs. Phelps was appeasing the Calvinist fathers—and thus earning her daughter's superior privilege of following the path the mother was most interested in.

25. When Avis' first baby comes, she is disappointed that it is a boy. Incompetent to take care of him, she lets him cry for six hours one night. With clever obtuseness, the author attributes the baby's crying to "reasons which were metaphysically satisfactory to himself" (pp. 278–279). Apparently, males are metaphysicians from the cradle up. The boy is said to cry "crossly," but the second child, a girl, cries "with a low, confiding wail." Avis can "never be impatient with her little girl's cry" (p. 330), but she suspects the boy of being secretly monstrous, a Rosemary's baby, and wonders darkly "what else he had inherited from his father besides his delicate lungs" (p. 326). She dutifully tries to overcome her distaste for the "clamorous selfism" (p. 320) he shares with his father.

26. Spring, "Elizabeth Stuart Phelps," pp. 571–573. Spring's reading of the unrevised ending of the novel is interesting: she apparently assumed that Isabel was *not* going to return to Osmond. Spring clearly knew Phelps well and had a great deal in common with her. Spring venerated her own mother and wrote a *Memorial of Eliza Butler Thompson. By Her Daughter* (New York: A.D.F. Randolph, 1879).

Constance Fenimore Woolson agreed with Spring's view that Isabel isn't "lovable" enough. Woolson wrote James in 1883 that Isabel did not exhibit a womanly love and pleaded with him to create a woman who would: "at any rate, let *her* love very much, and let us see that she does." Leon Edel, *Henry James: The Middle Years* (Philadelphia: Lippincott, 1962), p. 89.

Another contemporary reader besides Spring also found a comparison between Avis and Marcia in order. James Herbert Morse, "The Native Element in American Fiction: Since the War," *Century* (July 1883), 26:370–371, had a high opinion of Avis. Morse considered the heroine "fiercely characteristic of woman's mode of mental action" in New England. He saw that Phelps's men were "sticks" but found Avis "firm, strong, passionate, intense, conscientious, beautiful in a narrow way. . . . But Miss Phelps could not, by any possibility, draw Howells' Marcia Hubbard. She could not get down to her, or out to her."

7. HENRY JAMES AND W. D. HOWELLS AS SISSIES

1. Alexander Harvey, *William Dean Howells: A Study of the Achievement of a Literary Artist* (New York: Huebsch, 1917), pp. 179–180. Overall, Harvey had high praise for Howells, who read this first critical study of his work and

objected to being called a sissy; see his letters to William Griffith (August 19, 1917—at Harvard) and T. S. Perry (August 23, 1917—at Colby).

2. Quoted from Edwin H. Cady, *The Road to Realism: The Early Years 1837–1885 of William Dean Howells* (Syracuse: Syracuse University Press, 1956), p. 6.

3. *New Leaf Mills* (New York: Harper, 1913), p. 150. See also Howells, *My Year in a Log Cabin* (New York: Harper, 1902).

4. I see no reason to accept the assumption that justifies Edel's portrait of Mary James as sinister and manipulative—the assumption that all of James's fictional mothers are versions of his own. See Leon Edel, *Henry James: The Untried Years* (Philadelphia: Lippincott, 1953), pp. 41–55.

5. This is a key phrase in *A Small Boy and Others* (New York: Scribner, 1913), pp. 25, 26, 27.

6. Howells, *Years of My Youth* (Bloomington: Indiana University Press, 1975), pp. 92–93.

7. Kenneth S. Lynn, *William Dean Howells: An American Life* (New York: Harcourt Brace Jovanovich, 1971), p. 74; Gail Thain Parker, "William Dean Howells: Realism and Feminism," in Monroe Engel, ed., *Uses of Literature* (Cambridge: Harvard University Press, 1973), p. 150.

8. Howells, *Years of My Youth*, p. 141.

9. Howells, *Selected Letters* (Boston: Twayne, 1979), 1:73–74. Letter dated February 24, 1861.

10. *Ibid.*, p. 340. Letter dated September 22, 1869.

11. Quoted from Jay B. Hubbell, *Who Are the Major American Writers? A Study of the Changing Literary Canon* (Durham: Duke University Press, 1972), p. 120.

12. John William De Forest, *Miss Ravenel's Conversion from Secession to Loyalty* (Columbus, Ohio: Charles E. Merrill, 1969), pp. 95–96.

13. Howells, *A Fearful Responsibility* (Boston: Osgood, 1881), p. 3.

14. Howells, *Years of My Youth*, p. 138.

15. *Mark Twain—Howells Letters*, Henry Nash Smith and William M. Gibson, eds. (Cambridge: Harvard University Press, 1960), 2:503.

16. Much less flowery, however, than the cover of Frances E. Willard's *How to Win: A Book for Girls* (1887). Kate Sanborn's *The Wit of Women* (1885) had an amusing variation on the flowery cover—a grasshopper eating the regulation leaves. One edition of Howells' *Their Wedding Journey* has a cover with Cupid toting the luggage.

17. Paul Fatout, *Ambrose Bierce: The Devil's Lexicographer* (Norman: University of Oklahoma Press, 1951), p. 146.

18. *North American Review* (January 1874), 118:191.

19. The letter, at Harvard, was written August 21, 1876.

20. Eugene L. Didier, "William D. Howells," *A Primer of Criticism* (Baltimore: People's Publishing, 1883), as quoted by Clayton L. Eichelberger, *Published Comment on William Dean Howells through 1920: A Research Bibliography* (Boston: Hall, 1976), p. 37.

21. Hamlin Garland, *A Son of the Middle Border* (New York: Macmillan, 1919), p. 383.

22. The letter, at Harvard, was written December 6, 1886.

23. De Forest, *Miss Ravenel's Conversion*, p. 191.

24. Howells, "Police Report," *Atlantic* (January 1882), 49:14. Originally, in a letter to Aldrich, Howells called the madam a "hostess" (*Selected Letters,* 2:294).

25. Howells, *Years of My Youth*, p. 110.

26. *Ibid.*, p. 153.

27. Leon Edel, *Henry James: The Treacherous Years* (Philadelphia: Lippincott, 1969), p. 350.

28. Howells, *The Minister's Charge* (Boston: Houghton Mifflin, n.d.), p. 229.

29. Nina Baym, "Melville's Quarrel with Fiction," *PMLA* (October 1979), 94:909–923. On the cultivation of women readers, see Van Wyck Brooks, *New England: Indian Summer* (New York: Dutton, 1940), pp. 243–246.

30. For an account of the origins of British realism that highlights the influence of Mary Elizabeth Braddon's *Lady Audley's Secret*, see Christopher Heywood, "French and American sources of Victorian realism," *Comparative Criticism: A Yearbook* (1979), 1:107–126.

8. THE PORTRAIT OF A LADY

1. *Letters*, Leon Edel, ed. (Cambridge: Harvard University Press, 1975), 2:156, 231.

2. William Veeder, *Henry James—The Lessons of the Master: Popular Fiction and Personal Style in the Nineteenth Century* (Chicago: University of Chicago Press, 1975), p. 171.

3. See Nina Baym's review in *Journal of English and Germanic Philology* (July 1976), 75:465–467. What Veeder needed was the book Baym was writing at this time. His equation, popular equals conventional, overlooks the great originality of books like Evans' *St. Elmo* and the incredible diversity of popular books. He needed to isolate the appropriate popular genres that lay behind Howells and James. Unfortunately, *Woman's Fiction* would not appear until 1978. Still, I learned a great deal about James from Veeder's book. Also, Baym's review gave too little attention to Veeder's painstaking analysis of James's style.

In spite of the enormous number of articles and chapters on the *Portrait*, surprisingly few consider the novel against its historical background—the late 1870s and early 80s. No doubt this is partly because of the prevailing use of the 1908 version, which is *far* inferior to the 1881 edition; cf. Nina Baym's comparison of the way the early and late versions treat the themes of women and marriage, "Revision and Thematic Change in *The Portrait of a Lady*," *Modern Fiction Studies* (Summer 1976), 22:183–200.

4. *The Portrait of a Lady* (Boston: Osgood, 1881), p. 199. Except where noted, all quotations come from this edition. Louis Auchincloss has stressed the importance of Osmond's American origin in *Reading Henry James* (Minneapolis: University of Minnesota Press, 1975), pp. 66–67.

5. In his preface to the 1908 edition, James recalled his effort to justify

"organising an ado" about a girl protagonist; see Richard P. Blackmur, ed., *The Art of the Novel: Critical Prefaces* (New York: Scribner, 1934), p. 48. Yet there was nothing strange about putting a single girl at the center of a novel in the 1870s, when James first began the novel. By the time he wrote the preface, he had forgotten the original social and historical context.

6. Veeder, *Lessons*, pp. 84–86.

7. Elizabeth T. Spring, "Elizabeth Stuart Phelps," in Phelps et al., *Our Famous Women* (Hartford: Worthington, 1884), p. 572.

8. *North American Review* (January 1865), 100:281–282. For James's request to do the review, see *Letters*, 1:55.

9. In the New York Edition James sharpened the polarity by replacing "young girl" with "creature of conditions." *Portrait* (New York: Scribner, 1908), 3:69.

10. In his preface to *The American*, James admitted his oversight in failing to represent Newman and Claire's love for one another during their engagement. In the *Portrait*, the engaged couple's mutual love is again conspicuously absent.

11. Ralph is a later version of James's first novelistic hero, Roger Lawrence in *Watch and Ward*. Roger supports Nora and refrains from proposing because he wants "to leave her free"—*Atlantic* (October 1871), 28:417.

12. *Portrait* (1908), p. 434.

13. *Ibid.*, p. 436. The kiss or embrace was often seen as an act of capture around the turn of the century. In Edvard Munch's painting of a kiss, the woman seems to be absorbing, even sucking up, the man. This is similar to the narrator's sense of sexual contact in *The Sacred Fount*.

14. Many critics have mistakenly assumed that Isabel reciprocates Goodwood's desire. Richard Poirier offered a complicated version of this reading in *The Comic Sense of Henry James* (New York: Oxford University Press, 1960). Poirier saw her motives for refusing Goodwood as two-tiered: the obvious reason is that "she is simply not deeply enough in love with him" (p. 245); the covert reason is her fear of her own sexual desire. More recent critics who see that Goodwood represents a real threat to Isabel are Philip M. Weinstein, *Henry James and the Requirements of the Imagination* (Cambridge: Harvard University Press, 1971) and Judith Fryer, *The Faces of Eve: Women in the Nineteenth Century American Novel* (New York: Oxford University Press, 1976), pp. 136–137. Veeder makes the point that Goodwood and Osmond are finally alike. It should not be forgotten that the "deepest thing" in Isabel is a "belief that . . . she could" (but not a desire to) "give herself completely" (p. 44). I suspect that this "belief" belongs with her "factitious" theories. Thus, Isabel's last temptation turns out to be the readiness to let go. I see no reason to think that James shared the general view of his day—that this readiness was an essential female trait. James detested the idea, utterly conventional in many novels of the 1860s, that a Rochester easily and rightly sweeps a woman off her feet. James's review of Louisa M. Alcott's *Eight Cousins* in *Nation* (October 14, 1875), 21:250–251, ridiculed a version of the Rochester-type, as did his earlier review of the same author's *Moods* in *North American Review* (July 1865), 101:276–281.

15. Fryer, *Faces of Eve*, p. 126.
16. Horace E. Scudder, "*The Portrait of a Lady* and *Dr. Breen's Practice*," *Atlantic* (January 1882), 49:128.
17. The phrase comes from Elizabeth Sabiston, "The Prison of Womanhood," *Comparative Literature* (Fall 1973), 25:336–351. See also Annette Niemtzow, "Marriage and the New Woman in *The Portrait of a Lady*," *American Literature* (1975), 47:377–395.

9. THEIR WEDDING JOURNEY

1. The best discussion of Howells as subtle humorist is William M. Gibson, "W. D. Howells and 'The Ridiculous Human Heart,'" *Studies in American Humor* (April 1975), 2:32–45. Howells' delicate humor was regularly noted by reviewers from 1866 (*Venetian Life*) on. See Clayton L. Eichelberger, *Published Comment on William Dean Howells Through 1920: A Research Bibliography* (Boston: Hall, 1976), items 6, 7, 8, 10, 11, 12, 14, 15, 16, 20, 29, 31, 37, etc. A biographical sketch in the New York *Times*, February 18, 1881, p. 4, articulated the view of Howells that had become a formula—he was a master of "character-drawing set in dainty description and delicate humor" (Eichelberger, p. 23). Hence, readers were surprised, if not displeased, by *A Modern Instance*: "The Earlier and Later Work of Mr. Howells," *Lippincott's* (December 1882), 30:604–608, missed the charm of Howells' earlier books. To some extent Howells' early fastidiousness was diplomatic; as a westerner trying to make it in Boston, he had to tread lightly. For his sense of the obstacles in his way, see his *Literary Friends and Acquaintances* (Bloomington: Indiana University Press, 1968), and his account of Mark Twain's gaffe at the Whittier birthday dinner in *My Mark Twain: Reminiscences and Criticisms* (Baton Rouge: Louisiana State University Press, 1967), pp. 50–54. But the underlying reasons for Howells' delicate humor and sentiment must have involved his formed personality.
2. Howells, *Suburban Sketches* (Boston: Houghton Mifflin, 1883), p. 255.
3. The view that the source of Howells' creativity was his "Western" nature is a distortion. One of the first critics to express this view was V. F. Calverton, *The Liberation of American Literature* (New York: Scribners, 1932), p. 377: "Howells' adoption of realism as a literary philosophy was a distant outgrowth of the frontier force." This perspective either overlooks the fact that Howells was very fastidious, or else tends to regard this trait as a self-betrayal. For a much sounder view see Gregory L. Crider, "William Dean Howells and the Antiurban Tradition," *American Studies* (Spring 1978), 19:55–64.
4. Howells, *Venetian Life* (Boston: Osgood, 1875), pp. 42, 143.
5. Howells, *Their Wedding Journey* (Bloomington: Indiana University Press, 1968), p. 42.
6. Edwin H. Cady, *The Road to Realism: The Early Years 1837–1885 of William Dean Howells* (Syracuse, N.Y.: Syracuse University Press, 1956), was the first

to emphasize Howells' neuroticism. This theme was later developed in different ways by George C. Carrington, Jr., *The Immense Complex Drama: The World and Art of the Howells Novel* (Columbus: Ohio State University Press, 1966), and Kenneth S. Lynn, *William Dean Howells, An American Life* (New York: Harcourt Brace Jovanovich, 1971), pp. 253–254, 280–282, 364 (index entry under Howells for "neurotic history"). Carrington sees Howells as subject to existential angst, terror, demons, and other dark forces much in evidence in the 1950s and 60s; Lynn (like Cady) finds that Howells underwent nervous breakdowns at crucial points in his career, particularly as he neared the end of *A Modern Instance* and *The Rise of Silas Lapham*. There is no doubt Howells went through a crisis of some sort while writing the latter book. But a letter Howells wrote to his father during the illness that interrupted his work on *A Modern Instance* shows, as George Arms and Christoph K. Lohmann point out in *Selected Letters of W. D. Howells* (Boston: Twayne), 2:302, that Howells' problem was physical—probably a difficulty in urinating.

7. The chief study of Howells' treatment of marriage is Allen F. Stein, "Marriage in Howells's Novels," *American Literature* (January 1977), 48:501–524. Stein's basic idea is that "for Howells, ultimately, marriage offers, above all, a means of liberation from the prison of self" (p. 502). His main point about *Their Wedding Journey* is that marriage helps Basil and Isabel face the chaotic, threatening aspects of life. A review of Howells' *A Fearful Responsibility* said that Howells "excels in depicting the conjugal relationship, and the conversations between Elmore and his wife are the more delightful because the literary possibilities of the married state are commonly neglected." See "Recent Fiction," *Critic* (July 16, 1881), 1:191, as quoted by Eichelberger, *Published Comment*, p. 25. Two Howells novels that study marriage against a background of Shaker celibacy are *The Undiscovered Country* and *The Vacation of The Kelwyns*.

8. Basil "dutifully tried to imagine another issue to the disaster of the night, and to realize himself suddenly bereft of her who so filled his life." But he can't manage to frighten himself: "it was quite idle: where love was, life only was" (p. 50). Lynn, Carrington, and Edwin H. Cady, "Howells and Crane: Violence, Decorum and Reality," *The Light of Common Day* (Bloomington: Indiana University Press, 1971), pp. 161–181, all deal with Howells' fear of disaster. See also Kenneth Seib, "Uneasiness at Niagara: Howells' *Their Wedding Journey*," *Studies in American Fiction* (Spring 1976), 4:15–25. Clayton L. Eichelberger, "William Dean Howells: Perception and Ambivalence," in Matthew J. Bruccoli, ed., *The Chief Glory of Every People: Essays on Classic American Writers* (Carbondale: Southern Illinois University Press, 1973), pp. 121–127, is good on *Their Wedding Journey*.

9. See Clara M. Kirk, "Reality and Actuality in the March Family Narratives of W. D. Howells," *PMLA* (March 1959), 74:137–152.

10. So impressed was T. S. Perry by this episode that he spontaneously singled it out for praise six years after publication; see his February 6, 1878, letter to Howells at Harvard.

10. *A MODERN INSTANCE*

1. Edith Wharton, *The Age of Innocence* (New York: Scribner, 1920), p. 42.
2. *Interviews with William Dean Howells*, Ulrich Halfmann, ed. (University of Texas at Arlington: American Literary Realism, 1973), p. 82. The play Howells saw was not Euripedes' but Franz Grillparzer's, an Austrian; see Gerard M. Sweeney, "The *Medea* Howells Saw," *American Literature* (March 1970), 42:83–89, and Arms and Lohmann, *Selected Letters of W. D. Howells* (Boston: Twayne, 1979), 1:112, n. 3. William M. Gibson's good account of the genesis of the novel, Introduction to *A Modern Instance* (Cambridge: Houghton Mifflin, 1957), p. v, also notes Howells' experience with a quarreling couple at a farm near Shirley, Massachusetts, his much later novel, *The Vacation of the Kelwyns*, and the relevant data on Bret Harte (a possible model for Bartley). Kenneth S. Lynn, *William Dean Howells: An American Life* (New York: Harcourt Brace Jovanovich, 1971), p. 257, suggests without offering any evidence that Marcia was based on Elinor Howells. There is an impressive parallel between Marcia and Egeria Boynton in Howells' earlier novel, *The Undiscovered Country*; see Kermit Vanderbilt, *The Achievement of William Dean Howells* (Princeton: Princeton University Press, 1968), pp. 72–73. Olov W. Fryckstedt, *In Quest of America: A Study of Howells' Early Development as a Novelist* (Cambridge: Harvard University Press, 1958), pp. 241–242, sees in Bartley traces of George Eliot's Tito in *Romola*. For the most thorough account of the composition and reception of the novel, see George N. Bennett's introduction to the Indiana Edition (Bloomington: Indiana University Press, 1977). For Bennett the novel demonstrates Howells' maturity as a writer. For a detailed examination of the way Howells' illness interfered with his reading proof, see David J. Nordloh and David Kleinman, "Textual Commentary," in the Indiana Edition. All my quotations come from this edition.
3. I take the phrase from Jack London's *The Sea Wolf*, where Van Weyden's "pet, secret phrase" for Maud is "one small woman"; not coincidentally, this was also her father's name for her mother. Many contemporary reviews of *A Modern Instance* took for granted that the reader would recognize the typicality of the Hubbards' married life. "'Tis a sad tale, and o'er true," wrote the reviewer in the New Orleans *Daily Picayune*, August 6, 1882, p. 2, as quoted in Clayton L. Eichelberger, *Published Comment on William Dean Howells Through 1920: A Research Bibliography* (Boston: Hall, 1976), p. 30. The reviewer in the New York *Times*, October 15, 1882, p. 6, as quoted in Eichelberger, p. 32, wondered "why so much care and interest are bestowed on matters that happen to almost every couple." A women's magazine, *Cottage Hearth* (December 1882), 8:401, preferred fiction that had "the nobler and truer types of husband and wife" (Eichelberger, p. 35).
4. There is a useful discussion of this aspect of the novel in Paul John Eakin, *The New England Girl: Cultural Ideals in Hawthorne, Stowe, Howells and James* (Athens: University of Georgia Press, 1976), p. 108.

5. Elizabeth T. Spring, "Elizabeth Stuart Phelps," in Phelps et al., *Our Famous Women* (Hartford: Worthington, 1884), p. 572.

6. Eakin, *New England Girl*, pp. 105–107, interprets this scene well. See also Kenneth B. Eble, "Howells' Kisses," *American Quarterly* (Winter 1957), 9:441–447. Some other critics actually appear to find an intimation of fellatio in Marcia's act.

7. Gibson, "Introduction," p. xvi, and "Textual Note," p. xx in *A Modern Instance*; Lynn, *Howells*, pp. 258–259. Lynn makes the point about the opening paragraphs. Kermit Vanderbilt, *Achievement*, pp. 62–76, discusses Marcia's "Electra complex."

8. Henry Adams, "Primitive Rights of Women," *Historical Essays* (New York: Scribner's, 1891). It had been widely assumed that primitive women were the slaves of men. In 1860 a writer blandly announced, "In savage life she [woman] has always, by reason of her physical weakness, if from no other cause, been a slave; as civilization has advanced, her condition has improved." "Woman's Rights as to Labor and Property," *North American Review* (April 1860), 90:541. Sarah Josepha Hale tried to demonstrate the same thesis in *Woman's Record*. In reviewing Howells' novel in the *Atlantic* (November 1882), 50:711, Horace Scudder saw that Marcia's jealousy rendered her "more than half wild," but could not help objecting to her "savage" and "animalistic" qualities.

There is considerable tension in the novel between Marcia as pre-Christian pagan and Marcia as an instance of modern post-Puritan decay. Several critics have explicated the latter aspect, most notably Vanderbilt, *Achievement*, pp. 51–62, and earlier Edwin H. Cady, *The Road to Realism* (Syracuse: Syracuse University Press, 1956), pp. 206–216.

9. Elizabeth Stuart Phelps, *The Story of Avis* (Boston: Houghton Mifflin, n.d.), p. 201.

10. Letter dated July 15, 1914. Original at University of Southern California.

11. After completing the manuscript of the novel, Howells added the last two sentences of chapter 11, which reveal the innkeeper's "admiration" (pp. 125, 543) for Bartley's smartness.

12. I think Howells was indebted to Phelps's portrait of Ostrander. Like him, Bartley has great charm and versatility, is chronically self-indulgent, dependent, and unfaithful, and has a long standing connection with a "low" woman.

13. There is a parallel between Bartley and Horatio Alger. Michael Zuckerman argues that "beneath his [Alger's] paeans to manly vigor" there was "a lust for effeminate indulgence; beneath his celebration of self-reliance, a craving to be taken care of and a yearning to surrender the terrible burden of independence." "The Nursery Tales of Horatio Alger," *American Quarterly* (May 1972), 24:209. The reviewer for the New York *Daily Tribune*, October 15, 1882, p. 8, was not alone in considering Bartley to be Howells' "masterwork." See Eichelberger, *Published Comment*, p. 32. Mark Twain relished

Bartley's drunk scene; see *Mark Twain-Howells Letters*, Henry Nash Smith and William M. Gibson, eds. (Cambridge: Harvard University Press, 1960), 1:407–408. There is odd confirmation of Bartley's representative quality in a novel published twenty years later. The hero of Frank Norris's *The Pit* (1903) "never could rid himself of a surreptitious admiration for Bartley Hubbard. He, too, was 'smart' and 'alive.' He had the 'get there' to him. 'Why,' he would say, 'I know fifty boys just like him down there in La Salle Street [commodity exchange area]." *The Pit* (New York: Grove, 1956), p. 216.

14. Howells, *The Quality of Mercy* (New York: Harper, n.d.), p. 135.

15. James, *The American* (Boston: Houghton Mifflin, 1962), pp. 18–20, 31, 87; John Robert Moore, "An Imperfection in the Art of Henry James," *Nineteenth-Century Fiction* (March 1959) 13:351–356. For a recent sympathetic and uncritical reading, see R. W. Butterfield, *"The American,"* in John Goode, ed., *The Air of Reality: New Essays on Henry James* (London: Methuen, 1972).

16. My point here has nothing to do with Marxism or any other ideology that assigns a grand, inevitable "meaning" to history. Karl Popper's arguments in *The Open Society and Its Enemies* persuade me that history lacks "meaning" and can't be predicted.

17. In 1899, someone at the (Chicago) Twentieth Century Club asked Howells: "Will you solve the puzzle as to whether Marcia Hubbard and Halleck were married?" Howells replied, "Marcia did not marry Halleck. O, I never could see it that way. Such an outcome would have been perfectly right, but Halleck's character, I believe, would have made it impossible for him to marry a woman with whom he had been in love when she was another man's wife." Ulrich Halfmann, ed., *Interviews with William Dean Howells* (University of Texas at Arlington: American Literary Realism, 1973), p. 67. When the novel first appeared a reviewer for the Chicago *Daily Tribune*, October 14, 1882, p. 9, thought that "Halleck's falling in love with a married woman casts a yellow light on the story." Eichelberger, *Published Comment*, p. 32. See James Harwood Barnett, "Divorce and the American Divorce Novel 1858–1937: A Study of Literary Reflections of Social Influences," Ph.D. dissertation, University of Pennsylvania, 1939, ch. 3, and William L. O'Neill, "Divorce as a Moral Issue: A Hundred Years of Controversy," in Carol V. R. George, ed., *"Remember the Ladies"/New Perspectives on Women in American History* (Syracuse: Syracuse University Press, 1975). A French critic, Th. Bentzon, "Les nouveaux romanciers américaines/I./W. D. Howells," *Revue des Deux Mondes*, ser. 3 (January 1, 1883), 55:656, was amazed at Halleck's scrupulosity. Bentzon approved of Howells' mingling "des nuances les plus subtiles" with the "traits vigoureux d'un roman réaliste."

18. There is talk about the initials on p. 67. Henry Bird, whom Bartley knocks down, has the initials reversed. (Could this weak man's last name reproduce Avis?) Hannah Morrison's initials reverse Marcia Hubbard's. Originally it was to be Sally Morris; maybe Howells changed her name for consistency in the pattern of initials.

19. In a letter to Brander Matthews, July 22, 1911, Howells claimed to

have modeled Bartley on himself; see Mildred Howells, ed., *Life in Letters of William Dean Howells* (Garden City, N.Y.: Doubleday, Doran, 1928), 2:301. George C. Carrington, Jr., *The Immense Complex Drama: The World and Art of the Howells Novel* (Columbus: Ohio State University Press, 1966), pp. 72–74, sees Bartley as the "alter ego, the uncivilized, 'natural,' demonic, hidden half of the author" and Ben Halleck as "the civilized half, the surface half." I see the two characters as major social types reflecting a central masculine dilemma of the culture.

20. In an unpublished letter at Smith College written to a Mr. Garrison, Jan. 26, 1877.

21. The gentlemanly lover's name is Bartlett, close to Bartley. His friend, Cummings, a "slighter" man with "a very abstracted look and a dark, dreaming eye" (*A Counterfeit Presentment*, Boston: Osgood, 1877, p. 8), is a minister, like Ben Halleck at the end. The scoundrel never appears. The identical story would be embedded in *The Kentons* over twenty years later. In this novel there are many suggestions of a hidden bond connecting the jeering Trannel, the blackguard Bittridge, and the lighthearted minister-hero, Breckon. Breckon even "amuses himself in calling" Bittridge his "*alter ego.*" *The Kentons* (Bloomington: Indiana University Press, 1971), p. 227. On the excursion to Leyden, he is shocked to see himself in Trannel. He suggests to Ellen that what first attracted her to him was his resemblance to Bittridge—a "certain unseriousness" (p. 226). See Carrington, *Immense Complex Drama*, pp. 47–50, 113–114. Precisely the same material turns up in Faulkner's greatest work, *The Sound and the Fury*, where Quentin Compson and Dalton Ames correspond to Howells' paired men. Quentin suffers a masculine torment very similar to Ben Halleck's. One may note that Howells had an idiot brother who had to be locked in a barred room on occasion (Cady, *Road to Realism*, p. 44).

22. There is an old dispute whether Atherton speaks for the author. Cady, *Road to Realism*, pp. 211, 213, 214, had no use for the "stuffy," "icily Swedenborgian," "previously cocksure" lawyer and explained his presence by means of Howells' illness. Gibson, "Introduction," p. xiv, argued that Howells' "dramatic irony" proves that Atherton is simply "a respectable, hair-splitting snob." William McMurray, *The Literary Realism of William Dean Howells* (Carbondale: Southern Illinois University Press, 1967), pp. 35–42, makes the same interpretation. I would like to be able to accept this interpretation. But Atherton is allowed great insight and authority throughout the novel. I think he mirrors Howells' mind, "correct" moral principle undermined by saving doubt—"Atherton flung the letter upon the table, and drew a troubled sigh. 'Ah, I don't know! I don't know!'" (p. 453). Contemporary reviews show that Atherton was trusted. Even the notice the *Century* ran simultaneous with the final installment named Atherton as the moral spokesman; see "Topics of the Time/Mr. Howells on Divorce," *Century* (October 1882), 24:940–941. Of course the novel was anything but an anti-divorce tract. Yet Robert Louis Stevenson was not the only reader who was misled into thinking it was. See also Maurice Thompson, "A 'Modern Instance' of Criticism,"

Indianapolis Saturday Herald, August 18, 1883, p. 4, as summarized by Eichelberger, *Published Comment*, p. 41. Significantly, of all the book's reviewers, Thompson was in the best position to know Howells' mind; see Walter L. Fertig, "Maurice Thompson and *A Modern Instance*," *American Literature* (March 1966), 38:103–111. One modern critic who saw Atherton as spokesman was Fryckstedt, *In Quest of America*, p. 228. Vanderbilt, *Achievement*, pp. 86–88, and Lynn, *William Dean Howells*, pp. 265–266, both adopt qualified versions of this position.

23. In writing the courtroom scene, Howells visited Crawfordsville, Indiana, and got some help from the lawyer-writer, Maurice Thompson; see Fertig, "Maurice Thompson," pp. 103–111.

11. REALISM

1. René Wellek, *Concepts of Criticism* (New Haven: Yale University Press, 1963), pp. 240–241. E. B. Greenwood tried to invalidate Wellek's approach in "Reflections on Professor Wellek's Concept of Realism," *Neophilologus* (1962), 46(2):89–96. For rejoinder, see Wellek, "A Reply to E. B. Greenwood's Reflections," *Ibid.* (3):194–196.

2. The chief studies of American realism are: Everett Carter, *Howells and the Age of Realism* (Philadelphia: Lippincott, 1954); Robert P. Falk, "The Rise of Realism," Harry Hayden Clark, ed., *Transitions in American Literary History*, (Durham: Duke University Press, 1953), pp. 379–442; Warner Berthoff, *The Ferment of Realism* (New York: Free Press, 1965); Donald Pizer, *Realism and Naturalism in Nineteenth-Century American Literature* (Carbondale: Southern Illinois University Press, 1966); Harold H. Kolb, Jr., *The Illusion of Life: American Realism as a Literary Form* (Charlottesville: University Press of Virginia, 1969); Edwin H. Cady, *The Light of Common Day: Realism in American Fiction* (Bloomington: Indiana University Press, 1971); Olov W. Fryckstedt's survey of Howells' movement towards realism in *In Quest of America: A Study of Howells' Early Development as a Novelist* (Cambridge: Harvard University Press, 1958), ch. 4; C. Hugh Holman, *Windows on the World: Essays on American Social Fiction* (Knoxville: University of Tennessee Press, 1979).

For broader discussions of realism, see especially the summer 1951 issue of *Comparative Literature*; Damian Grant, *Realism* (London: Methuen, 1970); Erich Auerbach, *Mimesis: The Representation of Reality in Western Literature*, Willard Trask, trans. (Garden City, N.Y.: Doubleday, 1957); and Joseph Peter Stern, *On Realism* (London: Routledge and Kegan Paul, 1973). Wellek, "Auerbach's Special Realism," *Kenyon Review* (Spring 1954), 16:299–307, has shown that the concept of realism in Auerbach's superb book is somewhat contaminated with existentialism. Stern follows Auerbach in taking realism to be, not a period-concept, but "a perennial mode of representing the world and coming to terms with it" (p. 32). The strength of Stern's book is in its patient teasing out of the nuances of *realism* and its wide-ranging exploration of "the realistic mode" as a timeless quantity. I hope I am not flattering myself in thinking that one main difference between my and Stern's approach is similar to the difference, in biological nomenclature, between splitters and lumpers, I being the splitter. At any rate, Stern's is the best book on realism as a perennial mode of writing.

The Stalinist view of realism may be represented by the assertion in Boris Suchkov, *A History of Realism* (Moscow: Progress, 1973), p. 143: "It was the conflict between the individual and his environment that underlay the action in works of critical realism, and this reflected the process of atomisation of bourgeois society, since the gradual advance of alienation also entailed a widening of the gap between the individual and his environment. The conditions for genuinely epic literature were only created in our own time by socialist realism, the main feature of which is analysis and portrayal of the process of reconciliation of the individual and society as a result of socialist transformation of private ownership social relations." For an excellent analysis of critical realism *cum* Lukács versus socialist realism *cum* Gorky, see George Bisztray, *Marxist Models of Literary Realism* (New York: Columbia University Press, 1978).

Lukács for the most part fought socialist realism. Although I have taken more from this critic than from any other writer on realism, I have essentially reassembled certain fragments of his system for my own constructions. The finest quality of his work is what Bisztray calls its "theoretical-methodological clairvoyance" (*ibid,,* p. 96). I cannot accept his use of certain Marxist categories or the Hegelian concrete universal, or his ignoring folk and popular literature. Certain vital elements in Lukács' thought, such as his grasp of modern bourgeois decay, may be abstracted from their Marxist context and integrated in other systems. In particular, for the concept of the concrete universal as embodied in the historically significant character type, I substitute a particular culture's ideal gender role as embodied in a male or female character-type. See Georg Lukács, *Studies in European Realism: A Sociological Survey of the Writings of Balzac, Stendhal, Zola, Tolstoy, Gorki and Others*, Edith Bone, trans. (London: Hillway, 1950); *The Meaning of Contemporary Realism*, John and Necke Mander, trans. (London: Merlin Press, 1963); *The Historical Novel*, Hannah and Stanley Mitchell, trans. (London: Merlin Press, 1962).

For a recent defense of realism with which I am in full agreement, see Gerald Graff, "The Politics of Anti-Realism," *Salmagundi* (Summer-Fall 1978), no. 42, pp. 4–30.

3. A remark in an 1876 review by James illustrates his patronizing view of local color: "The author has bravely attempted to write a characteristic American novel, which should be a tale of civilization—be void of big-hearted backwoodsmen and of every form of 'dialect.'" Review of Charles Henry Doe's *Buffets* in "Recent Novels," *Nation* (January 13, 1876), 22:32. Howells was generally more favorable and discriminating. The same year, in accepting "Freedom Wheeler's Controversy with Providence" by Rose Terry Cooke (whom he did not always care for), he wrote: "I am very glad to accept your story which I think extremely well wrought throughout" (unpublished letter, June 6, 1876, owned by Connecticut Historical Society, Hartford). Ten years later he called this story "a masterpiece"—"Editor's Study," *Harper's* (February 1887), 74:484. Howells' support of various local and local color writers—E.

W. Howe, Cable, Murfree, Jewett, Wilkins Freeman, Woolson, etc.—is known. Less well-known is that the four most distinguished writers he singled out in his "Editor's Study" essay on the short story in America were all women local colorists—Cooke, Murfree, Jewett, Woolson. In fact, as Ann Douglas has pointed out, many of the local colorists were the impoverished though more polished heirs of the women novelists of the 1850s; see "The Literature of Impoverishment: The Women Local Colorists in America 1865–1914," *Women's Studies* (1972), 1(1):3–45. On the other hand, Claude M. Simpson, Jr., traced local color in part to frontier humor in his comprehensive introduction to *The Local Colorists: American Short Stories, 1857–1900* (New York: Harper, 1960). Douglas persuades me that the local-color short story was to a large extent a diminished version of the earlier women's novel, muted but better pitched; yet I think she underrates Jewett and Wilkins Freeman.

4. The proof-text here is James's review of *The Schönberg-Cotta Family* in *Nation* (September 14, 1865), 1:345. At this time James equated realism with local color and scorned both: "It is just now very much the fashion to discuss the so-called principle of realism, and we all know that there exists in France a school of art in which it is associated with great brilliancy and great immorality. The disciples of this school pursue, with an assiduity worthy of a better cause, the research of local colors, with which they have produced a number of curious effects. We believe, however, that the greatest successes in this line are reserved for that branch of the school which contains the most female writers; for if women are unable to draw, they notoriously can at all events paint, and this is what realism requires. For an exhibition of the true realistic *chique* we would accordingly refer that body of artists who are represented in France by MM. Flaubert and Gerome to that class of works which in our own literature are represented by the 'Daisy Chain' [by Charlotte Yonge] and 'The Wide, Wide World'" [by Susan Warner]. The sarcasm of this recommendation reflects Godkin's editorial policies and James's own early hostility to realism. James was saying that the final, absurd consequences of the realists' program could be foreseen in the unspeakably bad "domestic" novelists. One of several critics who take this passage to express *approval* is Henry Nash Smith, "The Scribbling Women and the Cosmic Success Story," *Critical Inquiry* (September 1974), 1:68.

5. Wellek, *Concepts of Criticism*, p. 255. Stern's analysis of realism offers an alternative, possibly preferable, response to Wellek from my own.

6. *North American Review* (January 1865), 100:272; italics James's.

7. John G. Cawelti, *Adventure, Mystery, and Romance: Formula Stories as Art and Popular Culture* (Chicago: University of Chicago Press, 1976), pp. 18, 19.

8. This is the flaw in Maurice Larkin's generally quite authoritative survey of European realism, *Man and Society in Nineteenth-Century Realism: Determinism and Literature* (London: Macmillan, 1977). An exaggerated view of the influence of science on realism has led an astonishing number of thinkers to declare that the obsolescence of nineteenth-century science has led to the obsolescence of realism.

9. Quoted from Cady, *Light of Common Day*, p. 70.

10. George William Curtis, "Editor's Literary Record," *Harper's Monthly*

(January 1883), 66:314–315, felt the "defects" of the hero and heroine of *Modern Instance* were "so palpable and obtrusive" that the "story fails to awaken genuine sympathy for any one of its actors." The reviewer in "Literature/*A Woman's Reason*," *Critic* (December 22, 1883), 3:518–519, regretted that this novel and *Modern Instance* did not "carry our imaginations and hold them long captive in spite of themselves" (Eichelberger, *Published Comment*, pp. 46–47).

11. Gary Stephens, "Haunted Americana: The Endurance of American Realism," *Partisan Review*, (1977), 44:71–84.

12. Cf. Stern, *On Realism*: "the democratic ideology" is "a more natural habitation for the practice of literary realism than any other ideology I know" (p. 57); and realism "cannot help being interested in the political scene" (p. 53).

13. Cf. Robert L. Caserio, *Plot, Story, and the Novel from Dickens and Poe to the Modern Period* (Princeton: Princeton University Press, 1979), p. xiii: "When writers and readers of novels lose interest in plot and story, they appear to lose faith in the meaning and the moral value of acts."

14. Among many modern instances, there is David Caute's *The Illusion: An Essay on Politics, Theatre and the Novel* (London: André Deutsch, 1971). This book attacks a premise of realism and naturalism—the idea that it is possible and okay for art to provide an illusion of life. Caute's essay is pervaded with the familiar hysteria that insists it is "radical," displays a commitment to something that is vague but very sweeping, admires Sartre, Brecht, and Chernyshevsky, but is afraid, finally, that there is nothing to be done after all. The author has a chronic impulse to undercut himself: "Let me offer an assertion which I shall instantly retract" (p. 21). He comes out fighting for the idea that literature must commit itself to social change, but rejects realism's mimesis of imperfect society precisely because this mimesis is a "mirage" (p. 96) that reenters the world and "reshapes" (p. 97) it. He argues for "the dialectical novel," which "must inevitably de-mystify fiction by recognising its fictitious nature" (p. 265). What sort of fiction does Caute like most at the end of his book? "In the political novel," he tells us, more truthfully than I think he realizes, "the allegory is the most commonly employed metaphor of alienation" (p. 259). He cites several modern allegories, singling out Orwell's *Animal Farm* for high marks. Further, he rather unoriginally sets anti-utopia as "the authentic political allegory of our age" (p. 260), with its "singular individual who has not yet succumbed or been crushed or been totally absorbed by the prevailing totalitarianism" (p. 261) I think Caute's book inadvertently supports my contention that allegory—and the praise of allegory—grows out of a desperate sense of helplessness.

15. T. S. Perry, "William Dean Howells," *Century* (March 1882), 23:683.

12. EASYGOING MEN AND DRESSY LADIES

1. *The Rise of Silas Lapham*, Walter J. Meserve and David J. Nordloh, eds. (Bloomington: Indiana University Press, 1971), p. 88. Subsequent references are to this edition.

2. See, e. g., Marcus Cunliffe, *The Literature of the United States* (Baltimore: Penguin, 1961), p. 198; Howells "contrive[s] a subplot that seems a little implausible."

3. James's praise ("Everything in *Silas Lapham* is superior—nothing more so than the whole picture of casual, female youth and contemporaneous 'engaging' one's self") points to Penelope more than to anyone else. Cited from "William Dean Howells," *Harper's Weekly*, (1886), 30:394. One of the rare reviews that praised Penelope's humor was in the British *Saturday Review*, (1885), 60:517.

4. W. A. Jones, "The Ladies' Library," *Graham's Magazine* (1842), 21:333.

5. Howells, *Their Wedding Journey* (Boston: Osgood, 1875), p. 80. It may be because of passages like this that Ernest Earnest, *The American Eve in Fact and Fiction, 1775–1914* (Urbana: University of Illinois Press, 1974), p. 66, writes: "In *The Rise of Silas Lapham* Penelope is said to have brought back amusing accounts of the church meetings she attended, but no Howells woman ever made a recorded witty remark." Or maybe Earnest has too lofty and excellent a standard of humor to enjoy Howells' many humorous women—Kitty Ellison in *A Chance Acquaintance*, Miss Woodburn in *A Hazard of New Fortunes*, Mrs. Denton in *The World of Chance*, Mrs. Durgin in *The Landlord at Lion's Head*. The *Nation* praised the first of these for "her charming humor" and called her "a real human being" rather than "the familiar lay-figure"—*Nation* (June 12, 1873), 16:405. Howells was alert to humor in fictional women. In rereading DeForest's *Kate Beaumont*, he showed much less interest in the nominal heroine, who had a "prevailing passivity," than in the secondary figure of Nellie Armitage—"absolute woman, and yet with rather more humor than is vouchsafed to most of her family," *Heroines of Fiction* (New York: Harper, 1901), 2:154.

6. Robert Barnwell Roosevelt, *Progressive Petticoats; or, Dressed to Death. An Autobiography of a Married Man* (New York: Carleton, 1874), pp. 9–10.

7. Kate Sanborn, *The Wit of Women* (New York: Funk, 1885), pp. 205–206.

8. Quoted from Louis J. Budd, "Mark Twain Talks Mostly about Humor and Humorists," *Studies in American Humor* (April 1974), 1:16.

9. H. W. Boynton, "American Humor," *Atlantic Monthly* (1902), 90:418.

10. Deanne Stillman and Anne Beatts, eds., *Titters* (New York: Macmillan, 1976), p. 3.

11. For the major surveys, see Constance Rourke, *American Humor* (Garden City, N.Y.: Doubleday, 1955); Walter Blair, *Native American Humor* (San Francisco: Chandler, 1960); Jessie Bier, *The Rise and Fall of American Humor* (New York: Holt, 1968); Louis D. Rubin, Jr., ed., *The Comic Imagination in American Literature* (New Brunswick: Rutgers University Press, 1973); Walter Blair and Hamlin Hill, *America's Humor: From Poor Richard to Doonesbury* (New York: Oxford University Press, 1978). The only books on women and humor in America are Sanborn, *Wit of Women* (1885); Martha Bensley Bruère and Mary Ritter Beard, *Laughing Their Way: Women's Humor in America* (New York: Macmillan, 1934); and a dissertation by Jane Anne Curry, "Women as Subjects and Writers of Nineteenth Century American Humor" (University of Michigan, 1975). On present-day obscene jokes told by women, see Carol

Mitchell, "Hostility and Aggression Toward Males in Female Joke Telling," *Frontiers* (Fall 1978), 3:19–23.

12. Walter Blair, *Horse Sense in American Humor* (Chicago: University of Chicago Press, 1942), p. 231.

13. Samuel S. Cox, *Why We Laugh* (New York: Harper, 1876). Like many later writers, Cox took it for granted that American humor was male. In arguing that a shallow mind can't be humorous, he wrote: "Genuine humor is founded on a deep, thoughtful, and manly character" (p. 17).

14. George W. Peck, *Peck's Bad Boy and His Pa* (Chicago: Belford, 1883), p. 14. Cox, pp. 60–61, saw the practical joker as a version of the cunning Yankee trader. Frank Norris regarded the adventurous boy of the boy books as a juvenile form of the average American businessman. William Dean Howells, *Criticism and Fiction*, and Frank Norris, *The Responsibilities of the Novelist* (New York: Hill & Wang, 1967), pp. 238–241.

15. Frances Trego Montgomery, *Billy Whiskers' Kids or; Day and Night:—A Sequel to "Billy Whiskers"* (New York: Diver, 1971).

16. Adeline D. T. Whitney, *The Gayworthys: A Story of Threads and Thrums* (Boston: Loring, 1865), p. 24.

17. Ann S. Stephens, *Esther: A Story of the Oregon Trail* (New York: Beadle, 1862), pp. 42, 44.

18. Mark Twain, *Innocents Abroad* (New York: Harper, 1907), 1:251. See also David Gray, "Murillo's 'Immaculate Conception'," *Atlantic* (November 1870), 26:599.

19. John William De Forest, *Kate Beaumont* (State College, Penn.: Bald Eagle Press, 1963), p. 421. Another woman compared to this Madonna in a nineteenth-century American novel is Bertie Patterson in *With the Procession* by Henry Blake Fuller (Chicago: University of Chicago Press, 1965), p. 185. First published 1895.

20. W. D. Howells, *The Shadow of a Dream and An Imperative Duty* (Bloomington: Indiana University Press, 1970), pp. 3, 18.

21. W. D. Howells, *Years of My Youth* (New York: Harper, 1916), p. 181.

22. Frances E. Willard, *How to Win: A Book for Girls* (New York: Funk and Wagnalls, 1887).

23. *The Dime Pocket Joke Book, No. 1* (New York: Beadle and Adams, 1875), p. 60. The final hint was: "And, above all, don't imagine that you must keep your lady-talk and gentleman-talk in separate budgets, labeled and sorted, unless you want the girls to laugh at your wishy-washy sentimentalisms. Talk to them in a frank, manly style, as you would to an intelligent gentleman" (p. 62).

24. Joseph Kirkland, *Zury, the Meanest Man in Spring County: A Novel of Western Life* (Urbana: University of Illinois Press, 1956), p. 525. On the ridicule of Anne's dress, see pp. 205–206. The novel came out in 1887.

25. Ann Stephens, *High Life in New York* (New York: Edward Stephens, 1843), p. 2.

26. W. D. Howells, *Suburban Sketches* (Boston: Houghton Mifflin, 1883), p. 137.

27. [Charles Henry Smith], *Bill Arp: So Called* (New York: Metropolitan Record Office, 1866), p. 6.

28. [Charles Farrar Browne], *Artemus Ward: His Book* (New York: Carleton, 1862), p. 175. Ward is seen as the average American man by Stanley T. Williams, "Artemus the Delicious," *Virginia Quarterly Review* (1952), 28:214–227, and by James C. Austin, *Artemus Ward* (New York: Twayne, 1964).

29. "Recollections of Nasby," *Indianapolis News*, March 13, 1888, as cited by John M. Harrison, *The Man Who Made Nasby, David Ross Locke* (Chapel Hill: University of North Carolina Press, 1969), p. 98.

30. [David Ross Locke], *The Struggles (Social, Financial and Political) of Petroleum V. Nasby* (Boston: Richardson, 1872), p. 34.

31. Mary Jane Holmes, *'Lena Rivers* (New York: Carleton, 1871), pp. 267–268.

32. *Dime Pocket Joke Book*, p. 49.

33. W. D. Howells, *Venetian Life* (Boston: Osgood, 1876), p. 342.

34. Susan Warner, *Queechy* (New York: Putnam, 1852), 2:285.

35. Susan Warner, *The Wide, Wide World* (Philadelphia: Lippincott, 1875), p. 55.

36. Maria Cummins, *The Lamplighter* (Boston: Jewett, 1854), p. 257.

37. Rebecca Harding Davis, "A Story of To-day," *Atlantic Monthly* (December 1861), 8:712. Davis once wrote, "I believe that Whitman simply was indecent as thousands of other men are indecent, who are coarse by nature and vulgar by breeding." "Some Hobgoblins in Literature," *Book Buyer* (April 1897), 14:231.

38. "Editor's Easy Chair," *Harper's New Monthly Magazine*, (1871), 42:614, 615. On Rip Van Winkle, see Leslie Fiedler, *Love and Death in the American Novel* (New York: Criterion, 1960), pp. 332–36. Jefferson's *Rip Van Winkle* opened in 1865, when the literary comedians were at their crest.

39. See Kenneth Lynn's *Mark Twain and Southwestern Humor* (Boston: Little, 1959), based on the contrast between the Self-Controlled Gentleman and the Clown: "The conflict between two radically different styles is the enduring drama of American humor, representing . . . a conflict between two utterly different concepts of what American life should be" (p. 168). For other versions of this general view, see James M. Cox, "Humor of the Old Southwest," and Louis D. Rubin, Jr., "'The Barber Kept on Shaving': The Two Perspectives of American Humor," in *Comic Imagination*. Cox: "First of all, there is Longstreet's own path, following the border between refinement and vernacular" (p. 107). Rubin: "Everyone of Mark Twain's major books is based squarely on the clash of cultural modes" (p. 390). The next chapter of this part develops a version of this general view.

13. TAKING DOWN THE BIG ONE

1. J. Hector St. John de Crèvecoeur, *Letters from An American Farmer* (London: Dent, 1926), pp. 51–52.

2. See Richard B. Lee and Irven DeVore, eds., *Man the Hunter* (Chicago:

Aldine, 1968), and Richard B. Lee and Irven DeVore, ed., *Kalahari Hunter-Gatherers: Studies of the !Kung San and their Neighbors* (Cambridge: Harvard University Press, 1976).

3. Richard Slotkin, *Regeneration through Violence: The Mythology of the American Frontier, 1600–1860* (Middletown, Conn.: Wesleyan University Press, 1973). A flaw in Slotkin's thesis is that his "American myth" applies mainly to men: the frontiersman may have been seen as a sort of Indian, but was his wife ever seen as a sort of squaw? Then there are the problems inherent in the myth and symbol school.

4. Charlton Laird, *Language in America* (New York: World, 1970), p. 365. In back of Dickens' interest lay James K. Paulding's 1830 play, *The Lion of the West*, which featured Nimrod Wildfire the Kentuckian. The English version of the play had the title, *The Kentuckian; or, a Trip to New York*. This version was frequently performed in London in the 1830s. See Nils Erik Enkvist, *Caricatures of Americans on the English Stage Prior to 1870*, in *Commentationes Humanarum Litterarum* (Helsingfors: 1953), 18(1):60–65; James N. Tidwell, ed., *The Lion of the West, Retitled The Kentuckian, or a Trip to New York* (Stanford: Stanford University Press, 1954); and Joseph J. Arpad, "John Wesley Jarvis, James Kirke Paulding and Colonel Nimrod Wildfire," *New York Folklore Quarterly* (June, 1965), 21:92–106.

5. Quoted from Christian Schultz, Jr., *Travels on an Inland Voyage* (New York: Isaac Riley, 1810), 2:145–146, by Walter Blair, *Native American Humor* (San Francisco: Chandler, 1960), p. 30. The best account of this early nineteenth-century American humor is by Walter Blair in Blair and Hamlin Hill, *America's Humor from Poor Richard to Doonesbury* (New York: Oxford University Press, 1978), pp. 92–142. Blair stresses the influence of a comic story-teller, John Wesley Jarvis, summarizes the ways in which David Crockett and Mike Fink were turned into comic demigods, and makes an extended comparison of the stock bragging Spaniard in seventeenth-century Italian commedia dell'arte and the fictionalized Davy Crockett.

6. Laird, *Language in America*, pp. 352–370, argues that backwoods tall talk was an amusement of idle newspapermen. John Q. Anderson, "Mike Hooter—The Making of a Myth," in M. Thomas Inge, ed., *The Frontier Humorists: Critical Views* (Hamden, Conn.: Archon, 1975), pp. 197-207, shows how two Southern writers transformed a living man into a conventional kind of legend James Atkins Shackford, *David Crockett: The Man and the Legend* (Chapel Hill: University of North Carolina Press, 1956), discusses the ways in which Crockett was publicized and exploited and made to resemble "the theoretical backwoodsman."

7. I have got several ideas from Neil Schmitz, "Tall Tale, Tall Talk: Pursuing the Lie in Jacksonian Literature," *American Literature* (January 1977), 48:471–491. Schmitz sees the lying inherent in tall talk as a way of coping with the existential angst people felt who lived in a hard and primitive world. Schmitz pushes this idea so hard he makes Jim Doggett in "The Big Bear of Arkansas" look more like Woody Allen than a man with "perfect confidence in himself." For an earlier absurdist approach to frontier humor, see Richard Boyd Hauck, *A Cheerful Nihilism: Confidence and "The Absurd" in*

American Humorous Fiction (Bloomington: Indiana University Press, 1971), ch. 3.

8. See Edwin H. Cady, *"The Batrachomyomachia* & American Fiction," *The Light of Common Day: Realism in American Fiction* (Bloomington: Indiana University Press, 1971).

9. Laird, *Language in America*, p. 357.

10. Augustus Baldwin Longstreet, "Georgia Theatrics," *Georgia Scenes*, as printed in Blair, *Native American Humor*, pp. 287–289.

11. "Bears in Arkansas," *Beadle's Illustrated Book of Fun, No. 2* (New York: Beadle, 1860), pp. 8–9. This collection reappeared as the *Jim Crow Joke Book* (New York: Beadle and Adams, 1875).

12. John William De Forest, *Kate Beaumont* (State College, Penn.: Bald Eagle Press, 1963), p. 114. The gyascutus or gyanosa was originally an imaginary circus beast.

13. *The Rise of Silas Lapham* (Cambridge: Houghton Mifflin, 1957), p. 169.

14. *Kate Beaumont*, pp. 275, 279.

15. A. J. Sowell, *Rangers and Pioneers in Texas* (San Antonio, 1884), p. 330, as quoted from Mody C. Boatright, *Folk Laughter on the American Frontier* (New York: Macmillan, 1949), pp. 30–31.

16. Chester Sullivan, *Sullivan's Hollow* (Jackson: University Press of Mississippi, 1978), p. 37. The original Sullivans were squatters on Choctaw land. Norris W. Yates has suggested that many of the sketches in *The Spirit of The Times* were about the "professional squatter and backwoods farmer-hunters." Yates, *William T. Porter and the Spirit of the Times* (Baton Rouge: Louisiana State University Press, 1957), p. 112.

17. Hauck, *Cheerful Nihilism*, p. 249. See the same author's dissertation, "The Literary Content of the New York *Spirit of the Times*, 1831–1856" (Urbana: University of Illinois, 1965). See also Yates, *William T. Porter*; Hennig Cohen and William B. Dillingham, eds., *Humor of the Old Southwest* (Boston: Houghton Mifflin, 1964); and Blair, *Native American Humor*.

18. The odd balance between identification and derision in American humor has often prevented Northern liberals from seeing the joke. Thus, Edmund Wilson, believing that Sut Lovingood was to be identified with his creator, George Washington Harris, denounced the humorist's cruelty. I for one can't say that Wilson was wrong; it seems only a step from Harris to the humorous masquerading of the early Klan. Albion Tourgee was not imagining things when he spotted a link between this organization in its early days and Southwestern humor; see *Bricks without Straw* (New York: Fords, Howard, and Hulbert, 1880), p. 415. Tourgee was a fine civil libertarian committed to freedmen's rights. For Wilson's views on Harris, see *Patriotic Gore* (London: André Deutsch, 1962), pp. 507–519.

19. *Spectator*, November 24, 1866, as quoted by Blair, *Native American Humor*, p. 116.

20. Noah Brooks, "Mark Twain in California," *Century*, (1898), N.S. 25, pp. 98–99, as quoted in *ibid.*, p. 149.

21. *Dr. Breen's Practice* (Boston: Houghton Mifflin, n.d.) pp. 211, 214. First published 1881. Grace Breen is utterly at sea with Maynard.

22. R. H. Newell, *The Orpheus C. Kerr Papers* (New York: Carleton, 1871), p. 60. ("Orpheus C. Kerr" = office-seeker.)

23. Mark Twain, *Roughing It* (New York: New American Library, 1962), ch. 24. There is a very interesting discussion of the way the *eiron*, or self-deprecating man, replaced the *alazon*, or boaster, in the 1850s and 60s in Blair and Hill, *America's Humor*, ch. 25, "Twilight of the Comic Demigods."

24. E. P. Thompson, "Time, Work-Discipline, and Industrial Capitalism," *Past and Present*, Vol. 38 (December 1967), contrasts the "task-orientation" of farming and craft industry to the "time-discipline" of factories. In preindustrial life, "the working-day lengthens or contracts according to the task" (p. 60) and social life is often integrated with work. See also Herbert G. Gutman, "Work, Culture, and Society in Industrializing America," *American Historical Review* (June 1973), 78:531–588.

14. PETTICOAT HUMOR

1. Rebecca Harding Davis, "Paul Blecker," *Atlantic* (June 1863), 11:677.

2. Henry James, *The Bostonians* (London: Macmillan, 1886), p. 18.

3. Henry James, *The Portrait of a Lady* (Boston: Houghton Mifflin, 1882), p. 79.

4. H. H. Boyesen, "Types of American Women," *Literary and Social Silhouettes* (New York: Harper, 1894), p. 14.

5. Elizabeth T Spring, "Elizabeth Stuart Phelps," in Elizabeth Stuart Phelps et al., *Our Famous Women* (Hartford. Worthington, 1884), p. 580.

6. Emily Thornwell, *The Lady's Guide to Perfect Gentility* (San Marino, Calif.. Huntington Library, 1973), n.p. Both the 1856 and 1884 editions carried this warning.

7. From Ethel Parton's unpublished biography as cited by Ann D. Wood, "The 'Scribbling Women' and Fanny Fern: Why Women Wrote," *American Quarterly* (1971), 23:4–5.

8. *The Complete Poetical Works of James Whitcomb Riley* (New York: Grosset, 1937), p. 371.

9. Susan Warner, *The Wide, Wide World* (Philadelphia: Lippincott, 1875), 1:304.

10. Ann Stephens, *High Life in New York* (New York· Edwards Stephens, 1843), p. 20.

11. Marietta Holley, *Samantha at Saratoga; or, "Racing after Fashion"* (n.p.: Edgewood, 1887), p. 46.

12. Howells, *Years of My Youth* (Bloomington: Indiana University Press, 1975), pp. 86, 19, 86.

13. Howells, *The Kentons*, George C. Carrington, Jr. and Ronald Gottesman, ed. (Bloomington: Indiana University Press, 1971), p. 222.

14. Mark Twain, *Sketches New and Old* (New York: Harper, 1907), p. 109. In a review, Howells called the sketch "a bit of *genre* romance which must read like an abuse of confidence to every husband and father." *My Mark*

Twain: Reminiscences and Criticisms, Marilyn Austin Baldwin, ed. (Baton Rouge: Louisiana State University Press, 1967), p. 103.

15. Henry Nash Smith and William M. Gibson, eds., *Mark Twain—Howells Letters*, (Cambridge: Harvard University Press, 1960), 1:317, 408. For the McWilliamses as modeled on the Clemenses, see *ibid.*, 1:277, 305–306. For the authors' resentment of their wives, see *ibid.*, 1:63–64, 220–221, 360, 449, 452; 2:658–659.

16. See Carroll Smith-Rosenberg's important article, "The Female World of Love and Ritual: Relations between Women in Nineteenth-Century America," *Signs* (1975), 1:1–29.

17. Oliver Bell Bunce, *Bachelor Bluff: His Opinions, Sentiments, and Disputations* (New York: Appleton, 1881), pp. 80, 79.

18. Eleanor Emmons Maccoby and Carol Nagy Jacklin, *The Psychology of Sex Differences* (Stanford: Stanford University Press, 1978), 1:214.

19. Oliver Bell Bunce, "Some Notions about Domestic Bliss," *Appleton's Journal* (March 12, 1870), 3:295.

20. *Beadle's Illustrated Book of Fun, No. 1* (New York: Beadle, 1860), p. 24.

21. *Ibid.*, pp. 16, 18. This and the preceding story were reprinted in *The Dime Pocket Joke Book, No. 1* (New York: Beadle and Adams, 1875).

22. The politics are reversed in the first dime novel, Ann Stephens, *Malaeska* (New York: Beadle, 1860). In this story the women are natural democrats, while the men and boys are almost all proud, conservative, and racist.

23. Robert Barnwell Roosevelt, *Progressive Petticoats; or, Dressed to Death. An Autobiography of a Married Man* (New York: Carleton, 1874), pp. 14, 123, 61, 63, 76, 244, 118, 54. The author was a sportsman, a reform Democrat in New York City, and the uncle of Theodore Roosevelt. Reviewing the book in *Nation* (February 25, 1875), 20:137, George Parsons Lathrop objected to "several passages of surprising coarseness."

24. Frances M. Whitcher, *The Widow Bedott Papers* (New York: Derby, 1856), pp. xiii–xiv.

25. J. C. Derby, *Fifty Years among Authors, Books & Publishers* (New York: Carleton, 1884), p. 414.

26. "Neil Burgess," New York *Mirror*, August 9, 1879, p. 6. (My notes are ambiguous; the date may be August 9, 1881). If the original interview on which this article was based was accurate, Locke wrote the play at a time when some extremely daring burlesques and opera bouffes were being performed. Lydia Thompson and her British Blondes hit New York in 1869. A later chapter gives a brief account of the wild fantasias to be seen on stage in those years. Cross-gender impersonations were a central feature in minstrel shows and variety.

27. Most of my information comes from the New York Public Library's Performing Arts Research Center at Lincoln Center, which has playbills and a publicity poster (featuring the romantic lead, apparently, instead of the Widow) in addition to files of the *Mirror*. See also John M. Harrison, *The Man Who Made Nasby, David Ross Locke* (Chapel Hill: University of North Carolina Press, 1969), pp. 240–243.

28. *Mirror*, August 9, 1879, p. 6. My notes are unclear on this point, but I think the synopsis was first published in the Providence *Journal*.

29. *Mirror*, August 9, 1879, p. 6.

30. George C. D. Odell, *Annals of the New York Stage* (New York: Columbia University Press, 1940), 12:41. Charles B. Bishop also played the Widow.

31. *Annals*, 11:42. For a photograph of Burgess as Widow Bedott, see *Annals*, 11:40. See also John Bouvé Clapp and Edwin Francis Edgett, *Players of the Present* (New York: Dunlap Society, 1899), pp. 46–47. Edgett had a lower opinion of Burgess than my other sources. In the *Dictionary of American Biography* (New York: Scribners, 1929), 3:276, he wrote that Burgess "burlesqued rather than interpreted the eccentric personalities of elderly women."

32. Quoted from Providence *Journal* by *Mirror*, August 9, 1879, p. 6.

33. *Mirror*, August 9, 1879, p. 6.

34. *Mirror*, March 20, 1880, p. 7.

35. George William Curtis, *The Potiphar Papers* (New York: Putnam, 1853). Howells met a Hungarian lady in Venice who owned this work, "which must have been inexpressibly amused and bewildered to find itself there." *Venetian Life* (Boston: Osgood, 1876), p. 430.

36. John William De Forest, *Honest John Vane* (New Haven: Richmond & Patten, 1875).

37. Collected in *Mark Twain's Library of Humor* (New York: Webster, 1888).

38. "The Husband's Friend," *Putnam's Magazine* (September 1857), 10:334–338.

39. George William Curtis, *Prue and I* (New York: Dix, Edwards, 1857), pp. 42–43.

40. *Nation* (October 5, 1871), 13:228.

41. Thomas Sergent Perry, "William Dean Howells," *Century* (March 1882), 23:681–682. In *Suburban Sketches* (Boston: Houghton Mifflin, 1883), p. 248, Howells himself referred to the "peculiar kind of drolling" he became famous for. The best example of this humor may be the passage in "At the Sign of the Savage" (collected with *A Fearful Responsibility*) where Mr. Kenton refuses to believe he is in the Black Forest. Henry James, "William Dean Howells," in *The American Essays*, Leon Edel, ed. (New York: Vintage, 1956), p. 155, understood that Howells was "a humorist himself" and "strong in the representation of humorists." Hamilton Wright Mabie, one of Howells' fiercest reviewers, allowed that humor was "the most real and the most distinctive" of his "gifts." "A Typical Novel," *Andover Review*, Vol. 4 (November 1885), as quoted from George J. Becker, ed., *Documents of Modern Literary Realism* (Princeton: Princeton University Press, 1963), p. 299. Mark Twain had high praise for Howells' humor: "I do not think any one else can play with humorous fancies so gracefully and delicately and deliciously as he does, nor has so many to play with, nor can come so near making them look as if they were doing the playing themselves and he was not aware that they were at it." "William Dean Howells," in Jane Benardete, ed., *American Realism* (New York: Capricorn, 1972), p. 127.

42. See *Mark Twain—Howells Letters*, 1:398–399. Howells may not have had a hand in placing his own work in the *Library of Humor* (see *Letters*, 2:549).

As for the arrangement, "when I had done my work according to tradition, with authors, times, and topics carefully studied in due sequence, [Mark Twain] tore it all apart" (*My Mark Twain: Reminiscences and Criticisms*, p. 17). I believe Howells had placed the sketch by Neal and the excerpt from *Their Wedding Journey* side by side under the "topic" of petticoat tyranny, and Mark Twain then interposed the episode from *Tom Sawyer*. Howells expressed a low view of Neal in "Editor's Easy Chair," *Harper's Monthly Magazine* (1911), 123:310. Another of Howells' sources was Stowe's *Pink and White Tyranny*, which Howells reviewed while writing *Their Wedding Journey*; see *Atlantic* (September 1871), 28:377–384. According to Nina Baym, *Woman's Fiction: A Guide to Novels by and about Women in America, 1820–1870* (Ithaca: Cornell University Press, 1978), p. 235, *Pink and White Tyranny* was about "a disastrous marriage between a noble but somewhat naive New England man . . . and a beautiful, social-climbing flirt."

43. Howells, *Their Wedding Journey* (Boston: Osgood, 1875), pp. 138–143. Reprinted in *Mark Twain's Library of Humor*, pp. 121–126.

44. *Wedding Journey*, pp. 158, 159. Reprinted under the title "At Niagara" in *Mark Twain's Library of Humor*, pp. 495–497. The quarrel episode was reprinted in this collection, pp. 592–595, under the title, "Their First Quarrel."

45. *Wedding Journey*, pp. 297, 298. This episode was given the title "Custom House Morals" in *Mark Twain's Library of Humor* (pp. 433–434) where it was brought to an end after Isabel's order, "you must slip out of it some way." Howells had a "fondness" for Basil and Isabel, and "it was with a pang that I learned from one of my later critics that Mrs. March was hateful to him because of her conscience, I believe" (a cancelled passage from the "Bibliographical" introduction to the 1911 edition). See "Autobiographical," *A Hazard of New Fortunes* (Bloomington: Indiana University Press, 1976), p. 502. Many of Howells' fiercest critics exhibit a comparable blindness.

15. FUNNY WOMEN

1. *Julia Newberry's Diary*, Margaret Ayer Barnes and Janet Ayer Fairbank, eds. (New York: Norton, 1933), p. xi.

2. H. H. Boyesen, "German and American Women," *Literary and Social Silhouettes* (New York: Harper, 1894), pp. 32–33.

3. Howells, *Selected Letters* (Boston: Twayne, 1979), 1:395, 396.

4. Henry Clay Lewis, "The Curious Widow," John Q. Anderson, ed., *Louisiana Swamp Doctor* (Baton Rouge: Louisiana State University Press, 1962), p. 121.

5. *Annie Kilburn* (New York: Harper, 1889), p. 49.

6. Fanny Fern, *Caper-Sauce: A Volume of Chit-Chat about Men, Women, and Things* (New York: Carleton, 1872), p. 51. The title of this book plays on the reprimand often applied to a mischievous girl—"saucebox" or "saucy."

7. Howells, "Mark Twain: An Inquiry," in *My Mark Twain: Reminiscences and Criticisms* (Baton Rouge: Louisiana State University Press, 1967), p. 153.

8. *The Dime Pocket Joke Book, No. 1* (New York: Beadle & Adams, 1875), p. 15.

9. See Cornelia Meigs, *A Critical History of Children's Literature* (New York: Macmillan, 1953), pp. 211–231.

10. Quoted by Kate Sanborn, "Frances E. Willard," *Our Famous Women* (Hartford: Worthington, 1884), p. 698. This passage seems remarkably well-composed for a diary entry. Willard herself quoted it in her 1887 book, *How to Win: A Book for Girls.*

11. Quoted from Sarah Josepha Hale, *Woman's Record* (New York: Harper, 1860), p. 578. Italics hers.

12. Louis J. Budd, "Mark Twain Talks Mostly about Humor and Humorists," *Studies in American Humor* (April 1974), 1:16. For much of her married and publishing life, Frances Whitcher lived in Elmira, New York—Olivia Langdon's hometown before she married Mark Twain.

13. Rev. of *The English Orphans, North American Review* (October 1855), 81:557.

14. Mary Jane Holmes, *'Lena Rivers* (New York: Miller, Orton, 1856) p. 407.

15. Mary Jane Holmes, *Tempest and Sunshine* (New York: Appleton, 1854), p. 57. Another humorous girl in the novel is Florence Woodburn (p. 372). The knife was the all-purpose table utensil:

I eat my peas with honey.
I've done it all my life.
It makes the peas taste funny,
But it keeps 'em on the knife.

16. Adeline D. T. Whitney, *The Gayworthys: A Story of Threads and Thrums* (Boston: Loring, 1865), pp. 24, 58, 214.

17. Written by a Rev. Mr. Mayo and quoted by Joseph B. Lyman in James Parton et al., *Eminent Women of the Age; Being Narratives of the Lives & Deeds of the Most Prominent Women of the Present Generation* (Hartford: Betts, 1868), p. 153; italics mine. The big joke in *'Lena Rivers* is the way the rank old grandmother embarrasses the genteel Mrs. Livingston.

18. Caroline Lee Hentz, *Aunt Patty's Scrap Bag; or, The Brothers. A Tale of Love and Jealousy* (Philadelphia: Peterson, n.d.), pp. 146, 158, 147, 185. Lyle H. Wright's very useful article, "A Few Observations on American Fiction, 1851–1875," *Proceedings of the American Antiquarian Society* (1955), 65:96, identifies this work as one of five books of humor written by women before 1875. The other four are Ann Stephens, *High Life in New York* (1843), Whitcher's *Widow Bedott Papers* (first published 1846–1850), Virginia W. Johnson, *Travels of an American Owl* (1871), and Marietta Holley, *My Opinions and Betsey Bobbet's* (1873). This list overlooks the writing of Gail Hamilton and Fanny Fern, and several novels with comic heroines and episodes, Southworth's *Hidden Hand*, Holmes's early novels, and some of Whitney's and Louisa May Alcott's books. There were also several humorous books for children written by women in the 1860s and 70s.

19. *Aunt Patty's Scrap Bag*, pp. 152, 161–162.

20. *The Pearl of Orr's Island* (Ridgewood, N.J.: Gregg, 1967), p. 20. Originally published 1862.

21. Maria S. Cummins, *The Lamplighter* (Boston: Jewett, 1854), pp. 152–153.

22. *Doctor Zay* (Boston: Houghton, 1882), p. 88. According to Christine Stansell, "Elizabeth Stuart Phelps: A Study in Female Rebellion," *Massachusetts Review* (1972), 13:239–256, the common pattern of Phelps's novels is that a superwoman figure tries to overthrow the male autocracy that deforms women's lives.

23. An early account of the Samantha books may be found in Walter Blair, *Horse Sense in American Humor* (Chicago: University of Chicago Press, 1942), pp. 231–239. A more extensive discussion is in Jane Anne Curry, "Women as Subjects and Writers of Nineteenth Century American Humor," diss. University of Michigan, 1975, ch. 6.

24. Marietta Holley, *Josiah Allen's Wife as a P.A. and P.I.: Samantha at the Centennial* (Hartford: American Publishing, 1877), p. 71. P.A. and P.I. stand for Promiscuous Adviser and Private Investigator. The value of this book as a report on the Centennial of 1876 is rather impaired by the publisher's ingenuous admission in Holley's next book that the previous one had been "written wholly from imagination and from reading the descriptions others gave—the author never having seen the Great Exhibition." "Publishers' Preface," *Samantha at Saratoga* (n.p.: Edgewood Publishing, 1887).

25. *Josiah Allen's Wife as a P. A.*, p. 402.

26. Funk and Wagnalls advertised Holley in the end papers of Frances E. Willard's *How To Win: A Book for Girls* by saying: "The strong feature of all Miss Holley's humor, is its moral tone."

27. Tony Pastor's Theatre, June 5, 1883, and Bijou Opera House, week ending April 7, 1883. All my information on *Vim* comes from the Performing Arts Research Center at Lincoln Center.

28. Boston Bijou Theatre, May 24, 1886.

29. Review of *Vim*, New York *Mirror*, April 28, 1888, p. 2.

30. Boston Bijou Theatre, May 17, 1886.

31. The poster, printed by the Courier Lithograph Company, Buffalo, is in the Performing Arts Research Center at Lincoln Center.

32. *Mirror*, p. 2.

33. Program, Boston Bijou Theatre, May 24, 1886.

34. "Editor's Study," *Harper's Monthly* (July 1889), 79:318.

35. "A Pleasure Exertion," *Mark Twain's Library of Humor* (New York: Webster, 1888), pp. 327–338. This account of a picnic where everything goes wrong came from *My Wayward Pardner; or, My Trials with Josiah, America, The Widow Bump, and Etcetery* (Hartford: American Publishing, 1880).

36. Howells, "Editor's Study," p. 318. Perhaps the play kept Holley's message. One surviving program for *Vim* asks a series of questions in one column:

Young man! How would you like it if you had to stay in the house nine days in the week and hear nothing but dissertations on shirt buttons and historical reminiscences about bursted suspender buttons?

How would you like it if every time your wife saved a few dollars she would come home at 1 o'clock in the morning with back teeth afloat, and pull every door in the neighborhood out by the roots?

Tony Pastor's New 14th St. Theatre, September 17, 1883.

37. Robert Barnwell Roosevelt, *Progressive Petticoats; or, Dressed to Death. An Autobiography of a Married Man* (New York: Carleton, 1874), p. 15.

38. Howells, *The Lady of the Aroostook* (Boston: Houghton Mifflin, 1882), p. 92.

39. *Atlantic* (1884), 53:399. The *Atlantic* had become a more conservative magazine after Howells resigned the editorship in 1881.

40. *Critic* (March 22, 1884), N.S. 1, p. 138.

41. *Critic* (March 29, 1884), N.S. 1, pp. 145–146. Rollins thought highly of Howells' realism; see her "Effie's Realistic Novel" in Jane Benardete, ed., *American Realism* (New York: Putnam, 1972).

42. "The Humor of Women," *Critic* (June 28, 1884), N.S. 1, p. 302.

43. Kate Sanborn, *Memories and Anecdotes* (New York: Putnam, 1915), p. 164. At her death in 1917, Sanborn was spoken of in several press notices "as the leading woman humorist of America." Edwin W. Sanborn, *Kate Sanborn/July 11, 1839/July 9, 1917* (Boston: McGrath-Sherrill, 1918), p. 63. When Mark Twain quit as humor editor of the *Galaxy* in 1871, Kate Sanborn was brought in after the editors failed to keep "The Club Room" going. She lasted "a little more than a year." Frank Luther Mott, *A History of American Magazines 1865–1885* (Cambridge: Harvard University Press, 1938), p. 368. Her favorite "funny man" was Charles H. Webb, author of *St. Tw'elmo*. She was a friend of Frances E. Willard, though without taking the pledge. *The Wit of Women* is not so amusing as her later books. Thirty years after compiling the book, she still felt defensive about it: "If a masculine book reviewer ever alluded to the book, it was with a sneer" (*Memories and Anecdotes*, p. 164).

44. Martha Bensley Bruère and Mary Ritter Beard, *Laughing Their Way: Women's Humor in America* (New York: Macmillan, 1934), deals with the highbrow origin of local color humor in ch. 1, "Ladies' Laughter." *The Wit of Women* (New York: Funk and Wagnall, 1885) included a great deal of dialect or local color humor written by ladies considerably more cultivated than their subjects: Katherine Sherwood (Bonner) McDowell, "Aunt Anniky's Teeth," from *Dialect Tales* (New York: Harper, 1883); Grace Greenwood, "Mistress O'Rafferty on the Woman Question"; Amanda T. Jones, "Dochther O'Flannigan and his Wondherful Cures"; Julia Pickering, "The Old-Time Religion"; Mary Noailles Murfree, "A Blacksmith in Love"; Constance Fenimore Woolson, "Miss Lois," from *Anne; A Novel* (New York: Harper, 1882); Sarah Orne Jewett, "The Circus at Denby"; Rose Terry Cooke, "A Gift Horse."

45. *Wit of Women*, pp. 103, 202, 203.

46. Rollins, "Woman's Sense of Humor," p. 146; italics mine. On the other hand, as Sanborn points out, some women writers showed "their sense of humor in ridiculing the foibles of their own sex" (p. 179). Examples in this collection are Rose Terry Cooke's "Miss Lucinda's Pig," from *Somebody's Neighbors* (Boston: Osgood, 1881), about a woman who can't bear to have a favorite pig butchered; Metta Victoria Victor's "Miss Slimmens Surprised. A Terrible Accident," about an old maid so frightened by a fire that she lets the eligible male boarders see her without her make-up; Mary Kyle Dallas, "Aunty Doleful's Visit" (Dallas succeeded Fanny Fern as correspondent on

the New York *Ledger*); and Mrs. Julia Schayer's "Struggling Genius," a playlet about a wife who tries to write fiction while caring for her children.

47. *Nation* (October 14, 1875), 21:251.

48. *Nation* (March 7, 1878), 26:172. The lady correspondents were probably Gail Hamilton and Fanny Fern, who could be much funnier than James gave them credit for. For other possible lady correspondents, see ch. 11, "Woman's Opportunity in Journalism," in Willard, *How To Win: A Book for Girls* (1887). This chapter is an excellent source on the many women in journalism. See also Jeannette Gilder's memoirs, *The Autobiography of a Tomboy* (New York: Doubleday, Page, 1900) and *The Tomboy at Work* (New York: Doubleday, Page, 1904).

49. My language comes from Eudora Welty, "Petrified Man," *Thirteen Stories* (New York: Harcourt, Brace, and World, 1965), p. 83.

16. FUNNY TOMBOYS

1. Ernest Earnest, *The American Eve in Fact and Fiction, 1775–1914* (Urbana: University of Illinois Press, 1974), p. 110.

2. Fanny Fern, *Caper-Sauce: A Volume of Chit-Chat about Men, Women, and Things* (New York: Carleton, 1872), p. 61. Fanny Fern's biographical sketch of Gail Hamilton emphasized her healthy, active, outdoor life as a child in rural New England and insisted that she was "no diseased, embryo saint." James Parton, et al., *Eminent Women of the Age; Being Narratives of the Lives and Deeds of the Most Prominent Women of the Present Generation* (Hartford: Betts, 1868), p. 218.

3. Sarah Orne Jewett, *The Country of the Pointed Firs* (Garden City, N.Y.: Doubleday, 1956), p. 58.

4. Cornelia Meigs, *A Critical History of Children's Literature* (New York: Macmillan, 1953), p. 222.

5. Henry Nash Smith, *Virgin Land: The American West As Symbol and Myth* (Cambridge: Harvard University Press, 1950), pp. 112–113. Smith's chapter "The Dime Novel Heroine" traces her generally back to Cooper; Southworth, Ouida, and the theatre would also be likely sources. Smith mentions several cross-dressing heroines, who undoubtedly appealed to male readers.

6. In the *National Union Catalog* the earliest certain date for the book version is 1888. I learned about *The Hidden Hand* from Helen Waite Papashvily's *All the Happy Endings* (New York: Harper, 1956), pp. 126–130.

7. Southworth, *The Hidden Hand; or, Capitola the Mad-Cap* (New York: Dillingham, 1888), p. 211. All citations are to this edition.

8. Bernard Sobel, *Burleycue: An Underground History of Burlesque Days* (New York: Farrar and Rinehart, 1931) and *A Pictorial History of Burlesque* (New York: Putnam, 1956); Irving Zeidman, *The American Burlesque Show* (New York: Hawthorn, 1967); Ann Corio with Joseph DiMona, *This Was Burlesque* (New York: Madison Square Press, 1968).

9. Sobel, *Burleycue*, p. 13. The burlesque Ixion may have derived from Benjamin Disraeli's jeu d'esprit of the 1830s, *Ixion in Heaven*.

10. Howells, "Some Lessons from the School of Morals," *Suburban Sketches* (Boston: Houghton Mifflin, 1883), p. 233. In a letter to his father Howells commented on the apparent objectivity of his piece on burlesque: "Of course I merely meant to describe the badness of the stage as nearly as I could, and so let the moral enforce itself. I felt that it would do no good for me to preach about it." *Selected Letters* (Boston: Twayne, 1979), 1:325. See also 1:313, 317.

11. Howells, "The New Taste in Theatricals," *Atlantic* (May 1869), 23:638. The sentence from which this phrase is taken was deleted in *Suburban Sketches*.

12. First produced in 1858, the full title of this work by W. B. English was *Three Fast Men, and the Female Robinson Crusoes.* Howells, *Selected Letters*, 1:317.

13. Howells was everywhere. His fiction actually reflects this change in burlesque. In *Their Wedding Journey* (1871), Basil and Isabel and the Ellisons have some amusing encounters with a troupe of English burlesque artistes. Isabel and Kitty Ellison are rather frightened by the actresses, while Basil and the narrator seem more sympathetic: "In their shabby bestowal in those mean upper rooms, their tawdry poverty, their merry submission to the errors and caprices of destiny, their mutual kindliness and careless friendship, these unprofitable devotees of the twinkling-footed burlesque seemed to be playing rather than living the life of strolling players." *Their Wedding Journey* (Boston: Osgood, 1875), p. 294. A decade later, in *A Modern Instance*, this happy bohemianism has become a cynical business. In the bar where Bartley gets drunk, there is a "manager of a variety combination playing at one of the theaters." When someone asks him what his new show has, the manager replies: "Legs, principally. . . . That's what the public wants. I give the public what it wants." Howells identifies this man with the same phrase that formed the title of the chapter on burlesque in *Suburban Sketches*: he is "the manager of a school of morals." *A Modern Instance* (Boston: Houghton Mifflin, 1957), pp. 212–213.

14. Constance Rourke, *Troupers of the Gold Coast, or the Rise of Lotta Crabtree* (New York: Harcourt, 1928), pp. 158, 205. One of the most important stars of the time was Adah Isaacs Menken, who was a tomboy in girlhood, had herself strapped to an actual horse in the role of Mazeppa, and displayed her prowess with firearms on the stage. In *Mazeppa* she wore breeches in the part of the masculine Cassimir and then switched to the famous scantily dressed female role. She had a husky voice and was apparently not a trained actress. After her New York opening in *Mazeppa* she wrote in her diary: "As for the *Ladies' Magazine*, I want no part of that flabby, sanctimonious collection of trash which good women read so avidly." Paul Lewis, *Queen of the Plaza: A Biography of Adah Isaacs Menken* (New York: Funk & Wagnalls, 1964), p. 20. Apparently, she was not a comic actress but a sort of bohemian Marilyn Monroe.

15. George C. D. Odell, *Annals of the New York Stage* (New York: Columbia University Press, 1931), 7:140, 147. Fanny Herring preceded Adah Menken in the role of Mazeppa (Lewis, *Queen of the Plaza*, p. 12).

16. [Robert Jones], *The Hidden Hand. A Drama, in Five Acts. Adapted from*

Mrs. Emma D. E. N. Southworth's Celebrated Novel of the Same Name, Published in the New York Ledger. With Cast of Characters, Stage Business, Etc., Etc., Correctly Marked (Printed, Not Published. 1867). An English dramatization is represented by C. H. Hazlewood, *Capitola; or, the Masked Mother, and the Hidden Hand. A Drama, In Three Acts* (London: Lacy, n.d.). The English play, performed in 1860, has melodrama but little of the original language or humor. A passage in Odell, 7:337, gives the title of a third version, *Capitola, The Heiress of the Hidden House.* Undoubtedly, there were many versions. Regis Louise Boyle, *Mrs. E. D. E. N. Southworth, Novelist: A Dissertation* (Washington, D.C.: Catholic University of America Press, 1939), p. 39, mentions a dramatization by a Weaver for presentation in Milwaukee in 1860.

17. Southworth, *Hidden Hand*, pp. 388, 389. My notes indicate that Jones's play retained the second speech. I do not remember whether he used the first speech.

18. [Jones], *Hidden Hand*, pp. 41–42.

19. Quoted from William Veeder, *Henry James—The Lessons of the Master: Popular Fiction and Personal Style in the Nineteenth Century* (Chicago: University of Chicago Press, 1975), p. 155. There is a good chapter on Linton in Vineta Colby, *The Singular Anomaly: Women Novelists of the Nineteenth Century* (New York: New York University Press, 1970).

20. Howells, rev. of *Modern Women, Atlantic* (November 1868), 22:640. Neither Howells nor James knew a woman wrote the book.

21. James, rev. of *Modern Women, Nation* (October 22, 1868), 7:333.

22. Miriam Harris, *Rutledge* (New York: Carleton, 1885), p. 265. The respectable author once publicly snubbed Adah Menken (Lewis, *Queen of the Plaza*, p. 108).

23. James, *Watch and Ward, Atlantic* (August 1871), 28:245, 246. This passage casts some light on James's phrase, "the decline of the sentiment of sex," in his 1883 notebook entry for *The Bostonians.*

24. John Hay, *The Bread-Winners* (New Haven: College and University Press, 1973), pp. 77–78.

17. PENELOPE LAPHAM IN *THE RISE OF SILAS LAPHAM*

1. According to Walter J. Meserve's introduction to *The Rise of Silas Lapham* (Bloomington: Indiana University Press, 1971), p. xvi, Howells began the novel in July 1884. All quotations come from this edition.

2. *Mark Twain—Howells Letters,* Henry Nash Smith and William M. Gibson, ed. (Cambridge: Harvard University Press, 1960), 2:492–493.

3. The *Critic* treated *Silas Lapham* rather coolly: "In fiction we are having really too much realism" (February 28, 1885, N.S. 3, p. 101, as quoted in Clayton L. Eichelberger, *Published Comment on William Dean Howells Through 1920: A Research Bibliography* [Boston: Hall, 1976], p. 52). Significantly, the *Critic* found it "beyond belief" that Tom should love "the half-cultivated" Penelope (September 12, 1885, N.S. 4, p. 122). See also item 327 in Eichelberger.

4. Howells, *Selected Letters* (Boston: Twayne, 1979), 1:396.
5. Howells, *A Foregone Conclusion* (Boston: Osgood, 1875), p. 66.
6. The reviewer for the *Nation* shared Mrs. Corey's distaste: "The most unpleasant and the most unnatural girl is Penelope Lapham..., ironically snubbing her relations, or urging her sister to inextinguishable laughter by mimicking their father" (October 22, 1885, 41:348). Actually, this highbrow reviewer disliked Penelope *because* she was natural. In *Cottage-Hearth: A Magazine of Home Arts and Home Culture*, the reviewer who considered Penelope "natural to the least detail" (October 1885, 11:326) wrote with greater accuracy. In Miriam Harris' popular novel, *Rutledge* (New York: Derby & Jackson, 1860), drawling speech is a salient trait in the disagreeable Grace, who, in the narrator's eyes, has "a sort of gutta-percha insensibility, a lazy coolness that I had not expected from her drawling, listless way" (p. 221). The narrator notices Grace's "pertness" (pp. 218, 221, 235) and sees her as pre-feminine: "nothing of the woman seemed developed in her but the sharpness." *Rutledge* is an extremely well-bred novel; it offers precisely the view of Grace that Mrs. Corey takes of Penelope.
7. Lapham "knew who the Coreys were ... and ... had long hated their name as a symbol of splendor which, unless he should live to see at least three generations of his descendants *gilded* with mineral paint, he could not hope to realize in his own" (p. 92; italics mine). In *The World of Chance* (New York: Harper, 1893), p. 350, a publisher announces the extent to which he intends to promote a possible bestseller by saying, "I'm simply going to paint the universe red."
8. Howells, *Venetian Life* (Boston: Osgood, 1875), p. 162.
9. Albion Tourgee, *Bricks without Straw: A Novel* (New York: Fords, Howard, & Hulbert, 1880), p. 19. "Peart" is applied to a man on p. 192.
10. Mary Jane Holmes, *Tempest and Sunshine* (New York: Appleton, 1854). An earlier novel, Caroline Lee Hentz's *Rena; or, the Snow Bird* (Philadelphia: Hart, 1851) seems close to Howells with its black-haired tomboy heroine contrasted with a blonde, conniving beauty.
11. Sarah Orne Jewett, *Deephaven and Other Stories* (New Haven: College and University Press, 1966), p. 137. First published in book form in 1877. In Marietta Holley, *Samantha among the Brethren* (New York: Funk and Wagnalls, 1890), pp. 190, 183, 191, a woman who is "pert," has common sense, and "likes a joke," is praised for being "smart to answer back and joke."
12. On women and self-sacrifice, see Edwin H. Cady, *The Road to Realism: The Early Years, 1837–1885, of William Dean Howells* (Syracuse: Syracuse University Press, 1956), pp. 232–234. For general discussions of Howells' women, see Edward Wagenknecht, *William Dean Howells: The Friendly Eye* (New York: Oxford University Press, 1969), pp. 156–170; William Wasserstrom, *Heiress of All the Ages* (Minneapolis: University of Minnesota Press, 1959); and Paul John Eakin, *The New England Girl: Cultural Ideals in Hawthorne, Stowe, Howells and James* (Athens: University of Georgia Press, 1974).
13. Henry James, *Watch and Ward, Atlantic* (August 1871), 28:245. Eakin's explanation for Penelope's melodramatic self-sacrifice is superficial. He

suggests it is "the psychology of the plain girl"—a "desire to become through identification with the heroines of fiction, the pretty girl she isn't in real life" (*New England Girl*, p. 122). One might believe this if Penelope tried to make herself prettier during her self-sacrificial phase. But prettiness seems the last thing on her mind.

14. For a rendering of a different sort of feminine nervous breakdown, see Howells' *A Counterfeit Presentment* and *The Kentons*.

15. Myself, in the original version of this chapter: "Nothing more is said of Penelope in the novel. Howells whisks her away by sleight of hand while distracting us with those timid social pieties that make us see that, finally, we cannot respect this man as we respect Thoreau. Worse, Howells invokes our pity for the Coreys' loss of their son in order to make us sympathize with their social rigidity." Alfred Habegger, "Nineteenth-Century American Humor: Easygoing Males, Anxious Ladies, and Penelope Lapham," *PLMA* (October 1976), 91:896.

16. Francis Hackett, *Horizons: A Book of Criticism* (New York: Huebsch, 1918), p. 24.

17. Howells, *Suburban Sketches* (Boston: Houghton Mifflin, 1883), pp. 141–144.

18. *Ibid.*, p. 74.

19. Marilyn Austin Baldwin, ed., *My Mark Twain: Reminiscences and Criticisms* (Baton Rouge: Louisiana State University Press, 1967), p. 117. In his introduction to *Artemus Ward's Best Stories* (New York: Harper, 1912), p. viii, Howells said that Artemus Ward's humor "reflected the dislike of the anti-slavery movement and of the other contemporary reforms." Still, Howells remembered enjoying Artemus Ward in the late 1850s, and in 1912 he felt that "Affairs around the Village Green" was better than anything by Mark Twain.

20. Howells, *Years of My Youth* (Bloomington: Indiana University Press, 1975), p. 16. In *New Leaf Mills* (New York: Harper, 1913), p. 65, the man corresponding to Howells' father has a "provisional levity tempering his final seriousness." Howells' bad men appear to have no final seriousness.

21. "Editor's Easy Chair," *Harper's Magazine* (1911), 123:311.

22. Howells, *Literature and Life: Studies* (New York: Harper, 1902), p. 29.

18. THE MALE RISK

1. An early book, full of certainty about the good times coming once sex roles are wiped out, is Janet Saltzman Chafetz, *Masculine/Feminine or Human? An Overview of the Sociology of Sex Roles* (Itasca, Ill.: Peacock, 1974). A much better book on the same subject is Carol Tavris and Carole Offir, *The Longest War: Sex Differences in Perspective* (New York: Harcourt Brace Jovanovich, 1977). For books specifically on men, two useful early collections are John W. Petras, ed., *Sex: Male/Gender: Masculine: Readings in Male Sexuality* (Port Washington, N.Y.: Alfred, 1975); Joseph H. Pleck and Jack Sawyer, ed., *Men and Masculinity* (Englewood Cliffs, N.J.: Prentice-Hall, 1974). For more

recent studies, see Mirra Komarovsky, *Dilemmas of Masculinity: A Study of College Youth* (New York: Norton, 1976); a special issue of *Journal of Social Issues* (1978), vol. 34, no. 1; Natalie Gittelson, *Dominus: A Woman Looks at Men's Lives* (New York: Farrar, Straus and Giroux, 1978). A useful survey of recent literature on men is James B. Harrison, "Review Essay/Men's Roles and Men's Lives," *Signs* (Winter 1978), 4:324–336. This essay illustrates the flaws evident in all too many discussions: a weak sense of history and popular literature, and a tendency to approach the subject from a fixed commitment to the progressive outlook associated with modern feminism. Graham John Barker-Benfield, *The Horrors of the Half-Known Life: Male Attitudes toward Women and Sexuality in Nineteenth-Century America* (New York: Harper, 1976), has these and other flaws. It is unfortunate that the one book dealing with 19th-century American masculinity should set out from a position of committed hostility to what the author calls the WASP male. Herb Goldberg, *The Hazards of Being Male: Surviving the Myth of Masculine Privilege* (New York: Nash, 1976) reacts too much against feminism but has one fairly well researched chapter, "The Hazards of Being Male," pp. 179–189.

It may be misleading to apply the fashionable term, machismo, to nineteenth-century American masculinity. Machismo means a very different thing in Mexico or any other Catholic Latin culture from what it is taken to mean in the United States. There is a good discussion of this question by Richard Basham, "Machismo," *Frontiers* (Spring 1976), 1:126–143. Basham sees machismo "as a response on the part of the male to what he perceives as a sexually superior and threatening aspect" of the female. Thus, a boy growing up in a machismo culture manages to establish his independence from his mother by overreacting and assuming a rigid, dominating persona. The weakness of this view is that it overlooks the positively attractive features of the macho life in the eyes of boys and young men: being cock of the walk presumably looks great to them. Also, *do* males really see females as "sexually superior" because they can give birth?

Phyllis Chesler's recent study of masculinity, *About Men* (New York: Simon and Schuster, 1978), has some good perceptions but is disfigured by an ugly combination of arrogance and ignorance. Chesler thinks that "all male blood that is shed is somehow experienced by men as a loss of sexual blood, as sexual mutilation" (p. 215). She believes that because men have a penis and women do not, "men come to share a belief that women are not really human beings" (p. 211).

2. Tavris and Offir, *Longest War*, pp. 99–101.

3. Robert J. Stoller, *Sex and Gender; on the Development of Masculinity and Femininity* (New York: Science House, 1968), 1:263–264.

4. Eleanor Emmons Maccoby and Carol Nagy Jacklin, *The Psychology of Sex Differences* (Stanford: Stanford University Press, 1978), 1:210–211, report an experiment demonstrating that boys tend more than girls to choose "peer associations and peer values when these conflicted with their own interests and values or with those of adults."

5. In *A Boy's Town/Described for "Harper's Young People"* (New York: Harper, 1890), pp. 5, 6, Howells (b. 1837) remembered the time one of his grand-

mothers brought him his "Philadelphia suit" from over the mountains: "it testified unmistakably to the boy's advance in years beyond the shameful period of skirts."

6. Fanny Fern, *Caper-Sauce: A Volume of Chit-Chat about Men, Women, and Things* (New York: Carleton, 1872), p. 121.

7. *Ibid.*, p. 279.

8. Kenneth E. Read, *The High Valley* (New York: Scribner, 1965), p. 172.

9. Southworth, *The Hidden Hand; or, Capitola the Mad-Cap* (New York: Dillingham, 1888), p. 79.

10. Maria S. Cummins, *The Lamplighter* (Boston: Jewett, 1854), pp. 215, 218. Stoller, *Sex and Gender*, ch. 8, discusses transsexualism in boys—an obsession with wearing girl's clothes, jewelry, cosmetics, etc. Stoller finds the explanation of this behavior in mothers who baby the boys and talk over "feminine matters" (p. 93) with them. The mother's motive in feminizing her son, he claims, is to "revenge herself on males" (p. 121).

11. *The Smithsonian Collection of Newspaper Comics*, Bill Blackbeard and Martin Williams, ed. (Washington, D.C.: Smithsonian Institution Press and Harry N. Abrams, 1977), pp. 19–20.

12. Edward W. Townsend, *"Chimmie Fadden"/Major Max/and Other Studies* (New York: Lovell, Coryell, 1895); *Chimmie Fadden Explains: Major Max Expounds* (n.p.: United States Book Company, 1895); *Chimmie Fadden and Mr. Paul* (New York: Century, 1902). On Mose, see Walter Blair and Hamlin Hill, *America's Humor from Poor Richard to Doonesbury* (New York: Oxford University Press, 1978), pp. 147–151. Bad boys were so common in early comic strips that the cigar-smoking Flip in *Little Nemo* audaciously denied belonging to the notorious brotherhood: "I'm not one of these Sunday supplement kids that play tricks on people." This episode first appeared November 4, 1906, and is reprinted in *Little Nemo* (New York: Nostalgia Press, 1972), p. 66.

13. Thomas Sergeant Perry, "Mark Twain," *Century* (May 1885), 30:171.

14. Howells, *A Boy's Town*, p. 193. It took a woman to give a plain, unshaded portrait of a man without ambition; see Sarah Orne Jewett's William Blackett in *The Country of the Pointed Firs*.

15. Joseph Kirkland, *Zury: The Meanest Man in Spring County: A Novel of Western Life* (Urbana: University of Illinois Press, 1956), p. 457.

19. THAT OLD GANG OF MINE

1. Emma D. E. N. Southworth, *Ishmael; or, In the Depths* (New York: Burt, n.d.), p. 423. Among Southworth's novels, this was her favorite.

2. Thomas Bailey Aldrich, *The Story of a Bad Boy* (Boston: Houghton Mifflin, 1897), p. 29. The pioneering study of boy gangs in America, J. Adams Puffer, *The Boy and His Gang* (Boston: Houghton Mifflin, 1912), pp. 9–10, considered Aldrich's novel "the most adequate account yet in print of a typical boys' gang, told with insight and skill. One can hardly imagine a better introduction to the ways of all boys than this story of a bad one."

Howells' review considered Tom Bailey a representative boy: "his ideas, impulses, and adventures here are those of the great average of boys"— *Atlantic* (January 1870), 25:124. In a letter to Aldrich Howells wrote, "I read your Bad Boy's Fourth of July adventures last, and was made to laugh beyond reason by them. It is the best part yet given—this installment. And I *did* like the other parts." *Selected Letters* (Boston: Twayne, 1979), 1:318.

3. Margaret Mead and Nicolas Calas, ed., *Primitive Heritage: An Anthropological Anthology* (New York: Random House, 1953). The story was originally collected by James R. Murie and published in 1914.

4. See Sam Pickering's account of war stories for boys written during the Civil War, "A Boy's Own War," *New England Quarterly* (September 1975), 48:362–377. Harry Castlemon was the pen name of Charles Fosdick; Oliver Optic, of William T. Adams.

5. Horace Scudder, "Recent Literature," *Atlantic* (January 1879), 43:124. Howells left Shillaber out of *Mark Twain's Library of Humor*. Howells also reviewed several boy books in the *Atlantic*: Warner's *Being a Boy* in December 1877, George Cary Eggleston's *The Signal Boys; or, Captain Sam's Company* in January 1878, and Oliver Wendell Holmes' poem *The School-Boy* in January 1879.

6. According to Frank Luther Mott, *Golden Multitudes* (New York: Macmillan, 1947), this book was one of the two bestselling books written by Americans in 1855.

7. Howells, *A Boy's Town/Described for "Harper's Young People"* (New York: 1890), p. 2.

8. Hamlin Garland, *Boy Life on the Prairie* (New York: Harper, 1899), p. viii.

9. Howells, "Bobby, Study of a Boy," *Ohio State Journal* (December 14, 1858), 22:1.

10. Kenneth S. Lynn, *William Dean Howells: An American Life* (New York: Harcourt Brace Jovanovich, 1971), pp. 48–51, gives too heavy stress to Howells' private fears. Lynn's error here is partly a consequence of his insistence that *A Boy's Town* should have been an autobiographical rather than an autosocial book. He sees (as I do not) an "elegiac blurriness" (p. 38) in the book and blames it on Howells' strategy of presenting his boyhood "as typifying a general pattern of youthful behavior, rather than as a series of experiences leading to the formation of his own very special personality" (p. 38). Lynn overlooks Howells' important statement immediately following the chapter titled "Fantasies and Superstitions": "I tell these things about my boy, not so much because they were peculiar to him as because I think they are, many of them, *common to all boys*" (p. 205; italics mine). Once again, Edwin H. Cady, *The Road to Realism* (Syracuse: Syracuse University Press, 1956), pp. 22–24, made the groundbreaking explorations of Howells' fears. Thomas Cooley, "The Wilderness Within: Howells's *A Boy's Town*," *American Literature* (January 1976), 47:583–598, develops the "neurotic" interpretation, stressing terror, looking at water-images, seeing few positive aspects in Howells' picture of boy life. Cooley points out that Howells wrote as a kind of anthropologist.

11. Howells, *Suburban Sketches* (Boston: Houghton Mifflin, 1883), p. 250. Older and wiser by the time he wrote *A Hazard of New Fortunes* and *A Boy's Town* twenty years later, Howells would capture the misery that moving can bring to children.

12. This boyhood independence carried over into Howells' attitudes toward Canada and England. In 1871, he rather foolishly belittled Canada for not severing its ties with the mother country: Canada had "the attitude of an overgrown, unmanly boy, clinging to the maternal skirts, and though spoilt and wilful, without any character of his own." Howells found Canada's loyalty "ignoble, like all voluntarily subordinate things." *Their Wedding Journey* (Bloomington: Indiana University Press, 1968), p. 135.

13. In Garland's *Boy Life on the Prairie*, Lincoln and the other boys "were ill at ease in parlors. Lincoln only knew one, in fact,—the Knapp's,—and that he visited very seldom. It had a dim light,—like a sacred place. . . . The girls in their best dresses awed him, however, and he escaped to the barn as soon as possible" (p. 346).

14. Howells, *Years of My Youth* (Bloomington: Indiana University Press, 1975), p. 86. The heroine of Garland's *Rose of Dutcher's Coolly* (1895) wants to swim with the boys but they throw mud at her when she approaches the water. Howells' and Garland's books show that the distinction between gender roles preceded industrialization.

15. Donald Symons, *The Evolution of Human Sexuality* (New York: Oxford University Press, 1979), p. 162. For a cross-cultural look at the male public world and the female private sphere, see *Woman, Culture, and Society*, Michelle Zimbalist Rosaldo and Louise Lamphere, eds. (Stanford: Stanford University Press, 1974). For a highly controversial defense of the idea that there exists a male bond different in kind from friendship between women, see Lionel Tiger, *Men in Groups* (New York: Random House, 1969).

16. Howells, *Years of My Youth*, pp. 14, 110.

17. Howells, *The Flight of Pony Baker: A Boy's Town Story* (New York: Harper, 1902). In "Mark Twain: An Inquiry" (1902), Howells speculated that his friend got his "instinct of right and wrong" from a *female* ancestor; see *My Mark Twain: Reminiscences and Criticisms* (Baton Rouge: Louisiana State University Press, 1967), pp. 153–154.

18. Bobby's dream is to be a circus performer: "at present, the principal object of Bobby's life is to stand upon his head, and play the bones at the same instant" ("Bobby," *Ohio State Journal*, p. 1). Howells never forgot the circus; according to a letter from R. W. Gilder to Howells (May 14, 1881, owned by Harvard), Howells must have broached the idea of an "essay on 'behind the scenes' at a great circus."

19. Howells, *Selected Letters*, 1:154, 321, 323.

20. AMBITION VS. SELFLESSNESS

1. James, *A Small Boy and Others* (New York: Scribner, 1913), p. 346; italics James's. In *A Boy's Town* (New York: Harper, 1890), p. 185, Howells had an

"ideal of glory" and was full of "gaudy purposes which he wished to make shine before men in their fulfillment."

2. Charles Neider, ed., *The Autobiography of Mark Twain* (New York: Harper, 1959), pp. 71, 50–58.

3. Sarah Orne Jewett, *The Country of the Pointed Firs and Other Stories* (Garden City, N.Y.: Doubleday, 1956), p. 290.

4. Sir William A. Craigie and James R. Hulbert, eds., *A Dictionary of American English* (Chicago: University of Chicago Press, 1942), 3:1373. J. G. Saxe wrote the couplet.

5. *The Rise of Silas Lapham* (Bloomington: Indiana University Press, 1971), p. 94.

6. Quoted from Andrew Turnbull, *Scott Fitzgerald* (New York: Scribner's, 1962), p. 28.

7. Ann Douglas, *The Feminization of American Culture* (New York: Avon, 1977), p. 212.

8. Howells, *Years of My Youth* (Bloomington: Indiana University Press, 1975), p. 11.

9. Howells, *My Literary Passions* (New York: Harper, 1910), p. 5.

10. Howells, *Years of My Youth*, p. 88.

11. Howells, "I Talk of Dreams," *Impressions and Experiences* (New York: Harper, 1896), pp. 112–113. In this essay Howells links sleep dreaming to criminality and primitive life.

12. Howells, *The World of Chance* (New York: Harper, 1893), pp. 202, 190–191. Scott A. Dennis, "*The World of Chance*: Howells' Hawthornian Self-Parody," *American Literature* (May 1980), 52:277–293, argues that Howells used material from his own life in this novel to express doubts about himself. For a woman's daydreams in Howells, see *Annie Kilburn* (New York: Harper, 1889), where the title character "indulged reveries so vivid that they seemed to weaken and exhaust her for the grapple with realities; the recollection of them abashed her in the presence of facts" (pp. 8–9). The one daydream Howells specifies involves her foolish dream of devoting herself to the Fall River millworkers: "She fell into one of those intense reveries of hers—a rapture in which she prefigured what should happen in that new life before her. At its end Mr. Peck stood beside her grave, reading the lesson of her work to the multitude of grateful and loving poor who thronged to pay the last tribute to her memory. Putney was there with his wife, and Lyra regretful of her lightness, and Mrs. Munger repentant of her mendacities. They talked together in awe-stricken murmurs of the noble career just ended" (p. 293). This fantasy is the obverse of the male fantasy of kingship.

13. Howells, *The Minister's Charge* (Bloomington: Indiana University Press, 1978), p. 262. First published 1887.

14. Howells, *The Kentons* (Bloomington: Indiana University Press, 1971), p. 196.

15. *Silas Lapham*, p. 20.

16. George Makepeace Towle, *American Society* (London: Chapman and Hall, 1870), 1:291. Towle wrote as an American attempting to explain his country to the English.

17. Howells, *The Son of Royal Langbrith* (Bloomington: Indiana University Press, 1969), p. 208. Howells' lament about his lost popularity in old age employed the image of statues: "I am comparatively a dead cult with my statues cut down and grass growing over them in the pale moonlight." *Life in Letters*, Mildred Howells, ed. (Garden City, N.Y.: Doubleday, Doran, 1928), 2:350.

18. Howells, "Glimpses of Central Park," *Impressions and Experiences*, p. 234.

19. The best survey of Howells' politics up to 1881 is Louis J. Budd, "Howells, the *Atlantic Monthly*, and Republicanism," *American Literature* (May 1952), 24:139–156. Before the Civil War Howells eulogized John Brown in a poem, "Old Brown," which he later refused to disown. He supported Lincoln in '60 and '64 and favored the impeachment of Andrew Johnson. He backed Grant in '68 and again in '72 in spite of the disclosures of corruption. In the 1874 midterm election, Howells "voted Republican, but . . . without intelligence or heart" (letter to William Cooper Howells, November 8, 1874, at Harvard). That same year he lost faith in Reconstruction. He voted for Hayes in '76 and Garfield in '80 and after his assassination was disturbed at the accession of Arthur, a spoilsman from the New York Custom House. Even in 1884, when the Mugwumps (including Mark Twain) deserted the Republican Party in order to support the Democratic Cleveland, Howells voted for Blaine.

20. Marrion Wilcox, "Works of William Dean Howells—(1860–96.)," *Harper's Weekly* (July 4, 1896), 40:656.

21. Howells, *Life in Letters*, 1:404. On Howells' radicalization, see Louis J. Budd's articles, "William Dean Howells' Debt to Tolstoy," *American Slavic and East European Review* (December 1950), 9:292–301, and "Altruism Arrives in America," *American Quarterly* (Spring 1956), 8:40–52; Everett Carter, *Howells and the Age of Realism* (Hamden, Conn.: Archon, 1966), pp. 170–224; Olov W. Fryckstedt, *In Quest of America: A Study of Howells's Early Development as a Novelist* (Cambridge: Harvard University Press, 1958), ch. 13; Clara Marburg Kirk, *W. D. Howells, Traveller from Altruria 1889–1894* (New Brunswick: Rutgers University Press, 1962); Robert L. Hough, *The Quiet Rebel: William Dean Howells as Social Commentator* (Lincoln: University of Nebraska Press, 1959).

22. Howells, *A Hazard of New Fortunes* (Bloomington: Indiana University Press, 1976), p. 184.

23. "New York Streets," *Impressions and Experiences*, pp. 270–271, 280. Perhaps Howells' heightened aversion to savagery explains his regret that the United States Army was not allowed to pursue the Cheyennes—"these idiotic murderers"—onto the reservation after Custer's Last Stand; see "Editor's Study," *Harper's* (January 1891), 72:316–317. At any rate, this was Howells at his worst.

24. *Life in Letters*, 1:408.

25. See the Fall 1978 issue of *CoEvolution Quarterly*, which was done by City Lights Books under the title *Journal for the Protection of All Beings*. In the article "The Ultimate Coalition," Robert Aitken, a Zen teacher, preaches that the only way to resist tyranny is "to shed the skin of the individual self" (p.

26). Most interesting is the conversation between Jack Kornfield, Lawrence Ferlinghetti, and Scoop Nisker, "Buddhism and Nuclear Politics," pp. 29–36, in which these three men manage with remarkable self-approval to weasel their way out of the essential inactivity of Buddhism.

26. Howells, *Their Wedding Journey* (Bloomington: Indiana University Press, 1968), p. 127.

27. James to Howells, July 20, 1880. Letter at Harvard. In Howells' *Three Villages* (Boston: Osgood, 1884), two of the villages were religious communes—the Shakers' Shirley, Massachusetts, and the Moravians' Gnadenhütten, Pennsylvania.

28. Howells, *Hazard*, p. 496.

29. Howells, *Annie Kilburn*, p. 239.

30. Howells, *World of Chance*, pp. 92, 90, 153.

31. Budd, "Howells' Debt to Tolstoy," pp. 292–301; Hough, *Quiet Rebel*, p. 31. See especially Edward Wagenknecht, *William Dean Howells: The Friendly Eye* (New York: Oxford University Press, 1969), ch. 5.

32. "Lyof N. Tolstoy," *North American Review* (1908), 188:851–852, 846.

33. James, *The American Essays*, Leon Edel, ed. (New York: Vintage, 1956), pp. 256–257. First published 1898.

21. "THE BEST MEN"

1. "Visit of Mark Twain/Wit and Humour," Sydney (Australia) *Morning Herald*, September 17, 1895, pp. 5–6, as quoted by Louis J. Budd, "Mark Twain Talks Mostly about Humor and Humorists," *Studies in American Humor* (April 1974), 1:13.

2. John G. Sproat, *"The Best Men:" Liberal Reformers in the Gilded Age* (New York: Oxford University Press, 1968). See also Stow Persons, *The Decline of American Gentility* (New York: Columbia University Press, 1973), and Edwin Harrison Cady, *The Gentleman in America: A Literary Study in American Culture* (Syracuse: Syracuse University Press, 1949). On the personal inadequacies of the "best man" who named the Gilded Age, see Eugene E. Leach, "Charles Dudley Warner's 'Little Journey in the World'," *New England Quarterly* (September 1980), 53:329–344.

3. Edith Wharton, *The Age of Innocence* (New York: New American Library, 1962), p. 106.

4. Geoffrey Blodgett, "Reform Thought and the Genteel Tradition," in H. Wayne Morgan, ed., *The Gilded Age* (Syracuse: Syracuse University Press, 1970), p. 56.

5. Thomas Wentworth Higginson, *Common Sense about Women* (Boston: Lee and Shepard, 1882), p. 24.

6. Blodgett, "Reform Thought," p. 70. According to Frank Luther Mott, *A History of American Magazines 1865–1885* (Cambridge: Harvard University Press, 1938), p. 339, the *Nation's* circulation didn't go above 12,000 in the nineteenth century.

7. The letter, dated February 4, 1877, is in the Watkinson Library, Hartford.

8. Quoted from Gerald Langford, *The Richard Harding Davis Years: A Biography of a Mother and Son* (New York: Holt, 1961), p. 54.

9. Stow Persons, *The Decline of American Gentility* (New York: Columbia University Press, 1973), p. 108. I am indebted to Persons for my information on male clubs.

10. See John P. Mallan, "Roosevelt, Brooks Adams, and Lea: The Warrior Critique of the Business Civilization," *American Quarterly* (Fall 1956), 8:216–230. It is noteworthy that although *The Bread-Winners* was published anonymously, it was obvious to readers that the author was masculine. See Charles Vandersee's excellent edition (New Haven: College and University Press, 1973), p. 149.

11. Blodgett, *"Reform Thought,"* p. 56.

12. *The Scarlet Letter* (Columbus: Ohio State University Press, 1962), p. 18. See Dixon Wecter, "The Hero and the American Artist," *South Atlantic Quarterly* (July 1942), 41:284, on the contrast between Hawthorne's good, weak characters and his evil, dominant ones.

13. Quoted from *United States Magazine* (September 1856), 3:242, by Frank Luther Mott, *A History of American Magazines 1850–1865* (Cambridge: Harvard University Press, 1938), pp. 47–48.

14. Howells, *Criticism and Fiction* (New York: Hill & Wang, 1967), pp. 124–125. Howells' aversion to heroism no doubt had something to do with his laudable aversion to the lawlessness of fighting, which is apparent in some of his antimilitaristic Civil War letters. In *The Leatherwood God* (New York: Century, 1916), p. 207, gentle Hughey Blake is disgusted when Jim Redfield tears a swatch of hair from Joseph Dylks's head: "To tear it right out of his head, that way, I couldn't; it went ag'in my stommick."

15. James, *The Bostonians* (Indianapolis: Bobbs-Merrill, 1976), ch. 34.

16. Higginson, "Americanism in Literature," *Atlantic* (January 1870), 25:60.

17. James, "Travelling Companions," *Atlantic* (November 1870), 26:600, (December 1870), p. 696.

18. *Suburban Sketches* (Boston: Osgood, 1872), p. 148. Howells assumes the point of view of a "mere aesthetic observer" on p. 197. The superiority of the unaccomplished ideal had been a major theme in George William Curtis' *Prue and I* and Ik Marvel's *Reveries of a Bachelor*.

19. Howells, *Indian Summer* (Bloomington: Indiana University Press, 1971), p. 42.

20. Howells, *The Lady of the Aroostook* (Boston: Houghton, Osgood, 1879), p. 115.

21. Howells, *A Fearful Responsibility and Other Stories* (Boston: Osgood, 1881), pp. 23, 42. Maurice Thompson wrote Howells that he and his wife "like the historian's wife. She is evidently a truly American woman." Letter dated June 9, 1881, at Harvard. Howells confessed to cowardice in his dream-life: "It has more than once been my fate to find myself during sleep in battle, where I behave with so little courage as to bring discredit upon our

flag and shame upon myself" "I Talk of Dreams," *Impressions and Experiences* (New York: Harper, 1896), p. 98. He also reported a dream in which the Duke of Wellington humiliated him (*ibid.*, pp. 96–98).

22. James, *Literary Reviews and Essays*, Albert Mordell, ed. (New York: Twayne, 1957), pp. 205–207. The discriminating author of "American Literature in England," *Blackwood's Magazine* (January 1883), 133:156, considered "Don Ippolito . . . by far the highest effort Mr. Howells has made." Howells had written his sister Annie in 1877 that *Foregone Conclusion* was "the best book I ever did or ever shall write." *Selected Letters* (Boston: Twayne, 1979), 2:157.

23. James, *Literary Reviews*, pp. 205, 206–207.

24. On the surface this name is inappropriate for the priest, who is spurned rather than spurns. (He is also compared to Joseph fleeing Potiphar's wife, p. 16.) However, just as Joseph was ridiculed for his purity, Hippolytus was sometimes seen as a distinctly unmanly figure. Hence Howells' choice of name.

25. James, "William Dean Howells," *Harper's Weekly* (June 19, 1886), 30:394.

26. Howells, *The Quality of Mercy* (New York: Harper, 1892), p. 223.

27. Ann Douglas, *The Feminization of American Culture* (New York: Avon, 1977), p. 48. For an opposing statement, arguing that liberal Protestantism did not feminize men, see David S. Reynolds, "The Feminization Controversy: Sexual Stereotypes and the Paradoxes of Piety in Nineteenth-Century America," *New England Quarterly* (March 1980), 53:96–106.

28. Howells, "The Country Printer," *Scribner's Magazine* (May 1893), 13:551. In *Years of My Youth* (Bloomington: Indiana University Press, 1975), p. 90, Howells recalled that the first friend of his youth had a "smooth, rich, girlish complexion."

22. THE PLOT WITH A SECRET

1. *The Complete Tales of Henry James*, Leon Edel, ed. (Philadelphia: Lippincott, 1962), 4:52.

2. James, *The American* (Boston: Houghton Mifflin, 1962), p. 42.

3. James, *The Ambassadors*, S. P. Rosenbaum, ed. (New York: Norton, 1964), p. 166. For a more extended analysis of the secret-plot in James, see my dissertation, "Secrecy in the Fiction of Henry James" (Stanford, 1967). For a structural analysis of the quest for a secret in James's post-1890 tales, see Tzvetan Todorov, "The Secret of Narrative," *The Poetics of Prose*, Richard Howard, trans. (Oxford: Blackwell, 1977).

4. *The Novels and Tales of Henry James* (New York: Scribner, 1909), 24:237.

5. See my "Reciprocity and the Market Place in *The Wings of the Dove* and *What Maisie Knew*," *Nineteenth-Century Fiction* (1971), 25:455–473.

6. "The port from which I set out was, I think, that of *the essential loneliness of my life*." Leon Edel, *Henry James: The Treacherous Years* (Philadelphia: Lippincott, 1969), p. 350.

7. In *The Tragic Muse* the fine soul is Nick Dormer; in *The Awkward Age*, Nanda Brookenham.

8. See Alan Friedman, *The Turn of the Novel* (New York: Oxford University Press, 1966). Robert L. Caserio, *Plot, Story, and the Novel: From Dickens and Poe to the Modern Period* (Princeton: Princeton University Press, 1979) builds on a powerful truth: "when writers and readers of novels lose interest in plot and story, they appear to lose faith in the meaning and the moral value of acts" (p. xiii). But what about a plot, like that in *The Ambassadors*, that denies the value of purposeful action and repeatedly pulls the rug out from under Strether? Caserio's chapter on James does not convince me that his late fiction affirms the value of action. There is good practical criticism in Maxwell Geismar, *Henry James and the Jacobites* (New York: Hill and Wang, 1965), marred by careless reading, rhetorical overkill, and a naive appropriation of Freud. A much finer discussion of the poor quality of James's writing is W. M. Spackman, "James, James," *On the Decay of Humanism* (New Brunswick: Rutgers University Press, 1967).

23. THE BOY WHO COULD NOT BECOME A MAN

1. Rev. of *Eight Cousins, Nation* (October 14, 1875), 21:250.

2. Henry James, *The Art of the Novel: Critical Prefaces*, Richard P. Blackmur, ed. (New York: Scribner, 1934), p. 143.

3. James, *Novels and Tales*, 11:152.

4. See Muriel G. Shine, *The Fictional Children of Henry James* (Chapel Hill: University of North Carolina Press, 1969), p. 172: "In the final analysis, his children are, without exception, deeply sentient miniature adults."

5. James, *Notes of a Son and Brother* (New York: Scribner, 1914), p. 454. Hereafter identified as *Notes*. For a good recent study of the boundaries between James's life and art, see Daniel J. Schneider, *The Crystal Cage: Adventures of the Imagination in the Fiction of Henry James* (Lawrence: Regents Press of Kansas, 1978), esp. ch. 1, "James's Sense of Life." Among those critics whose work represents an effort to discern the figure in the carpet in James, Schneider may well be the best. Yet the very limitation of this task reflects a refusal to accept James except on his own terms, a failure to move from exegesis to criticism.

6. James, *A Small Boy and Others* (New York: Scribner, 1913), p. 26. It is noteworthy that the titles of the two volumes of memoirs James lived to complete emphasize him as a male in relation to others.

7. Ora Segal, *The Lucid Reflector: The Observer in Henry James' Fiction* (New Haven: Yale University Press, 1969), p. xii.

8. Quoted from Leon Edel, *Henry James: The Untried Years* (Philadelphia: Lippincott, 1953), p. 137.

9. Henry James, *Letters*, Leon Edel, ed. (Cambridge: Harvard University Press, 1974), 1:22.

10. Edel, *Untried Years*, pp. 136–139.

11. Quentin Anderson, *The Imperial Self: An Essay in American Literary and*

Cultural History (New York: Knopf, 1971), pp. 15–16. Anderson cannily writes: "I take it to be fact that the authority of the father was not very firmly based in the life of the culture, however widely he was held to be an original source of authority" (p. 16).

12. Richard A. Hocks, *Henry James and Pragmatistic Thought: A Study in the Relationship between the Philosophy of William James and the Literary Art of Henry James* (Chapel Hill: University of North Carolina Press, 1974), does not convince me that Henry, in any usable sense of the word, understood William's pragmatism, or that the fiction somehow reproduces the philosophy. More than one writer has run aground trying to prove that Henry James was dramatizing someone else's ideas. Quentin Anderson's early book is the best example. There is a later instance in Cleanth Brooks, R. W. B. Lewis, and Robert Penn Warren, eds., *American Literature: The Makers and the Making* (New York: St. Martin's, 1974), which argues that James's life and work bear out his father's theory that one progresses from selfhood to society, from a selfish egotistic life to one full of the give-and-take of social relationships. One example is Fleda Vetch, whose "self-transcending nature enables her to see persons as persons, even Mrs. Gereth, even Mona Brigstock" (p. 1393). Similarly, "Merton Densher is at the end, we are to understand, an example of the redeemed form of man" (p. 1,396). But both Fleda and Merton are alone at the end; this is society?

13. James, *Watch and Ward, Atlantic* (August 1871), 28:244, 239, 243.

14. Mark Twain, "The Private History of a Campaign That Failed," *Century Magazine* (1885), 31:193–204.

15. Howells, *Years of My Youth* (Bloomington: Indiana University Press, 1975), p. 201.

16. "Every loyal American who went abroad during the first years of our great war felt bound to make himself some excuse for turning his back on his country in the hour of her trouble." Howells, *A Fearful Responsibility and Other Stories* (Boston: Osgood, 1881), p. 3.

17. Edel, *Untried Years*, pp. 179–181, 184–188, 226–238, and Daniel Aaron, *The Unwritten War: American Writers and the Civil War* (New York: Knopf, 1973), pp. 106–120. Is there a possibility that Hubert Lawrence corresponds to Wilky? Hubert is four years *younger* than Roger—*Atlantic* (August 1871), 28:243.

18. An exception is Robert K. Martin's valuable article "The 'High Felicity' of Comradeship: A New Reading of *Roderick Hudson*," *American Literary Realism* (Spring 1978), 11:100–108. Richard Hall, "An Obscure Hurt: The Sexuality of Henry James," *New Republic* (April 28, 1979) 180:25–31, (May 5, 1979), 180:25–29, sees a strong erotic love for William as the central force in Henry's life.

19. "The tale is altogether feminine.... We say this in spite of the pretty passage near the close about the Emperor Hadrian and the suicide of the beautiful Antinous, which appears rather to have been written by a young lady who had not a definite idea what she was saying than by a young man who had such an idea, and who was still determined to say it." *Nation* (June 7, 1877), 24:341.

20. *Nation* (October 22, 1868), 7:331.

21. "An American and an English Novel," *Nation* (December 21, 1876), 23:372. In *Roderick Hudson* meek Sam Singleton shows less promise but achieves more than Roderick, who has the "artistic temperament," something evidently not compatible with meekness for James in the mid-1870s. Sam is the new kind of artist—the hard empirical worker.

22. *Nation* (March 7, 1878), 26:172.

23. Henry James, *The Middle Years* (New York: Scribner, 1917), p. 33.

24. See Richard Poirier, *"The American," The Comic Sense of Henry James* (New York: Oxford University Press, 1967).

25. When Roger shaves off his beard, Nora thinks he looks "too fat." *Watch and Ward, Atlantic* (September 1871), 28:327.

26. Quoted from Jane Benardete, ed., *American Realism* (New York: Putnam, 1972), p. 227.

27. James, *The American Essays*, Leon Edel, ed. (New York: Vintage, 1956), pp. 202–203. First published 1898. The many ways in which James's images of the businessman in this essay anticipate "The Jolly Corner" support Edel's seeing this story as a major autobiographical document. The bad people in James's early novels (Sloper, Osmond) are often authoritarian men. The demon businessman and Howells' many businessmen-tyrants suggest that one of the reasons a distorted Freudian theory swept through American thought in the 1920s was that the Oedipus complex provided a means for confronting the specter that terrified other men besides James and Howells— American machismo. O'Neill was not the only writer who seized Freudian thought to write about the tyrannical father. Also, it is striking how both the Oedipus and the Electra complex were used in such a way as to practically leave out the mother. Frederick J. Hoffman, *Freudianism and the Literary Mind* (Baton Rouge: Louisiana State University Press, 1945), pp. 67–68, showed that the unconscious, in America, was often imagined as "brutal." Hoffman also points out how obsessed many twenties writers were with the hero who was "pale, shy, sensitive, given to much introspective brooding over the world, which struck him as being harsh and importunate" (p. 72). Normative masculinity still oppressed, just as in Howells and James.

28. Howells, *The Altrurian Romances* (Bloomington: Indiana University Press, 1968), p. 120.

29. Howells, *Years of My Youth*, p. 19.

30. James, *Watch and Ward, Atlantic* (August 1871), 28:232, 234.

31. Quoted from *Watch and Ward*, Leon Edel, ed. (New York: Grove, 1960), p. 6.

32. *Atlantic* (September 1871), 28:330. "You would have very soon confessed . . . that he had a true genius for his part, and that it became him better to play at manhood than at juvenility. He could never have been a ruddy-cheeked boy." Fenton's "almost feminine voice" is a reflection of his Southwestern speech.

33. J. A. Ward, *"Watch and Ward," The Search for Form* (Chapel Hill: University of North Carolina Press, 1967), pp. 60–76.

34. Edel, *Untried Years*, p. 325.

35. *Ibid.*, p. 327.

36. *Letters*, 1:214. James wrote this shortly before learning of her death.

37. James, *The Painter's Eye: Notes and Essays on the Pictorial Arts* (London: Hart-Davis, 1956), p. 80. James once referred to Hercules as his opposite (*Letters*, 2:94).

38. James, *Middle Years*, p. 76.

39. F. O. Matthiessen and Kenneth B. Murdock, eds., *The Notebooks of Henry James* (New York: Oxford University Press, 1961), p. 179.

40. Philip M. Weinstein, *Henry James and the Requirements of the Imagination* (Cambridge: Harvard University Press, 1971), pp. 72–79.

41. Quoted from Weinstein, p. 99.

42. Leon Edel, *Henry James: The Master* (Philadelphia: Lippincott, 1972), pp. 472–473.

43. Saul Rosenzweig, "The Ghost of Henry James," *Partisan Review* (1944), 11:436–455.

44. Quoted from Edel, *The Master*, p. 552. Mark L. Krupnick, "Henry James: The Artist as Emperor," *Novel* (1973), 6:257–265, has stressed the seriousness of James's Napoleonic delusion.

45. Quoted from a speech by Gabriel Nash in *The Tragic Muse* by Edel, *Untried Years*, p. 13.

24. "OBSERVING": THE VIEW FROM JAMES'S ROOM IN THE HOUSE OF FICTION

1. *Nation* (December 21, 1865), 1:787.

2. *Nation* (January 4, 1866), 2:21–22.

3. "The Passionate Pilgrim and Other Tales," in Albert Mordell, ed., *Discovery of a Genius* (New York: Twayne, 1961), pp. 73–74.

4. Howells, *A Chance Acquaintance* (Bloomington: Indiana University Press, 1971), p. 32.

5. *Letters*, Leon Edel, ed. (Cambridge: Harvard University Press, 1974), 1:401. As James read the novel, he "was hoping that it was she who was to affront him. She does, indeed, by her shabby clothes. . . ." Edel transcribes this incorrectly. In "Commentary," *Nineteenth Century Fiction* (September 1976), 31:244–247, Christoph K. Lohmann and George Arms expose the unreliability of Edel's edition.

6. Milly Theale is deceived by Mrs. Lowder's hospitality—"a fine floating gold-dust . . . that threw over the prospect a harmonising blur" (*Novels and Tales*, 19:168). Once Maggie Verver wakes up, she sees "realities looming through the golden mist" (*Novels and Tales*, 24:31).

7. James, *The Painter's Eye: Notes and Essays on the Pictorial Arts* (London: Hart-Davis, 1956), p. 19.

8. *Ibid.*, pp. 70, 210.

9. James, *Washington Square, The Europeans* (New York: Dell, 1959), pp. 208, 207. The Boston horsecar was apparently a major positive symbol for James's father; see Robert Falk, "Henry James's *The American* as a Centennial

Novel," in Joseph Waldmeir, ed., *Essays in Honor of Russel B. Nye* (East Lansing: Michigan State University Press, 1978), p. 35.

10. Howells, "By Horse-Car to Boston," *Suburban Sketches* (Boston: Houghton Mifflin, 1883), p. 113. First printed 1870. A reading of Howells' and James's writings on Italy will show that Howells, not James, is the exception to the usual American attitude summed up by Ann Douglas: American writers and tourists in Italy "concurred in slighting the political, intellectual, and domestic habits of the Italian people, even while they praised and envied the Italians' love of art and capacity for leisure. They unanimously resented the encroachments of the present on the classical past." *The Feminization of American Culture* (New York: Knopf, 1977), p. 283. See James L. Woodress, Jr., *Howells & Italy* (Durham: Duke University Press, 1952); Carl Maves, *Sensuous Pessimism: Italy in the Work of Henry James* (Bloomington: Indiana University Press 1973); Nathalia Wright, *American Novelists in Italy* (Philadelphia: University of Pennsylvania Press, 1965).

11. James, *Art of the Novel*, p. 121. The only *candid* photograph I've seen of James talking, where he is not aware of the camera, is in Carolyn G. Heilbrun, ed., *Lady Ottoline's Album* (New York: Knopf, 1976), p. 41, where James is holding forth with Ethel Sands and Lady Ottoline. He is looking down and at neither of the ladies, apparently gesturing by holding his left hand to his breast.

12. James, *The American Essays*, Leon Edel, ed. (New York: Vintage, 1956), pp. 272–273.

13. Gordon O. Taylor, *The Passages of Thought: Psychological Representation in the American Novel 1870–1900* (New York: Oxford University Press, 1969), p. 83.

14. William Veeder, *Henry James—The Lessons of the Master: Popular Fiction and Personal Style in the Nineteenth Century* (Chicago: University of Chicago Press, 1975), pp. 217–228. See also Ruth Bernard Yeazell, *Language and Knowledge in the Late Henry James* (Chicago: University of Chicago Press, 1976).

15. James E. Miller, Jr., "Henry James in Reality," *Critical Inquiry* (Spring 1976), 2:591.

16. H. E. Scudder, *"The Portrait of a Lady* and *Dr. Breen's Practice,"* *Atlantic* (January 1882), 49:128.

17. E.g., Peter Buitenhuis claims that the viewpoints of James's various characters "give a spectrum of opinion about America that amounts to one of the most comprehensive criticisms that any writer has made of his own country." *The Grasping Imagination: The American Writings of Henry James* (Toronto: University of Toronto Press, 1970), p. 4.

18. As James admitted in his preface: "The way things happen is frankly not the way in which they are represented as having happened, in Paris, to my hero" (*Novels and Tales*, 2:xviii). Two things should be noted: James's sense that the unreality was a flaw (p. xix), and the implication that his other books *do* generally represent the way things happen.

19. From "The Art of Fiction," in *The Future of the Novel*, Leon Edel, ed.

(New York: Random House, 1956), p. 12. James, of course, had a very big stake in the argument that you could know the world without being of it. Like Victorian women novelists, he lacked access to vast areas of masculine experience. Thus, his test case was a woman writer.

20. *The American* (Boston: Houghton Mifflin, 1962), p. 120. In his preface James admitted that it was a serious omission not to show the engaged couple together and alone (*Novels and Tales*, 2:xxi-xxii).

21. See Elsa Nettels, "William Dean Howells and the American Language," *New England Quarterly* (September 1980), 53:308-328.

22. *The Bostonians* (Indianapolis: Bobbs-Merrill, 1976), p. 436.

23. Hawthorne, *The Marble Faun* (Columbus: Ohio State University Press, 1968), p. 3.

24. James, *Hawthorne* (Ithaca: Cornell University Press, 1956), pp. 33, 34.

25. James W. Tuttleton, *The Novel of Manners in America* (Chapel Hill: University of North Carolina Press, 1972), pp. 70-79. Elsewhere, particularly pp. 7-27, Tuttleton sharply questions the idea that American society was so undeveloped that it afforded little material for the novelist. The best book on this subject is Nicolaus Mills, *American and English Fiction in the Nineteenth Century: An Antigenre Critique and Comparison* (Bloomington: Indiana University Press, 1973). Mills rigorously dismantles four widely held views closely associated with Trilling, Chase, and Bewley: 1) "The English novel did not survive in America because the texture of American society was too thin to support such an art form" (p. 22). 2) "The thinness of American society accounts not only for the absence of the English novel in America but provides a basic explanation for the form of American fiction" (p. 22). 3) "The historical uniqueness of America accounts for the uniqueness of American fiction" (p. 23). 4) "The complaints of American writers against American society are evidence that the texture of American society forced them to write romances rather than novels" (p. 24).

26. *The Scarlet Letter* (Columbus: Ohio State University Press, 1962), p. 37.

27. Daniel Aaron, *The Unwritten War: American Writers and the Civil War* (New York: Knopf, 1973), p. 335.

28. James, *Hawthorne*, p. 35.

29. *Scarlet Letter*, pp. 17, 18.

30. Robert Dusenbery, "Hawthorne's Merry Company: The Anatomy of Laughter in the Tales and Short Stories," *PMLA* (1967), 82:285-288.

31. Frank Norris' "A Deal in Wheat" shows the innermost circle; the monopolists who run the lives of farmers and food consumers turn out to be jovial laughers. In Herman Melville's *The Confidence Man* the jokes and tricks help define a satanic order manifest in male steamboat society. One of the best known secret societies in America was the Junto, organized by the one joker among our founding fathers, Benjamin Franklin.

32. James, *American Essays*, p. 211. James also enjoyed Grant's *Letters*, but again could not explain why, except by means of the fortuitous associations of Grant's fame (*ibid.*, pp. 208-209). James himself was much more aware of the serious disadvantages of alienation than his fond admirers seem to be.

In 1902 he advised Edith Wharton to write about America:
    There it is round you. Don't pass it by—the immediate, the real. . . .
Take hold of it and keep hold, and let it pull you where it will.
    What I would say in a word is: Profit, be warned, by my awful example
of exile and ignorance.
R. W. B. Lewis, *Edith Wharton: A Biography* (New York: Harper and Row,
1975), p. 127. In 1899 James earnestly advised William to make sure his sons
were immersed in American life; see Percy Lubbock, ed. *The Letters of Henry
James* (New York: Scribner, 1920), 1:316.

25. WHO MADE JAMES THE MODERN AMERICAN MASTER, AND WHY?

1. *The Genteel Tradition: Nine Essays by George Santayana* (Cambridge: Harvard University Press, 1967), pp. 39–40.
2. For differing positions on modernism, see Irving Howe, ed., *The Idea of the Modern in Literature and the Arts* (New York: Horizon, 1967); David Daiches, "What Was the Modern Novel?" *Critical Inquiry* (June 1975), 1:813–819; Lowry Nelson, Jr., "Now That It's Past Let's Call It Modernism," *Yale Review* (Winter 1979), 68:266–270. I find Yvor Winters' attack on Eliot correct in many ways; see "T. S. Eliot, or the Illusion of Reaction," *On Modern Poets* (New York: Meridian, 1959).
    On the continuities between nineteenth-century culture and modernism, see Robert Langbaum, *The Poetry of Experience: The Dramatic Monologue in Modern Literary Tradition* (New York: Random House, 1957) and Charles Altieri, "Arnold and Tennyson: The Plight of Victorian Lyricism as Context of Modernism," *Criticism* (Summer 1978), 20:281–306. Stow Persons, *The Decline of American Gentility* (New York: Columbia, 1973), p. vii, writes that "the successor to the nineteenth-century gentleman is the alienated intellectual."
    3. Modern art "can be comprehended only by people possessed of the peculiar gift of artistic sensibility—an art for artists and not for the masses, for 'quality' and not for hoi polloi." *The Dehumanization of Art*, as quoted in *Idea of the Modern*, p. 86.
    4. Quoted by Howe, *ibid.*, p. 16.
    5. Trilling, "On the Modern Element in Modern Literature," *The Idea of the Modern*, p. 82.
    6. Howe, "The Idea of the Modern," *ibid.*, p. 14.
    7. Leon Edel, *Henry James: The Master* (Philadelphia: Lippincott, 1972), pp. 388–425; Jay B. Hubbell, *Who are the Major American Writers? A Study of the Changing Literary Canon* (Durham: Duke University Press, 1972), pp. 130–132, *passim*.
    8. Norman Podhoretz, *Making It* (New York: Random House, 1967), p. 116. Podhoretz writes that "when the family spoke of itself or was spoken of as 'alienated,' the reference might be to any number of things, but the deepest thing of all was this: *They did not feel that they belonged to America or that America belonged to them*" (pp. 116–117). One may note in passing the pomposity of the notion that America might "belong" to an intellectual.

Podhoretz's career no doubt reveals the implicit and unacknowledged commitments of the Partisan Reviewers: his defense of President Reagan in the April 6, 1981, issue of *New York* makes explicit the closet conservatism of Rahv and Trilling.

9. Trilling, "On the Modern Element," *The Idea of the Modern*, p. 82.

10. Rahv, "On the Decline of Naturalism," *Partisan Review* (November/December 1942), 9:483, 493, 492. Rahv did insist on the value of realism, however.

11. Carroll Smith-Rosenberg, "The Female World of Love and Ritual: Relations between Women in Nineteenth-Century America," *Signs* (1975), 1:1–29. Rahv's quotations on *The Bostonians* come from his introduction to the 1945 Dial edition, pp. v–ix.

12. For Trilling's account of the book's origins and growth, see his introduction to *The Middle of the Journey* (New York: Scribner, 1976). For more sympathetic views of the novel than my own, see Quentin Anderson, "On *The Middle of the Journey*," in Quentin Anderson, Stephen Donadio, and Steven Marcus, eds., *Art, Politics and Will, Essays in Honor of Lionel Trilling* (New York: Basic Books, 1977), pp. 254–59, and William M. Chace, *Lionel Trilling: Criticism and Politics* (Stanford: Stanford University Press, 1980), ch. 4. See also Robert Boyers, *Lionel Trilling: Negative Capability and the Wisdom of Avoidance* (Columbia: University of Missouri Press, 1977), and the Spring 1978 issue of *Salmagundi*, devoted to Trilling. This issue has valuable assessments by Mark Shechner, Robert Langbaum, Helen Vendler, and Joseph Frank. Part of my own argument has been well put by the latter critic in "Lionel Trilling and the Conservative Imagination," *Salmagundi* (Spring 1978), no. 41, p. 33. Trying to explain the "anomaly" that Trilling became so influential in spite of his differences from the prevailing New Criticism, Frank writes:

> In defending the autonomy and integrity of the work of art, the New Critics were repulsing the claims of the liberals and radicals to appropriate it for social or political ends; their influence was part of the wave of disillusionment with politics that marked the generation of the fifties. And, though Lionel Trilling approached art with overt moral and historical assumptions, the substance of what he had to say was by no means dissimilar to what the New Critics were advocating in their own way. For the pervasive disillusionment with politics was given its most sensitive, subtle, and judiciously circumspect expression in the criticism of Lionel Trilling—and this is the real answer to the anomaly of his success.

13. Trilling, "*The Bostonians*," *The Opposing Self* (New York: Harcourt Brace Jovanovich, 1977), pp. 98–100. Irving Howe's introduction to his 1956 Modern Library edition of the novel corrected Trilling's distorted view of Basil, but gave extreme emphasis to the irony in James's treatment of him (pp. xvi, xxv–xxvi). Howe perceived that the novel did not involve "any notions about 'eternal' wars between the sexes" (p. xvii). Yet Howe retained Rahv's view that Olive was lesbian.

14. Letter to John Hay, dated May 13, 1885. See George Monteiro, *Henry*

James and John Hay: The Record of a Friendship (Providence: Brown University Press, 1965), p. 97. James's confession also undercuts Rahv's view that America is "rendered" with "an exceptionally acute observation of people and places" (Introduction, p. viii), in *The Bostonians*.

15. Trilling, *"The Bostonians," Opposing Self*, p. 94. Although Irving Howe revised Trilling's view of Basil Ransom, Howe accepted his (and Rahv's) opinion that *The Bostonians* is a brilliant work of social realism about an uprooted society. The formula with which Howe reconciled the novel's increasing privatism in books Second and Third with his own socialism is worth noting: Howe insisted that the point of the book, its "great stroke" (p. xxvi), is to show how public ideology infects private life. Howe's improved version of the *Partisan Review* line, widely circulated in an inexpensive Modern Library edition, overlooks James's decreasing distance from Basil in the latter half of the book and takes on faith the *accuracy* of James's representation of American ideologies.

16. Trilling, "William Dean Howells and the Roots of Modern Taste," *Opposing Self*.

17. Alfred Kazin, *New York Jew* (New York: Knopf, 1978), pp. 46–47. Duck Caldwell, the only nonintellectual rural male gentile in *The Middle of the Journey*, seems exceptionally crude and cruel.

18. Trilling, "Introduction," *Middle of the Journey*, pp. xxi, xx.

19. See Alfred Habegger, "The Disunity of *The Bostonians*," *Nineteenth-Century Fiction* (1969), 24:193–209; Martin Green, "Henry James and the Great Tradition," *Re-appraisals: Some Commonsense Readings in American Literature* (New York: Norton, 1965); W. M. Spackman, "James, James," *On the Decay of Humanism* (New Brunswick: Rutgers University Press, 1967).

Index

Aaron, Daniel, 261, 286, 313*n*4

Adams, Henry, 105, 238, 248, 271, 291; *Democracy*, 235; *The Education of Henry Adams*, 266; "Primitive Rights of Women," 88–89, 100

Adams, Marian ("Clover"), 60–61

Adams, William T. (pseud. Oliver Optic), 209

Aitken, Robert, 352*n*25

Alcott, Bronson, 58

Alcott, Louisa May, 159, 339*n*18; *Eight Cousins*, 170, 319*n*14; *Little Women*, 118–19, 141, 172, 181, 306*n*4; *Moods*, 173, 319*n*14

Alden, John, 20, 21

Aldrich, Thomas Bailey: "Mlle. Olympe Zabriski," 31–32; *The Story of a Bad Boy*, 117, 139, 307–9, 310, 315

Alger, Horatio, 209, 323*n*13

Alice Doesn't Live Here Any More (movie), 158

Allegory, 111–12, 329*n*14

Allen, Gracie, 144

Allen, Samantha, *see* Holley, Marietta

Allen, Woody, 333*n*7

Altieri, Charles, 362*n*2

Andersen, Hans Christian, 282

Anderson, Hendrik, 273

Anderson, John Q., 333*n*6

Anderson, Quentin, 259, 356*n*11, 357*n*12, 363*n*12

Anthony, Susan B., 148, 164

Antinous, 262, 357*n*19

Appleton's Journal, 25

Arms, George, 321*n*6, 322*n*2, 359*n*5

Arp, Bill, 122, 137

Arthur, Chester A., 352*n*19

Atlantic Monthly, 45–46, 59, 209, 279, 341*n*39

Auchincloss, Louis, 274, 318*n*4

Auerbach, Erich, 326*n*2

Austin, James C., 332*n*28

Ball, Lucille, 148

Balzac, Honoré de, ix, xi

Bancroft, George, 222

Barker-Benfield, Graham John, 347*n*1

Barlow, Joel, *The Hasty Pudding*, 130

Basham, Richard, 347*n*1

Baym, Nina, 6, 8, 16, 66, 306*n*4, 311*n*11, 315*n*19, 318*n*3, 338*n*42

Beadle's joke books, 121, 123, 125, 132, 145–47, 159, 331*n*23

Beard, Mary Ritter, 341*n*44

Beatts, Anne, 117, 330*n*10

Beecher, Catherine, 19, 159–60

Beer, Thomas, 313*n*4

Bellamy, Edward, 231

Belle Hélène, La (opera bouffe), 179

Bellini, Giovanni, 276

Bennett, George N., 322*n*2

Bentzon, Th., 324*n*17

Bewley, Marius, 361*n*25

Bierce, Ambrose, 61

Bishop, Charles B., 337*n*30

Bisztray, George, 327*n*2

Blaine, James G., 60, 235, 352*n*19

Blair, Walter, 129, 333*n*5, 335*n*23, 340*n*23

Blanc, Mel, 203

Blankenship, Tom, 205

Bliss, Elisha, 164

Blodgett, Geoffrey, 236–37, 239

365

168–171, 184; Capitola, 173–77; deadpan speech, 126, 137–38; drawling, 137, 185, 187; in girlhood, 157, 159–61, 170–71; literary comedians, 122–23, 135–38; masculine self-ridicule, x, 11, 130–31, 133, 136, 164, 170; of the Old Southwest, x, 131–32, 135–38, 169, 334*n*18; Penelope Lapham, 115, 183–95; and politics, 117, 145–47; wise old woman, 157–58, 161–71; *see also under* Femininity; Howells; Masculinity; *and* Masculinity, bragging
"Husband's Friend, The" (humorous sketch), 152

I Love Lucy (TV series), 148
Industrialization, 22–23, 94–95, 126, 138, 201, 266, 308*n*5
Ingraham, Joseph II., *The Prince of the House of David*, 209–10
Initials, The, 4
Ivanhoe (burlesque), 178
Ixion (burlesque), 177, 178–79

Jacklin, Carol Nagy, 145, 347*n*4
Jackson, Helen Hunt, 263
James, Garth Wilkinson ("Wilky"— brother), 260–61, 276–77, 279, 357*n*17
James, Henry
— *topics:* boyhood, 256–59; and business, 23–24, 258, 263–66; and combat, 257, 261–62, 265–67, 273; disinterest in ordinary life, 274–75, 288; effeminacy, xi, 56–61, 240–41, 263; "essential loneliness," 64, 255, 271; and Europe, 252–54, 258–59, 270–71; fantasies, xiii, 76–79, 221, 254–55, 268, 273, 279; fear of American masculinity, 77, 78, 285; frustrated efforts to pass as a man, 246–47, 256–73; on Howells, 105, 115, 229, 234, 244, 246–47, 275, 330*n*3, 337*n*41, 359*n*5; and local color, 104, 327*n*3; observing, 73, 74, 78, 257, 270, 274–88;